I0814706

A KILLING IN CANNABIS

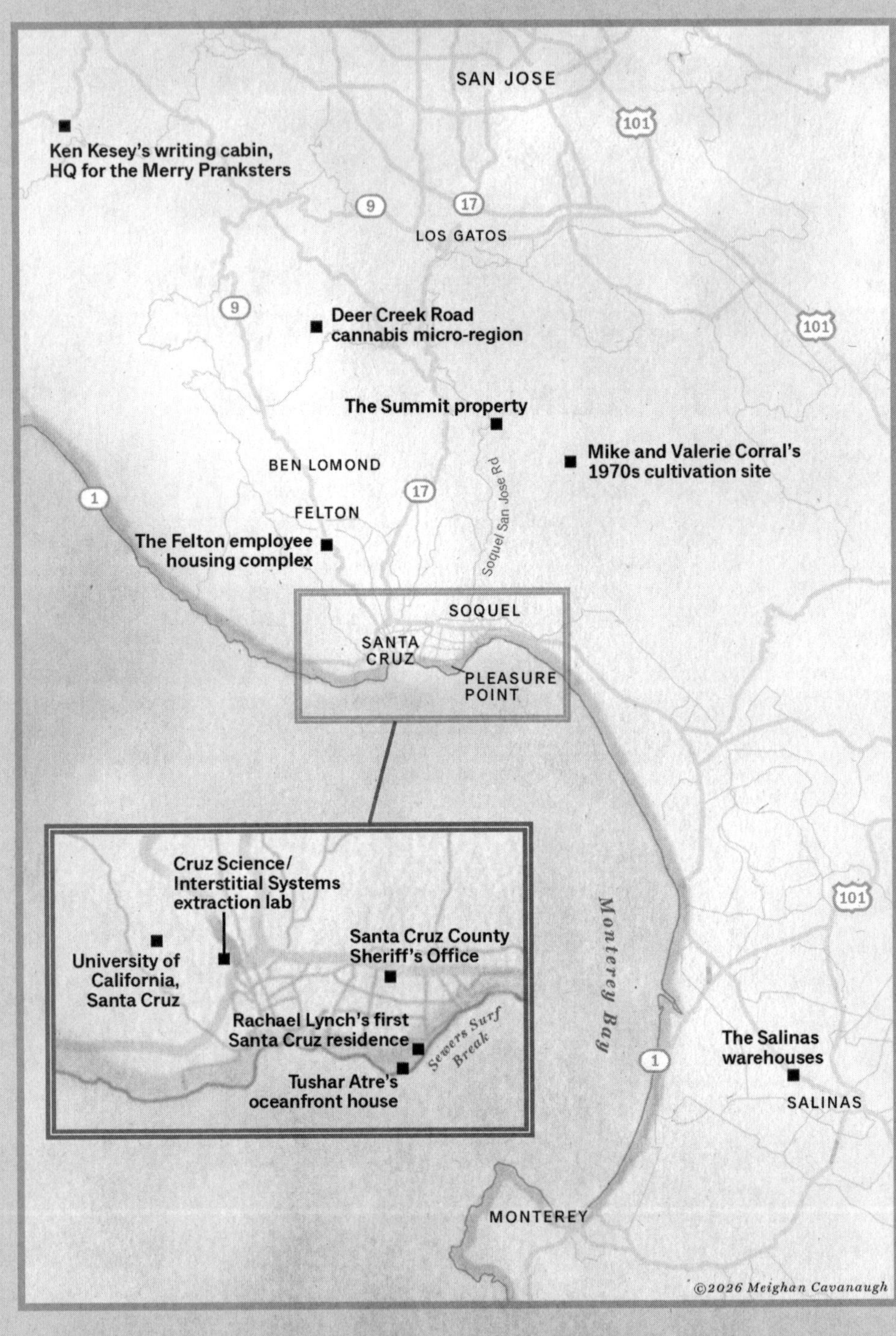

SAN JOSE
101
Ken Kesey's writing cabin,
HQ for the Merry Pranksters
9
17
LOS GATOS
9
Deer Creek Road
cannabis micro-region
101
The Summit property
Mike and Valerie Corral's
1970s cultivation site
BEN LOMOND
Soquel San Jose Rd
17
1
FELTON
The Felton employee
housing complex
SOQUEL
SANTA
CRUZ
PLEASURE
POINT
Cruz Science/
Interstitial Systems
extraction lab
Santa Cruz County
Sheriff's Office
University of
California,
Santa Cruz
Rachael Lynch's first
Santa Cruz residence
Sewers Surf
Break
Tushar Atre's
oceanfront house
Monterey Bay
101
1
The Salinas
warehouses
SALINAS
MONTEREY
©2026 Meighan Cavanaugh

A KILLING IN CANNABIS

A True Story of Love, Murder, and California Weed

Scott Eden

S&G

Spiegel & Grau, New York
www.spiegelandgrau.com

Interior design by Meighan Cavanaugh

Library of Congress Cataloging-in-Publication Data
Available Upon Request

ISBN 978-1-954118-62-1 (hardcover)
ISBN 978-1-954118-88-1 (eBook)

Printed in the United States

First Edition
10 9 8 7 6 5 4 3 2 1

For Leyla

Almost invariably the inebriation is of the most cheerful kind, causing the person to sing and dance, to eat food with great relish, and to seek aphrodisiac enjoyments. In persons of a quarrelsome disposition it occasions, as might be expected, an exasperation of their natural tendency.

—W. B. O'Shaughnessy, MD, "On the preparations of the Indian hemp, or Gunjah" (1838)

The need for mystery is greater than the need for an answer.

—Ken Kesey, *The Paris Review*, Issue 130

A KILLING IN CANNABIS

1. Persons of Interest

October 1, 2019

There are good trips, and there are bad trips. Some end in feelings of transcendence, others in feelings of madness and doom. Science still doesn't know why. An entire neurological system, the endocannabinoid system—its name based on the botanical term for a genus of psychotropic plant (*Cannabis*) first ingested by humans in a time before history—wasn't discovered until 1988. Since then researchers have found that the body manufactures its own cannabinoid molecules, which attach to their own cannabinoid receptors, whenever something new, important, or meaningful is encountered. On the level of the cell, cannabinoids, it would seem, help create meaning.

When you take a toke, the heat from the flame transmutes the plant's inert acid form of tetrahydrocannabinol, or THC, into its psychoactive doppelgänger, delta-9-THC, the molecules of which enter the lungs, then the bloodstream. Fewer than 1 percent will make it across the blood-brain barrier. But that's more than enough to do the trick. There, the delta-9-THC molecules find and attach to the brain's native endocannabinoid receptors, billions of them, unleashing cascades of neural reactions that are, in turn, intensified or muted or complexly adjusted by an unknown number of *other* cannabinoids—for THC is but one in an enigmatic host of cannabinoids found in weed. As of this writing, 301 have been discovered. Many more almost certainly exist, their effects shrouded in mystery.

A whole subindustry has arisen to isolate, understand, and commercialize them. It's almost as though this plant and its molecules have evolved expressly to couple with the cogwheels of the human mind. As the cascades continue, they provoke blasts of dopamine that drench your prefrontal cortex, the brain's most-evolved district, your center for abstract thought, your intellectual bastion, inducing euphoria and hedonic delight, and, at the very highest doses, possible hallucination and psychosis.

In the amygdala, which regulates fear, the neural cascade encounters—or produces—a paradox. THC calms neurons that would otherwise excite anxiety yet also blocks neurons that would otherwise calm it. Are you relaxed? Are you paranoid? Normal stimuli become hilarious. Or sinister. Why one and not the other? Here we reach the limit of the current state of the knowledge. In the end—or is it the beginning?—these forces may join to suck the mind into the thought flumes that form the lived experience—the addled, joyful profundity, or the addled, metaphysical panic—of being high.

What kind of trip will it be?

Just after 10:00 a.m. on the first day of October 2019, on a deeply forested tract of private land almost exactly equidistant between the surf breaks of Santa Cruz, California, to the south and the megalopolitan sprawl of Silicon Valley on the plain to the north, a posse of sheriff's deputies began their approach. Each had a sidearm clasped in both hands. Their movements were cautious, painstaking. So much so that the scene felt choreographed, like a piece of theatrical stage blocking. They were crouched low behind a two-tone bulletproof Ford Interceptor, green and white, the words *Santa Cruz County Sheriff* decal'd on the doors, which crept forward inch by inch at the slowest pace. The day was otherwise cheerful; sunshine dappled through evergreen boughs. Against the possibility of gunfire, the cops were using the Ford as a shield.

Almost seven hours earlier, 911 dispatchers had received a panicked call: A group of assailants had invaded an oceanfront house on Santa Cruz's affluent Pleasure Point Drive, which runs along cliffs overlooking

Monterey Bay, and kidnapped the homeowner. The 911 call had been made by a group of the owners' visiting houseguests. The commotion had awoken some of them in their bedrooms, but they had remained there, too afraid to intervene. Footage obtained from nearby surveillance cameras—multiple officers were even now combing over the video at headquarters, all hands on deck—showed three figures taking the man away in what the deputies at first believed was the victim's own white BMW X3 SUV.

Now the BMW had been located, parked mutely up a switchbacking driveway on this undeveloped sixty-acre property, in a part of the Santa Cruz Mountains known as the Summit, where deputies from all points in the county were now swarming in their patrol cars. The property, as it happened, was also owned by the victim.

Tushar Atre. Fifty-year-old male. Indian American. Five nine, 165 pounds. Eyes a shocking emerald green. His most striking feature by far. The one that people would most often remark on after first meeting him. With his piercing gaze, he'd been known to freeze people momentarily in place, like a mesmerist. At one time he had a thick chunk of black mad-scientist hair, but once it started to recede, he shaved his head clean. He'd crossed into late middle age but looked much younger. Fit as a sensei. In fact, he trained at a local dojo. Avid mountain biker. Obsessed surfer. A couple of the deputies knew him from the lineup at the breaks on Santa Cruz's east side. Unmarried, lifelong bachelor. No known children. Always had girlfriends, though. Seemed always to be dating attractive younger women. Occasionally took off to spend months chasing waves around the world at some of the greatest surf spots, endless summering it. Guy was living the dream.

From back East originally, New York City suburbs, but he'd been a Santa Cruz resident for more than twenty years. Well-known figure in the community. Rich. Like so many in Santa Cruz now, he'd made his money in tech. Founder and CEO of AtreNet, a private company, a kind of design agency that built websites for other tech companies all over Silicon Valley. He was the charismatic center of a loyal circle of surfing tech-industry friends, all of whom had become practitioners of a kind of heady lifestyle discipline, a philosophy of hyperfocus, first formulated by Hungarian psychologist Mihaly Csikszentmihalyi in 1990, called "the flow." Atre had long lived in one or another of several houses near the ocean in Santa Cruz so he could put on his 4/3 wet suit at home and walk down to the rocks beneath the cliffs early each morning, break of dawn, dawn patrol, and paddle out and join the lineup and catch waves in the bracing, often sub-sixty-degree Pacific, where he'd absorb the sea's mineral vigors and commune with the otters and seals and birds and catch more waves, he and his friends working their minds, bodies, and selves into a kind of adrenal rapture. After surfing, after meditation, the flow state would be achieved. Then Atre and his friends would retire to their desks and go to work, focused, enthralled, relentless—ten, twelve, fourteen hours without pause—applying their energies to their various start-ups and inventions and business ideas. Atre had a large personality. He dressed quirkily—he wanted to stand out, but not too much—flat-brimmed trucker hats that he crumpled so the brims were no longer flat, board shorts, hiking sneakers, tech-wool hiking socks that he pulled up to his knees. He often worked late into the night and when he grew tired just fell into bed and slept in his clothes. He had a black, off-kilter sense of humor, was a rabble-rouser, a rogue, and was more fun to be around, his loyal friends believed, than anyone they had ever met in their lives. They begged to hang out with him. Often they brought their kids when they came over to hang out, and the kids loved Tushar, too. He kept a trampoline in his yard and skateboards, Onewheels, mountain bikes, cruisers, electric bikes, and other expensive vehicular toys. He'd let anyone borrow anything at any time. He kept a local lending library of surfboards (soft tops, fish boards, longboards, shortboards, guns, for any size person and all levels of ability) in an unlocked storage closet under the ocean-facing deck at his house, for anyone to take out into the breaks beyond. People who knew him described him as "childlike" and "an eager puppy" and "super juiced" and "*super* fired up" and "shameless" and "pretty ADHD" and "definitely crazy." He had his houses outfitted with hatches and trapdoors, secret passages and lofts, all of it ensconced in shiplap, cozy like the cabin of a yacht made of teak, like a fort. Kids went bananas when they saw these hideaways. It was as though Atre's life itself was an act of fort building, of cool curation. He was a patron of the local arts. He was a huge Wes Anderson fan. At one time he had a Wes Anderson mood board. Like an Anderson protagonist, he had a restless energy that demanded he always be building something, pursuing some new project. Buying homes and renovating them and flipping them. Converting a van into a surf-safari camper. Learning to play guitar on acoustic instruments handmade by a local luthier. Foraging for edible mushrooms in the redwood forests and then developing recipes around them. He knew wines, California wines, obscure coastal range pinot noirs, and paired them well. He experimented with growing the best weed he could, in small amounts, in his garden, or in a small grow room he fashioned out of a closet, not to sell but to share with his circle of attractive and successful and interesting and unconventional friends, all living their best lives with blue Pacific views in the fizzy coastal air under the golden light of the California sun.

RECENTLY, THOUGH, ATRE HAD DECIDED to make a change. Conjuring all his powers for one last big swing, he'd undertaken a major new project. He'd founded a weed company.

In the paperwork it was called Interstitial Systems, but its d/b/a was Cruz Science, one of the hundreds of cannabis start-ups launched in the state between 2017 and 2018 to exploit the opportunities presented by Proposition 64, passed by California voters on November 8, 2016, when weed in the nation's richest and most populous state was legalized for recreational use, sale, distribution, production, and cultivation. They were calling it the *dawn of a new industry*. They were calling it an *unprecedented opportunity*, the beginning of the end of prohibition, and Tushar Atre and his late-stage-capitalist cohort, trained in the most competitive and fortune-making business environment the world has ever known—Silicon Valley—were coming for cannabis. Silicon Valley interests had, after all, largely bankrolled the later phases of the cannabis legalization effort in California. Sean Parker, the Napster guy, the early-Facebook-investor guy, was the campaign's biggest donor. Tech entrepreneurs eyeing cannabis resembled the ship captains of the age of exploration. Cannabis, to them, was a resource-rich land inhabited by primitives. If they could position themselves among the first movers, they could come in and conquer and build themselves an empire.

Befitting his Silicon Valley background, Atre had entered what might be considered cannabis's high-tech sector, which also happened to be its hardest-core sector: not farming, not retail, but so-called manufacturing. That is, using chemistry to transform raw biomass—pot plant material—into the oils, waxes, butters, crystals, and cakes that contain THC in its purest, most concentrated form, and that serve as the base ingredients in today's innumerable cannabis products, including vape pens, gummies, cookies, beverages, and even skin creams. The process, called extraction, is borrowed partly from food science and partly from petroleum refining and partly from the fluid mechanics of HVAC engineering. It's also the descendant of the ancient craft of hashish preparation. In the decades before legalization, outlaw engineers had pioneered the techniques of extraction in secrecy. Sometimes they blew themselves to pieces or set themselves aflame or got themselves arrested on felony narcotics-production charges, for the process of decocting the highest-quality elixirs required the use of highly flammable hydrocarbons and thus was more dangerous even than the cooking of meth—and just as illicit.

Tushar Atre had big ambitions. He didn't just want to take this outlawry into the light. He wanted his company to extract oil from a thousand pounds of biomass per day, which would have made Cruz Science one of the largest cannabis oil manufacturers in California and thus the world. He'd promised as much to his investors, a venture capital outfit specializing in cannabis start-ups, which had injected $4.25 million in a Series A round into Cruz Science earlier in 2019. Atre wanted his company to reside at the cutting edge. He dreamed of establishing a hard-science research institute, an R&D lab that could isolate obscure cannabinoids in order to figure out what they did to the brain and then commercialize them. He began to think of his company as a weed biotech firm. He employed an organic chemist and several students at the University of California, Santa Cruz. In spirited brainstorming sessions, he talked about analyzing cannabis tissue cultures, with the aim of understanding the plant's DNA. He talked about applying to the Drug Enforcement Administration to be included on its short list of approved suppliers of cannabis products for scientific research. At times his staff had to slow down his febrile Silicon Valley mind.

The Cruz Science lab was housed inside a converted automotive repair shop at 211 Fern Street, in an industrial section of Santa Cruz city. Earlier on the morning of October 1, not long after the 911 call, police officers had rushed to the building and searched it. No one was inside. Instead, they found a gleaming state-of-the-art facility, filled to the rafters with chrome and brass and glass contraptions, giant flasks and beakers, stainless steel explosion-proof rooms, pipes and valves and dials and switches. It was steampunk. It might have been designed by Willy Wonka.

A tall muscular man with swept-back silver hair, expensive sunglasses, and an overall Hollywood air arrived in his Tesla at 211 Fern Street just before 9:00 a.m. His name was Alex Rowland. He was supposed to meet Atre at this address at this time, but instead there was a policeman standing sentry outside. What was going on? Rowland, another Bay Area tech entrepreneur in the legal weed business, was Atre's trading partner, competitor, and coinvestor in a *second* cannabis venture that Atre was pursuing, this one involving the extraction of CBD from tremendous quantities of hemp. Mr. Atre was missing, the cop finally divulged. The sheriff's office was investigating. That's all he was at liberty to say. Rowland's heart went into his throat. Robberies were a rite of passage in the weed business, he knew, but this was next level—a *dramatic escalation* were the words that came to mind. Still, it hadn't yet occurred to him that he might never see his friend and business partner again.

Investigators had been busy in the hours after Atre's kidnapping. Each of the four people who'd been sleeping inside the house on Pleasure Point Drive that night gave lengthy statements to police. The houseguests were all on the Cruz Science payroll. This was another of Atre's quirks. First at AtreNet, now at Cruz Science, he had a tendency to hire young people, or those without familial attachments, and put them up at his houses, striving to nurture a convivial, communal, collegial work-life dynamic. The houseguests were all engineers or technicians from out of town, contractors Atre had recruited to help build and run Fern Street's extraction machines. Interstitial Systems had officially existed since May 2017, yet these four were all recent hires. One had been on staff for less than a week.

Sheriff's deputies had also started contacting as many other Cruz Science employees and business associates as they could. Soon they'd hear that one associate, a local weed entrepreneur named Latif Horst, who spoke, incongruously, in a slick British accent, had argued with Atre the day before his disappearance. They would learn about a group of Samoan men who operated an auto repair shop and another business of an ambiguous nature out of one of Atre's Salinas warehouses. They would learn that Atre had not one, not two, but *three* disgruntled former partners in Cruz Science. All of these people—the former partners, the Samoans, Latif Horst, the houseguests at the time of the home invasion, Alex Rowland, and many Cruz Science employees—would become persons of interest in the case.

Before the sun had risen in Santa Cruz, a sheriff's deputy had also placed a call to Atre's latest girlfriend, or possibly now ex-girlfriend, Rachael Lynch. She was, at any rate, not living in Santa Cruz any longer but in western Massachusetts, and was some kind of marijuana entrepreneur herself. Overcome with anguish at the news of his disappearance, Lynch said she'd been having disturbing premonitions about Atre these last few weeks. But then, over the course of the call, she grew hostile, agitated. She said that she, too, was Atre's business partner. She started yelling at the deputy, saying the cops needed to search *all Tushar's properties*, especially the Summit property, immediately. *Why were they wasting time? Here's the address! Go! Now!* In a report, the deputies would later note that Lynch was "not cooperative." She, too, became a person of interest.

When the deputies arrived at Atre's mountain property, they prepared themselves for a number of possible outcomes: a hostage situation, a rescue mission, a gunfight? The footage from the security cameras on the neighboring houses would show three men walking down the sidewalk of Pleasure Point Drive at 3:00 a.m. wearing gloves, hoodies, baseball caps, and N95-style face masks. One of them carried an assault rifle, later determined to be an AR-15, its strap slung high across his chest. Another carried a black duffel bag. The suspects appeared to have tactical experience. The active theory was that the assailants were career burglars or career thugs or worse. It wasn't a leap to consider the possibility that Atre was taken out by a professional hit.

The sheriff's office certainly knew that an enormous marijuana black market—orders of magnitude larger than its aboveboard counterpart—still thrived in California, despite legalization or maybe because of it. Taxes and other costs were so high for legal operators that they often sold their products into the black market just to stay in business. The black market's profit margins were much greater. Weed remained federally illegal, which meant that interstate commerce in weed remained federally illegal, a statutory incoherence that spawned certain financial opportunities. The prices for weed and its derivatives in states (and nations) that had yet to legalize were far higher than in California, sometimes by a factor of ten or more. The black market existed expressly to exploit these market inefficiencies. And the cannabis black market, a diverse shadow economy of long standing, still included elements of violent organized crime. Had Tushar Atre ever done business with anyone dangerous? Already the sheriffs had called in for support: A no-fly zone for commercial and private aircraft had been established overhead, and a team of militarized SWAT guys in black body armor were on their way.

Leading the approach to the BMW was a young, skinny deputy named Daniel Robbins, whose father had made his name as the county's top narcotics cop during the years of full-scale weed prohibition. In the 1980s and 1990s, the elder Robbins and other officers created havoc among Santa Cruz's pot smugglers and dealers and growers, of which there were many, for the region had long been a hub of the weed and illicit drugs trade. Here, in the rugged, remote Santa Cruz Mountains, one of California's coastal ranges, the counterculture had found one of its first bucolic, dharma-bum milieus. In the mid 1960s, the novelist Ken Kesey kept his famous writing cabin in La Honda, in the northwest part of the range, where he threw his wild hallucinogenic parties and incubated the Merry Pranksters and its house band, the Grateful Dead. With Kesey's crowd providing the initial demand, some of the earliest commercial marijuana crops in the US were planted in the Santa Cruz Mountains. Nestled in these cloistered reaches, hippie spiritual communes proliferated, along with their secret gardens. Hillbilly hippies with dreadlock beards buried safes in the woods containing hundreds of thousands of dollars in cash. In the hills, in the hollows, up the draws and the old dirt logging roads, hidden in the chaparral above the fog line, growing and selling weed became a way of life, woven into the community and its economy. It was a dynamic analogous to deep Appalachia, with its moonshiners and revenuers and don't-tread-on-me pride. To generations of people in the weed business in Santa Cruz, there was no greater enemy than the Santa Cruz County Sheriff's Office.

Now, crouched behind a Ford Interceptor, Robbins took in the property. In addition to the white BMW there were four other vehicles parked in close proximity: two classic Jeep Wagoneers from the 1990s and two Toyota Tacomas—including one that Atre had reported stolen back in December. Rising around them in all directions were stands of towering redwoods. The cars were situated on a little plateau, almost a peninsula, surrounded on three sides by downward sloping terrain. At the back of the peninsula, near a cluster of redwoods, stood a giant tepee, at least twenty feet high. Elsewhere there was a large yurt and a well-built outdoor kitchen framed in redwood timbers. The place had Wes Anderson vibes. You could have glamped there. But it also meant there were many places for assailants to hide.

One by one, Robbins and his team peeled away from their redoubt behind the Interceptor and cleared the pickups and the Wagoneers. They were on the lookout for bodies, cop speak not for corpses but live human beings, armed and dangerous. They carefully approached the BMW. The driver's side window was partially open. Robbins looked inside. Empty. Along the length of the passenger door, however, he saw what appeared to be blood. A dark reddish splotch, possibly a palm print, stood out like graffiti against the BMW's gleaming white finish, just above the gas cap. And along the length of the passenger door was a reddish-brown horizontal smear.

Robbins noticed something else, something he hadn't observed on a previous visit to the property a year earlier, when he'd come to investigate the theft of the Tacoma. On the other side of a shallow gully shrouded by large trees was a clearing several football fields in size, like a meadow. But the meadow was planted with a crop, hundreds of plants, it looked like, in swollen October bloom, tall gangly stalks with colas blossoming from their branches. This property was not the site of a state-licensed cannabis cultivation. Atre, it seemed, was growing black market weed on a commercial scale.

Robbins heard a shout from one of his deputies, who directed the others' attention down a slope about ten yards from the plateau. Amid the underbrush and atop the pine straw duff and in sight of the marijuana, they saw a flash of bright red. Not blood. It was a pair of athletic shorts. And legs with black socks pulled up to the knees, no shoes on the feet. And an olive-colored sweatshirt on the torso of a man lying on his side, his hands bound behind his back with plastic flex-cuffs. There was blood and matter on the duff around his clean-shaven head, which was turned toward the ground so you couldn't fully see his face, just part of his profile, the crown of his skull almost touching the trunk of a young redwood tree. No need to bring in the paramedics. As Robbins would later say in court, "He was clearly, clearly deceased."

Robbins told the other deputies to stand back. They had to preserve the integrity of the scene for the forensic people and the detectives, though the cause of death was immediately plain. A single circular entrance wound dotted the back of the dead man's skull. Atre had been shot, execution style.

2. Dropping In

One spring day in 2016, Cynthia E. collapsed at her house in South Pomfret, Vermont. An ambulance, a hospital stay, a diagnosis—stage-four endometrial cancer—and just like that, at sixty-five years old, Rachael's mother was dying. At the time Rachael was thirty and living in Arcata, on the coast of Humboldt County, in far Northern California. Her business over the previous three years had been strong. She'd saved a lot of cash, so it was no problem for her to quit Humboldt, where things had gotten a little dicey for her anyway, and take a long vacation with her mother, a professional artist who was also Rachael's best friend. Cynthia had divorced Rachael's father when Rachael was just three, never remarried, raised six children on her own in tiny South Pomfret, and now was in a fight for her life against this virulent and unfair disease.

Ever since Rachael was a little girl running around those same Vermont woods, she believed she had the gift of intuition—inherited, indeed, from her wise mother. And even before her mother's diagnosis, her intuition had been compelling her toward a specific beach town on the central California coast, a sunny Pacific place, far from the bitter New England winter, that now seemed perfect for Cynthia, too: Santa Cruz.

She found a rental on Airbnb. Small but stylish, it had two bedrooms, a balcony, a hot tub. It was the upstairs unit in a multiunit house on Thirty-Eighth Avenue, in the heart of a trendy neighborhood, Pleasure Point, full of renovated beach shacks, slender-trunked Mexican fan palms that soared into a dome of baby blue sky, and aromatic jacaranda trees that burst into grape-soda phantasms of billowing purple every spring. Better yet, the apartment was just two blocks from picturesque cliffs atop which you could gaze out at the sets of uncannily uniform waves rolling in from beyond the horizon and corduroying whole nautical acres of Monterey Bay. Surfers were all over the place: in the water, paddling out, dropping in, shredding, wiping out, climbing down into the water from the rocky cliffs, milling around on the street corners, their black wet suits half off, clouds of marijuana smoke hovering over their heads, gearing up behind meticulously restored VW Buses and camper vans, or commuting to the breaks on their bikes, surfboards clasped under their arms.

The apartment's host, according to the Airbnb listing, was a man named Tushar Atre. Cynthia met him first. She was the only one home when he came by to see how his new guests were settling in. Immediately disarming, he was able to persuade Cynthia—whose hip often pained her because of the cancer—to let him, a stranger, take her to one of his favorite spots in all of the Santa Cruz Mountains, a spiritual retreat a few miles away called Land of Medicine Buddha. It was, he said, a peaceful forest refuge for meditation and healing. There they strolled arm in arm on hushed, densely shadowed paths that forked and wove among giant redwoods and temples with colorful prayer flags. They spun the prayer wheels and read the inscriptions. They dwelt at the shrine of Ksitigarbha, described by a nearby sign as one of the eight great students of the Buddha, who had a "deep relationship with beings of the earth—humans, and especially with the hungry ghosts and hell beings." Reciting his mantra helped "avert danger." Another temple contained a large bell meant to honor Namgyalma, the deity of longevity. Cynthia gonged it. In front of the fat golden Ksitigarbha statue, Tushar snapped a selfie: he in a trucker cap and an olive-colored sweatshirt, she in a headscarf and a pair of purple-tinted folk singer sunglasses, both smiling warmly into the lens.

Cynthia, of course, relayed all of this to Rachael when she returned home, rolling up to the curb outside in the white BMW X3 she'd bought used in Arcata a year or two before. Tushar may have been older, her mother said, but he was altogether charming and apparently single. Rachael rolled her eyes.

Two days later, Cynthia heard Tushar spelunking down in the garage. At the time, he didn't live at the beach, so he used the Thirty-Eighth Avenue house as a storage place for his many boards and wet suits. *He's here!* Cynthia whispered loudly to Rachael across the room. Then Cynthia opened the front door, poked her head out, and yoo-hooed in flirtatious singsong down to the man in the courtyard below. *Tushar! Rachael's here today! Come meet my daughter!*

Tushar bounded up the exterior staircase and saw Rachael for the first time. She was tall and slender, with blue-green eyes, high cheekbones, and long light-brown hair. Rachael, for her part, was embarrassed by her mother's meddling. He was their landlord. Give him some space. But she said hello and made small talk about, what else, surfing. She mentioned that she'd recently bought a wet suit. Would she like to go out and surf with him? he asked. Right now. This morning. He had a board she could use! Her first reaction was no. She really didn't want to deal with some smitten landlord right now, her mother sick, this guy trying to barge into her life. But. . . . It was true. . . . He *didn't* look forty-seven. He was about her height but strapping, with a surfer's lats and V-shaped torso. And . . . you know . . . she *was* planning to take surfing lessons anyway . . . and she'd always viewed life as an *adventure*, and here was another one presenting itself. When she told this story many years later, she described something like clouds parting. She could hear her inner voice instructing her: "Say yes to things like this!"

They practiced their pop-ups on the living room floor then walked down Thirty-Eighth Avenue toward the ocean. She had never surfed before in her life, but for reasons unclear to her, she allowed Tushar to think that she had. But whatever. She was a superb swimmer. She was in good shape. How hard could this be?

The first bad sign was the crowd. Or the lack of one. Huge winter storms had been pounding Santa Cruz all that week, mothering swells that had attracted droves of surfers from all over the Bay Area. Pleasure Point had been like a surfer convention. But now almost all of them were gone. Why?

The second bad sign was their launch point. They had to set off into the water from a pile of jagged rocks at the bottom of a cliff. Apparently, from this spot, you had to just leap headfirst into the water and onto your board and start paddling. This wasn't just any water, though. It was a boiling, seething, high tide maelstrom of snot-green sea. But she did leap, following Tushar's wordless lead after waiting for an angry mass of a wave to explode into the rocks. Later she would learn that the reason so few surfers were out there on this day was that the waves, though big, were crumbly, mushy, closed out—crappy, in other words, and dangerous, and the water was nasty and polluted with runoff from the previous night's mighty rains. But now here she was lying prone on this plank with a roaring foaming wall of white water careening toward her. *Dive!* she heard him yell above the sea's din, and she did as she was told, did what she saw him do, performing her first ever duck dive, an advanced and technically challenging maneuver in which, right at the base of a crashing wave, you push down on your board with all your might, making the buoyant thing submerge so you can slip underwater, below the surface turbulence, and advance to safety beyond the peril of the break—in this case, a point break on the east side of Santa Cruz, one of the most famous surf spots in the world. Up into the air and breathing again, she sees Tushar calmly paddling in front of her and, again, she follows his lead. He offers little guidance—zero guidance, actually—and she is terrified but keeps following him through a channel of relative calm, out to where the biggest waves are breaking. And finally she shouts above the sea roar: *I've never done this before!* And he looks over his shoulder, surprised, but then they spot a big wave in the distance—she better get ready *now*, it's her time *now*—and he's yelling for her to paddle like hell, and he's close enough to give her board a powerful shove, and suddenly she's flying on top of this thing, paddling like hell, gazing down its steep face, and all around her it's a chaos of elemental oceanic force and velocity and mass—this monster that's risen up and taken her and is now apparently trying to kill her, and despite all this mayhem she has the presence of mind to try to execute the pop-up like they'd practiced on the living room floor, and she does that, she pops up, and she's standing, and in her memory of this moment she can hear Tushar's voice singing in exuberant ululation, but then in that exact same instant, her balance, this vanishing nanosecond of balance, is lost, and she is no longer standing, she's plunging headfirst into the turbulent sea.

AFTERWARD TUSHAR TOOK HER OUT TO LUNCH, and they talked about the excitement of the morning. Why hadn't she told him she was a total surfing novice? Well, how could *he* have been so . . . unmindful? . . . as to bring anyone but a total expert into those fiendish conditions. On this occasion at least, beginner's luck seemed real.

Tushar steered the conversation. He was blunt. His Airbnb was not cheap: forty-two hundred dollars a month. Yet Rachael had wanted to pay all four months up front in cash. Her offer made him curious, made him think she had a story to tell. She could see the intrigue in his eyes, his widening Cheshire cat grin. How was it that a young person like her was able to pay such a large sum in cash?

She dreaded this sort of question. It was tantamount to asking what she did for a living. And she didn't like telling people what she did for a living. Answering truthfully often turned her into something like a celebrity. People wanted to be her friend, wanted access to her product, her know-how, and sometimes her money. Or people would become judgmental. And so with Tushar she danced around it, played coy. *Hmm, how am I paying in cash? Maybe I just withdrew it from the bank? Maybe I'm trying to avoid taxes?*

No, seriously, he said.

She told him she was an entrepreneur.

What kind of entrepreneur?

She ran her own businesses up north, she said.

Where up north?

Humboldt, she said. And instantly she knew this was like saying Wall Street or Hollywood or Silicon Valley. You tell people you work in those places, it goes without saying you're in finance, movies, tech. She'd been cornered.

OK, she said. *I'm in cannabis.*

Now his curiosity was really amped. He pressed her for more, and eventually she relented. She told him about her career as a pot farmer in the wilds of the so-called Emerald Triangle, the three vast counties in northernmost California—Humboldt, Mendocino, Trinity—that together formed one of, if not the, most productive marijuana-growing regions in the world. But she wasn't just any self-taught pot farmer, she bragged. She had a degree in environmental science and was an agriculturalist certified in permaculture. She told him about being the only woman growing weed on a backwoods hill otherwise full of stoner dudes bursting with unvented testosterone. About managing a staff of ne'er-do-wells and the management lessons she gleaned from that experience. About the neighboring grow operated by a Mexican drug cartel. About flipping boxes—a *box* in the lexicon meant a hundred pounds of pot; *flipping* meant brokering, selling, dealing. About how she sold most of her weed back East. About how she'd pursued a career, basically, as a drug dealer, but also as an entrepreneur and start-up founder in the vast, unregulated, underground, male-dominated economy of American weed. And about how, after her mother became ill, Rachael had quit the business to take care of her.

Her stories bewitched him. He wanted to know more, more, more. Because, he said, legalization in California had come, and it was a gigantic opportunity, and he, too, had been thinking—for quite a while now!—about getting into the cannabis business.

Yeah, she said, *you and everybody else.*

What are your dreams? he asked her. *What would you do if you could do anything in cannabis?*

She did have ideas, she did have dreams, but she had no desire to share them with someone she'd known for just a few hours.

All she wanted him to know for now was that she could easily cover the monthly rent in cash, and she had a lot more behind that.

By the way, she told him, something other than the prime location had drawn her to select his Airbnb above similarly priced places in Santa Cruz: The numerology of the monthly rent figure. Forty-two hundred, a multiple of four twenty—4:20, the stoner's hour.

Tushar grinned.

AFTER THAT DAY, Tushar kept coming around. He wanted Rachael to sit down with him so he could pick her brain. It was sort of getting on her nerves . . . and sort of not. He seemed like a fun guy to hang out with; the promise of thrills and mischief surrounded him. She liked his unique style, outdoorsy surfer: the hiking socks and sneakers, the loudly colorful board shorts, and the same T-shirts all the time, like the one that said across the front, "Find what you love and let it kill you." It could have been his mantra. He was passionate about things, and he wanted to know all about her cannabis ideas. She, on the other hand, wasn't sure if this interest in her entrepreneurial vision was just a pretense for his flirting or if it was the other way around: The flirting was the pretense.

One day a bunch of workers appeared on the property, carpenters and other tradespeople, there ostensibly to remodel the other units. Then Tushar started working from the house, conducting business from its garage, which he'd converted into a kind of office. He was the founder and CEO of AtreNet, which designed websites for Silicon Valley start-ups, software companies mostly, and so Tushar was always on the phone dealing with clients and managing employees. More than once, Rachael and her mother overheard him screaming into the phone in fits of rage.

Finally Rachael succumbed to his persistence. He invited her to his main residence, a bungalow in the prosperous village of Los Gatos, situated on the northern flank of the Santa Cruz Mountains, its real estate among the priciest in the Bay Area, its streets lined with live oak and date palms, Teslas and Land Rovers. It was the kind of Silicon Valley town that appeared to be populated entirely by tech lords, their attorneys, and exes who'd taken half.

Rachael had just completed an urgent errand up north. Her mother had had a string of good days, so Rachael felt comfortable leaving her alone at the beach for a day or two so she could shoot up to Arcata. She had stored around a hundred pounds of pot up there with trusted associates, a pair of brothers now in their sixties, also commercial pot growers, who knew how to keep weed safe from the crews of professional bandits who plagued the business. One of the brothers was the former chieftain of the Fog Dogs, a Humboldt biker gang said to be affiliated with the Hells Angels. To Rachael, though, they were less chain-whip, dirty-thunder outlaws and more grandpa Santas with Harley hobbies. It turns out Rachael was not *entirely* retired. She needed to sell the weed, remnants of her 2016 harvests, before the quality degraded.

She'd gone up there, successfully dealt with the stash, and was on her way back to Santa Cruz when Tushar called. Los Gatos, not far off Route 17, the road to Santa Cruz from Silicon Valley, was right on her way.

After she arrived, Tushar poured them glasses of wine and took her on a tour of the premises. The house itself was a century-old Craftsman jewel box he'd bought a few years earlier. He'd renovated the place and refitted it like a kid's fort, with secret hatches and ladders and nooks and hideaways. He showed her the small backyard where he'd been growing small ganja yields, experimenting with various strains and growing techniques. Then he handed her a jar of some of his nuggets. What did she think?

The buds looked OK, if a little brown and shaggily untrimmed in that homegrown way. But when she uncapped the jar and took a whiff, instead of a tangy herbaceous blast, there was only the barest trace of a scent. She rolled a joint with bits of the crumbling flower and sampled it. She wasn't impressed. Somehow he'd botched the curing process, a notoriously tricky but critical phase of weed production.

Well, this was just one of his many tinkerer's hobbies. He wasn't a pro like her. He grew it so he could give it away to friends. Gift weed. He said he'd been growing on and off since his college years, and then he began telling her his personal weed story. Everyone in cannabis had one, and there was a sameness to them: the first puffs as a teen, the surreptitious attempts to grow a few feeble specimens in bedroom closets, the high school dope dealing, selling eighths to other teenagers in the parking lots of Taco Bells. . . .

But Tushar's story was different. After high school in Rye, New York, the Westchester suburbs, he went to college at NYU—this was in the late 1980s, early '90s—but he'd never smoked weed; he was, in fact, *anti-stoner*, did not vibe at all with the drug's hippie connotations. His scene was more downtown hipster. He got heavily into urban biking, racing all over the city, until the day—June 6, 1990—when he was shooting down Broadway and a car clipped him and he crashed to the street, and the truck that was right behind him had no time to stop. He was rushed to the hospital. He had emergency surgery. It was bad. The doctors told his parents to prepare for the worst. But of course he didn't die. He fought. He defied expectations. And while he was in the hospital recovering, he got to talking to a chaplain—a Catholic priest, Tushar said—who told him that a good way to stimulate his appetite (because other drugs were suppressing it) was with, yes, weed. Despite his prejudice, Tushar told Rachael, he took the chaplain's advice. And he immediately found that smoking a little marijuana did make him hungry. (He had to be careful, though, with pot's paranoia-inducing effects.) Still, Tushar being Tushar, he made a study of it. Why not grow it himself instead of enriching a bunch of drug dealers?

He experimented in his college apartment near NYU, cultivating various strains. He harvested tiny amounts. He smoked some and gave some away. And sold some, too. Already in college he'd built a little fake-ID business, he told Rachael, peddling fraudulent driver's licenses to the underaged of NYC. His weed growing went on for a while until the day his mother visited his apartment and discovered his closet jungled over with this fragrant green psychotropic profusion. She was not just appalled; she was furious. *Keep that up*, she said, *and you will receive no further financial support from us.* His mother was an executive at IBM, a database scientist, an Indian woman who had risen up a corporate ladder dominated by white men. She was by far the most influential figure in young Tushar's life. Admittedly and without question, Tushar was a mama's boy.

So that was the end of that. Life went on. He graduated and eventually made his way to Silicon Valley, where, with his mother's connections in the software industry, he launched the business that would become AtreNet. Designing and building websites for tech start-ups. It proved lucrative. And he found that he excelled at sales, buddying up with tech CEOs and chief marketing officers and getting them to pay handsomely for his firm's services. For sure the business had fat profit margins. It financed his great life. But it was also proving to be, after twenty years, boring. Tushar was bored. So, *so* bored. After a career in marketing and branding, he wanted to *make* something. He wanted to pull the levers in the chocolate factory, so to speak, and see the candy bars coming out the other end. . . .

He may not have come out and said it in so many words, but to Rachael it was clear. AtreNet was his mom's company. It had been her idea. Her connections had made it possible. In its early stages, she'd even moved to Santa Cruz to help birth the company, Tushar's entrepreneurial doula. "I used the name Atre not because it's my last name, but because it's her last name," he'd told the *Santa Cruz Sentinel*. For the better part of AtreNet's existence, for most of his career, he'd essentially been working for his mom. He was approaching fifty; it was now or never. It was time to prove himself. To become an adult. Become his *own* man. He wanted—needed—to build a business himself. He wanted, he *needed*, to change his life.

Hanging on a wall in Tushar's house was a whiteboard. He sat down cross-legged on the floor in front of it and handed Rachael a marker. *Remember that entrepreneurial dream you were telling me about?* he said. *Draw it for me now.*

Her ideas. Her vision for a cannabis enterprise. She even had a name for it. Benevolence Bound. *Bound* as in headed toward a destination, a journey with an end goal, but also *bound* as in tied, as in shackled, to doing good. She'd been thinking about this for years, dreaming about it, *manifesting it*. She'd actually sketched out a graphic version of her plan just the previous summer, in the pages of her journal, like an illustrated business proposal. At the whiteboard, standing in front of Tushar, she sketched something similar. First, the necessary facilities. A central farm on which to grow cannabis from seed. No buying of baby plants from a nursery. This business would be seed to sale. Vertically integrated. Also a processing facility to extract and isolate THC and other cannabinoid molecules from plants she'd grown herself, turning those isolates into powders that could be encapsulated in pills so that consistent dosages of THC and CBD and CBN and other cannabinoids might be administered to people in physical pain. Medicine. This plant was medicine. *Bioactive* medicine. Why not also have a testing facility to determine potencies? How about a batch of warehouses for storage of raw materials, for use as a distribution hub, and also extra space so that the business could be *scaled up*? Why not be prepared? The state-by-state legalization of weed was just the beginning. The final brick in the wall of US marijuana prohibition—that the federal government still outlawed the sale of weed between states—would eventually be removed. And when that wall finally toppled, the real cannabis boom would begin, especially for weed brands that were already established, and especially—*especially*—for established weed brands in that greatest of all the weed-producing states, California. What an enormous opportunity! She felt like she was pitching Tushar on something he'd already agreed to buy, but she kept going, saying: *We'll need to scale this thing up!* Why not have a building that could serve as employee housing? Why not hire and train nurses in the administration of this profound therapeutic substance to a population addicted catastrophically to opioids? Why not clinical trials? Why not FDA approval? Why not? Why not?

Sitting in front of the whiteboard, Tushar appeared riveted. She remembers him saying: *I want to do this with you*. She remembers looking at him, not sure what his angle was, if he was humoring her, bullshitting her, trying to get her in the sack. He said: *What if I give you the money to make all of this happen?* She remembers replying, *Well, I don't take partners.* She had taken partners before. It almost never ended well. Any time business had gone bad for her, humans were to blame, not the plants. But he persisted, wouldn't let it go, kept trying to figure out how they could get going ASAP. He was thinking out loud here, spitballing. What if they started growing weed somewhere *right now*? He would fund the planting. Sure it would be unlicensed, but who cared? Or he could stake her a hundred grand and she could use that money to buy and sell weed on the black market, just like she was doing now anyway, and they could use the profit from that to seed the legal start-up! *No, no, no*, she remembers saying. *If* they were going to do this, he absolutely *should not* put his clean money toward any kind of black market business. She told him, *I see that you want to make money—but that's all I see*.

Their dialogue went on for hours, deep into the night. She slept over but did not sleep with him. At some point, she explained to him her "theory of the plant." Cannabis gives more than it receives. It has evolved alongside humans. It has this enormous range of uses. For example—she was lecturing him now—it's one of the few plants that can be used to create a substitute for mother's milk. Cannabis when it's growing also gives off heat, she said—waves, *vibes*. Science has proven this, she claimed. And so all of this together had convinced her that the cannabis plant contained its own karma—it radiated karmic energy, produced karmic beauty, and if you tried to use this plant only to make money, if you used it only to feed your ego, then you were *raping* the plant. You were blocking its value, inhibiting its vibes, preventing it from adding to the beauty of the world. You were creating bad karma.

And Tushar agreed with all of that. *Agreed!* he kept saying. *Agreed!* He totally understood . . . and he loved her ideas. Medicine. Science. Technology. Yes. Seed to sale. Yes. Best of all: doing something good in the world, good *for* the world, for once in his life. Not only causing no harm, but adding to the world's store of good. Was it corny? Maybe. But so what! The stakes were too high. They couldn't be any higher!

With his phone he took a picture of Rachael's whiteboard renderings, and in the days and weeks to come, he appeared unable to think of anything else. Every chance he got, he came over to the Airbnb to talk cannabis business with her. The first step was finding a farm, a piece of property for which they could seek a cultivation license. It would be legal. And he kept talking about what Rachael had said, about her theory of the plant, about his role in this whole thing. There was a kind of math to his altruism. He said, *If I help you develop your ideas, I know I'll be helping the world. Therefore, helping you helps me go to heaven.* If he could just help Rachael, he would *get into heaven*. Those were the words he used. As far as Rachael knew, Tushar had no religion, wasn't spiritual at all. Mocked it, even. But now he seemed dead serious. The way he talked, it was like he was desperate to save his soul.

3. The Houseguests

October 1, 2019

They were still wearing their pajamas and sleeping clothes when deputies escorted them out of the house at 3034 Pleasure Point Drive and drove them in patrol cars through the early-morning dark to the headquarters building of the Santa Cruz County Sheriff's Office. In a quirk of the local districting, Pleasure Point Drive was not located within the borders of the City of Santa Cruz, but instead in an unincorporated part of the county. And so the task of solving Atre's murder had fallen to the sheriff.

At HQ, deputies politely ushered each of the four houseguests into separate rooms. The guests had already spoken to the uniformed deputies who'd responded to the 911 call, but now they were told they needed to give formal statements to the plainclothes detectives just assigned to the case.

Two of the four houseguests were partners in both senses of the word, a husband-and-wife team of engineers who ran a firm based in Penn Valley, California, in the Sierra Nevada foothills. The Ides were their names: Neil and Diana Ide. For the last month, the couple had been working inside Atre's extraction facility at 211 Fern Street, in the final stages of the project Atre had hired them to execute: Design and assemble a massive machine that used ethanol as the solvent to extract oil from cannabis plant matter. With its valves and piping and chimneys, this was the monstrous

Willy Wonkan apparatus that nearly filled the Fern Street interior. Atre's strategy was scale, Mr. Ide said. Atre wanted this thing to excrete such prodigious volumes that his company would dominate the market for cannabis oil.

While the Ides finished the job, Atre had insisted that the couple stay in the guest suite he'd fashioned below the main house at 3034, under the deck. The suite had its own entrance, bathroom, kitchenette, and a balcony overlooking the sea. Yesterday, Monday, after the day's work, around 5:00 p.m., the Ides had said good night to Atre at the lab—and that was the last time they ever saw him. The couple came home to their suite, where they had dinner, read for a bit, turned out the lights, bedtime. But then, at 2:57 a.m., Diana nudged Neil awake. They could hear shouting in the main house above, clamorous noises. They could hear, in Neil's words, "shit being thrown around," heavy objects, maybe furniture, slamming to the floor. It sounded like a fight, "like a real conflict." Bald, bespectacled, skinny, in his late thirties, Neil resembled one of those pocket-protector NASA engineers of Apollo missions of yore. He and Diana had a five-year-old daughter staying back home with their grandma, four hours north, while they finished the Cruz Science job. The little girl and Grandma were *just here* in Santa Cruz, had stayed in that very house, had *just left* yesterday after visiting for the weekend. *No way* was Neil Ide going upstairs and inserting himself into whatever dangerous event was unfolding up there. He and Diana sat upright in the bed, motionless, listening, waiting for it to be over. . . .

The other two houseguests were Stephanie Murri, who went by the nickname Murphy, and her assistant, Christopher Berry. At the sheriff's office, Murphy Murri told the detective taking her statement that she was, essentially, Atre's new head of extraction. She was a contractor, though, a consultant, not a salaried employee, and had just begun her work with Atre a month ago, commuting to Santa Cruz from her home outside of Denver. She had other clients, too. She traveled around the nation training and consulting with extractors. When she flew out to Santa Cruz for the very first time, in late August or early September, she'd met Atre as well as his girlfriend, a woman named Rachael, at the 3034 house. The way Tushar and Rachael told it, they'd met some years earlier, prior to California legalization, tech bro and cannabis girl, had fallen in love and gone into business. Now they were turning it into a licensed thing, and Atre needed Murri to help get the Fern Street lab ready, at long last, to push out big volumes.

Detectives would soon learn that Murphy Murri was a well-known figure in her field, a leading innovator in the preparation of high-quality cannabis concentrates, particularly an increasingly popular product known as live resin. With her bottle blond hair, nose piercing, gleaming white teeth, and tattooed arms, she had become something of a social media star, with more than twenty thousand Instagram followers. In the videos she posted frequently, she liked to wear a white lab coat. Three weeks later, she would post a photo of a fresh tattoo on her shoulder blade: a cartoon skull framed by the words *Live Resin or Die Tryin*. The photo received nearly a thousand likes.

At the sheriff's office Murri told the detective that she had spent the previous eighteen or so hours at the Fern Street lab, most of it with her assistant, Chris, running batches of biomass through its two functioning extraction units, loading them up for more runs the following day, then scrubbing the whole place down in preparation for a visit from an important customer, also the very next day. By the time they returned to the Pleasure Point house, it was after midnight, and they were exhausted. They assumed Atre was home, as well, asleep in his own bedroom, his vintage Porsche parked in the garage. He'd been working with them at the lab until about 9:30. He was tired, he told them. *See you guys tomorrow*, he'd said. They never saw him again.

Murri's suite, like the Ides', had its own private entrance. Atre had created these units so they could be rented on Airbnb. After crashing into bed, Murri told the detective, she'd slept right through everything, oblivious, her room soundproofed by the Pacific's white noise.

In the last of the four interview rooms, Chris Berry gave his statement to Detective Erik Miyoshi. At forty-one, Miyoshi was both a late bloomer and a fast riser as a law enforcement officer. He'd been on the force for just six years before being elevated to detective in 2018. Tushar Atre was Miyoshi's first murder case in a leadership role. At the table, Berry looked worn down and freaked out. An extraction technician who'd worked with Murri on previous consulting projects, Berry was in his mid-thirties, and based in Sacramento. He'd been hired by Murri for the Cruz Science job only the previous week. The day of the murder, Monday, was his *first official day* at Fern Street after signing his employment contract! He barely knew Tushar Atre at all. He'd worked nonstop with Murri into the night, and when they got back to Pleasure Point, they went to Murri's room, took a few puffs from cannabis vapes as they planned the next day's work, before Berry retired to his own bedroom inside the main house. It shared a wall with Atre's master suite. Drained from the day's labors, Berry took a shower, lay down, and then screwed earplugs into his ears. He was dropping off, about to slide into unconsciousness, when he became aware of voices—raised and angry voices. He sat up and took out the plugs. He thought he heard an unfamiliar voice shout, "Get on your stomach!" and, "Put your hands behind your back!" He heard a male voice that sounded like Atre's say, calmly, "How can we make things right?" He heard, "Open the safe!" He heard a sequence of beeps, as though from the depression of electronic keypad buttons. He heard, "Where is it?" and, "Where are they?" Then all the voices and all the sounds seemed to move in a tumult through the house and out the front door and into the street. He thought he heard a car engine start, maybe two car engines. He heard a voice shrieking in terror or pain or both. He heard the same voice scream, "Help me!" And he heard the same voice call out his name—"Chris! Chris!" But through all the shouting and all the racket, Berry had been too frightened to move—he assumed the invaders were coming for him next—so he waited and waited until he was sure there were no more voices, no more car engines. He told Miyoshi that he'd made sure the front door was locked behind him when he'd come back from Fern Street; Atre must have let these people in, must have known them. Finally, Berry left his room and darted over to Murri's suite, trembling and bumbling, and woke her up and delivered the inconceivable news. Atre had been kidnapped! To Murri this came across as *a preposterous combination of words*. They'd just seen him! They *had plans*! They had *stuff to do*! In this state of semidenial, they walked outside and down to the Ides' suite. They knocked on the Ides' door. Inside, they all conferred in a panic—the Ides were convinced that whoever had taken Atre had taken him to the Cruz Science lab, had wanted something that was there. Neil grabbed his wife's phone and dialed 911.

According to detectives' later calculations, twenty-nine minutes had elapsed since the assailants had taken Atre from the house, vanishing with him into the Santa Cruz dark.

4. Call Ben Rice

Was she falling in love with him or with the idea of running a cannabis business with him? Maybe it didn't matter. Maybe it was the same thing. It was all happening so quickly. A cannabis partnership was in the works. The whole endeavor seemed poised somewhere between the real and the pretend. But life was an adventure, right? (*Say yes to things like this.*)

They began searching for land in Santa Cruz. Their real estate agent, whose long black hair was streaked with bolts of white, had a witchy, earth mother vibe. She seemed to know everyone who was anyone in Santa Cruz weed, one of the many legitimate businesspeople in California—Realtors, lawyers, accountants, electricians, carpenters, equipment suppliers, hydroponic storekeepers, a vast vibrant ecosystem—who earned some portion of their incomes from those who were directly engaged in growing and selling weed. She suggested they focus their efforts on a subregion of the Santa Cruz Mountains known as the Summit, so-called because it encompassed the highest point in the range, Loma Prieta Peak. At an elevation of nearly four thousand feet, rugged and remote, the Summit was also home to a section of the San Andreas Fault—the epicenter of the 1989 earthquake was, in fact, at Loma Prieta—and had long attracted pot cultivators, a historic weed-growing region within a historic weed-growing region.

Rachael in this period was full of optimism bordering on euphoria. "My dream farm is coming," she wrote in her journal in March 2017. "Tushar is a great and good friend" whose "support . . . lifts me high enough to not falter so easily anymore. However long it takes I will get there, where I can be proud to watch a benevolent business run behind our wonderful partnership." They had long brainstorming sessions. Tushar at one point entered her dreams. With the poor spelling that Tushar would later make fun of, she wrote in her journal, "I drempt that I jumped across a babbling brook onto some nice moss only to be caught by Tushar. He stabilized me by my arms, and I woke up."

For his part, Tushar took to sleeping overnight in the garage he'd converted into an office. He had his workers haul a bed into the garage, build a bathroom, and install a shower. He'd also fallen in love with Rachael's dog, Hashtag, and was already telling her how badly he wanted children—three children, he said—and he spun a scene involving the whole family jumping on the bed and laughing and laughing. Suddenly it was like he'd moved in. Late one night about a month after they'd first met, Rachael stole quietly downstairs to his makeshift suite. Tushar never locked his door, so she just sauntered inside, where she found him sitting up in bed, his laptop open, doing AtreNet work. She got in beside him and said something like: *Are we doing business? OK, let's do business.* Tushar killed the lights. Now they were both kinds of partner.

AT SOME POINT in early 2017, they sat down with Ben Rice, the best-known weed lawyer in Santa Cruz. Tall and wiry, with a mop of steel gray hair and a matching chevron mustache, Rice was an old progressive, one of the phalanx of activist attorneys in the Bay Area who'd gone to battle across decades against the square forces of marijuana prohibition. He had a robust criminal-defense practice, representing weed growers, extractors, and dealers against a spectrum of felony charges. The sheriff had long joked that Rice had the biggest business card in all of Santa Cruz County. When deputies would fly over the mountains looking for illegal pot farms to raid, they would sometimes encounter sheets of plywood spray-painted with the words: *Call Ben Rice*. Though he grew up in the Bay Area, Rice came from a family of Boston Brahmins. His father and grandfather were Harvard men, but young Ben chose a different path. In 1966, after ignoring the draft, Rice went west, not east, a surfer (and part-time construction worker) bumming on the beaches of Hawaii. Then came a complicated series of events that would change his life. It all started with a chance encounter with a group of young GIs who wanted to know if hip-looking Ben could help them score one last lid of grass before they shipped out for 'Nam, Ben saying *sure man*, but the GIs weren't GIs, they turned out to be undercover federal agents, *you're under arrest*, and then a federal marijuana charge, and probation, and then refuge in a tree house commune on Kauai, and a second marijuana bust, and representation by a talented young lawyer who got Rice's case dropped and whose groovy persona inspired Rice to seek a career in the law. The case, though dismissed, was still a violation of his probation, so he skipped on those charges, which led to a year on the lam—living under an alias, harbored for a time in Berkeley by the Students for a Democratic Society, the left-wing activist group, while he planned an escape overseas, until finally he turned himself in after the FBI threatened to indict his lifelong Republican mother on charges of aiding and abetting her fugitive son.

These were the kinds of bananas stories that lurked inside the biographies of just about everyone involved in the weed trade in this part of California, it seemed. Very few people today knew about Ben Rice's colorful past; now he was simply an elder statesman of local cannabis jurisprudence. For a fee, people wanting to enter the cannabis business could come to his office and receive an hour-long lecture on "how to stay out of trouble, what the rules were, where the soft edges were and where the hard edges were," as he later explained it. In the months immediately before and after the ballot ratification of Prop 64 in 2016, a stream of hopeful weed entrepreneurs sought Ben Rice's counsel, including Tushar and Rachael.

One thing to understand, Rice would explain, was that 2017 was a year of transition, a bridge between the earlier era of medical marijuana and the brave new world of recreational use brought into being by Prop 64. The earlier era had begun twenty years before, with the passage of Proposition 215, which led to the pioneering Compassionate Use Act, making California the first state in the nation to legalize cannabis for medical purposes. In the "215 era," as it came to be known, only a person with a qualifying disorder could legally use pot. A doctor was supposed to examine you and then write you a "recommendation." Not a prescription, mind you, since cannabis, of course, was not an FDA-approved drug. But with this document in hand, you could get your pot in one of two ways. You could grow it yourself, in limited quantities that varied wildly depending on local rules (zero plants in conservative counties, or as many as ninety-nine plants per person in permissive counties such as, yes, Santa Cruz) or you could join a patients' collective. There were two kinds of collectives: retail collectives—known as clubs or dispensaries—or farm collectives. The farms were supposed to grow only enough cannabis for each member who'd pick up their allotments at the end of every harvest. According to the spirit of the law, the collectives were to be small and nonprofit. But, of course, more animal spirits soon prevailed. The loopholes and soft spots and gray areas were obvious. Dispensaries and cultivators came to have hundreds and then thousands of collective members, many of whom were just names taken from a telephone book. Collectives morphed into vast, quasi-legal, for-profit enterprises. Many neglected to pay income taxes. Many began "exporting" their products to other states, and even to other countries, a commercial act that law enforcement bodies interpreted not as exportation but as narcotics trafficking. The medical marijuana regime of California quickly graduated from gray market into black. Great illicit fortunes were made.

The era of the collective would, on January 1, 2018, soon be coming to an end. For now, in early 2017, growers were still operating under the 215 nonprofit-collective rules. You also had to abide by the local statutes, of course. And when it came to the statutes of Santa Cruz County, the main thing to know was that . . . well, things were kind of *unstable*. The county board of supervisors was still hashing out policy that would locally regulate recreational pot production and sales, but the county was far less permissive than it used to be. The ninety-nine-plant-per-person rule was a thing of the past. If you wanted to cultivate in the county now, you had to register with the county government and go through a commercial-development permit process. You had to pay attention to what your property was zoned for. The Summit, for example, had very different zoning than down in South County, where the big commercial ag districts were located, near the border with Monterey County, real Steinbeck country down there. Berry juggernaut Driscoll's owned enormous tracts, from the foothills right up to the beach dunes. It was much easier to get a cultivation permit in South County. Elsewhere, up in the hills, some parcels were zoned for *residential* agriculture, the hereditament of 1970s coastal-California progressivism, the back-to-the-land/*Whole Earth Catalog* movement. Residential ag zoning, that was good, because it meant you'd be a big step closer to getting a permit, albeit for a smaller parcel.

Rice had a tendency to digress. But Tushar and Rachael got the drift. They, in turn, made an impression on Rice. The lawyer believed he had spoken to two "lovers," who "seemed very bright and friendly and interested" and "wanted to get into the cannabis world of Santa Cruz in a large way, and in a good way." Rice maintained an email list of five hundred to six hundred people, pot growers all, to which he would blast out warnings when necessary—if, say, he caught wind that the sheriff was flying around the county looking for pot farms to raid. Rice took down Tushar's new Interstitial email address and added him to his list.

•

ONE DAY not long after they began searching for farmland in the Santa Cruz Mountains, Tushar stopped by the Airbnb and announced nonchalantly, *That was our new partner, Evan Scott.* It took Rachael a second to understand who the hell he was talking about. Earlier that day, she'd gone out onto the balcony and looked down the stairs and seen Tushar with a young guy, scruffy beard, in good shape, looked to be in his late twenties, early thirties. Tushar had called up to her, *Rachael, this is Evan. Evan, this is Rachael*. The guy was speechless, his jaw dropped, and Rachael said, *Nice to meet you?* And Tushar elbowed the guy to speak up, introduce himself.

So Evan Scott is in the industry, Tushar was explaining to her now, alone with her in the apartment. *He's an extractor, a master extractor, who's also a dealer of the material we want to make. I met him surfing. I approached him for us, for what we want to do. And*, Tushar added, *he's going to be our partner. Our new partner*.

Rachael listened without comment. She said nothing until, later that night, she crept down again to Tushar's darkened unit and climbed into bed with him, and in a single movement straddled his torso and pumped down on his chest with both hands. He started awake, a frightened grunt escaping his lungs—*huh!*—and suddenly he was upright looking into her eyes. She said, *I could have pistol-whipped you today!* His face wore a look of total confusion. *Fuck. You. You fucking invited another person into our partnership?* she said. *Who are you? Are you my partner? Or are you just some guy using me, and now you've got your* real *partner?* The light of comprehension coming into his eyes, Tushar started to speak, but she wasn't finished. *This is what it's like! It's fucking dangerous in this industry! You have no locks on your door! I just came in here and you didn't even wake up! You just did the* wrong thing *by going off and getting another partner without even consulting me! That's, like, the* opposite *of being somebody's partner!* But Tushar was smiling now, his hand on her leg, that look on his face. . . . Jesus Christ, she knew that look. . . . *Wow*, he finally said, his voice low. *This is pretty sexy. . . .*

5. A New Partner

They called this break Sewers. East side of Santa Cruz, off Pleasure Point, gnarly. Named after an ancient underwater pipe that had once disgorged the town's sewage into Monterey Bay. Supposedly. Now the water was full of kelp and surfers and other marine mammals. Clustered in the water in their black wet suits, the surfers looked from a distance like clans of black sea lions. Evan Scott was among them, sitting on his board along with one of his best salesmen, as Scott referred to his dealers, a kid named Deva. Deva was Indian American, from Santa Cruz, and named for the class of benevolent Hindu celestial beings; he also happened to be a supremely talented surfer who was considering turning pro. Evan and Deva were chitchatting, waiting for their turn to drop in.

Evan had a problem. Over the last decade or so, he'd earned a lot of cash. He'd earned these profits by producing and selling a cannabis extract known, alternately, as crude oil, or hash oil, or butane hash oil, and its refined, liquid, almost-pure-THC form, known as distillate. Operating a network of clandestine extraction labs—his specialty was hiding them inside shipping containers buried in the ground—he was the CEO of his own literally underworld company. He needed to find a way to put his money on the books.

The previous year, Evan Scott's various labs had, in total, gone through a quarter million pounds of trim, one of the terms for the pot plant matter, the cannabis biomass, from which extractors wrested the golden, highly valuable hash oil. The extraction method that yielded the purest and thus the highest-priced oil required liquified petroleum gases—hydrocarbons—as solvents. Very basically, you soaked the trim in butane or propane, which dissolved the herb's precious cannabinoids, drawing them out of the plant matter until only the essential oil remained. You could then distill that oil in a secondary process that resulted in an even purer form of extract—distillate—which is what went into vape pens, the vaporizer devices that had lately become so popular. At just twenty-eight, Evan was one of the local pioneers in this technical and dangerous trade, which had over the previous decade taken a spectacular technological leap, incorporating methods and materials and equipment never before used in the history of hash making.

These innovations had occurred despite the fact that the production of hash oil was illegal in California. "Every person who manufactures, compounds, converts, produces, derives, processes, or prepares, either directly or indirectly by chemical extraction . . . any controlled substance . . . shall be punished by imprisonment . . . for three, five, or seven years," read the statute. And the accused hash maker was subject to enhanced punishments if the extraction process took place within three hundred feet of a residence. Like others, Scott had learned the hash-making craft by trial and error and through a shadowy, informal apprenticeship system. The craft's practitioners formed a kind of secretive guild whose heritage stretched back centuries and across oceans to the hashish-producing tribes of the Rif Mountains in Morocco and the charas makers of the Nepalese highlands. In twenty-first-century California, the craft still included masters and apprentices and initiation rites, often unplanned and involving police raids or the accidental ignition of highly volatile media. Ropes of glutinous hashish syrup had once erupted like a geyser from the vessel of a primitive extraction system Evan was then operating, coating his face and sealing his eyelids shut.

But that accident had occurred long ago, years before he'd mastered the necessary skills and scaled up to take advantage of skyrocketing prices for the superpotent THC extracts that people had come to smoke from glass pipes using culinary blowtorches, like crack. Indeed, crack was to cocaine as these cannabis extracts, called dabs, were to the dried buds that got rolled into joints or pushed into bowls. A closer analogy was smoking hashish from a water pipe, à la *Alice in Wonderland*'s slow-talking Caterpillar taking puffs while lounging on the cap of the mushroom: A dab rig was like a space-age hookah. A few hits from the rig, with its small lump of blondish concentrate heated by the torch to more than five hundred degrees Fahrenheit, could induce a special kind of catatonia, ambushing the smoker's brains until he was falling into the cushions of his couch, sucked into the pillows and springs and deeper davenport structures as if by some psychotropic gravity. *Couch lock* was the term stoners used for this condition. In the early 2010s, prices for such extracts had reached disorienting heights: thirty-five thousand dollars a kilo wholesale in some places. In Santa Cruz there were extractor kids who were millionaires without bank accounts. Talk about theft risk. The smarter ones knew they had to do *something* with all that freaking cash!

Was this money laundering? Evan Scott preferred to think of it as investing. Diversifying. He was considering buying real estate. But there were other possibilities, other opportunities, perhaps once-in-a-lifetime opportunities, akin to getting in early on the Internet's first wave. Recreational legalization was coming. A licit corporate industry, the conventional wisdom went, would eventually rout what the square world called the black market, but what long-time participants often referred to euphemistically as the "traditional market"—a catchall term that encompassed everything from old hippie growers out in the sticks to young street pushers in the big cities. Evan had a deep allegiance to the traditional market, had friends on both the Deadhead and the hip-hop sides of things. But he also knew that successful people had to change with the times. He wasn't *married* to the traditional market. Maybe, therefore, he ought to prepare to ride the approaching entrepreneurial wave and plow his cash into a legal start-up weed company. Maybe *that* was the move. But how?

Long ago he'd decided to leave no paper trail. Since becoming an adult in the eyes of the law, he'd striven to keep his name, his identity, his very existence off the grid, invisible to the prying eyes of any government authority that might grow curious about his business endeavors. He had precisely no credit history. He'd never had a credit card, never had a bank account—in his own name, that is. And so he felt somewhat out of his depth when it came to the normal, aboveboard business world. What he needed was a guide, a mentor.

The answer came via the lineup at Sewers, via Deva. Submerged to his chest on his short board, Deva mentioned that he knew someone. Knew him from surfing right here on the east side. Silicon Valley entrepreneur, built apps or something. Indian American like Deva, among the few in the Santa Cruz surfing community.

When they first met in person, Evan recognized the guy. *This guy!* Evan said to himself. *I know this guy!* In the waters off Pleasure Point, this guy was somewhat infamous. The local surf scene had always had a reputation for insularity, its surfers as hostile as they were skilled. In the parking areas, local surfers had been known to slash the tires of unfamiliar cars. Outsiders paddling out for the first time had been pelted with stones or punched in the face or dragged off their boards or worse. So when an invasion of rich kooks from Silicon Valley began infesting the Santa Cruz breaks twenty years ago, the aggressive traits already encoded in the DNA of the area's surfing clans really kicked in.

Tushar, of course, was among the invaders from "over the hill," as locals referred to Silicon Valley. Like many tech dudes, he rode a longboard, scorned by some as the board of the poser. Worse, Tushar seemed to pay little heed to the ancient behavioral codes of the waterman. He was, in Evan's mind, "kind of a psycho out there." He was the type of surfer other surfers had to watch out for so they didn't get run over by the bastard. He was dangerous. On the other hand, he dropped into waves that most other surfers judged substandard and would gladly suffer the consequences, wrecking hard. He didn't care about raising the hackles of the locals, and he didn't care about wiping out. He seemed to have no fear, which earned him Evan's respect. Tushar, Evan said, was an *interesting person*.

After Deva introduced them, they took to surfing together in the early mornings, often at Sewers. One day in the lineup, Tushar revealed to Evan that he'd developed a bit of secret knowledge. He knew how to commune with the otters. A population of the carnivorous sea weasels lived prominently among the kelp fields right in the middle of the surf breaks off Pleasure Point, presenting yet another challenge—reefs, currents, sharks. One of the Pleasure Point otters, a female, would become world-famous. Emerging suddenly from beneath the surface, her head sometimes wreathed in red-brown kelpweed, she would hop onto the boards of surfers in the lineup. This particular creature's behavior was highly unusual, however. Cagey, twitchy, suspicious, otters normally kept their distance and dove away like lightning at the slightest human approach. But Tushar said he'd formed a method for getting close to these anxious beings—right up to their whiskers, near enough for a kiss. *Bullshit*, Evan said. So Tushar proposed a game. First person to squeeze an otter's paw wins. Evan had grown up in Florence, Montana, population 821, so he'd done a lot of dumb shit with animals in his life. *OK*, he said, *let's do it!* Then Tushar revealed the secret; it wouldn't have been sporting not to: *Do not look at the animal*, he said. That was the trick. *Do not make eye contact with the animal.* If you don't, the otter will allow you to come right up to it—*watch me*—and then Tushar made his move, looking off but paddling right up to one of the cute marine ferrets lolling in the sun, and he did it—he squeezed one if its weirdly squishy paws. Tushar's face for an instant carried the look of victory, but then the otter lunged and snapped and sank its fangs into his hand. Back on land, a doctor wrote him a script. The bite wound was infected.

•

When Evan eventually sat down with Tushar to discuss the cannabis business, Tushar said he'd never heard of extraction. Did not know that cannabis could be processed, let alone that its essential oils held economic value. Deva was at the meeting, too, the three of them dining at one of Tushar's favorite restaurants, Café Sparrow.

Evan was a little surprised by Tushar's ignorance. How could he not know about hash oil? So Evan explained. He touched on the basic science of how the stuff was made, the manufacturing process, the biomass inputs—

No, Tushar said. He wanted his cannabis start-up to be a *cultivation* company. Growing weed and selling flower and building a brand had more financial promise than whatever Evan was talking about. Extraction seemed too complex and therefore vulnerable to a ferocious burn rate. Growing was simpler. Growing was well understood. Growing was where the money was. That's how he'd seeded his tech company, Tushar eventually disclosed to Evan in confidential tones. Grew it and sold it in New York City when he was in college, where he was more than just a dorm-room dealer. He'd made enough to come west in the nineties and parlay his bankroll into his own dot-com start-up, which he then turned into a cash-flow beast.

Evan didn't quite know what to make of all of that. Seeded his start-up with proceeds from pot dealing back East? He'd heard similar tales before. Everyone in weed had an origin story. Needed one. The cannabis business was swarming with guys like Tushar—wealthy entrepreneurs sensing in legalized weed another exploitable opportunity. The legacy operators had coined or perhaps borrowed a term for these intruders, who were like the tech bros crowding the Pleasure Point lineups with their foam-top kook boards. Because quite a few of them seemed to come from privileged upbringings and have names like Chad, they were called Chads. Tushar, to Evan, was an absolute Chad, albeit a pretty cool one. Another thing about Chads was that, striving for authenticity, flailing for cool, they often felt the need to exaggerate or even fabricate black market bullet points on their résumés.

Evan put his bullshit radar on pause. He told Tushar, *You've got it wrong. There's more upside in manufacturing compared to growing. I'm going to break this down for you.* And he took a napkin and jotted some figures and sketched a little chart. Fixed costs. Variable costs. Inputs. Outputs. Wholesale prices. Profit margins. Upside.

Tushar said, *What the fuck is this?*

And Evan said, *These are the numbers. The numbers I deal with.* It was, basically, the Q1 earnings report from Evan's s existing extraction operation, with projections for the rest of the year.

Tushar was silent. He stared at the napkin, studying the figures. Then he started nodding.

That, Tushar said at last, *is the best, and the shittiest, pitch deck I've ever seen*.

WEEKS WENT BY BEFORE THEY MET AGAIN. Or was it months? Evan can't totally be sure. His memory for dates is vague. A lot has happened in the intervening years, including, soon after Tushar's murder, leaving California and disappearing to Fiji. But Evan remembers Tushar calling him and texting him until Evan eventually accepted an invitation to come over to his house in Los Gatos. Evan was fried that day. He'd been up all night at a wild party—one of the weed-scene raves the area was famous for. But he rallied, and in Los Gatos they rode around the side streets on Tushar's Onewheels, a kind of electric skateboard crossed with a unicycle, and Tushar gave a tour of the house: a wine cellar, an attic space like a ship's cabin, a gallery of pictures, his collection of Wes Anderson memorabilia, including a pair of unworn and apparently vintage Adidas sneakers that said "Zissou" on the uppers. And a girlfriend. Or was it an ex-girlfriend? Unclear. A woman, anyhow, was hanging out at the house, name began with a *B*? Small and cute. She worked in the tech industry, as well, had gone to Stanford or Berkeley. What was weird was that she appeared to live in the house *next door*.

Tushar seemed to have a bunch of crazy projects he was pursuing. He showed Evan the new grow room under construction, a small one, just one or two lights. Out in his backyard, he'd also once planted a few seedlings, he said, experimenting with some cannabis gardening.

Finally they spoke about their partnership. It was a handshake deal. Evan, of course, had always worked that way. The traditional market could *only* work that way. No paper trails. But there was a lot to do, a lot to pay for. They needed to buy property, equipment. They needed to fund the long, arduous licensing and permitting process. Evan would contribute his extraction know-how and his black market cash to the partnership, with the cash eventually coming out the other side as equity in a licensed cannabis start-up. Tushar would contribute his entrepreneurial know-how and his legal cash, which would result in the same: fifty-fifty. They shook hands, smiling and laughing. Each had found his mentor, his guide, as they plunged into the other's strange new world.

On the day that Evan first met Rachael he was cruising around Pleasure Point on his new Onewheel, a gift from Tushar. Evan also lived in the neighborhood, and he liked to use the electric unicycle, such an echt Bay Area conveyance, to run errands and commute to the house on Thirty-Eighth Avenue where Tushar had converted the garage into an airy, inviting workplace for their start-up.

They now had a name for it: Interstitial Systems. Tushar's idea, the strange word *interstitial* being a favorite of his, *the space in between*. In the context of their business, Tushar explained, it referred to the intervening time between cannabis prohibition and cannabis legalization, which was exactly where they sat at this moment. Pretty clever, Evan thought. Anyway, it was a temporary name, a paperwork name. When the time came, they'd figure out something else for the d/b/a.

As Evan rolled up to the house, he saw two young women standing in Tushar's driveway. He stepped off the board and stared for a second.

Who were these visions? He remembers, for some reason, that the one who turned out to be Rachael was wearing white pants. Tushar at some point materialized in the middle of this scene. Evan could already detect something between the two, a spark.

Tushar told Evan that Rachael was an accomplished grower of fine cannabis with experience in the Emerald Triangle. She'd come down here to spend time with her ailing mother, and she was going to cultivate again, in Santa Cruz, with Tushar's backing. *Cool, cool*, Evan said. *None of my business, but cool, cool.* Confiding to Evan, Tushar said he wasn't entirely sure himself, actually. He'd fallen hard for this woman, no doubt about that. He was in love. But maybe this was a dumb move, going into business with her. What did Evan think? Should Tushar trust her? Was she who she said she was? Evan had his doubts, but he dodged the question. *Not my business.*

6. The Safe

October 1, 2019

By the time Sgt. Nick Baldrige got back to town after his brief examination of the murder scene at the Summit, multiple deputies were searching the victim's oceanfront house at 3034 Pleasure Point Drive. Baldrige had just made sergeant three years earlier. He'd been working long hours on the narcotics investigation team and was getting a little paunchy now in the early stages of middle age. He stepped over the yellow tape and entered the front door to a busy house. It was, it must be said, a spectacular venue for a crime scene. A wall of windows faced the sea, making it feel as though you were suspended in some kind of hovercraft right over the breaks.

A handful of Baldrige's colleagues were already on the premises, looking through the house. There was John Habermehl and Chris Jones, and soon Ryan Fulton would arrive. A few CSIs were there, too, working a bedroom in the back, which turned out to be the decedent's master suite. The house had not been ransacked. No cabinet doors hanging open, no drawers yanked out of desks, no overturned furniture, despite what the Ides had said they'd heard. No evidence of struggle or signs of violence, at least not in the home's interior. Outside, in the driveway, however, deputies had found a single gray sock, like a tech-wool hiking sock, and farther away, out on the street, multiple pools of what appeared to be blood. CSI was working on all that, too. Adjacent to the bedroom was a big dressing area with a bathroom, multiple vanities and mirrors, and two separate closets, one containing clothes and one containing almost nothing except a safe. A big gun safe. Size of a refrigerator. Its door was closed and locked, with no scratches or dents, no indication that anyone had tried to break it open. The forensic people had already come through for possible prints, and a locksmith was coming to crack the thing.

That took a while. The safecrackers used a large drill to bore a hole through the thick door. Lots of noise and smoke and the sharp tang of hot metal. When it was open, the detectives didn't find guns. Instead, they found stacks of US currency—eighty-two thousand dollars and change. They booked the cash into evidence. But that wasn't all. The safe contained another, more surprising thing: a large number of jars, and also little glass vials, filled with a viscous honey-brown fluid, some of which was later determined to be BHO, butane hash oil, and some possibly distillate. More of this stuff was discovered elsewhere in the bedroom and later also in the garage at the 3034 house: maybe a dozen one-liter jars. All told, it came to at least thirty-four kilograms of cannabis extract, worth, by some estimates, more than four hundred thousand dollars wholesale. According to California's cannabis regulations, extracts made at licensed facilities could only be stored at licensed facilities. This, the detectives determined, was likely illegal product, contraband hash oil.

If the people who'd invaded Atre's house had been seeking a large amount of cash or drugs, they'd missed a half-million-dollar trove.

7. Being Values

Rachael didn't need this shit. After learning about Evan Scott, she was ready to walk away from it all—the budding business partnership and the budding romance. She was in Santa Cruz to take care of her dying mother. But Tushar had a way. He was a fortress of optimism. Everything was always going to be OK. *Nothing has changed*, he told her. They were building this business together. Evan Scott was simply the extraction arm. And he was homegrown just like her. *Homegrown* was Rachael's word for a non-Chad, someone with deep experience in the traditional market. *Experience is everything*, Tushar said. Together, she and Evan would give the start-up double authenticity.

And so she began to adjust her thinking. They *did* need an extraction expert, after all, and if you couldn't pay an extractor a salary because you were a start-up and didn't have enough working capital, then you paid the person in sweat equity. Rachael was a grower, not an extractor. In the org chart in her mind, Evan Scott would be head of extraction. She was head of cultivation.

But there was another reason she stuck with it. This driven, forceful, optimistic man she was falling in love with was also naive; he didn't understand the world he was entering, didn't know just how coded and hazardous it could be. There were unspoken rules, cryptic signs that only the initiated could read. She felt she needed to protect him.

•

Early one morning Cynthia's cell phone rang, waking her up. It was Tushar. He was upset. He usually rose before dawn, joining the Pleasure Point dawn patrol if the waves were any good, and would be showered, dressed, and at work, attacking the day before 8:00 a.m. Today was no exception. Tushar and Cynthia had developed a friendship of their own. He liked talking to her. She was interesting, educated, worldly. Her father, Rachael's grandfather, had been a high-level automotive executive who'd raised his children in New England, but also on extended assignments in Libya, Switzerland, and Penang. She'd gone to Mount Holyoke, the elite Massachusetts women's college, alma mater of Emily Dickinson, one of poetry-loving Tushar's favorite poets. Tushar was impressed with Cynthia's career as an artist. For many years, Cynthia had run her own company, designing logos for other businesses. She also had her own line of successful coloring books for adults, was indeed semifamous among the ardent fans of that genre. Her style was a cross between Victorian botanical prints and the psychedelia of sixties rock posters. Always looking for fresh design ideas for his AtreNet clients, Tushar had persuaded Cynthia to make a few digital illustrations, and he loved them, but she'd forgotten to send them to him, and now here he was, agitated, with a client meeting in a few minutes, and *where were the drawings, Cynthia!*

After the call, Cynthia looked tired, like she was in pain. Rachael asked her what was wrong, and Cynthia replied, *You know, Rachael, I think I just want to go home.*

Rachael was enraged. Here again was Tushar being Tushar, the boss who routinely demeaned and humiliated his AtreNet "underlings"—his word—who once told Rachael that fear was the best motivational tool. Tushar had a real talent for breaking people down. He seemed to enjoy it. Even before the early-morning phone call, Cynthia had picked up on this, too. It was surprising, her mother had said, that Tushar—so charismatic and curious and sensitive most of the time—could also be so *mean*.

But then Rachael wasn't feeling well herself. She lay down. Aches, cough, fever. She had the flu. And of course Tushar swooped in, transforming into his other self, charming, generous, flower bouquets arriving for mother and daughter, chicken soup for Rachael in bed. They didn't want immunocompromised Cynthia to catch whatever she had, so Tushar replaced Rachael as Cynthia's caregiver for a week, feeding her, accompanying her on walks, making sure she took her meds. Coming to the rescue, Tushar nursed both women and won them back.

In their apartment one evening after Rachael had recovered, Tushar apologized for the angry early-morning call. *I don't know why I do things like that*, he said.

Not long before her cancer diagnosis, Cynthia had picked up another line of business, hanging a shingle in South Pomfret: "Transformational Life Coaching." It seemed natural. People had always been drawn to her. Relatives, friends, neighbors sought her out for advice. She had an aura. Maybe it was her physical appearance. There was no other way to put it: She was cute. Copiously, almost preternaturally cute, with a round face, soft features, deep dimples, big lovable eyes—and plump. Just being around her was soothing.

Now, she went into her belongings and pulled out some worksheets. She asked both Tushar and Rachael to fill them out. She had read deeply in the work of Abraham Maslow, a pioneer in the field of humanistic psychology. Maslow was famous for his "hierarchy of needs," his ideas on self-actualization, and his "Being-values," a set of abstract qualities that he defined, such as "Truth" ("honesty . . . nakedness") and "Wholeness" ("unity, integrity . . . interconnectedness"). To Maslow's original fourteen values, Cynthia had added two of her own invention, including "Order," which she defined as "structure . . . rightness, nothing superfluous, sequentiality, lawfulness." The values were a tool meant to analyze and provide insight into behaviors and personality types. A client would rate each of the sixteen values on a scale of one to ten, and from most to least important to them.

Tushar was normally dismissive of pop psychology, but he loved this exercise. In Maslow's values, he saw a way to *quantify* personality, to *extract data* from character, to convert human beings into spreadsheet cells so you could understand them better.

After they were done, Cynthia studied their worksheets and wrote comments in the margins. Which values were assets to them? Which might present problems in the future? Cynthia had an additional twist on Maslow. In her interpretation, each value had a light and a dark side, could go in either a positive or negative direction. Tushar had "Aliveness" ("spontaneity . . . exuberance") at the top of his list, for example. "Be careful not to hold Rachael and others to your same standard of aliveness," Cynthia advised him. In many ways, the couple's values aligned. Both had "Truth" ("honesty, reality, nakedness") rated and ranked high. "Be careful not to compete in this area and realize that one person's truth may be different than yours," Cynthia wrote. But in other ways they diverged. Tushar had "Order" rated highly, Rachael not so much. "Order could be a source of tension," Cynthia warned. "Pick your battles."

In March and April 2017, they got down to business. As they prepared to file the governing documents, Tushar suggested a name: Interstitial Systems. A temporary name, just for the paperwork, it came from surfing, he explained to Rachael. It was his word for the slightly lower-quality waves that arrived *in between* the better waves in a set and that, therefore, hardly any other surfers wanted to ride. Tushar found that he could have these interstitial waves all to himself, could catch more of them during a session, thus maximizing his time in the water. Tushar always working the angles.

For the extraction lab, they went looking for a building in a nonresidential area of Santa Cruz. They looked for a structure with a permitting history that entailed the use or storage of corrosive or explosive chemicals and found just such a place: a former auto repair shop at 211 Fern Street, in a section of town that was zoned for light industry. Nearby were a metal fabricator, a machine shop, and the Santa Cruz Costco's vast parking area. A "massage parlor" was across the street. *Perfect*. List price: $1.3 million.

With a soupçon of regret, Tushar sold a pied-à-terre penthouse he owned in San Francisco for $2.7 million, almost sixty thousand less than what he'd paid for it just a year before, making him perhaps the first person in modern history ever to lose money on SF real estate, but, hey, they needed the capital. He was considering selling the Los Gatos bungalow for the same reason.

Tushar and Rachael continued, meanwhile, to scour the Summit for land. That spring their real estate agent brought their attention to a parcel that had come on the market. It was much larger than other places they were considering, and hence more costly: 24575 Soquel San Jose Road, sixty acres in total, the asking price almost three million dollars. When they visited, they were struck. The land was totally undeveloped and chiefly forest: Douglas fir, madrone, California live oak, and huge redwoods clustered together in those mysterious fairy circle groupings, like the silent votaries of a forgotten religion. As if in a cathedral's nave, the forest dimmed the day into a permanent dusk. In one section of the tract, the trees parted to reveal an expansive green alpine meadow, six acres in size just by itself, as open to the sky as Driscoll's strawberry fields down on the coastal plain. Perfect for growing! There was also a creek and a pond and a vigorous natural spring that produced forty gallons of water per minute, extremely valuable in drought-stricken California. Later, Tushar and Rachael would hear that the location had been, in the centuries before European settlement, an ancient gathering place for the various tribes of the Ohlone peoples—perhaps even, it was said in whispers, a *burial ground*. This information troubled Tushar. If the county learned about any kind of Native American historicity attached to the property, surely they'd prohibit all land development or use, and the place would immediately be thronged with batteries of righteous UCSC anthropologists. *So let's keep that quiet!* Tushar took to calling the property the Shire, a nod to the idyllic homeland of J. R. R. Tolkien's pipe-smoking hobbits.

Not long after, Rachael brought Cynthia to see the parcels they were considering buying, including the Shire. Rachael drove slowly up the Soquel San Jose Road—so-called because it connects the village of Soquel, just down the coast from Santa Cruz, with the Silicon Valley city of San Jose—a route that Tushar and Rachael would travel countless times over the next two years, a twisting road that curved this way and that, past Soquel High, past the Everett Family Farm stand, past the intersection with Laurel Glen Road, where the sheriff's office had recently conducted raids of pot farms, past Casalegno's coffee shop and country store, whose proprietor's cannabis garden had once been raided, past the Subud Santa Cruz spiritual center, past the mysterious Dharma Ridge Educational Collective, whose entranceway was plastered with angry "Warning/No Trespassing" notices, past the road leading to the place owned by Bob Hoffman, aka Bonefire Bob, an anarcho-artist whose claim to fame was the fabrication of "light-weight personal, recreational flamethrowers," past the signs for the turnoff to Silver Mountain Vineyards, climbing nearly two thousand vertical feet until they arrived at the main entrance to the Shire.

The driveway's switchbacks laddered up a steep hillside, and the vehicle jounced, causing Cynthia to wince in pain. Finally they crested at a kind of plateau, the spot where Tushar would eventually set up his beloved tepee. Suddenly Cynthia had a feeling, an intuitive frisson. *This*, she told Rachael, *is worthy of your dreams!* But she hadn't even seen the best parts yet, so slowly, slowly Rachael maneuvered the car over the ruts of the dirt track that led to the full-sun meadow, where Rachael would eventually cultivate a crop of more than a thousand cannabis plants, harvesting hundreds of thousands of dollars' worth of cannabis flower. The view extended to a distant ridge jagged with evergreen pinnacles. *This is it*,

Cynthia said again. *I feel it. This is your property.* They stood there, admiring the meadow, the woods, the sage-like coniferous smells, the whispering quiet, the soft forest air. On the way back down, they paused again at the plateau where Tushar's tepee would one day rise. When Rachael put the car in park, she looked over and saw that her mother was crying. *What's going on?* Rachael asked, alarmed. *Are you OK? Are you hurting?* Cynthia collected herself and told Rachael that she'd been overcome by an even stronger feeling. It was almost a vision. Of transformation, of death. And then she pointed down the length of the plateau. *I saw my stone there*, she said. *I saw my grave.*

8. Blindfold

Tushar wanted to do a test. Like a proof of concept. He was adamant: He wanted to observe for himself the whole process of setting up a hydrocarbon extraction system from scratch. It would be like building a scale model or a prototype. Participating in the assembly and then the operation of a small extraction system, being *hands-on*, would give Tushar invaluable experience where currently he had none. Experience and knowledge he would need if he were going to be the founder of a licensed cannabis-manufacturing company—or cofounder, with Evan Scott.

The obvious next question was: OK, where? The answer came from Tushar. *Why not use the house right here? On Thirty-Eighth Avenue!* His own house! The Airbnb house!

This, to Evan, seemed insane. Not least because doing so would be an unambiguous felony. Wasn't the whole point of the partnership to *get away* from the black market? The beach houses of Pleasure Point sat on tiny lots, were maybe fifteen feet apart. And persons were present at all times, everywhere. The commission of a felony was one thing. Certainly Evan was no stranger to those risks. But extracting right smack in the middle of a residential neighborhood? When Evan put himself at such risk, he did so in the middle of nowhere and literally underground. Now they'd be doing it in a place with many, many possible informants.

The other weird thing was that Tushar said he *hated* the black market. He spoke about it as if it was offensive to him. His goal, it seemed, was to conquer the black market. With weed prohibition falling away, Tushar and his fellow Chads from the corporate world would build their legal weed empires while simultaneously vanquishing the drug dealers and black marketeers who'd had free rein to profit from cannabis for far too long. Tushar seemed to believe that prohibition had led to artificially inflated weed prices and artificially low expenses (no taxes!), and, hence, profit margins so wide that any imbecile could make money at it. It was time for the pros to take over. But it was looking like the only way to conquer the black market was, as a temporary and unfortunate first step, to participate in it.

And so they would put a lab at the house on Thirty-Eighth. They would keep it small, keep the workload light. They could hide it in the living room of the downstairs unit. Though the main purpose of the lab would be R&D, they would need to sell *some* of its output on the black market. How else to know if your products were any good? Selling the product, getting feedback, then adjusting and tweaking: This was the iterative Silicon Valley way, the process of product development that Tushar knew so well. Also: Why leave money on the table? Any cash they brought in from black market sales could be plowed back into the business. Tushar would shut down the Airbnb listings. No more vacation renters, except Rachael and Cynthia of course. In fact, the lab operation itself could pay him rent, and Tushar could book that rent as part of the property's income, allowing him to pay taxes on it, the dirty money coming out clean. They would keep the circle of knowledge tight. They would not reference the lab in any form of digital communication. Evan would stop using his Android with its crappy security and start using the new iPhone Tushar had bought him. Tushar, in turn, would use a safe to store the oil and cash. And, above all, the lab would be *temporary*. Soon they would move into one of their other facilities, the ones they were seeking local permits and state licenses for: 211 Fern Street in Santa Cruz, or possibly a complex of warehouses near Salinas that Tushar was also contemplating buying.

The idea of a secret extraction system churning out hash oil at the house on Thirty-Eighth freaked out someone else, too: one of Tushar's finance guys, a data analyst from back East, who had a master's in economics and had worked for a hedge fund before Tushar recruited him to AtreNet. Along the way, Tushar repurposed the finance guy, who enjoyed weed as much as anyone, to help out with the cannabis start-up, Interstitial Systems. He later recalled how Tushar explained this strange name to him in almost religio-industrial terms: In manufacturing, you bring separate things together to make something else, and right before you make it, there's the interstitial moment! *Oh-kay*, the finance guy thought. Interesting. When he learned that Tushar was having a secret lab installed at the Thirty-Eighth Avenue house, he shook his head. This was a *dangerously bad use case* for this property. *It's a fucking beach house, dude*, he thought. *Put a pool table in there!*

INSTEAD OF A POOL TABLE, Tushar and Evan wanted a state-of-the-art crude-oil-producing machine. They also wanted a distillation system, which would further refine the crude oil into a substance of even greater potency, distillate. The goal was to get as close to 100 percent THC as possible. The methods were roughly analogous to the two-step process for producing almost any kind of distilled spirit. First you brewed a beer-like liquid from your grain or fruit of choice. That was the crude oil. Then you distilled it into whiskey or brandy. Distillate.

Evan, of course, knew some guys. Locally, there was Elliot Kremerman, who happened to be one of the largest underground vendors of cannabis-extraction equipment and supplies in the country. Kremerman operated out of a commercial building in Scotts Valley, a town right off Route 17 not far from Santa Cruz, in the foothills on the ocean-facing side of the range. Kremerman didn't exactly have a big sign on the awning of a storefront, though his supply company did have a name: Summit Research. Was this purposefully vague? Research? What kind of research? The fact was, Kremerman's business did carry certain risks. The pieces of equipment and the chemicals he sold—components any extractor would need to build and operate a lab, minus the biomass itself—all came from other industries, legitimate industries. It wasn't illegal, obviously, to sell these items. It was arguably risky to sell them to people you knew to be involved in illicit profit-seeking activities. The real risk was to Kremerman's customers. If, for instance, law enforcement were ever to visit Summit Research and pressure its owner into giving up the names of his clients, that could be bad. Which is why Elliot did not keep a client list, did not maintain a database that contained any customer information. Many of the people who did business with him never even entered Summit Research; they sent proxies. Very few used their real names.

By March 2017, however, when Tushar and Evan visited Summit Research, the passage of Proposition 64 had slackened the hunger of law enforcement for black market weed busts. So the partners felt OK using their real names. Kremerman's place was more than just a store; it was an inventor's workshop. All around them were elaborate Rube Goldberg–esque contraptions. One showpiece apparatus consisted of a series of globular flasks the size of medicine balls connected to vertical and horizontal glass tubes like smoothbores, all of it hooked up to a vacuum pump. It could have been the prototype of a weapon invented by a supervillain to extort the world's governments, but it was a cannabis-distillation system, Kremerman said, his biggest unit.

Kremerman was, like so many of these Santa Cruz weed operators, surprisingly young. And also like so many of them, he had a vivid biography. Born behind the Iron Curtain, in Vilnius, Lithuania, in 1984, he emigrated with his family to the United States when he was still a toddler; eventually they settled in Los Gatos. By the time he was a teenager, Kremerman had found his way into the Santa Cruz surf-and-pot demimonde on the other side of the hill. He took stabs at making his own hashish, honing his skills under the tutelage of a certain obscure Bay Area hashish master, who has since, Kremerman claims, vanished. Kremerman spent a lot of time in the Santa Cruz Mountains, and over the years, his expertise widened. He experimented, trial and error, in volatile hydrocarbon extraction and worked as a kind of consultant, teaching others how to build their own systems. Wookiee training sessions, they were called, after Chewbacca's species in *Star Wars*. Wookiee had become a stoner label for the kinds of people, almost always male, almost always hirsute, who grew weed or made hash in secrecy in remote places, chiefly arboreal. "Lord of the Wooks," as one admirer described Kremerman. People began traveling from all over the country to be trained by Kremerman. "I always looked at extraction as, like, alchemy," said one of those Wooks. "You take a plant and turn it into different substances, different states. Turn it into a gas to a liquid to a goo to an oil—you take the plant through the gambit of existence. I thought we were wizards."

Around 2013, however, Kremerman got spooked. He caught wind of a DEA investigation. Undercover agents were attending hash-making events and meetups in other parts of California. How long before they started signing up for training programs like his? Kremerman had become especially adept at the preparation of a form of homogenized hash oil known as shatter. It looked like golden glass. You smoked hunks of it out of dab rigs. Would-be Wookiees were flocking to his shatter-making academy, but he shut it down just in time. Nine people were eventually arrested. The feds, as they do, had given the case a title: Operation Shattered Dreams. Even before the crackdown, Kremerman had decided to shift his business. Instead of mining gold himself or teaching people how to mine, he would sell them picks and shovels of his own design.

Burly as a Balkan grappler, Kremerman spoke so rapidly it was hard to keep up. He also had a deep, tubercular, but festive laugh, birthed from a prodigious torso and the near-constant inhalation of vapor and fume from whatever he was smoking at the moment. After a rough spell in his youth, Kremerman had gone California sober—no intoxicants except weed. Tushar was fascinated by Kremerman. They became friends. Kremerman even took up surfing again, heading out regularly to the lineup with Evan and Tushar, the sight of this happy 270-pound ogre sheathed in a wet suit, popping up and carving—or attempting to carve—causing a minor uproar at the Pleasure Point breaks.

Evan and Tushar spent more than a hundred thousand dollars at Summit Research. They bought glassware, filtration media, and a distillation apparatus of Kremerman's own design. For the extraction itself, Evan built a unit out of parts, assembling it at the house. They began conducting experimental runs but soon enough agreed that they ought to upgrade to a larger, more cutting-edge machine. For this, Evan knew a guy, too. He was based in Seattle and had, since 2013, been designing and building extraction systems in Washington State, where recreational weed had been legal since 2012. But he also did business, on the down-low, with extractors in other places where legalization had yet to come. The company was called Bizzybee, and the engineer behind it, a computer scientist who used to work for Microsoft, was named Boris Kogon.

A MONTH LATER, Tushar picked up Kogon and two of his technicians at the San Jose airport. Kogon had earlier shipped the big machinery by air freight. He was almost the same age as Tushar, forty-eight, and had wire-rimmed glasses and flecks of gray in his goatee and in his dark, close-cropped hair. He looked scholarly, well-read, which he was—a fact he made sure to let you know, relentlessly, once you got to talking to him. In Seattle a few weeks earlier, Tushar and Evan had met with Kogon at his workshop, where Evan gave Kogon feedback and tweaked some of the designs. They all had dinner at an expensive restaurant near Pike Place. Later that night, Tushar emailed Rachael, describing Kogon as "the sensei master scientist." He and Evan, he wrote, had had their "r&d minds blown."

In Santa Cruz, Kogon and his crew and Evan and Tushar all gathered at Evan's rental unit above the Point Market—a neighborhood institution—that had long served as the headquarters of his underground empire. It was also across the street from the oceanfront house at 3034 Pleasure Point Drive that Tushar would, less than a year later, purchase and renovate. Evan's apartment/office was a dealmaking hub, a spot for selling extracts, buying biomass, selling vape cartridges, buying pot, dealing pot, all black market. Inside was a reception area, and beyond that a conference room with a table that could seat twenty, and a product room where flower and extracts were stored and sampled, and living quarters with a kitchen. Completing the scene was a big deck outside with an outstanding view of the surf breaks. Here Evan would occasionally put up brokers or other pot people traveling to town on business from afar. *Welcome to Santa Cruz!* Thus the place above the Point Market was—in an expression widely used in the weed trade but appropriated from African American street slang—a *trap house*. Evan later calculated that, over the course of his career, he sold more than forty million dollars' worth of product from the apartment above the Point Market.

Kogon and his technicians were supposed to stay overnight at the apartment while spending their two contractual days in Santa Cruz installing the Bizzybee unit and then training the new client on its proper operation. As the Seattleites were getting settled—Kogon not exactly thrilled with the accommodations, no toilet paper, he recalled, no bath towels, the place lacking the basic amenities "to sleep like a decent human being"—Tushar debriefed them on the nature of the installation site. They would be setting up the machine inside a vacation-rental house he owned not far away—a house that, Tushar said, he was in the middle of remodeling. It would be a *test* lab, Tushar went on, nervously; it would exist in this house just long enough to do a couple of *test runs*. That it was also a *trap* lab—unlicensed and hence illegal—did not bother Boris Kogon. It did, however, seem to bother Tushar Atre. He was worried about the neighbors, he said. Kogon thought to himself: *Well, why are you doing this then, if you're so bothered about it?* Tushar's anxiety seemed to bloom right there in the Point Market apartment. "I mean, Tushar's a tech entrepreneur; he's not a drug dealer," Kogon recalled. "But he's doing some trap shit, but he's not comfortable *doing* the trap shit! He's like a fucking anxious mess! And he's taking his anxiety out on me. So that's when he tells me he's going to blindfold me to take me to his trap spot."

Suddenly dangling from Tushar's hands were what appeared to be bolts of dark cloth—*were those pillowcases?* Evan Scott thought. Glances were exchanged. Mouths fell open. Someone burst into laughter, then someone else. Funny joke, Tushar! *Hilarious*, man.

But Tushar's face did not change. His look was intense. *I'm serious*, he said. *I'm going to have to blindfold you.*

Everyone turned to Boris Kogon. Despite the fact that he was a computer scientist and AI expert who was once ascendant up the Microsoft corporate ladder, this was a man who'd spent time in federal prison. This was a man who, for years, had no fixed address, no credit history, no dotted-line identity. He couch surfed when he wasn't living out of rooms in luxury hotels. He did drug deals out of the suites. "The nicer the hotel, the less likely they are to fuck with you," he said. He preferred Ws. This type of criminal life was an unlikely turn for Boris Kogon, who'd grown up in an upper-middle-class neighborhood in Seattle, a nice ("but precocious") Jewish boy. His father was an anesthesiologist, his mother a neurobiologist at the University of Washington. He graduated from an elite private school and studied computer science at the University of Washington. But then in 1995 he went with friends to Burning Man, consumed a large quantity of psychedelics, and embarked on a transcendental journey—"I could *see* math; I could *see* physics; the world was, like, overlaid with fractals and formulas," at the end of which he experienced a kind of conversion, his "self-deceptions stripped away." He dropped out of college. Now a committed psychonaut, he descended deeply into the West Coast rave scene, eventually meeting a retired Navy SEAL who'd recently launched a second career in large-scale weed brokering. The SEAL became Boris's benefactor. Eventually Boris began smuggling weed into the United States from British Columbia, at the time a giant producer of bulk indoor marijuana. He drove the stuff to Chicago, to

L.A. He was a "bulk wholesale middleman." He branched out beyond weed. He built a psychedelic-mushroom farm in Gualala, California. But it wasn't all mind-expanding fun. He did a few stints in rehab. His parents disowned him. A snitch led to a DEA bust, which led to a conviction in 2004 (he pleaded guilty) on one count of conspiracy to distribute marijuana, which led to a year in prison—minimum security, but still. After his release, he went straight and eventually made his way back to school, to UDub, earning his degree and then somehow talking his way into the job at Microsoft. He was, however, still a stoner. Through a friend who was a hash-oil maker, he became fascinated by the science of extraction. He created an anonymous account on a new social media platform, Instagram, just then attracting a cohort of brash dab makers and hashish boffins—"a demographic that I call hash nerds"—newly emboldened by weed-decrim movements in states around the country, who no longer feared the wrath of the law. His handle was @bizzybee. He started building his own small BHO-extraction machines, running biomass through them, and posting videos of the process on his Instagram account. In part because of his "weird sense of humor and dorky jokes," his posts went viral, at least within the community of hash nerds, and his audience expanded to such a degree (about ten thousand followers) that he decided to launch his own company. He named it after his Instagram handle. The business took off. Revenue was doubling year over year. Bizzybee was becoming "the first, like, legal thing that's really succeeded for me in my life." Kogon had remade himself, had come back from the nadir. And now here he was in Santa Cruz in this shitty apartment with this paranoid motherfucker telling him he needed to put a pillowcase over his head.

Fuck you is how Kogon responded. He moved toward the door. "Tushar is Indian of the Brahman caste, and he was raised wealthy," Kogon said. "I'm a Jew, with all the baggage that entails. I'm also a Kohen, and, like, the Kohanim are the priests of the temple. Basically, wealthy Brahman Indians and Jewish kids have something in common. They both think they're the smartest people in the room. And are really good at arguing. And had a lot of high expectations from their parents. So we were perfect headbutting material."

Tushar relented on the blindfolds. The peace, however, did not last. On the way to the Thirty-Eighth Avenue house, Tushar told Kogon that he had it on good information that Kogon was being followed. *What the fuck is this now? Followed?* Followed by whom, Kogon wanted to know. *I can't tell you that*, Tushar said. The implication was that the entity following Kogon was a federal law enforcement agency. "So that kind of went around in circles for a while," Kogon recalled. "I felt like he was probably fucking with me. Something about eating a lot of psychedelics makes you pretty aware of the games other people play."

And then they arrived at the Thirty-Eighth Avenue house, ready to work. *No cell phones*, Tushar said. In fact, *could all of you give me your cell phones now, please?* Again, Kogon wasn't having it. *You're not taking my fucking phone*, he said. OK, fine, they could keep their phones on their persons, Tushar said, but they had to turn off the location services. And then power down their devices completely. Absolutely, definitely, without question: They were *not* allowed to take photos or record videos. Tushar didn't want anyone finding out the location of his . . . *test lab*. He did not want Kogon posting shit on Instagram. Despite the fact that sharing just this sort of thing online—the assembly of one of his big machines in the wild for a customer—was a crucial form of Bizzybee marketing, Kogon reluctantly agreed.

Everyone got to work. The extractor's components were going in, hoses and plugs, coils and gauges, and eight shiny stainless steel cylinders, each about four feet high—columns, they called them. Arranged vertically, the columns were what you packed your biomass into, then permeated with your solvent, your hydrocarbon gas, your butane, which the system was designed to recover and then reuse after each batch, no gas escaping from this sealed appliance—a closed-loop system.

As it came together, the Bizzybee unit was turning out to be not as small as they'd expected. Kogon called this particular model the "Bizzy Beest." It was the largest unit Kogon had at that point designed, and its columns and appendages and ducts and siphons filled up a swath of the living room. Meanwhile, Evan and his foreman, Ryan, were busy installing the Kremerman distillation rig in one of the bedrooms. At one point, taking a break, Evan came into the main area and saw Kogon with his cell phone out, pointed at the Bizzy Beest, engaged in the forbidden act.

Kogon and his crew had just finished setting it up and were conducting an initial run with a tiny batch of biomass. Hash oil was about to squirt for the first time from the endmost nozzle of the system. For extremely online Boris Kogon, the temptation was strong. "I just couldn't resist," he said. "And I pulled out my phone. And I took a fucking video." Tushar had stepped outside to take a call, but just as Kogon whipped out his phone, he returned.

Evan winced. He could see Tushar's expression darken and knew instantly what was about to happen: Tushar was entering "psycholand." He made a move toward Kogon. *I said no phones!* He snatched the device from Kogon's hand and jumped into a martial arts stance, squaring off as if for hand-to-hand combat. Kogon's technicians were physically large people, and also veterans of the legacy cannabis trade. "Seattle OGs," Evan called them. They got between the two men but Tushar showed no fear, yelling at Kogon, *I'm going to punch you in the fucking face!* Then everyone was barking at one another, a brawl a real possibility, until finally Tushar tossed the phone back to Kogon.

Kogon told his crew to pack up their tools. That was the last time he saw Tushar alive.

9. The Casings

October 1, 2019

By early afternoon, Dr. Lauren Zephro had taken control of the crime scene. Among the deputies in their uniforms milling around the woods on the Summit property, Zephro stood out. Nearly six feet tall, her long blond hair pulled back into a ponytail, she circled the spot where the body of Tushar Atre had lain before being taken away to the coroner for autopsy, supervising her small team of criminalists, almost all of them women. The rest of Zephro's CSI team was down at the other crime scene, in Pleasure Point, the decedent's home by the ocean.

Zephro, a civilian employee of the sheriff's department, was its forensic services director. She was joined by Detective Ryan Fulton, who'd just returned to the Summit after a trip down to help with the search of Atre's home, the search that had yielded the safe full of money and hash oil. Fulton was yet another green investigator on the Atre case, only recently promoted to detective and assigned to narcotics. Already Zephro and her team had found and studied tire tracks, shoe impressions. One of the criminalists handed Fulton a metal detector and instructed him on how to use it. Turn it on, pretty self-explanatory after that. Waving the instrument over the ground, Fulton worked his way slowly around the white BMW. Then he made his way down the incline toward the spot where the victim's body had lain. Soon the machine made its warning noise, and Zephro came over and bent to the ground and carefully manipulated the pine straw and decomposing tree matter until she and Fulton saw it flashing there, the brass of a casing from a discharged round of ammunition. This happened five times. Five casings. Five evidence markers, little hard-plastic A-frames, green with black numbers on them—2 through 6—placed at the spots on the forest floor from which Zephro had plucked the casings. They took out a measuring tape. Someone took photographs. The first casing was thirteen feet (approximately) from where the body had lain; the second, third, and fourth were incrementally closer; and the final one was within two feet of where the decedent had fallen. Just by sight, Fulton could tell the caliber of these cartridges: .223, a rifle round first developed by Remington in the 1950s and now widely used as ammunition for the semiautomatic AR-15. Arms manufacturers almost always etch a so-called headstamp code onto the baseplates of their casings. Before Fulton dropped each casing into a special evidence envelope, he and Zephro turned the cylinders over and looked. The metal read LC + 17, indicating that these cartridges were manufactured in 2017 at the Lake City Army Ammunition Plant, a government-owned small-arms production facility in Independence, Missouri, that supplies the soldiers of the United States Army.

10. Alternative Therapies

Not long after Cynthia's vision at the Summit, Tushar received a tip from a friend, a rich tech exec named Sunny whose mother had also been diagnosed with terminal cancer. Sunny had heard about a doctor with a clinic in Los Gatos, and he'd taken his mom there, and now here she was a year later, still with us, still going strong, all thanks to the plant-based therapeutic innovations of the amazing Dr. Bomi Joseph.

That was the name they knew him by: *Bomi Joseph*. At Dr. Bomi Joseph's clinic, Peak Health Center, Rachael and Cynthia soon learned that his proprietary treatment involved CBD, but not just any CBD—CBD and a host of other *bioactive* cannabinoids derived from a novel form of hops. Some kind of hybrid of hops and cannabis, apparently. Bomi Joseph was preparing to apply for a patent. He showed them some of the paperwork.

Cynthia had stopped chemo after arriving in Santa Cruz. The side effects were too harsh, the benefits approaching zero. She was losing weight, losing energy, losing life. She and Rachael—especially Rachael—were desperate, primed for alternatives. Already, Rachael was giving Cynthia doses of so-called Rick Simpson Oil, a hash-oil-based tincture first formulated by an eponymous Canadian electrical engineer and widely believed (without evidence) to be a cure for cancer. So why not also give Dr. Bomi Joseph's cannabinoid extract a try? There appeared to be no downside. The treatment had no side effects, Bomi said. An assistant—she appeared to be a nurse—discussed dosages with Rachael and Cynthia, who were impressed by Bomi's knowledge and presentation, as polished as a TED Talk. At the first mention of cannabinoids, Rachael's entrepreneurial ears had perked up. Here was an inventor extracting essences from plants and making those elixirs into medicines available to a needful public. Just like she and Tushar were doing, or wanted to do. It seemed like destiny had brought them together. She arranged for Tushar and Bomi to meet.

Peak Health occupied a building in a corporate park in Los Gatos. It included a showroom filled with tablets, gel caps, creams, salves, all in brown bottles with handsome, Whole Foods–ready packaging. In the back of the showroom was a small warehouse packed with boxes and, in the corner, a sparring gym. Like Tushar, Bomi was an avid practitioner of martial arts, in Bomi's case karate. A decade older than Tushar, Bomi was a little bug-eyed, and his teeth were a little snaggled, and his hair was thinning, but he was svelte and spry and bursting with energy.

In a conference room at Peak Health, Bomi told Tushar the story of his novel therapy. He spoke with an accent; he was from the tropical state of Kerala, he said, though he'd resided in the United States for more than thirty years. In a village in Kerala, his uncle had worked as an apothecary, an expert in the preparation of herbal therapies from the ancient Hindu folk medicine tradition known as Ayurveda. The uncle's Ayurveda pharmacy eventually went out of business, but not before Bomi had gone home and rescued its library of original therapeutic manuscripts. These became the basis of Peak Health. With Dr. Bomi Joseph as its chief executive, Peak Health combined ancient wisdom with "modern clinical research."

Bomi Joseph said he and his partners in India, a group of highly trained scientists, had succeeded in locating a rare, marvelous, cannabinoid-expressing hop variant: *Humulus yunnanensis*. They found it growing in the highlands of the Indian Himalayan state of Arunachal Pradesh, in the far northeastern flange of the country, a region encircled by ominous, forbidden lands: Myanmar to the south, the Kingdom of Bhutan to the west, and, to the north, occupied Tibet. China itself claimed Arunachal Pradesh as its own. Obscure rebel groups lurked in its mountains. Detachments of the Indian army were stationed in redoubts spread along the Himalayan escarpment. Bomi's group had discovered specimens containing "unusually high cannabinoid content" but without THC, as Bomi's patent documents would later declare. The lack of THC was a good thing, of course. That's precisely what Bomi was after. To the FDA, hops was a foodstuff, a flavoring agent, not a scheduled drug substance, which meant fewer regulations, less government red tape. Bomi and his partners selected the specimens with the highest cannabinoid content, took cuttings, grew them and bred them, and voilà, Bomi Joseph had his new plant, which he had trademarked under the name Kriya. The word meant "action" in Sanskrit and appeared to be an homage to the discipline of Kriya Yoga. *Kriya hops*.

There was no cure for cancer, Bomi was careful to say. And so his Kriya extracts were not a cure. But the body of traditional knowledge in India made it clear. Ayurveda masters had long used *Humulus* tinctures (extractions, really) to treat diseases. In layman's terms, Bomi told them, the active cannabinoid molecules in this extract had the ability to make cancer cells "forget" to defend themselves. That's how Rachael remembers Bomi phrasing it. Forgetful cancer cells. And when the cancer cells forgot to defend themselves, the body's own immune system could attack them, beating back the disease. No guarantees, of course, Bomi Joseph said.

AFTER THEIR FIRST MEETING, Tushar and Bomi Joseph became fast friends. Tushar told Rachael that he felt Bomi Joseph could be a potential partner. Tushar brought him to see the Shire. There was talk of Bomi putting up money to help with the purchase of the property, where perhaps they could grow Kriya hops for Peak Health.

In April, Tushar and Rachael entered a contract to buy the Shire. During the negotiation, Rachael wrote a letter appealing to the sellers: "I hope these 60 acres to be a noteworthy example of environmental stewardship and agricultural management.... We want it to be a place in Santa Cruz County that a person could visit for a weekend and write a book about."

But the negotiations dragged on. She and Tushar couldn't quite pull the trigger. As the spring planting season arrived, Evan and Tushar asked Rachael if she wanted to grow this year. She hadn't really considered it; she was so focused on her mother, on the start-up, and on the negotiations for the land. But Evan knew a guy with a spot. He lived up a winding back road near the mountain town of Ben Lomond. Tushar cosigned on the idea: Rachael should grow this year. He wanted to be able to show—to customers, to the wider weed world—that one of his partners was actively cultivating cannabis biomass.

THE GUY HAD A WEIRD NICKNAME, Bamm Bamm, so called because he had a certain Neolithic look. One of the many hirsute heirs to the area's aging hippies, he had long, thick dreads with what appeared to be tiny animal bones—the tibiae and fibulae of small terrestrial vertebrates?—woven into them. Bamm Bamm also had an affinity for firearms, so Rachael took to calling him Bang Bang. She was put off by the guy and his apparent gun fetish, but she did a deal with him anyway. Maybe because she couldn't resist the lure of cultivation, or the promise of turning a quick black market buck, or maybe because she knew she needed to do this to keep Tushar happy, Rachael changed her mind. She would plant a small crop of marijuana on Bang Bang/Bamm Bamm's property in the woods. After the harvest, they would split the crop's yield down the middle. Rachael would take a somewhat hands-off approach. During her days in the Emerald Triangle, she had a trusted ally, a grower named Hank. Hank was an old schoolmate from Vermont. They had reconnected by chance in California after Hank had migrated west, drawn to the weed trade just like her.

Rachael put Hank in charge of the Bang Bang grow. She would oversee things from afar.

Meanwhile, Cynthia began taking Bomi Joseph's Kriya hops pills, and she actually started feeling better! More energy, less pain. A bottle of thirty tablets lasted two weeks and cost around two hundred dollars per bottle. When her supply ran out, they ordered more from Peak Health's online store. *No problem*, Bomi Joseph said. He was only too happy to provide, to help, to heal.

11. Illuminati

Two weeks before his high school graduation, Christopher Daly, class of 1974, left home and hitchhiked across the country. He'd grown up in the middle-class New Jersey suburbs. His father worked on Wall Street; his mother was a teacher. They'd recently divorced. By the time he was seventeen, Chris Daly had already discovered weed, acid, and mescaline while hanging out in Greenwich Village. He'd already been *selling* weed, hash, and peyote; he was a high school dope dealer. Recently, he'd assembled a rudimentary hash-oil-extraction apparatus in his mom's basement, carefully following the instructions outlined in a now-cult-classic underground handbook, *Cannabis Alchemy*, written by one D. Gold, the pseudonym of a secretive Berkeley chemist.

"The body of the plant itself serves as a link between the physical plane and a host of Spirits of exceptional wisdom and subtlety," the mysterious D. Gold wrote, as if speaking directly to Chris Daly of River Vale, New Jersey, age seventeen. "When the plant is ingested, these qualities are manifested in the mind of the worshipper, unlocking the storehouse of Wisdom within and revealing the hidden springs of pleasure."

Daly had also already read *The Tibetan Book of the Dead*, *Siddhartha*, and *The Doors of Perception*; he'd read Ken Kesey's *One Flew Over the Cuckoo's Nest*, Tom Wolfe's *The Electric Kool-Aid Acid Test*, Timothy Leary's *Terra II . . . A Way Out*, and Abbie Hoffman's *Steal This Book*—which he did steal, from a shopping mall in Nanuet, New York. High on mescaline one night, Daly had had a vision of his future self. *Go to California. . . . Build a cabin deep in the woods. . . . Grow weed!* A varsity letterman on the cross-country team, he was lean and handsome and hungry for adventure. He was primed. He wanted nothing more than to turn on, tune in, drop out, and have as much sex as possible with girls of a complementary mindset. One of his best friends back home, Robert Koenig—son of jazz clarinetist George Koenig, who played in Benny Goodman's orchestra, who'd jammed with Lionel Hampton and Louis Armstrong, who therefore had smoked copious amounts of reefer and told stories to the boys about scoring from his main man in Harlem—had already left for California days earlier.

Seven years after the Summer of Love, a generation of disaffected youth was still heading west to those groovy naked climes next to the Pacific where you could live free, free from your parents, "free of all the old middle-class Freudian hang-ups," where you could escape all those *bad trips* by seeking out and reveling in the *good trips*.

Daly met up with Koenig near an ashram in the Sierra Nevada run by the famed American swami Kriyananda, who had studied under the Indian founder of Kriya Yoga. The Kriya ashram was adjacent to a kind of informal commune in Malakoff Diggins State Historic Park—a place bearing some resemblance to the "Malakoff Diggings" commune mentioned briefly in Joan Didion's seminal 1967 essay "Slouching Towards Bethlehem," which explored the world of teenage hippie runaways in San Francisco's Haight-Ashbury district.

The summer of 1974 evolved into a whole psychedelic odyssey of escapades and misadventures. Chris Daly and Robert Koenig had visions while they roamed the wasteland moonscape where hydraulic gold miners in the 1850s had blasted away the hillsides hoping to make a killing. They smoked hashish so potent that someone in their delirium accidentally set a madrone grove on fire. Koenig and his girl got out of there, hitching rides until they were picked up by a guy who had property up a ridge not too far from Boulder Creek, California, near the headwaters of the San Lorenzo River, the main riparian artery of the Santa Cruz Mountains.

Near the confluence of Bear Creek, which flows into the San Lorenzo, and Deer Creek, a narrow, fast-moving stream that plunges more than a thousand vertical feet in the space of two miles—that's where Daly and Koenig eventually ended up. At first they lived on land owned by a Zen Buddhist named Neil Plante, his old lady, Joyce, and a collection of like-minded young people. Call it a commune. Everyone was a back-to-the-lander—one of the 1960s counterculture's many submovements, in which young people, following utopian impulses, were taking up subsistence farming, living off the land, off the grid, subscribing to the *Whole Earth Catalog*, and following the teachings of Alan Chadwick, a horticulturist at the University of California, Santa Cruz, known as the father of organic farming.

Before long, Daly and Koenig decided that Deer Creek was the place for them. No one else was living in the canyon except the Plante group and an old couple—actual Okies, who'd migrated to California from Oklahoma in the *Grapes of Wrath* years. But Daly heard tell of other hippies who'd been growing pot in the Santa Cruz Mountains before he and Koenig arrived. Famously, over in La Honda, in the westernmost part of the range, the Merry Pranksters were headquartered at Ken Kesey's writing cabin. On the land surrounding the cabin, the Pranksters had for years grown a small amount of weed for their own stash. Kesey's former girlfriend Carolyn Adams, aka Mountain Girl, the celebrity Prankster and hippie who would go on to marry the Grateful Dead's Jerry Garcia, had turned herself into a practiced grower. A few years later, in 1977, she would leverage her fame by publishing her own weed-cultivation manual, *The Primo Plant*. In its pages, she made sure to emphasize that her advice was meant for hobbyist gardeners wishing to produce "home-grown grass" at a small and definitely not commercial scale, for their own personal smoking pleasure. That's how it went for most of the communes and experiments in collective living popping up across the Santa Cruz

Mountains and beyond since the early 1960s: back-to-the-landers growing cannabis alongside herbs and vegetables, for their own use or to barter.

But Daly and Koenig had other ideas. They were at the vanguard of a new wave of hippie migrants. Many, like Daly, had been teenage pot dealers back home. They had a crucial risk tolerance, a certain mercantile instinct. Far from fearing the outlaw life, they felt it was the only way forward. They also had what amounted to an astute business insight (though they never would have called it that). It was, in hindsight, crushingly obvious. Almost all the weed consumed in the United States at the time was smuggled in from other countries—chiefly Mexico, from which came the infamous, low-grade brick weed, flowers and stems and leaves and seeds pressed into dense blocks of biomass for ease of transport. The brick was overwhelmed with seeds; practically half its weight was seed. So the American weed market had a quality problem. Higher-quality pot was available from Mexico as well as Colombia, Panama, Thailand, and Afghanistan, all of it smuggled into the country in increasingly elaborate, expensive, and dangerous operations. And so the American weed market also had a supply-chain-efficiency problem. As Daly knew from New Jersey, where he was both consumer and retailer, demand for weed in the United States was absolutely exploding along with the coming of age of his enormous generation, the baby boomers. Why not meet the new demand for pot by growing it domestically? Why not pursue, for fun and profit, an outlaw career as a pot farmer?

If Daly and Koenig had more commercial sense than their predecessor growers in the Santa Cruz Mountains, it wasn't by much. Their motive was a *modest* profit, they told themselves. Just enough to live on. Just enough to cover the cost of the next season's planting, and maybe one day purchase their own land to grow weed and construct cabins on, proper shelter. In time, they made the happy discovery that high-quality California bud could fetch twelve hundred dollars a pound wholesale. If combined with other sources of income, like selling firewood or compost or trimming trees, growing and selling just ten pounds of weed could generate more than enough income to underwrite a year of life in Santa Cruz County for young, single, resourceful fellows such as themselves. Daly studied topographic maps. He hiked every trail in the Deer Creek and Bear Creek drainages, on the hunt for southern-facing ridges with easy access to water. He eventually found a steep but arable eleven-acre tract of raw land, approached the owner, and did a deal for eighteen thousand dollars, using an inheritance from his late grandmother as well as proceeds from the sale of previous crops he'd grown guerrilla style—that is, on public lands or on other people's property but without their knowledge. Eighteen thousand for eleven acres was pricey; in the middle 1970s the going rate for undeveloped land in the Santa Cruz Mountains was about a thousand dollars an acre. But Daly was willing to overpay for the sun and the water.

Within a few years, Daly and Koenig were going big. Their stuff, their primo stuff, was now fetching two thousand dollars a pound. Grow and sell just three dozen pounds in a year—*not bad!* They were, sort of, relatively speaking, getting rich. And they sort of liked it. By now the pair was delving deeper into Eastern thought and mystical practices: Koenig especially sought the counsel of an assortment of swamis, gurus, shamans, and kahunas. All of this plus their typical experimental consumption of the full psychedelic cornucopia—LSD, MDMA, peyote, mushrooms, morning glories, baby woodrose, and homemade hashish of the highest obtainable potency. A roly-poly young man with long blond hair and a matching beard, Koenig was as charming as he was spiritual. He refused to kill the rattlesnakes that roamed their cannabis gardens. Instead, he seemed to pacify them with his very presence; then he picked them up and peacefully removed them.

The money was pouring in. They forged relationships with the area's biggest broker-dealers, including a guy known as Alba Mark, who had strong links to the California rock scene. Almost all of Daly's weed in the mid- to late seventies went through Alba Mark and into the lungs and minds of famous bands, including *the* Band, and especially its guitarist and leader Robbie Robertson, who, Daly says, was a fan of his stuff. But then came the 1980s and, into the Oval Office, a certain former Hollywood actor who hated weed and loved cops. The State of California, in 1983, started CAMP, the Campaign Against Marijuana Planting, a task force of federal, state, and local law enforcement bent on crushing the nation's domestic reefer production. CAMP would become infamous, a gestapo to the hippie cultivators of California. On the autumnal equinox of 1983, Daly heard the rhythmic thud of rotor blades. He climbed to the top of a tall fir tree on his property and saw what appeared to be a Bell UH-1 Iroquois, the iconic Huey of the US Army, swooping back and forth in the air above Deer Creek like something out of *Apocalypse Now*. The next day, cops rappelled from the Huey on ropes and destroyed Koenig's huge crop of killer weed. He lost everything but avoided arrest. Other growers were also raided. Daly, for his part, climbed down from the tree and immediately harvested all that he could—maybe sixty pounds—from his crop, staying up all night and stuffing the colas into bags, and the bags into the back of a friend's Volkswagen Microbus.

For a number of years Daly cut back production, but by 1986 he was ready to go big again. The end users of his product had changed. Fewer rock stars, more of the high-strung technologists over the hill who, busy launching start-ups and inventing gizmos, wanted weed as a mellowing agent to calm their febrile minds, or for the opposite effect: to induce inspiration. Daly was fetching four hundred dollars *an ounce* wholesale, the prices driven higher by CAMP's success in eradicating supply, his weed then worth almost as much as gold. Soon, the boom times drew a different drug, cocaine, into the country. Long an important smuggling port, Santa Cruz in the 1980s was awash in cocaine. Weed dealers became coke dealers. Weed users became coke users. Daly had a sweet hookup: a man in the Colombian diplomatic corps. His coke was pure; it had a faint pink color. In one year, Daly spent thirty thousand dollars on the pink coke, which went up his nose. Not, in retrospect, a great investment! Meanwhile, he finally completed the construction of his Deer Creek homestead, a ramshackle three-story Robinson Crusoe villa, post and beam, made almost entirely out of old-growth-redwood lumber that he'd harvested from fallen trees on his land. The house had wide redwood-plank floors and a huge redwood-timber deck with a tub in which Daly would pour hot water and soak in the evenings while gazing west over the treetops toward the setting sun.

The life paths of the old friends from New Jersey would, at this point, substantially fork. In 1990, Koenig would flee Santa Cruz in the wake of a major police raid on a bulk-psilocybin-production facility that Koenig was operating. He went north, relocating to the Emerald Triangle, where, hidden inside greenhouses in the remote forests there, he soon built an even more lucrative underground empire of weed. Koenig later told Daly he was making more than a million dollars a year. (Koenig denies this.) He had a share in a ranch that covered two thousand acres and comprised the point at which the borders of Humboldt, Mendocino, and Trinity counties met, the circumcenter of the Emerald Triangle. As Koenig's fortunes soared, Daly's plunged. For most of the nineties, Daly went straight, taking a regular job as a carpenter for a Bay Area municipal agency. He was a single dad, raising his young son after the boy's mother ran off with another man. At some point, methamphetamines came into the country. A biker who lived on Deer Creek Road built a meth lab. Daly got addicted to the biker's stuff. "I did meth once," Daly would later say. "For ten years." Eventually he kicked the addiction. For a time Daly and Koenig kept in touch. For a time Daly had a role in his friend's black market empire. Koenig had a stepdaughter who now worked in the family business. The business had become one of the main weed suppliers to a well-known Hollywood dealer who sported a thick beard and Turkic mustache and looked like the Zig-Zag man. Daly helped Koenig's stepdaughter move the Hollywood weight and collect the cash, which Daly then buried for Koenig in ammo cases on his Deer Creek land. Accounting discrepancies would eventually emerge when it came to the precise sums Daly had secreted for Koenig in these makeshift Santa Cruz Mountains vaults.

Later there would be still other betrayals, and more hurt feelings, and nearly half a century after leaving home for a life in California grass, for a life that was free of all the old middle-class hangups, the old friends were no longer so.

EVAN SCOTT HAD DONE BUSINESS with Ginny Namaste Stone for years. He'd even once met her legendary pot-mogul stepfather, Robert Koenig. After spending time with her stepfather in Humboldt County, Ginny had come down to Santa Cruz and started growing herself, eventually founding several indoor-cannabis-cultivation companies, including Rattlesnake Ridge and Stone Madrone Farms.

Long before meeting Tushar, Evan had interactions with a network of major weed players from all over California, a network so powerful and secretive that some people liked to call it the Cannabis Illuminati. Every so often, meetings were convened during which the group's members would try to agree on such things as pricing and supply in the cannabis black market—a sort of weed OPEC. But the group was on the verge of irrelevance. Recreational legalization had radically altered the status quo.

Partly as a way to stay relevant in these times of drastic change, a local Santa Cruz version of the Illuminati had formed. The group consisted of a handful of Santa Cruz weed entrepreneurs representing the full spectrum of cannabis business sectors, among them Ginny Stone, of the storied Koenig weed family, and Evan Scott, the specialist extractor, as well as his new partner Tushar Atre. The leader of the group, its founder and soul, was a black market wholesaler. Like a latter-day Alba Mark, he specialized in selling the high-quality pot grown by Santa Cruz producers. Aside from Tushar, all the members of the group had operated in the 215 era, and most (but not all) had been raided or investigated or charged with felony weed-related crimes at some point in their careers. They called themselves the Pharmers Group.

At a meeting in June 2017, they all sat around the conference table at Evan's Point Market office. Earlier in the day, Ginny Stone had given some of the Pharmers Group members a tour of her indoor grow rooms inside Building 28 of a former concrete plant in the old port town of Moss Landing, an ancient smugglers' moorage halfway between Santa Cruz and the Monterey Peninsula. The members of the Pharmers Group had big ambitions. They would join forces to create a licensed distribution enterprise built around the idea of forming a kind of Santa Cruz appellation that played up and took advantage of the region's deep cannabis history and lore. Giddy optimism was in the air. If they could capture just 1 percent of the projected market for California cannabis, within five years the company would have annual revenue of forty-seven million dollars. Then they could sell the whole thing to the highest bidder among whatever giant, acquisitive cannabis conglomerates existed then—and not have to work for the rest of their lives.

Tushar seemed game. By now, the trap lab at the Thirty-Eighth Avenue house was operational. Evan Scott and his people were experimenting and R&Ding and pumping out pretty substantial amounts of black market oil. No way was Tushar bringing anyone from the Pharmers Group to see that. But he did offer up AtreNet's website-design services to the group. He also told the other members that he was meeting with "a VC" in July, and he wanted to take this particular venture capital executive to visit Ginny Stone's indoor grow at Moss Landing. Oozing Silicon Valley vibes, Tushar suggested that the VC might be interested in funding the Pharmers Group in an early seed round. He thought it would be great if the Pharmers Group could make a two-minute video, a pitch for investors, that would demonstrate "business flow from harvest to dispensary shelves." Brainstorming sessions ensued at the Point Market office, the members breaking down ideas on whiteboards.

Privately, though, Tushar seemed ambivalent about the Pharmers Group, unsure that this thing was worth his and Evan's time. On the other hand, why not see if they could get something out of it? Maybe Evan could emerge as the group's leader, pushing the founder aside? Maybe, Tushar said, they could glean some business info from these guys and then just dispense with them. Maybe this could be fun after all. Divide and conquer, right?

12. The Girlfriend

October 2, 2019

Or was it ex-girlfriend? After flying in from the East Coast, she came to the sheriff's office straight from the airport, and she came with a lawyer. A veteran Santa Cruz criminal-defense attorney: Peter A. Leeming. Played a role in the fight to get medical marijuana legalized. Compatriot and friend of the area's highest-profile marijuana attorney, Mr. Ben Rice.

The morning after the discovery of Tushar Atre's body, Mr. Leeming sat beside Rachael Lynch and across a table from Detective Erik Miyoshi and his partner, Detective Ethan Rumrill, newly promoted, yet another rookie detective on the case.

Lynch looked tired. No surprise there. But she talked and talked. The interview lasted many hours before they all agreed to pick it up again the next day, let her get some sleep. She talked about how she first met Atre, renting one of his properties in 2017, about how she and Atre were not just in a "romantic relationship" but a "business relationship," about how Atre had promised to put her name on the title to the Summit property. But she also talked about how Atre was a "very controlling man" who "manipulat[ed] her financially." At the time of his death they were in a business dispute of some kind. She accused him of defrauding her.

At the prodding of detectives, she dished on others. She was skeptical of quite a few of the people who worked with or for Atre, Miyoshi recalled. There was a "running theme" of Atre withholding full payment for work as a form of "leverage." She named the head of a team of handymen that Atre employed pretty much full time. She named Adam Jones, a "random" person Atre had hired off of Craigslist to trim trees at the Summit property. Jones had stolen one of Atre's Toyota pickup trucks in December and had run him over with it at the Summit property! Atre had filed a police report, she believed. She mentioned a young employee who'd gone crazy at the Cruz Science lab one day not long before the murder and smashed a computer. And she named Evan Scott, a former partner of Atre's with whom he'd had a falling out.

The names kept coming. The proprietor of an auto-body repair shop—101 Collision & Restoration—turned out to be Atre's tenant. The owner was a mechanic named Elijah Esteban, and his shop occupied one end of an industrial building or warehouse that was part of a complex of three such buildings near the city of Salinas, in Monterey County. Atre had owned this complex since 2017—it was somehow related to his cannabis business—and he'd started renting the spot to Esteban in October 2018. The Santa Cruz County Sheriff's Office (SCSO) had sent cops down there as part of the search for Atre in the hours after his kidnapping.

Lynch told detectives that Esteban "did not like" Tushar, though she wasn't entirely sure why. Possibly because of "rent issues."

Also, she said there had been an act of vandalism at the Salinas complex at one point. One of the buildings had been damaged, and its exterior graffitied with some kind of symbol; she didn't know what it meant. And also, she continued, one of the tenants in these buildings—not Esteban, a different tenant—had at one point threatened Tushar's life.

Lynch even remembered a phrase the threatener had used when delivering the menacing remark: "He deserves to die."

13. Fresh Frozen

A large delivery arrived at the Thirty-Eighth Avenue house in late spring: a series of coolers packed with dry ice and containing around a thousand pounds of frozen cannabis. Tushar was there. Evan Scott was out of town.

The extraction machines at the house had been up and running for weeks. For raw material, they had tapped into Evan's network—more than a hundred farmers and brokers from all over the state. The biomass they obtained typically took the form of trim. Trim is a by-product of cultivation. Before cannabis flowers can go to market, they need to be dried or cured. Before they can be cured, they need to be trimmed. A freshly harvested cannabis cola is like a hairy vegetal phallus, bearded with bracts and glumes. And so you go into that thing with a pair of little scissors, snipping and pruning the tiny leaves that protrude from the colas. The clippings and parings that result from this work are, in aggregate, *trim*—the basic raw material, the biomass, from which hash oil is most often wrung.

But what had arrived at the house wasn't trim. The coolers were filled instead with the entire unmanicured tops of weed plants—colas, stems, leaves, bracts, and all—frozen solid. Tushar was baffled. What to do with this *frozen stuff*? Biomass had never arrived at the house in this form before. Evan's standard operating procedure called for all trim to be dried before loading it into the extraction machine. And so the obvious thing to do was *defrost* the weed. And then dry it out. Right?

Somehow Tushar got it into his head that the best way to go about this was to buy a bunch of hanging drying racks, the ones with a series of flat discoid platforms vertically arrayed and framed in mesh netting. Racks like these are often used to dry any kind of flower or herb; smaller versions hang over kitchen counters as onion storage. Tushar suspended dozens of such racks all over the apartment, and onto each platform he placed a hunk of frozen cannabis. He also plugged in a bunch of dehumidifiers, started those things going. Soon enough, the frozen hunks began to melt, water leaking onto the floors, blobs of heavy glaucous protoplasm oozing from platters all over the apartment—what the *fuck* was this? A goddamn mess was what this was. Tushar was not pleased.

He had a lot of other things going on. These were busy times. Tushar had recently closed on the purchase of another property: a complex of three cavernous warehouse buildings on a lonely strip of highway just outside the town of Salinas. A spur of the Union Pacific Railroad ran adjacent to the warehouses. Broccoli farms and lettuce fields and artichoke plantations spread in all directions across the flat land, migrant workers hunkered down over the crop rows. The long, narrow swale of the Salinas Valley was poised to become a major region for weed cultivation. By the summer of 2017, a group of ambitious pot farmers were preparing to grow more cannabis here than had ever been grown in one place before in human history. Much of the cultivation would take place inside huge greenhouses once used by some of the biggest growers of cut flowers in the world. The Monterey flower industry had collapsed in the 1990s—a victim of NAFTA—and its greenhouses had fallen into flamboyant decay, glass shattered, iron warped, foundations cracked, like crystal palaces after a world war. Then a group of shrewd go-getters had glimpsed an opportunity. They leased the moldering greenhouses from their desperate owners at super-low rates, then turned around and subleased the buildings at ten times the price to optimistic cannabis growers preparing for legalization.

To the pot farmers, flush with investment money, the rents were unbelievably cheap. More than a million square feet of growing space, it was predicted, would come online the following year, 2018. Greenhouse weed had a reputation for being mediocre, but it was perfect as a raw material for manufacturers of hash oil. All those big corporate growers would want a nearby oil factory to sell their mediocre weed to. Enter Tushar Atre and Interstitial Systems, whose newly acquired complex sat just a few miles from the greenhouse district.

That was the idea, anyway. Eventually build a giant extraction lab inside the warehouse complex. But, for now, in this transitional phase, this *interstitial period* before the big farms came online, Tushar and Evan decided to waste no time in putting the Salinas warehouses to use. In one of the buildings, the one at the southern end, they began creating a new and larger trap lab. In Evan Scott style, the extraction systems would operate inside explosion-proof rooms inside shipping containers that sat on the concrete slab floor inside the warehouse—a hash-oil-production Matryoshka doll. This would allow them to vacate the Thirty-Eighth Avenue house at last, mitigating Tushar's anxiety.

The frozen weed now in thaw at the Thirty-Eighth Avenue house had come from one of Evan's longtime suppliers, a guy everybody called Odie. Like the dog in *Garfield*. Evan knew him fairly well, knew that his real name was Danny O'Brien. A name as Hibernian as a Boston cop's, but as far as Evan knew, Odie was not Irish. He was, Evan believed, Filipino. And possibly an orphan, but adopted and raised by a big family in Salinas, the Estebans. And as far as Evan knew, the Estebans didn't identify as Latino, or only as Latino. They identified as Samoan. Odie himself could have passed for a Pacific Islander. He was shorter than the other guys in the family but solidly built, with Polynesian tattoos and long black hair. The Estebans were a big family, many siblings and cousins in Odie's generation, and many children of those siblings and cousins in the next generation. In Latino-dominated Salinas, the Estebans stood out. Some members of the family were involved in the cannabis trade, though mostly indirectly. The Estebans of Salinas had become well-known for their security services, standing sentry like bouncers at the gates of cannabis farms throughout Monterey and Santa Cruz counties. Armed robberies and inside jobs had long plagued this cash-only weed business. The Samoans provided protection.

Unlike most of his relatives, however, Odie was *directly* involved in weed. He was a broker who had access to many of the region's biggest cannabis cultivators. The weed he'd delivered to Tushar had been fronted to Odie by one of those pot farms, where it had been flash frozen onsite. Buying, selling, trading, Odie stood between grower and extractor. There were three basic ways to structure deals between an extractor and a biomass source: The extractor could just buy it outright, which required capital. Or the extractor could use his production facility to make oil from a supplier's trim, the supplier paying him a fee, a toll, for the service; this was called toll processing. Or, lastly, the extractor and the supplier could do a split, wherein extractor and supplier each got half the quantity of the oil produced, and each sold their portion on their own. In this third method, no cash was exchanged. This was Evan's favorite type of transaction, and that was how they'd done their deal with Odie: a split. At forty-three, Odie was an OG, as seasoned a player in weed as there was. He'd been at it for more than two decades. Odie would have known that a split was like a simple version of a call option on a commodities future. It was a bet that the price of hash oil would rise. And in this case, there was good reason to believe that it would.

When Evan arrived back in Santa Cruz, he went to the Thirty-Eighth Avenue house and gazed upon the scene with shock and horror. Odie's weed had arrived in a form known as fresh frozen. At the time, a novel cannabis extract was exploding in popularity: They were calling it live resin, and you made it by extracting it from fresh frozen, by putting the gelid biomass directly into a super-chilled extraction column. Live resin was prized because the process of its manufacture from the whole plant better preserved the flavor and aroma profile of the original flower.

Everyone wanted it. It was fetching top dollar. But now all of that was fucked. A thousand pounds of fresh frozen, spoiled. Tushar, for his part, was furious. Why hadn't this been *explained to him*?! Total communication breakdown! Evan tried to salvage the product, but the yield was predictably dismal.

And then there was Odie, who, to Evan, seemed suspicious. Did Odie think this was a scheme to defraud him? Trim suppliers and extractors were constantly having disputes of this kind, Evan knew, and would have to litigate these matters in their own ways, which sometimes entailed large men who also worked as security guards. How would Evan and Tushar make this right? Evan wound up just paying Odie for a little more than the value of the raw material—somewhere between sixty and eighty grand, according to what Evan Scott remembers today. But Odie, of course, would have made more if he'd been able to execute his call option by receiving his portion of the live resin and then selling it on the open market.

Odie said he wanted to see Evan and Tushar in person. His adoptive brother Elijah owned an auto-body shop in Salinas—101 Collision & Restoration, it was called—which Odie sometimes used as a kind of office or business spot. *Let's meet there*, he said.

14. Mothers

Spring rolled into summer, and the news came from back East: Shaku was coming. Shakuntala Atre, Tushar's mother, was coming to visit her son in California. She would stay for several weeks, through Tushar's forty-eighth birthday, on the first of August.

Tushar had told Rachael some of his mother's story. She was a formidable woman who had recently taken to writing her memoirs. "Chapter one describes Panvel, the Indian village near Mumbai where the author grew up, and the *wada* or walled compound in which she and her family lived," reads part of a summary of the memoirs on Shaku's personal website. Born on September 11, 1940—India still a British colony, India still with its princely states and maharajas—Shaku came from a family of Brahmans, the uppermost caste, the descendants of ancient priests, keepers of sacred knowledge, but also poets, mathematicians, philosophers, kings. Inside the *wada* there were courtyards and vestibules and balconies and servants. Outside the *wada*, there was water, mud, and many village children, "the children of Panvel living gloriously free and happy lives, but lives that are entwined with the harsh reality of lice, snakes, sickness, and possible death." Her girlhood, she wrote, was defined by water. Monsoon rains inundated the land, and the streets of the village ran like rivers. "Sometimes," Shaku wrote, "you could hear a frog at a distance pleading for an escape when it was swallowed by a water snake."

She may have been a child prodigy. At ten, she became entranced by a giant globe at her school that depicted the size of the British Empire. She decided: *I want to see the world*. She wanted to learn English, but English was only taught to boys, so she convinced her mother to force a nearby boys' school to enroll her. After tearing through the curriculum there, she began undergraduate studies in physics and mathematics, age fifteen, at the University of Pune. By the time she was twenty-one she had acquired a master's in statistics and an intellectual curiosity that could not be satisfied by any of her home country's institutions. In India at that time, for a young woman even of her high station, this was highly unusual. More unusual still, Tushar told Rachael, was Shaku's decision to renounce an arranged marriage. She told her own mother: Inform all suitors that *their* family, the groom's family, must pay a dowry to *her* family, the bride's—reversing the direction of that ancient nuptial financial transaction. "I'm going to make a lot of money," Shaku explained. A man eight years older than she, from a family Shaku knew growing up, had won a scholarship to pursue graduate studies in Vienna. He wrote her letters asking for her hand in marriage. Without consulting her family, she said yes. This was her chance—her chance to leave India, to prove herself in the world. She taught herself German, then won a scholarship to Heidelberg University, the oldest and most venerable of German universities. When she arrived in 1962, she and Prabhakar Atre, who would become Tushar's father, were married in Germany. They left scandal in their wake; according to the story Tushar told Rachael, both had been betrothed to others back home.

A doctoral student in physics, Shaku learned computer programming as a way to carry out astronomical-scale calculations, and soon she fell in love with the field. In the breaks between semesters, she worked at an engineering firm, writing custom software programs on an IBM mainframe. IBM's German office found out about her and recruited her. The hiring officer informed her that the company had offices in 120 countries. *That will do*, Shaku said. She still wanted to see the world.

On August 1, 1969, in a village called Dagersheim, in the home of a midwife, Shaku gave birth to her green-eyed son. When he emerged into the world, he made no sound, as if unsurprised, as if he had been here before. "The doctor was worried and splashed water on him," Shaku later wrote. "He cried and we sighed with relief." They named him Tushar—"fine mist of water" in Hindi.

Two years later, Tushar's parents immigrated to New York—Queens, specifically.

Now came the incident that would enter Atre family legend. For some reason, IBM couldn't—or wouldn't—transfer Shaku from Germany to the New York office. Worse, the New York office was not, at this time, hiring. Caught up in a Gordian tangle of red tape reminiscent of the dreaded Indian bureaucracy, Shaku refused to be deterred. In New York she took her sword to the knot. From a telephone booth at Forty-Second Street and Third Avenue, beneath the tower that housed IBM's New York City offices, she somehow managed to get through to the office of Thomas Watson Jr., chief executive officer, chairman of the board, and son of the company's founder. She didn't speak to Watson, but to one of his aides. It is difficult to imagine today the all-encompassing might of early-1970s IBM. The very definition of blue chip, it was the second most profitable company in the world and one of the largest by stock-market capitalization. It employed more than 270,000 people. It dominated the computer industry to such a degree that it essentially was the computer industry. Its machines were the machines then guiding the missions to the moon. Moving out of mainframes and into personal computing—which it was, in 1971, in the middle of inventing—it had just released the floppy disk. The company would never again be so powerful as it was at that moment in May 1971 when Shaku Atre explained her situation to Watson's aide as taxi horns bleated in the background and an operator informed her of the need to insert another ten cents if she wanted her call to continue. She was out of coins. Quickly she told the aide to please call her back at this number, please. Which he did do, and then he asked Shaku if she could come to Armonk.

"What is Armonk?"

Armonk was the town in Westchester County where IBM had recently erected a multibillion-dollar campus as its world headquarters.

Shaku said she couldn't. Could Watson's man come down to IBM's city office, underneath which she was then standing in a phone booth? He said yes. The next morning, a different aide showed up, he in a dark mid-century suit and tie, she in a sari of blazing-bright color. Despite the sartorial disparities, by the end of the interview Shaku was sitting at a desk inside the Midtown skyscraper, the newest member of the IBM division that administered to clients outside the United States. She made the blazing sari her uniform, and, in it, she strove to climb the corporate mountain. For ten years she moved through various roles until she quit in 1981 to start her own consulting business. This she lucratively operated, in one form or another, for the rest of her career, advising clients (AT&T and the FBI, among them) on the architecture of their databases. She wrote textbooks and became a sought-after keynote speaker at technology conferences. In the late 1990s, she and her husband moved from the family home in Rye, New York, to Santa Cruz to help young Tushar launch AtreNet, a business that was to a great degree Shaku's idea.

His parents stayed in Santa Cruz until 2007, when they returned to New York City to be closer to Tushar's younger sister and their first grandchildren. But Shaku would come back to visit Tushar in California quite often, and now she was on her way again, her impending arrival causing a certain disturbance in the atmosphere above Pleasure Point, as though Tushar were a teenager who'd thrown a raging keg party at home, and whose parents were now returning from vacation. Rachael did not yet fully grasp the degree to which Shaku despised weed, considered it an intoxicant fit only for the underclasses, and did not know that Tushar was, consequently, trying to keep the fact that he was launching a cannabis start-up a secret from his mother.

Anyway, it didn't matter: Tushar had already had the trap lab dismantled and relocated to one of the industrial buildings he'd bought near

Salinas. Once Shaku was in Santa Cruz, Tushar arranged for the mothers to meet. They escorted slow-moving Cynthia down to the bustling Verve coffee shop in the center of Pleasure Point. Cynthia gave Shaku a hand-drawn greeting card, and Shaku accepted it courteously, expressing thanks, but not opening it, setting it aside, and then not really addressing Cynthia for the rest of the visit, incurious, it seemed to Rachael, about Cynthia, her life, her illness. The meeting grew awkward, strangely formal, the politeness forced. Shaku told stories about her interesting, enterprising life . . . stories that illustrated the toughness it took to succeed as an immigrant in America.

Rachael left the café feeling a little depressed and a little irritated. Back home, sometime later, she could hear Tushar yelling at someone in another part of the Thirty-Eighth Avenue house. Soon, it became clear he was yelling at his mother. Rachael walked downstairs and saw Tushar bent low, screaming into the face of this tiny, seventy-six-year-old woman, spit flying, blind with rage. After it was over and Tushar had left the room, Rachael approached Shaku and made an attempt to comfort her. But Shaku was standing there cold-eyed, without emotion, and suddenly Rachael realized that this had probably happened many times before, Tushar losing himself in spasms of fury, and that Shaku had on those occasions reacted in the same way she did this time: She'd let Tushar rage and done nothing, let him feel like there were no repercussions for his loss of control. Which meant that Shaku had also, in a way, enabled it, had allowed her son to believe he was an invulnerable prince who could lose control without consequence. Which meant Tushar was a danger not only to others but to himself. Which was not a great way of being if you were starting out in the weed business. She told Shaku, *You created a monster*.

15. The Compliance Manager

October 2, 2019

She'd only been working with the victim for less than a week, she said, and she was freaked out. She had *just seen him.* Had just seen him at Fern Street the day before. *See you tomorrow*, she'd told him!

Detective Baldrige was on the phone with the freaked-out person. A Santa Cruz resident, she'd met Atre through a mutual friend, a local surfer who owned a company here in town, a surfboard-wax brand, a *sustainable* wax made out of seaweed, or something. She described herself as a "lab safety and compliance specialist." According to her LinkedIn, she'd worked for a pair of alt-therapy herbal-supplement brands in Santa Cruz, companies that promised "bioenergetic scans" and "microbiome-balancing formulations." Zero experience in the cannabis business. Atre had hired her to handle compliance for the Cruz Science start-up—to make sure the Fern Street facility was continually up to snuff with the local and state cannabis regulators. Atre had been running her ragged, pushing her hard. So much so that she had to put her foot down. Literally had to stare him down and say: *Dude, I'm not going to be one of your employees who's on call, like, twenty-four hours a day*. But Atre was cool with that. He laughed and told her: *OK, OK, I get it.*

There were other weird things, though, she told Baldrige. The lab was a "free for all," with "people coming in and out all the time." She couldn't keep them straight, didn't know who they were, why they were there. It was apparent to her that Atre was playing things fast and loose. To her knowledge, the company had yet to generate revenue. Yet here were all these people, coming and going.

After that initial call with Baldrige, she would stay in contact with the sheriff's office, sharing information whenever she thought of something. She'd heard from other Cruz Science employees, for example, that there were shady things going on. Things Atre had never mentioned to her. Like that he basically had a side business—a black market side business. There was some other facility, a huge facility, in another county? She was confused, her mind spiraling with rumors she'd heard, conspiracy theories, and she was scared for her own safety. The deputies attempted to reassure her, but she was not reassured.

16. Sons of Samoa

For their highly anticipated meeting with Odie, Evan and Tushar trekked down to Salinas, to the auto repair shop owned by Odie's brother, or adoptive brother Elijah Esteban. The shop occupied a low-slung commercial building next to a mobile home park on a dusty stretch of ag-zone right off the 101, the highway that runs nearly the length of California from Los Angeles to the Oregon border. Here, on the poured-concrete floor of 101 Collision & Restoration, amid cracked-up automobiles in various stages of repair, Evan and Tushar listened to Odie. A few other large, massively biceps'd men—Odie's brothers or cousins or nephews or a mix of all of the above—were there, including Elijah, the shop's proprietor, and also a guy called LaLa, who worked as a security guard or, some said, as an "enforcer." Odie, a little shorter and smaller than the rest, wore his hair in long cornrows. A chain of what looked like mala beads encircled his neck. He greeted his guests with warmth and good cheer.

Evan had visited Elijah's 101 shop on weed business before. Because of its proximity to the increasing number of giant cannabis farms in the Salinas Valley—farms that Odie traded with—Odie used the shop as a meeting place and a business address. And yet despite Odie's good humor, tension hung in the air. Evan and Tushar thought that the fresh-frozen mishap had irritated him, but that wasn't what Odie wanted to talk about. Instead, he wanted to talk about his new brand.

He was calling it Island Pharmz. An homage, clearly, to his adoptive Oceania brotherhood. With the coming of legalization, Odie didn't want to just broker weed anymore. A consummate middleman, an expert in the buying and selling of weed, both flower and trim, he knew all the biggest growers and extractors. He knew all the buyers—including California's medical dispensaries, many of which were soon to become legal retail outlets of recreational weed for any person over twenty-one. Why not repackage and rebrand the flower he'd been buying all along from these growers as Island Pharmz flower? Why not repackage and rebrand the extracts he'd been acquiring all along from these Santa Cruz white boys with their chemistry sets as Island Pharmz extracts? To get it going, he would need to devise a marketing and branding strategy. How perfect was it that one of his longtime trading partners, Evan Scott, had teamed up with this Chad named Tushar, who was also a tech guy, an Internet guy, a marketing guy? Could this Mr. Tushar Atre help Odie with the Island Pharmz brand?

ODIE WANTED TO TALK ABOUT SOMETHING ELSE, TOO. Weed brands had existed for many decades in California, even going back to the days of total prohibition. But in the Prop 215 era, especially as recreational legalization approached, weed producers were jockeying to establish their brands in the public eye, developing ever more sophisticated packaging and logos and marketing strategies. Sensing another opportunity, Evan Scott had recently developed a scheme. Swimming in trim sources, swimming in oil, Evan would front product to these brands—oil, shatter, distillate, whatever they wanted. Instead of receiving cash for the product, he would strike profit-sharing agreements with the brands, taking equity stakes in the companies, effectively. Evan called it "funding from the back end." Such deals were lucrative—more lucrative than standard biomass deals with farmers or brokers. And it was good for the start-up brands—who were often cash poor—too. Indeed, Evan told Tushar, he'd drawn inspiration for the idea from the venture capitalists on the other side of the hill. Instead of infusing a start-up with cash, he was infusing it with product. Product, in this case, was the capital.

Before ever meeting Tushar, Evan had already been funding Island Pharmz with product. Now Odie wanted to know: Would the Tushar-Evan partnership want to do the same?

PEOPLE IN THE WEED BUSINESS had good things to say about Odie, for the most part. He was "a nice guy," "a supercool guy," "an awesome guy . . . who was dealt a shit ton of bad cards." An alcoholic father, abuse, abandonment, violence. He'd seen a lot in life, it was true, had suffered his fair share of hard luck and struggle. He felt his life story could be a book or a movie. Taken in by the Esteban family, he was "adopted, raised Islander, raised up on the east side of ghetto Salinas," as he once described it. But now, at last, in middle age, his prospects were on the rise. Marijuana legalization was a ticket out of his old life and might even make him rich. Like Samoan football stars drafted into the NFL, like the rappers Odie knew who'd gone from the streets to the jet set—marijuana was about to give him his turn. How odd it seemed, how fucked-up ironic: The very activity that had sent him away to prison for all those years—basically the same thing, anyway—was going to be his financial salvation. Odie was fairly open about his past, but in addition to all the good things people had to say about Odie, they also warned: *Don't poke around too much.*

If Tushar had poked around, he would have learned that certain adoptive relatives of Odie's were well-known not just to the region's cannabis operators, but also to the Salinas Police Department; the Monterey County Sheriff's Office; the California Bureau of Investigation; the US Bureau of Alcohol, Tobacco, Firearms and Explosives; the FBI; the DEA; and the offices of the US Attorneys of at least five states. If law enforcement was to be believed, some of the brothers may also have been members of a gang that had originally formed in the Islander enclaves of Long Beach and Carson in the 1980s, a group called the Sons of Samoa, or S.O.S.—a Samoan Mafia that was also, at least according to police agencies, affiliated with the Crips, the famous L.A. street gang. In Salinas, the Sons of Samoa would have rubbed shoulders with an assortment of Latino street gangs, including the Norteños, the Northerners, who in turn were ruled over by the notorious prison gang Nuestra Familia. In California's prisons, incarcerated members of the S.O.S. would have mingled among the same. If law enforcement was to be believed, the Norteños and Nuestra Familia were affiliated with at least two Mexican drug-trafficking organizations: the Jalisco New Generation cartel and the La Familia Michoacana.

In July 2000, when he was twenty-six years old, Danny O'Brien pleaded guilty to trafficking meth. He and two of his adoptive Salinas brothers had been caught with three pounds of the stuff in, of all places, Smith County, Mississippi. Other Esteban brothers were also busted for selling meth in 2003 in San Jose. Included in that case's diverse array of charges were illegal possession of a machine gun, illegal possession of a firearm silencer, illegal possession of the kind of firearm silencer that has no serial number, and illegal possession of firearms on which the serial numbers had been "obliterated," though some of these gun charges were later dropped. When the time came for parole, one of the special conditions for one of the brothers' supervisory release was "shall not associate with Sons of Samoa gang." For his part, Odie spent nearly ten years in federal prison. (Elijah Esteban, the auto-repair shop owner, was not involved in any of these cases and has never been charged with any crimes.)

Odie began the long journey toward entrepreneurship in 2009, while on probation. He worked for Waste Management. He worked as a security guard. He had five daughters he was struggling to maintain relationships with. Time after time on his obligatory visits to his probation officer, he tested positive for cannabinoids. He violated the terms of his supervisory release so frequently that a judge at one point ordered him back into custody for nine days. He was ordered to rehab. He skipped rehab. He smoked weed so much, he told the judge, because of the stress he was under. Through it all, however, Odie held down jobs and earned. He also sold weed and earned even more, eventually conceiving the Island Pharmz brand as a way to go legit and make it big. Which is how he found himself in 2017 standing in his brother's auto-body shop, talking to this Chad Tushar Atre.

Odie may not have come out and said it during the meeting at the shop, but when it came to Island Pharmz, Evan could see there was a catch. The California regulations were such that a felony conviction for trafficking hard drugs (i.e., meth) would make it very difficult for Odie to obtain a cannabis license in California. And yet there were ways around this, maybe. He could make a deal, for example, with someone who had a clean record. When that clean-record person applied for and obtained the desired license, Odie could be his behind-the-scenes business partner. Tushar, of course, had a clean record. So did Evan. Maybe someone like Tushar/Evan could, therefore, invest in Island Pharmz, a brand founded by a reformed and totally rehabilitated black market businessperson, in the way Evan talked about? And maybe then Island Pharmz could piggyback on Tushar's license and, under that license number, totally legally sell the amazing products of Odie's amazing brand with all its street cred and authenticity?

The meeting ended with good feelings but no resolution, just an acknowledgment of good ideas and a pledge to keep in touch, Odie and his brothers and Tushar and Evan shaking hands and bro hugging.

Not two minutes out the door, on the drive back to Santa Cruz, Tushar was shaking his head. No way. He was not going into business with those guys. Tushar, Evan could tell, was scared of them.

17. Forty-Eighth

Horses! Tushar wanted to buy Rachael some horses. Rachael was an experienced horsewoman, having ridden from a young age in Vermont. Tushar said they could stable the animals at the barnlike outbuilding on the odd but picturesque mountain property he'd recently bought on Highway 9 very near the town of Felton. About fifteen miles southwest of the Summit property, the Felton place abutted Henry Cowell Redwoods State Park, where a labyrinth of horse trails wove through the forest. Rachael had to talk him out of it. Did he know how much work it took, caring for horses? She was not about to take that on. And so instead Tushar sent the squad of handymen he employed pretty much full time to the Felton building to gut renovate the place. Tushar and Evan were getting ready to install another small extraction lab there.

Then came Tushar's birthday. August 1, 2017. He was turning forty-eight and was going to have a party. For the occasion, he had his custom-made dining cart backed up into the yard at the Felton house. The cart was pretty amazing. It had previously served as a kind of mobile greenhouse in which Tushar had grown a few cannabis plants in the backyard of his Los Gatos bungalow. But he'd since had it repurposed. Wood paneling. Wooden stools that swung out on hinges. Wooden tables, wooden booths, and the original greenhouse roof. It was like a miniature dining car on an old-time train. Rachael festooned the place with balloons, a

"Happy Birthday" banner. She'd bought a cake with Tushar's name written in frosting. A few of Tushar's Silicon Valley friends arrived. One of them brought his little kids. Evan was there, too. Rachael had made peace with Evan, whom she'd seen having deep conversations with her mom once or twice at the house on Thirty-Eighth. She wasn't sure what to think about that. Cynthia was not at the party. She had good days and bad days, and today was a bad day. But Shaku was there, telling stories. Rachael was self-conscious, first birthday with a new boyfriend, and she wanted to make a good impression, but was worried about how her lowbrow birthday decorations would be received by all these people, most importantly Shaku.

After dinner, she sneaked out to the temporary kitchen they'd set up in the house, lit the candles, and walked back to the dining cart carrying the cake on its platter. Everyone was singing "Happy Birthday." As she climbed the steps to the cart, her foot caught and the cake slid off the platter, landing face down, the candles buried in a sickening confectionary heap. Rachael stared down at the wreckage. There was an excruciating moment of silence. But then the little kids grabbed hunks of cake from the floor and shouted, *It's OK! It's good, see?* Everybody laughed, and Tushar joined the children, taking a handful of ruined cake and tucking into it happily like a hungry galoot. He looked up and gave her that warm, serene smile of his, telling her quietly, *It's great, it's great. Thank you.*

WHAT WASN'T GREAT WAS HER DEAL WITH BAMM BAMM, aka Bang Bang. She'd made a mistake. She shouldn't have been so hands-off, shouldn't even have gone into business with him in the first place. Bamm Bamm had been light on capital. That was the reason, he'd said, that he'd needed to take on a partner at all. The question was: If he was such a great grower of cannabis, why was he so light on capital? But, encouraged by Evan and Tushar, Rachael had forged ahead anyway. Per her agreement with the guy, Rachael fronted all the money for the grow's overhead—clones, soil, fertilizer. Bamm Bamm's property didn't have a well. So they had to import water, too, at great expense. Total costs were close to fifty thousand dollars. Per their agreement, Bamm Bamm would pay her back for half the expenditures once they sold the resulting pounds. Then there was the twenty thousand dollars she'd promised Hank, who was supervising the grow.

By mid-August, the deal was falling apart. It had become clear to Rachael that Hank and Bamm Bamm had spent more than they should have. At harvest time, the yield turned out to be mediocre, maybe sixty pounds, and the profit margin vanished. So Bamm Bamm told her he was seizing the crop in its entirety. The guy was stiffing her. She'd had a similarly bad experience with a growing partner in the Emerald Triangle, and fuck if it wasn't happening again. She drove up Highway 9 to the property one day to confront this hippie gun freak. Tough over the phone, he was meeker in person. Bamm Bamm's non-weed business was jewelry making. Crystals and energy stones and whatever. He offered Rachael a diamond ring of his own design as compensation. She knew a little about diamonds. She could tell the piece wasn't worth anywhere near half the grow's expenses. *Well, that's all I have*, Bamm Bamm pleaded.

When she told Tushar what was happening, he was predictably pissed. *Let's sue the bastard!* he said. Of course filing a lawsuit wouldn't be possible. Rachael and Bamm Bamm had in fact signed a contract, but they were engaged in unlawful business activities. In this deal, everyone's hands were unclean.

She had no choice but to let it go. And, anyway, her mind was elsewhere. Cynthia had taken a turn for the worse.

18. The Footage

Early October 2019

The homes along Pleasure Point Drive did not lack for security cameras. Perhaps the only residence on this short lane of multimillion-dollar properties without such video surveillance was, typical luck, the one belonging to the victim.

The neighbors' cameras had captured multiple angles of the front of the Atre property, but there was no video recording of the events that had taken place inside the house in the earliest hours of October 1. Now, at SCSO headquarters, Erik Miyoshi was screening the pertinent footage downloaded from those cameras.

Time stamp 2:47:56 a.m.: In the grainy night vision black and white of all CCTV footage, the street lamps cast a pallid, spectral glow. Three figures emerge from an alleyway on the north side of Pleasure Point Drive. They cross the street. They walk single file along the south sidewalk toward the victim's house. Young guys. Two of them are slender, wearing skinny jeans or tapered sweatpants. The first guy wears a baseball cap. The other two guys are in hoodies with the hoods up. The guy in the rear, heavier set than the others, has an assault rifle slung over his shoulder. An N95 mask covers his face. The middle guy carries a duffel bag that looks empty, but maybe not, hard to say. Halos of pixilation surround the three figures. The distance of the cameras from the three men and the muddy quality of the recording meant there was no hope of scoring IDs. You could, however, just barely make out that the middle guy is wearing what appears to be a pair of Vans, the skateboarder shoe. And, as it happens, they'd found footprints with the unmistakable Vans waffle iron sole patterns in the dirt around the BMW at the Summit crime scene.

Time stamp 2:48:12 a.m.: The guys vanish out of the frame. Fast-forward, fast-forward, nothing, nothing . . . and then, thirteen minutes later, time stamp 3:01:43 on the same camera, the victim races into the frame, hands restrained behind his back. He is running hard. He is escaping! Something falls from his mouth. Later the detectives would come to believe that Atre had spit out a sock used to gag him. You knew the outcome but were rooting for him anyway. *Go, go, go!* A fraction of a second later, one of the three guys sprints into the frame like a linebacker and tackles the victim headlong in the middle of Pleasure Point Drive. Another guy is right behind him, coming to assist, and something about the way the perps move in this whole sequence suggests to Miyoshi that they "had some form of tactical experience." Possibly law enforcement, but more likely military. Miyoshi could just tell.

19. A Warning

By August, Evan had been coming around the house on Thirty-Eighth so often he'd gotten to know Cynthia pretty well. They'd roll a joint from Rachael's stash and then enjoy it while sitting on the balcony, gazing across the rooftops and the palms toward the sea. Cynthia would wear her turban and sunglasses, a shawl over her shoulders. Occasionally their conversations went deep. Career, love, family. Death. Evan believed that Cynthia was one of the sweetest people he'd ever met, but also wise. He sought her advice.

Evan, in turn, entertained Cynthia with bits and pieces of his story: He was born during a blizzard on a ranch in Montana. His father was a gunsmith and a wildcat miner of gold and Yogo sapphires. The Scott family ranch was bought with the sapphires. Raised in the small town of Florence, he'd grown up on four-wheelers and snowmobiles, not surfboards or skateboards. The first cannabis plant he ever saw was deep in the woods outside Florence, near Bitterroot National Forest—spectacular country, big of sky, filled with trout streams, stands of spruce and Douglas fir, alpine meadows ablaze with summer wildflowers, herds of elk, the occasional grizzly, and craggy peaks rising above ten thousand feet. Evan Scott was eleven when he and a friend, exploring in the forest, stumbled on a small dilapidated cabin, more shack than cabin. To the boys it seemed abandoned, except for this verdant garden abloom with all manner of herbs and vegetables, including specimens of a strange, cartoonish plant, huge bushes taller than they were. Opening the cabin's unlocked door, they stepped inside. It was dark. As their eyes adjusted they saw a kitchen, a stove, rough furniture, maybe two or three other rooms back there. They wandered through the darkness, touching objects, examining them. Then suddenly out popped a woman in a flash of movement: *It's the witch!* They screamed and they ran. Local folklore had long told of an old woman, a hermit, who lived alone in the woods. Local folklore called her a witch. *Don't go to the witch's house!* And so no one ever did. But the boys eventually stopped running and returned to the cabin and befriended the old lady. She was unkempt, with long fingernails and broken teeth. Witchlike! But she was kind and generous—and also an old hippie and longtime cultivator of weed. She had encouraged the witch lore, Evan would learn, in order to discourage unwanted visitors to her property.

When Evan got a little older, seventh grade maybe, he tried to sell some of the crone's weed. He found buyers among some high school kids, but they gave him a wedgie and stole it from him. That was his first weed deal.

From a young age Evan had an anti-authority streak. He got his driver's license at thirteen, the driving age in Montana if you lived on a ranch. A year later, he ran away from home because his mother didn't like that he had an older girlfriend, and he stayed away from home forever after that. He lived in a kind of communal house rented by young people in their late teens and early twenties, not far from his parents' place, and continued to attend his same high school. Now that he was out from under his parents' roof, he said, his relationship with them greatly improved.

With the guidance of the old lady in the woods, Evan and friends started growing small cannabis crops nearby, guerrilla grows. But winter comes early in Montana. Frosts in August would sometimes kill the plants. To rescue the THC from this frostbit weed, Evan took to making hash oil from it. The old lady had a method for using butter to remove the resins that sugar cannabis flowers. But Evan, a mechanically minded ranch kid, figured out that certain petroleum-derived gases might work even better as solvents. He read up on how big industry extracted glucose from sugarcane. Hexane was the answer. He didn't have access to any hexane, but he could easily obtain propane, which he employed in a rudimentary extraction process known as open blasting. In a tube, you blasted the weed with a stream of gaseous solvent, which separated the THC-rich trichomes from other plant matter. You had to do it outside so the gas would just dissipate into the surrounding troposphere. Around the same time, about a thousand miles to the southwest, Elliot Kremerman and his Wookiee cohort were experimenting with the same open-blasting techniques in the Santa Cruz Mountains. Evan's efforts produced a primitive form of oil, an unappealing if potent hashish goo, for which, alas, there wasn't much of a market.

After high school, Evan moved to Coeur d'Alene, Idaho, to study automotive engineering at North Idaho College. A gearhead, he liked to buy junkers and fix them up. In Idaho, he got a job as a dishwasher at a restaurant called Bistro on Spruce. One night, one of the cooks told him he should quit this dead-end job: *Come to California this summer*, the cook said. *Work for just one week there and you'll have enough money to live on for the next six months.* Evan laughed at the guy. But that night, after work, he went out to the lake with some friends, ate mushrooms, and had a revelatory experience. *Why would you laugh in someone's face like that? This could change your life.* Tripping, he made his decision.

The cook brought Evan to a place on a dirt road off Highway 9, some miles from the town of Boulder Creek, where an outdoor cannabis farm sprawled on a sun-splashed hillside of the Santa Cruz Mountains. Evan worked as a trimmer, a trimmigrant. And, just as the cook had foretold, he did earn enough to finance the next six months of his life. Of course he couldn't resist returning the next year. This time, he was paid in cash as well as product. The year after that, the farm's proprietors fronted Evan weed, which he took back to Idaho to sell. The same pound that cost a thousand dollars wholesale in California could fetch four grand in Idaho.

He began going back and forth, back and forth, no longer a trimmer but a broker, building his bankroll and smuggling back more weed each time.

Eventually, he followed a path that many others had and would follow. He moved to Santa Cruz. He learned to surf, became obsessed with surfing, and used his weed profits to take monthslong surf trips around the world. Not yet twenty-three, he seemed to have achieved the good life. But then, just like that, it all fell apart. The cook from Bistro on Spruce, who had become his weed-trafficking partner, disappeared. As Evan would discover, the cook had gotten hooked on opioids, had stolen cash and weed, had been approached by narcs and had ratted out their clique of black market peers. Arrests and indictments came down. Evan was sure he was next. He stopped selling weed and fled to Thailand where a friend—yet another Santa Cruz pot dealer—had opened a tiki bar on a beach near Phucket. Evan stayed there nearly a year until he determined the coast was clear.

Returning to Santa Cruz, he had to start all over again, from the bottom: trimming. Evan hated trimming. But he had the good fortune to find work as a trimmer at a cannabis operation controlled by a pair of identical twins. The twins' grow sites included a parcel of land way up in the mountains near the terminus of Deer Creek Road, a now notorious road that twisted and turned through rugged terrain. On either side lived reclusive hippie marijuana barons and meth-cooking outlaw bikers and psychedelic gangsters and drug addicts of every category. People were scared of Deer Creek Road. Outsiders stayed away from Deer Creek Road. As with the old lady in the woods, this was partly by design. Chris Daly, for example, paved the section of Deer Creek Road that abutted his gate with spent shell casings. It was a warning, rooted in aesthetics. Daly just thought it looked cool! By this point, circa 2010, his shoulder-length hair was going gray. He was bandy-legged. He'd become something of a hermit, not leaving his homestead for months at a time for fear that intruders might steal his crop of primo, sun-grown, high-potency flower. Most people now knew him by the gonzo, Prankster-ish nickname he'd given himself:

Professor Wingnuttt. Three *T*s. He still consumed quantities of psychedelic drugs, which may have taken a toll. He believed in chemtrails. But he also liked to write poems and jam with friends on his vintage Les Paul, and he still grew commercial quantities of weed—though compared to the ambitious newcomers swarming into the county, like Evan's identical twins, his grow was tiny.

If the first wave of cannabis migration into the Santa Cruz Mountains had occurred during the seventies, the second wave occurred almost forty years later. Two things happened. In 2009, the Obama administration's Department of Justice issued the first of several memos that essentially told federal law enforcement agencies to stand down from investigating cannabis operators in states where the plant was legal for medical uses, as long as those operators were following state statutes, weren't selling their weed out of state, and weren't breaking other laws, like owning unlicensed guns. And then, in 2011 a local ordinance passed by Santa Cruz County's board of supervisors created a regulatory regime under which nonprofit medical marijuana collectives could grow weed at scale. The Santa Cruz County Sheriff's Office pulled back, for the moment, on weed busts. A joke spread locally. Q: Where's the best place to hide your cocaine in Santa Cruz County? A: Inside your bag of weed! Santa Cruz was hailed as the Amsterdam of California. Would-be weed entrepreneurs flocked to the county from across the country and around the world. Daly and others called it the Green Gold Rush. This was peak 215.

In the montane setting around Boulder Creek, in the drainages of Mount Bielawski, Castle Rock, Goat Rock, Fat Buck Ridge, Eagle Rock, and Ben Lomond Mountain, the newcomers discovered the same qualities that Daly and his cohort had recognized long ago: a remote place that was nonetheless within a thirty-minute drive of a major US metropolis. A rugged place where you could hide large numbers of fragrant virescent flowering annuals. The newcomers were not exactly students of Alan Chadwick, the UCSC-affiliated father of organic farming. Cannabis is a thirsty plant. The newcomers drew so much water from the local watershed that springs ran dry. Cannabis is a hungry plant. The newcomers used so much chemical fertilizer that it helped fuel algal blooms in Monterey Bay. Cannabis attracts pests. The newcomers used banned pesticides and fungicides and laid down so much d-CON to curb the rats that routinely plague pot farms that the rodent's main predator, the red-tailed hawk, was locally depopulated. They clear-cut portions of the forest. "Land rape," Chris Daly called it. Along Deer Creek alone there were newcomers from all over the world: Russians, Romanians, Israelis, and, allegedly, the mafias of several nations. In the wider Boulder Creek area there were said to be New York Gambinos, a Chinese triad, Mexican cartels, yakuza. Yakuza's presence in Santa Cruz, circa 2011 and 2012, was facilitated by an unlikely middleman: a Silicon Valley "tech geek" who'd once lived in Japan and was affiliated with a well-known video game company. Talk about profit margins: In Japan, they were big. Effective law enforcement in Japan made pot so scarce there that high-quality California flower could fetch as much as thirty thousand dollars a pound. Yakuza would come to Santa Cruz with suitcases of clean, crisp hundred-dollar bills and buy whole crops at a time. It seemed that pot was growing everywhere in the county, outside and indoors. In barns, car-repair garages, homes, warehouses. In a warehouse literally next door to the Santa Cruz County Sheriff's Office. On a parcel of land that abutted the vacation home of the Santa Cruz County administrative officer. When families from San Jose and other Silicon Valley towns went into the mountains in December to buy their Christmas trees from one of the huge, well-known Christmas tree farms there, they did not know that about a month earlier, in the rows between the conical evergreens, thousands upon thousands of pot plants had just been harvested.

And then there were the twins, who hailed from Southern California and were the sons of a person who had achieved great success in a challenging profession that the twins would rather not reveal. Together the brothers built an operation that became one of the most significant movers of weight in all of Santa Cruz and perhaps the state. One twin had gone to a well-known California university, majoring in a field relevant to the cultivation of plants; the other had studied science at a college in the East, but joined forces with his brother in Santa Cruz after graduation. When the financial crisis struck in late 2007, the twins figured out an angle. They leased homes from homeowners with underwater mortgages and, within a short time, had indoor weed crops secreted away in residential neighborhoods all over Santa Cruz. They weren't alone. "What we did in Santa Cruz was kind of unique," one such weed entrepreneur recalls, "in the sense that a bunch of stoner kids were able to lock down one of the most expensive real estate markets in the world." A few scares and brushes with the law ensued. Friends and associates got pinched. For a year, the twins left the business, got legit jobs, but they couldn't stay away. The price of weed was just too high. When they came back, they were done with the puny grow rooms all over town. They wanted to go big. Really big. They acquired whole tracts of Santa Cruz Mountain hillsides. They eventually had five hills, including the one near the top of Deer Creek Road. They graded and terraced the steep land. The twins had a saying, according to an associate: *Whoever has the most plants wins.* They wanted to win. They wanted to crush it. Mt. Crushmore is what people started calling the twins' massive pot farm on the hill up Deer Creek Road, just above Chris Daly's place.

The twins' empire eventually came to include an investment in a sixty-five-acre weed ranch in the hills above the town of Ben Lomond. Sunny clearings on the property were planted with cannabis. Seven greenhouses had been erected and planted with cannabis. Other buildings on the property—including portions of a five-thousand-square-foot lodge, built as a vacation house by the former resident, the scion of a Bay Area industrial fortune—were given over to indoor grow rooms. An immense garage where the scion housed his Lamborghinis became a cannabis-flower-curing facility. A barn was outfitted with extraction labs. Evan Scott began working at one of those labs. Workers often camped at the ranch or lived in one or another of its permanent dwellings, which included a tree house. Parties were thrown at the ranch, outdoor techno raves or blissed-out jam band festivals on stages with sound systems. A supercross track was carved into an undulating section of the property. Dirt bikes buzzed and soared in great leaping arcs through the air. The ranch was leased from the scion. The lessee was a native Santa Cruzan named Todd Iles (pronounced "aisles"), a concrete pourer and contractor, at least as far as the IRS knew. Fit and sun splashed, he had a mop of blond hair and wore flat-brimmed trucker caps. Iles was a totally surfer-looking California dude except that he didn't surf anymore. Or smoke weed. He preferred IPAs. He'd been enticed into the cannabis trade by the high profits he saw people raking in all around him. Iles had developed the sixty-five acres as a weed property; in 2015, the twins came in as his partners.

Todd Iles was the one who saved Evan's ass. This was not long after Evan returned to Santa Cruz from Thailand. He was broke, was about to crawl home to Montana for good, but was introduced to Iles through a friend, and they hit it off. Iles agreed to fund Evan's first independent forays into extraction. The partnership was soon profitable enough that Evan branched out. This was the time when most growers still considered trim a waste product. They burned it. Or composted it. Or baled it up and tossed it over hillsides. Or gave it away for free to these young extractors like Evan coming around asking for it. (In time, growers would wise up, and trim would come to have a market price.) Cops and courts in Santa Cruz, Amsterdamish though they may have been, still treated hydrocarbon hash-oil production with as much severity as meth production. Evan started installing his labs inside shipping containers. You could buy these things for cheap, like a couple grand. They were small and mobile. Then he found amenable landowners in the mountains and leased little sections of their properties for his containers. This turned out to be not clandestine enough. Aircraft still surveilled from above. Satellites, too: Search warrants had been obtained using probable cause raised by the orbital photography of Google Maps. So Evan started digging holes and burying the shipping containers. These subterranean chambers were elaborately wired and vented. They were powered by gasoline generators, which Evan also buried. He was operating his own literally underground empire of hash. At the height of his business, 2015, he claims to have had as many as twenty containers buried in remote places around Santa Cruz County and more than one hundred people working for him. By 2015, his spots were annually processing more than a hundred thousand pounds of biomass, trim he procured from all over California, not just Santa Cruz. He says his operation was grossing more than twenty million dollars a year.

The amounts were large enough that he got into crypto. Large enough that he made pilgrimages around the world: Fiji; China; the Amazon rainforests of northern Peru, where he drank ayahuasca and visited coca farms; and to the Rif Mountains of Morocco, where he spent days with isolated Berber tribesmen, who produced hashish by hand in a tradition that stretched back centuries. Large enough that he needed to do *something* with all that cash. And then he met Tushar Atre.

In California, running trap labs remained a dangerous business, not just because of the cops but also the robbers. Evan convinced two friends, veterans of the wars in Iraq and Afghanistan, to come to Santa Cruz and serve as his security team. Evan would later keep the existence of his team of ex-military guys a secret from Tushar.

TOWARD THE END OF THE SUMMER OF 2017, Evan and Cynthia sat on the balcony at the Thirty-Eighth house, smoking a joint.

The way Evan remembers it, Cynthia had an even more sagacious air than usual, as if to say, I don't have a lot of time left, so here are a few lessons I've learned. She gave him a drawing she'd made for him and said many things, but the one line he remembered most was: *Be careful who you bring into your life*. At the time he took this as a general piece of wisdom. Only later did it occur to him: She was warning him about Tushar.

20. A Passing

The time had come. In September, Rachael took Cynthia back to Vermont. She was bringing her mother home to die. Tushar joined them and, despite the somber journey, was his typical relentlessly positive self. The trees on the hills around South Pomfret were in the early stages of their blazing autumnal turning. Rachael and Tushar settled Cynthia in the rambling white-clapboard farmhouse. Before long Cynthia was too weak to leave her bed. But she didn't want to go to the hospital; she wanted to die in her home. Her other children and family and friends came to see her. The house was busy and full.

For months Tushar had been planning something special, a week-long trip to Europe with Rachael for her birthday. Rachael was hesitant, afraid her mother was close to death. But Tushar pressed, told her Cynthia would be OK; she was a fighter. Cynthia, for her part, wouldn't hear of Rachael canceling the trip. *Go!* she told Rachael. *I'll be here when you get back*. And so they went. In Barcelona they were greeted by a photographer and a sound man, a makeup artist and a hair stylist, all hired by Tushar. Rachael had once joked about making a documentary about her zany life in weed. Tushar loved that idea! Her life *was* zany! He always said that Rachael was *undiscovered*. And so this was his gift to her: two Spanish guys following them around Barcelona, snapping glam shots of her in front of famous landmarks, or zipping around on a Vespa, or standing at tapas bars eating *jamón* and sipping cava. It embarrassed Rachael, but she also loved it because Tushar loved it. Then they flew to Paris (without the crew) and did the touristy things. They went to the Louvre and the Eiffel Tower, and they strolled along the Seine. They went clothes shopping, and he bought her a dress. For Rachael the trip was a struggle, clouded as it was with worry about Cynthia.

Soon enough, the dreaded phone call came. Cynthia was not well. They flew back to the States immediately.

At the house, Cynthia summoned Tushar to her bedroom. For twenty minutes, thirty minutes, they conferred privately. When he emerged, he was choking back tears. He did not divulge what they'd spoken about, and Rachael, already grief-stricken, did not press. She spent her mother's final hours at her bedside. Cynthia died on October 29. She was sixty-seven years old.

The funeral was at a Unitarian church in the nearby town of Woodstock. One by one her children went to the lectern to speak. When it was Rachael's turn, a beam of sunlight shone through the church windows into her eyes. She had to squint. Standing there, facing everyone, she couldn't get through her speech. She broke down in sobs. As she walked back to her pew, what she felt was: *I am nothing without you. I don't know how to be in the world without you.*

She returned to her seat next to Tushar. The Beatles' "Let It Be" played, at Cynthia's request. Tushar held Rachael and told her she was amazing. The whole moment was amazing. It was as though God had come through the window and shone his light on her.

21. The BMW

October 3, 2019

Detective Ryan Fulton stood at the Summit property like an irritated sentinel, making sure this numbnuts tow truck crew didn't lay a goddamn finger on any part of this vehicle. Sling the tow straps onto the tires and that's it. Any goddamn finger laid on this vehicle risked besmirching what amounted to a giant Bavarian-motorcar hunk of evidence, perhaps the most important evidence outside of the body itself, or the weapon itself, should one ever be located. Any goddamn finger could ruin the vehicle's prosecutorial utility. This was forensic recovery, a no-touch towing process.

The tow crew and their SCSO minder delivered the 2008 white BMW X3 SUV, registered to Rachael Lynch, the victim's girlfriend—or was it ex-girlfriend?—to the sheriff's office for a painstaking forensic examination. No keys had been recovered, so a deputy had to find the nearest BMW dealer, flash a badge, and procure a universal.

On the morning of October 3, one of Lauren Zephro's criminalists, May Cheung, donned a white lab coat, snapped on gloves, and approached the vehicle bay in the SCSO's state-of-the-art, climate-controlled, limited-access forensic garage lab, erected at great cost to area taxpayers. It would take Cheung and a colleague six weeks to give the BMW the full monty. They worked from the outside in, methodically documenting whatever struck them as out of the ordinary, such as the "multiple areas" of "blood stain patterns"—or, rather, patterns created by a substance that appeared to be blood—on the passenger side of the car. Using sterile water and sterile cotton swabs, they collected specimens from all exterior surfaces likely to have encountered the hands of the perps, taking so-called "touch DNA samples." Like her boss, Lauren Zephro, Cheung was a fingerprint specialist. She scrutinized every square centimeter of the exterior panels of the vehicle, sticking little colored Post-it notes wherever she saw spots of interest. Perhaps the most significant was located above the BMW's gas-cap cover on the passenger side: a possible palm print. Cheung dusted the areas with black powder to "recover additional ridge detail" possibly made by the creases, arcs, loops, and whorls on the palmar side of the human hand.

Then she moved to the vehicle's interior, breaking down the work into quadrants, repeating the search for latent prints, the swabbing for touch DNA. Her search also turned up two water bottles, a phone charger, but no weapons, no ammunition. In the rear, the seats had been folded down and several pieces of furniture stored inside, a small chest of drawers, a small side table, a small wooden chair. And, in the front, she noticed more of what appeared to be blood. Much more. It was splashed on the leather of the bucket seat, the glass of the front windshield, the passenger headrest, the metal headrest post, and the steering wheel—an ostentation of blood, which suggested the violence that had occurred even before the final, mortal shooting of Tushar Atre at the Summit.

22. Two Sharks

While Tushar was sightseeing in Paris with Rachael, a carefully worded email arrived in Tushar's inbox. He'd been expelled from the Pharmers Group. The stated reason was a bland *moving in a different direction*, but Evan knew the real reason.

After a brief honeymoon period, Tushar had managed to insult almost everyone. His Machiavellian strategies to divide and conquer had not so much backfired as fizzled. He came off as sexist and condescending to the women in the group, including Ginny Stone and another experienced cultivator who'd been growing in the mountains almost as long as Chris Daly and Robert Koenig.

Tushar had also exaggerated Interstitial's numbers. Overpromising was, evidently, a Tushar strategy. To growers who wanted to do business with them, Tushar had more than once overstated their lab's capabilities. Always pushing the envelope: Was this a Silicon Valley trait? The Pharmers Group had supposedly sniffed out the dubious projections. That's when they sent the expulsion email.

Tushar wrote off the whole thing as a clash of cultures. A bunch of traditional market blunderers naive to the ways of the legit start-up world. When he returned to Santa Cruz from Vermont, he didn't seem to care about the expulsion. Evan, for his part, was embarrassed about it, but he was also glad to be done with the Pharmers Group. Too many cooks in that kitchen.

•

AS TIME WENT ON, Tushar's anxiety seemed to worsen. He would shush people whenever the conversation turned to black market business. *Power off your phones! Step away from your phones!* It was possible to hack these things and turn them into recording devices, he said. He would descend into fits of anger, then he'd calm down, regain control, and want to push forward, keep trapping, exhilarated, it seemed, by the act of breaking the law, and also by the money flowing in from it. One day he'd be a mess of nervous anger; the next he'd be riding high on the trap life. Tushar had had a nickname since high school: Two Sharks. You never knew which shark you were gonna get.

And trap they did. Tushar hired electricians to rewire the southernmost of the Salinas warehouses, installing a new heavy-duty service panel so they could jack the amperage to industrial levels. Evan ordered six shipping containers and positioned them across the darkened warehouse floor. It made the space look like a CIA black site. One container held the distillation unit they'd bought from Elliot Kremerman. Two containers were used as storage (one for trim, the other for finished product). One container they used as an office, and the final two housed a pair of extraction machines, including Kogon's Bizzy Beest. Each of those two containers was outfitted with an explosion-proof room, which meant that they were equipped with safety features: fans, vents, alarms, and automatic shutdown mechanisms designed to prevent explosions in the event of a hydrocarbon leak. Leaks were how accidents typically happened. Butane and propane are heavier than air. If a leak went undetected, the gases would sink to the floor, gather, and pool, creating a shipping container-sized bomb. In preparation for its use in cannabis extraction, propane is purged of mercaptan, the chemical ingredient that's added to the consumer product so you can smell it in case of a leak. A careless trap extractor would, therefore, be none the wiser as the gas spewed and sank and built at floor level as he went on running batches of biomass through the machine. If something sparked—a door closing, metal on metal, static on clothes, or some fool lighting a cigarette or joint—the gas would ignite instantly, and the resulting sudden pressure change could literally blow roofs off buildings. For years, black market extractors had been accidentally self-immolating and raising roofs all over Santa Cruz. Extractors had been airlifted to Bay Area burn units, saved, released, and prosecuted. Extractors lying unconscious in hospital beds had notes pinned above their IV machines instructing law enforcement that the patient was "represented by counsel. Do not ask any questions. Call Ben Rice."

By October, the Salinas lab was churning out hash oil and distillate. More than a thousand pounds of biomass were going through the machines' pipes and columns weekly, according to Evan Scott, yielding hundreds of kilos of oil. Crude oil prices had declined somewhat since peak 215, owing chiefly to greater supply. But the market was robust enough that Evan could unload the product easily. Even by Tushar's high standards, the resulting cash flow was pleasing. Their monthly revenue run rate that fall was clocking in at around three hundred thousand dollars. Woo! Let's party! And party they did.

Evan's birthday, his twenty-ninth, was in November, and Tushar threw him a real bash. He rented out an entire spa, a cross between a Japanese Zen garden and a vodka-soaked Russian bath, with hot tubs and saunas, steam rooms and cold pools, waterfalls and chill-out spots. Tushar had it catered with tables of food and drink and invited a bunch of Evan's weed-biz friends, men and women. Poor Rachael was still grieving in Vermont, probably for the best. Dozens of people, some of them naked, paraded around like they owned the place. Evan felt it was one of the nicest things anyone had ever done for him, and they partied into the wee hours, soaking and swimming, dancing and drinking, smoking, snorting, dropping—a smorgasbord of agents for the achievement of altered states. . . .

Altered states. In the daylight hours, Tushar continued to suffer from bouts of paranoia. To deal with the workload at the Salinas warehouse, Evan had brought in a whole staff of people to work the extraction systems there, and Tushar began to suspect some of them of who knows what hidden betrayals. Evan had a right-hand man, his lab foreman, and Tushar would tell the guy off, saying he was playing things too loose and was going to get them all busted! The foreman, previously stable as granite, experienced some sort of breakdown himself. He walked into traffic one afternoon in Pleasure Point, and stripped off his clothes until he was stark naked. Trying to talk sense into him, someone told him he looked like hell; he needed to come out of the road, put on his clothes, and get some rest, but instead he lifted his head to the sky and screamed: *I'm in the best shape of my life!* Evan sent the guy home to Idaho. Had Tushar driven him crazy?

With Tushar behaving so erratically, Evan decided to employ what he called "emissaries" or "straw men" to deal with some of the big weed growers who provided their biomass. He didn't want Tushar fucking up these relationships. One of the biggest weed tycoons in Santa Cruz, kind of a legend, was a guy known as Big J. Evan intended to keep Tushar and Big J far, far apart.

23. Trap Queen

In Vermont Rachael grieved. She hunkered down in Cynthia's farmhouse, wrapped herself in blankets, and drew the curtains. She spent much of the day sleeping. She succumbed to long crying jags. *Why did you have to be so damn wise?* she railed at Cynthia. Her thoughts ran in circles. What was she supposed to do now? Why even go on? How far from grief was madness?

Rachael's sister came by the house and began to sort through Cynthia's things. Rachael couldn't bring herself to look through the accumulated matter of her mother's life. But her sister made a discovery. Twenty thousand dollars in cash, the bills banded neatly together inside a manila envelope labeled in a precise hand "This Is Rachael's Money." Rachael knew what it was but was in no hurry to find the rest. Two more weeks passed. Rachael's aunt, Cynthia's sister, arrived for a long visit to help clean out the house. Slowly Rachael roused herself. She began sorting through the stuff in her mother's bedroom. At one point, heavy with emotion, she lay down on the floor and rolled onto her side, and from this position she could see a stack of shoeboxes rising in the shadows of the bedroom closet. She sat up and started opening the boxes. Some contained shoes. One didn't. Inside were stacks of cash. *Oh God*, Rachael thought. This was what her mother was trying to tell her a few days before she died, when she could no longer speak and was lying in bed, pointing to the closet with an urgent look. Cynthia was trying to tell her about this cash. Rachael counted it out: thirty-eight thousand dollars.

There was more of it in the house, and still more—much more—buried in the woods out back. When Rachael's interstate traffic in weed had begun to generate large sums, she had turned to her mother. Almost all the weed Rachael grew in the Emerald Triangle she'd sell in New England through trusted associates, friends from her youth who'd become pot dealers, basically. Sometimes Rachael would drive the cash from these drug sales to Cynthia's house. Rachael also rented a PO box at the South Pomfret post office. Sometimes she'd ship cash and weed through the mail, which Cynthia would retrieve. Cynthia was a fastidious woman. She kept a ledger. She purchased paper money bands on Amazon in denominations of one thousand dollars, two thousand dollars, five thousand dollars, and ten thousand dollars.

Before she got sick, Cynthia had visited Rachael in the Emerald Triangle, where Rachael's crew of friends and workers on her pot farms liked to listen to hip-hop and R&B. Cynthia toured the cannabis gardens. From the playlist, her mother had some favorites, including Rihanna's "Desperado," and also the New Jersey rapper and singer and convicted crack dealer Fetty Wap's 2015 hit single "Trap Queen." Cynthia, they decided then and there, was Rachael's trap queen.

Eventually, however, Cynthia grew uncomfortable with the sums of illicit cash in the closets of her home. And so Rachael explained to her how to bury the money. Put it into Ziploc bags. Put the bags into Tupperware containers. Put the containers into garbage bags. Dig a hole in the loose soil in the woods behind the house, cover the containers well, and mark them in some subtle way but not so subtle that you forget the location! Three times Cynthia dug holes and buried Tupperware containers stuffed with Rachael's cash. Then she got uncomfortable again. *You have more than two hundred thousand dollars here according to my books*, Cynthia said.

What? Books? You're keeping a record?

Yes, Cynthia said. *Of course I'm keeping a record!*

Rachael made her mother aware of the fact that a record such as this could be used as evidence against her, against them, and so Cynthia destroyed the ledger, and Rachael lost track of just how much money she had saved, and then Cynthia fell ill, and they moved to Santa Cruz, and Tushar came into their lives.

AS WINTER APPROACHED, Tushar called Rachael from Santa Cruz. He had some good news. The property was theirs.

He meant the Shire. The sixty acres at the Summit. The place where Cynthia had had her vision. Since April they'd dithered, uncertain, indecisive. They'd extended the sales contract something like eleven times. But now, Tushar was saying, he'd done the deed. He'd put down the million bucks necessary to consummate the acquisition. The sellers would hold the note for the balance, another $1.4 million. Interest payments of $4,666.67 due monthly. Balloon payments of a quarter million due every year in December for the next four years, and four hundred thousand dollars in the fifth. Tushar had put AtreNet on the title as the property's owner, but that was just a formality. Really, Tushar and Rachael together were the owners. Tushar told her: When she got back to Santa Cruz, they could start working on it, developing their plan for a home and a business, a farm! *OK*, she whispered into the phone and not much more. She was still deep in her grief, sleeping most of the day. But soon she had the thought: What the fuck did Tushar just do? What did *she* just do? Was she really now in debt, along with her lover, to the tune of 1.4 million plus interest?

The sleepiness fell away. The sadness retreated, just a little. She pulled on boots and grabbed a shovel and tromped out into the cold December woods. She knew the spots. Putting the blade to the hard earth, stomping on the blade to drive it through, she eventually hit plastic. If there ever was a time to tap into her savings, her dirty money, now was it.

•

WHEN RACHAEL RETURNED TO SANTA CRUZ, Tushar took her to Big Sur. It was Christmastime. He'd booked them a cabin at the Post Ranch Inn, a resort perched on cliffs overlooking the sea, two thousand dollars a night, a millionaire's hallucination of rustic Bohemia, just up the road from the Esalen Institute. At first she was indifferent—not in any mood to celebrate Christmas or anything else—but then she loved it. *You took me to the perfect place to be sad* and *happy*, she told Tushar. Just the two of them, hardly anyone else around, taking hikes through the silent misty cypress groves, taking soaks in the warm infinity pools, gazing at the crashing waves a thousand feet below, cuddling in their cabin by the fire, crying, the sadness still swarming over her at unpredictable moments. On Christmas Day, they exchanged gifts. He gave her a strand of pearls. She gave him one of those Santa Claus hats with a fake beard attached. She was embarrassed by the disparity. He didn't care. He laughed and said, *I love this!* And he put it on, and they took selfies, each wearing the absurd headdress in turn.

Around this time, Tushar told her that he and Evan might be on the verge of separating. Rachael spoke her mind. If Evan wanted to walk away, let him. She'd been clear from the start: She never wanted a third partner. She wanted to build this enterprise with Tushar, just the two of them, in love and business. She told him, *At the end of a good day, I want to look into your eyes and high-five with you. No one else.* She also sort of didn't care one way or the other. Cynthia's death was having that effect, too. She was having a hard time caring about anything.

Through all these mixed emotions there was, however, something else Rachael was feeling. A sense of foreboding. An intuition that splitting with Evan Scott would, somehow, come back to haunt them all. But she ignored it.

24. The Lab

October 2019

The detectives needed someone to explain what the hell they were looking at. The inside of 211 Fern Street was a mad scientist's lair of incomprehensible machines. The aroma was powerful, like a surfeit of skunks had crawled in there and gone on some mad bender. But these premises were now integral to the investigation, and the detectives needed a crash course on the victim's business, how it worked, how the wider licensed weed industry worked. Operational security in the Atre case was a top priority. The circle of knowledge on this case had to be extremely tight. So the detectives invited one of their own to Fern Street to give them a lesson.

For almost thirty years Steve Carney had been a cop somewhere in Santa Cruz County, most of it with the sheriff's office, most of it investigating drug dealers, most of them of the marijuana kind. Though Santa Cruz's institutions have a deep liberal tradition, conservatism lurks in the ranks of law enforcement. Carney was part of a long line of fervent Santa Cruz weed cops. He'd come up under a pair of decorated officers: Terry Parker and Steven Robbins, whose long résumés included a blockbuster 1988 bust that involved a smuggling ring, a remote cove, a fishing vessel, and twelve tons of pot from Thailand in vacuum-sealed bags labeled "Golden Dragon."

Carney had served in the early 2000s on the infamous task force CAMP, rappelling off helicopters into cannabis fields, hacking down crops, and chasing growers into the woods. Of all the weed cops ever to patrol this patch of California, Carney ranked up there with Parker and Robbins on a list of the most hated. Among the county's weed bootleggers, it was impossible to find a good word for poor Steve Carney. He was underhanded, fraudulent, a criminal himself, they said. There were allegations of illegal search warrants, mysteriously disappearing cash, outright theft. His career, they said, was a secret history of corruption and cover-ups. Carney saw the vitriol directed his way as a sign that he was doing his job. Ben Rice, the preeminent marijuana lawyer, seemed to agree. They had over the years evolved a certain mutual respect. Their careers had become almost symbiotic. So many of Rice's clients had been busted by Carney that a large part of Rice's practice could be attributed to the career of Steve Carney.

In 2018, Carney took his weed cop know-how in a slightly new direction. He moved over to Santa Cruz County's newly created cannabis licensing office as head of enforcement. His job now was, in some ways, no different than it had been in the 215 era: root out the black market weed trade. But it differed in one important way: Very few of his cases would now wind up in the criminal courts (unless they involved violence, or truly enormous quantities of pot, or volatile hydrocarbons in unlicensed labs). Instead, Carney and the CLO were empowered to curtail black market weed through the use of a different stick: the civil fine. The main deterrent to unlicensed weed growers and dealers was no longer prison or felony convictions; it was the possibility of having to pay enormous financial penalties, in some cases upward of a million dollars.

Carney was in his mid-fifties, physically fit, with a shaved head and sharp features that gave him a vaguely raptorial look. At 211 Fern Street, Carney and his civilian colleague Sam LoForti, the cannabis licensing manager for Santa Cruz County, walked the detectives around the facility, explaining this and that. When they reached the storage vaults—designed, according to state regulation, to hold raw material and finished product—they opened the doors and came face-to-face with a mountain of black plastic garbage bags containing what looked like a thousand pounds of trim, at least. Biomass, Carney explained, awaiting transformation into hash oil. Each of the bags bore a tag, as proscribed by state regulation. On the tag was the name of the cultivator or distribution outfit that had ostensibly grown the weed or facilitated its transit. The tags on all the bags bore the same name and license number: Monterey Botanicals Processing, of Salinas, California.

Weird coincidence. Carney knew this name, this company. Knew its owner, a man that Carney had been investigating for almost a year. Target's name was Joshua Rich, one of the more prominent weed magnates in Santa Cruz. Very few people in the weed trade knew Josh Rich by his Christian name, however. Mostly they knew him by a nickname. Big J.

Just six months earlier, Carney and a platoon of SCSO deputies, state law enforcement officers, and federal IRS agents had descended on Big J's many weed businesses—indoor and outdoor grows, cannabis distribution hubs—in both Santa Cruz and Monterey counties, bearing search warrants. They went inside the buildings and started hauling out records.

Both figuratively and metaphorically, Big J was, indeed, big. Six feet six inches tall, he'd been selling pot from his base in Santa Cruz since the 1990s. The SCSO had actually busted him once before, years earlier, in 2002, when Big J's business was much smaller. Over the decades, however, he'd become a major 215-era mover and shaker. Like all 215-era movers and shakers he swore that his businesses hewed meticulously to the medical marijuana laws of the state of California. He ran collectives. He served chronically and terminally ill patients in need of the deep analgesic powers of this magnificent herb. He considered himself a patriot, battling the forces of repression. When the ground shifted with Prop 64, Big J had gone all in on building a licensed cannabis empire. He'd obtained at least twenty-four cannabis licenses from the state, mostly for cultivation, under a host of names—Rooted Republic, Monterey Botanicals, Round Valley Inc., and more.

Carney was coy about how or why, in late 2018, he came to be interested in Big J's sprawling operation. A tip from the post office is all he would say. The focus of the tip involved the massive use of money orders, a venerable method for paying bills in an industry where banking was still, even with legalization, onerous. But it was also a venerable method for paying bills with cash obtained through illicit trading—for money laundering. In Big J's case, Carney's team suspected, the tycoon was growing pot on unlicensed farms, where costs were much lower, owing to the lack of regulation, and then "inverting" all or most of that weed into his legal operation. The allegations were somewhat counterintuitive—growing black market weed and then selling it on the legal market? But the scheme was allegedly designed to juice profits. If you snuck a bunch of unlicensed pot onto the books of your licensed company, you could save yourself a lot of money.

Big J countered that this whole thing was a catch-22 created by government incompetence. Santa Cruz County had botched its regulatory rollout so badly that Big J and other cultivators had essentially been forced to grow weed without licenses! And now the county was shaking them down.

Big J and Santa Cruz County quickly settled the case, the defendant and his handful of partners agreeing to a fine of just over $750,000 in a deal negotiated by a team of lawyers that included none other than Ben Rice. When Big J paid the fine, he paid in cash, the bill-counting machines at the County building whirring on and on.

But there was something else that struck Carney as weird. Some weeks before Atre's murder, a vehicle had pulled up in front of a grow operated by a former business partner of Big J's, in Watsonville, a town in the southern part of the county. Armed men wearing masks emerged from the vehicle, entered the building, put the grow's workers, at gunpoint, into a storage container at the back of the property, locked it, and made off with a lot of cannabis. By all appearances, it was a professional heist. Two violent criminal acts in the weed business, near in time, linked at least superficially by these bags bearing the name of a Big J company.

Weird.

25. Revolt

Rigny is what he called himself, and what everyone in the lab called him. He was one of the technicians who operated the extraction machines at the Salinas warehouse, and he came to see Evan soon after the holidays, in January 2018. He was nervous. He wanted to get something off his chest. Would Evan promise not to hurt him if he told the truth? To which Evan responded, *Come on man, that's not my MO. I've never hurt anyone in my life.*

The thing that Rigny wanted to get off his chest was that, for a few weeks now, Tushar had been secretly paying him to spy on Evan. As soon as he said it, Evan recalled that Rigny had sort of been following him around the lab lately. Rigny's brief was that he would give Tushar a detailed report of Evan's methods for running the lab, which, Rigny said, he had not yet delivered. Tushar even had a very specific list of items he wanted Rigny to observe and report on. But why? Why would Tushar go through this kind of strange, almost childish subterfuge? Rigny had a theory about that, which was why he'd decided to come clean to Evan. Rigny said he thought Tushar was planning to cut Evan out of the company.

At first, Evan didn't believe it. They'd been making great progress! Clearing regulatory hurdles! They were on the verge of obtaining use permits from the City of Santa Cruz to operate a volatile cannabis-oil-manufacturing facility at 211 Fern Street, across from the massage parlor. They'd recently had the structure gutted to the studs. They were on the verge of submitting their applications to Sacramento for the big ones: their California state cannabis-manufacturing and -distribution licenses. They'd hired engineers, a consultant, an architect. Evan was in the middle of drawing up designs for the hash works of his dreams. They were on the verge of moving all the extraction and distillation equipment from Salinas to Fern Street, which meant they were about to shut down the trap lab and cease illicit production, directing all their energies toward the licensed operation. They were on the cusp of what Tushar was calling their "liberation" from the black market. Interstitial would soon be an obsolete name; they'd have to come up with a new one. Tushar was considering Rachael's idea to call it Benevolence Bound. Rachael had recently demanded to be made a partner in the licensed manufacturing entity, too. Evan and Tushar had looked at each other and noncommittally bottled the conversation, but whatever. They were on the verge of achieving their goal! *So what the hell was going on now?*

As it happened, a company-wide meeting had already been scheduled for later that day inside the shell of 211 Fern, where transparent plastic sheeting hung over the walls' exposed studs. Tushar arrived early. Chairs were arranged in a large circle for the staff—a little more than twenty people. As soon as everyone had settled in, Tushar stood up. *Sorry, guys*, he said, *but . . . the business is gonna be taking a little hiatus*. As they got Fern Street ready to make the transition into the legal market, Tushar went on, they were going to have to hit the pause button. And so he and Evan weren't going to be able to pay them for some time, and when it was time to start working again, they'd probably have to pay everybody a little bit less than what they'd been earning because, as everyone knew, the legal market was going to be challenging, the profit margins far narrower than what they'd gotten used to all these years.

In disbelief, Evan listened from his chair. This was the first he was hearing of any of this. . . .

When Tushar finished, a worker named Jordan stood up. Jordan was an old hand in Santa Cruz extraction, had worked with Evan for years. He didn't hold back. Tushar was *a terrible boss, a terrible person*, Jordan said, *a soulless Silicon Valley fuck*. And Jordan wouldn't be working for him anymore, not ever. He quit.

A chorus of concurring voices rose from the circle. The person next to Jordan stood up and said something similar. Then the next person and the next person after that, a wave of discontented avowal moving around the circle, like a session of embittered group therapy. It dawned on Evan that the staff had planned this revolt. And he should have known; he should have realized how much damage Tushar's managerial style had caused. As the staff one by one described their mistreatment—how Tushar had threatened to withhold paychecks, called them incompetent weed rats, etc.—Evan sank into his chair. He should have known! He thought of his Idaho friend, seemingly driven crazy by Tushar. He thought of Cynthia's coded warning. He thought of the time Tushar had said he wished he could *own slaves* like his extended family in India owned them, Tushar eliding his tenses so that Evan was uncertain if Tushar meant his family owned slaves in some distant historical past or *owned them now*! How could Evan have ignored all of that? But Tushar had always treated him so well, he was such a blast to hang out with, they were good friends, the money was rolling in, the project was developing fast—and so he'd been blind to it all. He felt sick to his stomach. He was certain his turn was next: When they finished roasting Tushar, the people in the circle would roast him.

But they didn't. Instead, Tushar went around the room and attacked each staffer in kind. *You suck, you suck, you suck*. He got into the face of an eighteen-year-old kid and urged the kid to consider suicide.

Then Tushar shut down the meeting and asked to speak to Evan in private. *What about you?* Tushar said when they were alone. *Are we still partners?*

Evan did not hold back. He confronted Tushar with Rigny's revelations. But Tushar, looking shocked, denied everything. These people were *crazy*! They were *liars*! They were black market shitbags! *Don't fuck all this up, all that we've built, over a bunch of employees*, Tushar said. *They're just people.*

Was Tushar gaslighting him? In the end, it didn't matter. After the meeting, Evan rushed down to the Salinas warehouses to find that the place had been padlocked. But luckily, earlier that day, several trusted staffers had, of their own accord, rescued the Bizzybee system and other key equipment from the warehouse and moved it all to a different location. So at least Evan had that. But he'd put most of his life savings into the partnership with Tushar. All on a handshake deal. He looked around the desolate parking lot in front of the warehouse, the artichoke fields across the highway. He'd been scammed before. He'd been robbed before. But never like this. Tushar had scammed him in the most charming way possible.

26. The Cloud

October 21, 2019

They never found the victim's cell phone. Much later, detectives would learn that one of the perps had likely walked out onto the deck during the home invasion and flung the device into the churning sea.

So they had to obtain a search warrant for his phone records. In response, Apple's general counsel's office, which dealt with who knows how many of these requests from law enforcement agencies nationwide every year, ordered a download of the victim's iCloud account onto an external hard drive. The drive contained everything that had been stored on Atre's iPhone. Texts, emails, notes, calendars, voicemails, photos, videos, apps. A digital forensic criminalist processed the materials and gave them to Detective Ethan Rumrill in a format that he was able to read on his laptop.

On his laptop, Rumrill saw many interesting things. Images and recordings of men planting what appeared to be a large quantity of marijuana plants outdoors in an apparently remote location. Shipping containers that closely resembled those the detectives had seen on the victim's property at the Summit, the site of his death. Tushar Atre himself, getting his hands dirty and pitching in with the planting. In one video, a young white guy was pounding fence posts into the ground, wearing Vans sneakers, totally inappropriate footwear for this kind of work!

The photos and videos documented the creation of a pot farm. An unlicensed one, it seemed. There was no record of Atre or any of his entities or surrogates or associates holding or even applying for a cannabis-cultivation license from state regulatory authorities. The photos and videos were all time-stamped July and August 2019—just three months earlier. And the GPS location information in the metadata all told the same story. Atre had been operating a pot farm right smack in the densely forested swath between the Soquel San Jose Road and Skyland Road and Highland Way—the heart of the heart of the Summit.

27. Summit

In 1973, Valerie Leveroni was a twenty-year-old college student, driving through the Nevada desert with a friend and rolling a joint in the passenger seat of her Volkswagen Beetle, when an airplane—specifically, a P-51 Mustang, the American fighter-plane workhorse of the Second World War—came screaming across the sky. The Mustang swooped so low and at such great speed that its airflow distortion lifted the Bug from the road and sent it cartwheeling across the pan of the desert, a giant mechanized tumbleweed shedding debris.

She was rescued from the wreckage and treated at a hospital in Reno for traumatic brain injuries. The pilot, a rich man's son, had been flying that low to the ground because he was practicing for the upcoming Reno Air Races. Valerie would go on to experience frequent grand mal seizures, as many as five in a day, and chronic debilitating headaches. Effectively, she now had epilepsy, that spooky disease that had given rise in premodern times to witch panics and witch hunts. She had to abandon her studies at the University of Nevada. She could feel the seizures' imminent arrival—her aura—two or three seconds before succumbing to the electromagnetic storms in her skull. The pharmaceuticals prescribed to her—Mysoline, Dilantin, Valium, Percodan, phenobarbital—made her feel like she was walking through an oceanic dreamworld in one of those weighted diving suits. She became addicted to the Valium, Percodan, and phenobarbital.

Her neurologists believed her brain would never heal. This was as good as it would get for her for the rest of her life. "But the thing is, I was twenty. What twenty-year-old believes that anybody else knows anything? I was like, 'What the fuck does anybody else know about me?'" She refused to submit to the authorized prognosis. Not long after the accident, she met a handsome, hip, long-haired photographer, three years her senior, from San Jose. Mike Corral didn't just love pot. He was on a personal quest to re-create the high he'd felt when he'd smoked a joint for the second time, at age fifteen, a blissful, nearly psychedelic high that he later described as a "*divine-experience* experience." He fell in love with Valerie and started researching epilepsy at the local public library, where he remembers eventually coming across an article in a scientific journal that detailed recent research findings: marijuana used to treat laboratory-induced seizures in rats. He stood up from the table. *Let's try weed!*

Valerie liked to smoke, of course. She had, after all, been rolling a joint at the very moment that the warplane had sucked the Beetle into the air and turned her life into a nightmare. When the aura came over her, Mike would be ready right beside her with a spliff. They worked out a regular cannabis-consumption regimen. Within three years, Valerie was off all prescribed meds, and the grand mal seizures had stopped completely.

For their own supply, the couple cultivated a small pot garden. This way, they could control the cost and quality and potency of the product. Mike was the gardener. He read deeply on the subject in those full-prohibition days, including Bill Drake's seminal *The Cultivator's Handbook of Marijuana* (1970) and the pseudonymous Mary Jane Superweed's *The Complete Cannabis Cultivator* (1969), early underground instructional tomes passed around secretly in counterculture circles. He and Valerie had been living in Campbell, near San Jose, but soon they decided to move to the country: the Santa Cruz Mountains. They'd heard about a specific subregion of the range, remote, rugged, isolated, that sat almost at its exact geographic center. The San Andreas Fault ran right through on its way up the San Francisco Peninsula and under the waves and into the sea to delineate tectonically the Pacific Ring of Fire. The San Andreas Fault zone had, in fact, created the area's ruggedness, and therefore its isolation, which in turn, in the early 1970s, began to attract the sorts of young people who were looking to grow marijuana away from prying eyes. By January 1975, the Corrals were there. The region was called the Summit.

They found a few acres with a small cabin down a dirt track off Highland Way. They used part of Valerie's settlement money from the accident to buy it from a man rumored to be a heroin dealer. If Valerie and Mike had been able to time travel forty-three years into the future as they hiked west from their property through the forest, in a little more than two miles they would have come upon the land owned by Tushar Atre.

The couple's new property had no electricity. This was "part of the healing process," Valerie said. "Get away from all electromagnetic waves." The parcel stood at fifteen hundred feet of elevation. This, too, was part of the plan. It was above the typical highest reaches of the marine layer, safe from the fog, which creates the humid conditions necessary to incubate the dreaded powdery mildew, which is hell on weed. Laguna Creek, a tributary of Soquel Creek, ran through a canyon at the edge of their property. On heavy-marine-layer days, the canyon would fill with dense white vapor like a heavenly carpet as Mike Corral stood at the lip of the gorge next to his garden of blossoming medicine.

The more he got into the gardening of weed, the more fascinated he became. Mike began studying cannabis genetics, cannabis breeding. He and Val met other local cannabis geneticists. An explosion of innovation in illicit plants and fungi in Santa Cruz mirrored the innovations then occurring on the other side of the hill. Sometimes the two intermingled. Around this same time, not twenty miles away, Steve Jobs was in his parent's garage, getting high and brainstorming Apple.

Where did Jobs get his weed? Which strains was he smoking? By 1975, the longtime smuggling hub of Santa Cruz was, like a souk at the end of the Silk Road, a cosmopolitan hodgepodge of cannabis strains arriving from all over the world. Smugglers coming up from Latin America and hippies seeking enlightenment on central Asia's Hippie Trail were bringing cannabis flower into the United States, flowers that were, more often than not, loaded with seeds. Minds blown, hungry now for the best stuff, the dynamite stuff, American strain hunters began spreading out to all points of the globe, infiltrating isolated villages and agrarian settlements, sometimes with sensitivity and grace, sometimes not, on the hunt for landrace strains, the local varieties that local peoples—their healers, sages, shamans, and sorceresses—had bred for centuries, selecting for the heartiest and/or the most sublime traits. From Mexico, Panama, Colombia, Jamaica, Malawi, Afghanistan, Nepal, India, they brought into Santa Cruz a diversity of genes. A coterie of young cannabis breeders went to work.

Mike Corral was one of them. He and Valerie had connections to a handful of strain hunters and drug smugglers, including Big Bill, who specialized in weed from Malawi, which he smuggled into California swaddled in banana leaf parcels, the parcels stuffed inside East African settees and divans, the furniture he was ostensibly importing. There was Miles Morgan, who was like someone out of a Jimmy Buffett fantasy. Miles Morgan was not his real name; he'd invented the alias for himself—Miles because he logged so many of them flying to Colombia to obtain product there, and Morgan because he was drunk a lot of the time on his favorite rum. Johnny Chesko was another friend of the Corrals', a smuggler and drug dealer, "a fucking total outlaw," Valerie says with great admiration. For his straight job, Chesko worked as a film-set builder for Hollywood studios. He was also a close confidant of Henry Miller, eventually serving as a sort of gonzo valet for the aging novelist when he lived in Big Sur and Los Angeles at the end of his life.

The community of breeders forming in Santa Cruz at this time seemed to be focused at or near the region of the Summit. They even had an anthem: The Doobie Brothers' "Neal's Fandango," released in 1975, with its lyrics about Loma Prieta and the "hills above Santa Cruz" and the journeys of Neal Cassady, the Jack Kerouac and Ken Kesey intimate who was also an early smuggler of weed, and hence genetics, from Mexico into Santa Cruz. Two mysterious partner-breeders—known to many people only by their initials, G.B. and R.L.—crossed landrace Mexican and Colombian and Thai genes to create a cultivar they dubbed the Original Haze, or just Haze. David Watson, who grew up in Los Angeles, migrated north in 1972 with his new bride, eventually making a home in the southern foothills of the Santa Cruz Mountains. Inside a barn on an apple orchard near the town of Freedom, Watson set up the rough-hewn botanical laboratory from which he would make history. He brought together the cultivars that he believed produced the best psychotropic effects, along with genes that would make the plants mature earlier, faster. He was innovating in response to the drug war. The less time it took for cannabis plants to bud, the less opportunity for cops to find and destroy clandestine cultivations. He hybridized an Afghani cultivar (which may have come into Santa Cruz via the Brotherhood of Eternal Love, the madcap surfer LSD cult who were also prolific strain hunters in Asia) with one from South America called Colombian Gold. Then he crossed that hybrid with a third cultivar, Acapulco Gold, the legendary Mexican primo weed of the 1960s and 1970s. When the flowers first began to bloom on his new creation, they bore an aroma distinctly similar to that of the irritant perfume sprayed from the anal glands of *M. mephitis*, the skunk. He called his cultivar Skunk.

Watson, known to his customers by the *nom de guerre* Jingles, was now a distributor of cannabis genetics, selling his seeds to the burgeoning number of pot farmers in Santa Cruz and beyond. It was perhaps inevitable that Terry Parker, described as the most weed-hating cop in Santa Cruz County, would soon be hot on David Watson's trail. From an altitude of fifteen hundred feet, Parker sat in the county's airplane, binoculars pressed to his eyes, as it buzzed Watson's property. That same year, 1982, Watson was charged with felony possession of marijuana for sale and felony cultivation of same. The prosecutors wanted him to snitch. Watson later described his response: "I looked at 'em straight in the eyes, and I said, 'Hey listen. You can lock me up in prison for the rest of my life. You can do the same thing to my wife. You can throw my kids in an orphanage. But I will *never* cooperate with you, so fuck off.'" During a hearing in his case, Watson cleared his throat and addressed the court and proceeded to give a kind of pro-cannabis sermon. In the end, he convinced the judge that the 236 plants he'd been growing in his greenhouse were for personal use—indeed, for personal scientific use. A marijuana researcher, he was trying to find cannabis strains that showed superior medicinal traits. "Which was the truth," Watson later recalled. "I mean, I was also selling to recreational users. But I didn't bother mentioning that!" The judge gave him community service, but Watson knew that Parker and the prosecutors would not stand down. And so he decided to "get the hell out of Dodge." He'd recently learned that Holland had legalized the production and sale of cannabis seeds. When a sheriff's deputy showed up at his old Santa Cruz address in 1985 with a warrant, no one was home. Watson had already moved with his family to Amsterdam. He brought his Skunk seeds with him and lived there for the rest of his life. Much lore has arisen around the origins of Haze and Skunk, perhaps the most iconic weed strains of all time. It is not an exaggeration to say that the cultivars created by Watson and the Haze Brothers went on to form the genetic foundations of the majority of strains found in US dispensaries today. From Amsterdam, Watson continued to study cannabis genetics until his death in 2025. He never looked back. "You can't do science, good science, when you're a fucking outlaw," he said.

One of Watson's closest allies was a 1976 graduate of the University of California, Santa Cruz, named Robert Connell Clarke, a botany major who'd converted his undergraduate dissertation into a booklet, a treatise on the botany and ecology of cannabis, which he printed himself and circulated. It, too, became a sought-after underground cannabis text. Part botanist, part anthropologist, Clarke would go on to dedicate his life to cannabis research, tracing the plant's origins and migrations across time and the globe: how it evolved before humans domesticated it, how it was further transformed once in human hands—the ethnobotany of weed.

In the 1970s, the young breeders of Santa Cruz were working chiefly with DNA obtained from seeds smuggled into the United States from Latin America, Mexico especially. The best weed in Mexico, such as Acapulco Gold, was grown by isolated, close-knit communities of armed *paisanos* on high-altitude farms in the Sierra Madre del Sur. Cannabis entered Mexico from the Caribbean, where, starting in the eighteenth century, indentured servants from India had brought seeds with them—first to Jamaica, where, in addition to genetics, they also brought with them the term ganja. Cannabis is also believed to have entered Mexico from Colombia and Brazil, where the plant was grown for its medicinal properties by communities of enslaved or formerly enslaved African peoples, the seeds possibly having been transported across the Atlantic on Portuguese slave ships, but also later obtained through trade. Cannabis cultivation in Africa began at least by the year 700, in Kenya. Some researchers believe that cannabis was first smoked in Africa, in water pipes. (Clarke is not one of those researchers.) Cannabis seeds and plants were carried to North and East Africa across the Mediterranean and Red Seas in the dhows of ancient Arab seafarers, following the course of the conquering armies of Islam. Despite the later tabooing of drug cannabis by some adherents of the prophet Muhammed, the Quran contains no reference to the substance. The ascetic monk Haydar, founder of the mystical Sufis, is said to have discovered hashish in the year 1155, but hashish use in Arab cultures likely predates Islam itself. Hashish in Arabic originally meant "grass" or "herb," later coming to refer specifically to the highly intoxicating resins of the cannabis plant. In Arab cultures, the substance is interwoven with storytelling. The Old Arabic word *banj*—which derives from the Hindu word *bhang*, which, in Hindi, meant psychoactive cannabis—often appears in classical Islamic literature as a plot device for narrative turns into lawbreaking, murder, and black magic. Marco Polo was the first to describe an esoteric sect of Islamic fundamentalists led by Ḥasan-e Ṣabbāḥ, the legendary Old Man of the Mountain, who, Marco Polo alleged, initiated new recruits by feeding them great quantities of hashish at his fortress, Alamut, perched high on a cliff in the rocky, imposing Alborz mountains of Persia. In the luxurious gardens of Ḥasan's Xanadu-like fortress, the recruits' minds dissolved as they lounged on divans and cavorted with a harem of staggering diversity. Afterward, the initiated soldiers stopped at nothing to accomplish the Old Man's bidding, which was, chiefly, the murder of theopolitical rivals. Garroting, stabbing, and poisoning were their typical methods. They waged war against, among others, the Christian Crusaders. The consensus among modern historians is that Marco Polo was, as far as the story of Ḥasan's hashish initiation ritual went, full of shit. But they agree that the Arabic name given to the murderous sect by its enemies—Hashshashin, "the hashish eaters"—evolved over time until it became, in English, *assassin*.

The Arab world, in turn, likely discovered cannabis from trading partners in India. The earliest archaeobotanical evidence of cannabis use in India dates to around three thousand years ago, in the Indus Valley. India's cannabis culture is ancient, sophisticated, complex. Possible references to it famously appear in the Vedic texts. The sacred beverage *soma* may have included psychoactive cannabis as one of its ingredients. Other discoveries suggest that an ancient cult of shamans inhaled smoke from the burning plant in psychotropic rituals at least twenty-five hundred years ago in western China. Genomic studies led by a team of Swiss and Chinese scientists would eventually point to what is now China's Yunnan province as the place where human beings first domesticated cannabis more than twelve thousand years ago, before written language, before human beings developed (some have posited) consciousness. These prehistoric domesticators would likely have been already gathering wild cannabis in order to exploit its beneficial fibrous qualities, only later discovering, probably by accident, possibly by noticing the gluey residue that stuck to their fingers after they'd handled the plant, that if cooked and eaten, or if burned and its fumes inhaled, a person would undergo a mysterious transformation, a rearrangement of the self that perhaps brought one closer to an apprehension of the sublime—to a hearing of the ur-stories of the eternal beings who fashioned all that is out of all that isn't, who split the sky from the earth and the fire from the waters.

As Robert Clarke's own research would eventually determine, cannabis experienced multiple domestication events after human beings first encountered the species before the end of the last ice ages. The glaciers would have chased the plant south from its temperate continental homelands in Central and Eastern Asia—the plant having emerged between two or three million years ago, breaking off from its cousin, hops—into numerous Himalayan valleys, into refugia, where it sheltered from the cold and underwent further natural selection, acclimating to new, arid climates and coming into contact with human populations and undergoing still further change. Clarke's research has pointed to one of those refugia in particular, northeast of the Indus Valley, as the home of the genetic progenitors of much of the psychoactive cannabis on earth today, set in the rocky soil and dry, thin air of the foothills of a stupendous mountain range, its highest peaks surmounting twenty thousand feet, widely regarded as the most isolated and treacherous mountain range in the world, which touches what are now parts of Afghanistan, Pakistan, and Tajikistan: the Hindu Kush.

In late-twentieth-century Californian English, *kush* would become one of the myriad slang terms for psychoactive cannabis. In fourteenth-century Persian, the language of Ibn Battuta, the Islamic explorer and writer who first used the name in writing to refer to the mountain range, *Hindu kush* meant "Indian killer."

In late September 1978, just as the plants were about to reach full maturation before harvest season, the Santa Cruz County Sheriff's Office raided a series of pot farms at the Summit. Profits were such that people had gone big up there, had become ambitious. Someone, for example, had carved a small air strip in the forest so that product could be flown out directly from the source. Mike and Valerie's plot escaped notice. But many of their neighbors went into hiding, or were arrested. In the aftermath of the raids, Chris Daly swung over from his home base on Deer Creek Road—he was acquainted with a few of the Summit growers who'd been raided—and walked among the wreckage. His interests were both forensic and venial. He wanted to see if the cops had missed any weed. Except for two measly buds resting on a table in a cook shack, they hadn't. They'd hacked down every last bush with machetes and hauled away the bounty, leaving behind a vast cemetery of stems protruding from the ground at odd angles.

Then came the night of October 17. With large amounts of weed curing and drying in sheds and barns, in the wee hours, a group of local teenage boys came skulking through the woods. Most were armed with shotguns. One carried a .22-caliber AR-15 semiautomatic rifle. They were looking to pull off a weed heist. They came to the property of Dennis Johnson, whom everyone knew as Rabbit. He was cultivating one of the larger pot crops in the area, just down the road from Valerie and Mike's place. "After crossing posted barricades and evading a primitive tin-can alarm system," as an appellate court later set the scene in a summary of the case, the kids came to Rabbit's garden. One of their guns misfired. Rabbit had dealt with thieves before. Now he grabbed a shotgun and stole toward the place where he thought the sound of the blast had come from. One of the teenagers spied Rabbit approaching. The boy, Norman Dillon, fired his rifle nine times and transformed himself from a pot thief into a killer. Rabbit died. First-degree murder, a jury found. Though Norman Dillon was sentenced to life in prison without parole, the charges were reversed on appeal, and he wound up spending six years behind bars.

THE CORRALS LEFT THE SUMMIT IN 1985. Their story after that is well-known: They moved to another part of the Santa Cruz Mountains, twenty miles west of the Summit, also remote, also forested, and continued to grow weed there. They thought they had forged a fragile truce with local law enforcement, but then a raid of their small garden by the SCSO in 1992 politicized the Corrals. One of their lawyers had the idea of fighting the case with a so-called medical necessity defense. For more than a decade, Valerie and Mike had already been sharing their weed with other people diagnosed with epilepsy, or who were experiencing pain that weed could help alleviate. Now they got organized. They formed their famous nonprofit collective, which they called the Wo/Men's Alliance for Medical Marijuana, WAMM. Mike cultivated WAMM's inventory using his prized genetics, the hybrids he'd bred and the cultivars he'd kept going from the original Malawi and Afghan landraces he'd obtained from his smuggler pals. Members gathered at a community center in downtown Santa Cruz to pick up their allotments. The psychedelic pioneer Ram Dass joined as a member. Soon WAMM teamed up with Dennis Peron, a Vietnam vet and San Francisco pot dealer turned cannabis and AIDS activist, who had already mobilized platoons of highly skilled gay attorneys and professionals from the Bay Area to obtain weed for AIDS patients. Together, Peron, the Corrals, and others wrote Proposition 215, got it on the ballet, and campaigned for its passage. It passed, 55 percent to 44 percent, in November 1996, the first loosened brick in the wall of American cannabis prohibition.

Then George W. Bush came into the White House, and the DEA, reenergized in its attitudes toward marijuana, trained its sights on WAMM. In 2002, a militarized SWAT team of federal agents swarmed the Corrals' mountain parcel and destroyed the year's harvest. The Corrals were never charged with a crime. Instead, they sued the federal government over the raid, undertaking a seven-year court struggle led by an elite unit of marijuana-law attorneys—including, of course, Ben Rice. If the case didn't technically set a legal precedent, it did establish a kind of shield from federal prosecution that would, eventually, help clear the way for states to legalize cannabis (first medically, then recreationally) despite the awkward fact that growing and buying and selling the plant's bounty remained a federal crime.

There would, however, be vicious ironies. Profiteering would come to dominate the 215 era despite its progressive, collectivist, even anti-capitalist underpinnings. By the time Prop 64 came on the ballot, the Corrals were exhausted. Already they had divorced, creating a leadership crisis at WAMM. Then recreational legalization dealt the group a fundamental blow. With Prop 64, California's new cannabis laws banned all medical collectives. Extinguished as a nonprofit weed-providing service, WAMM struggled to reinvent itself. There was infighting and controversy. Legalization and what it has wrought sometimes made Val gloomy. "I think capitalism is a fucked system," she said. "Over time, it devours itself."

She has, in the meanwhile, pursued a second vocation. She has become a kind of attendant for the terminally sick and the dying. *The Tibetan Book of the Dead* is one of her sacred manuals. So is Timothy Leary's *The Psychedelic Experience: A Manual Based on the Tibetan Book of the Dead*. So are the mystical poems of Rumi. As part of her practice, she will administer psychedelic drugs, mostly psilocybin, to the dying, and strive to support them as they make their elemental journey into the beyond. Recently, it was Johnny Chesko's time. Valerie was sitting at his deathbed when he took a tab of LSD in preparation for whatever would come next.

28. Driving Off a Cliff

By mid-July 2018, more than a thousand cannabis plants were growing on the sixty-acre property at the Summit. Long ago they'd stopped calling it the Shire; now it was just the Summit. Tushar had woken up that morning with his knee aching. He was irritable—that much was clear. And pessimistic, and growing more so by the day. The business wasn't being properly managed, he said. Was Rachael's pot farm actually going to turn a profit, as she'd promised it would?

Since the start of the year they'd been dividing their labors. Tushar was handling the creation of the licensed extraction lab at 211 Fern Street. Rachael was handling the development of the Summit parcel. Nearly six months had passed since the breakup with Evan Scott.

Because they had no cultivation license, the cannabis farm was just an experiment, they told each other. Just an effort to get things going. And why shouldn't Rachael sell what she harvested, after all? She could sell it through her black market connections back East. After some rough calculations, Rachael figured a thousand plants could conservatively yield eight hundred pounds of dry flower, which she could unload for more than a thousand bucks a pound, so revenue of more than eight hundred thousand dollars. Figure a quarter million in costs to develop the farm and harvest the crop and service the monthly interest on the Summit property. That would mean a profit of . . . more than half a mil! It was Rachael's idea:

They could use the proceeds from the sale of the harvest to pay the first annual $250,000 balloon payment they owed to the former owner of the Summit property, who held the $1.4 million note. The additional benefit to this plan was that Rachael could metamorphose all the cash she'd saved over the years into legitimate equity in a huge and very valuable piece of land. At some point, Tushar suggested, the land could be subdivided and parcels could be sold as homesteads to other Silicon Valley millionaires.

Was this money laundering? According to Rachael, she and Tushar never discussed this fraught topic. And yet it seemed to influence their decisions: They planned to pay taxes on any profits from the sale of the Summit weed. There were accounting stratagems that enabled you to do this. Also, the grow belonged to Rachael. Tushar referred to it as her "garden," her farm. She had spent her money—mostly the money buried in the ground in Vermont—to pay for the farming costs. And so Tushar, at least, was protected; he could claim to have no knowledge of the weed. He merely owned the land. Or, rather, AtreNet did. Meanwhile, they could claim that they were assiduously working to get the Summit property zoned and permitted and licensed as a proper, legal cannabis-cultivation site. Paired with the licensed cannabis-oil-extraction lab at 211 Fern Street, which was still under construction, they were shooting for vertical integration. That's what Rachael believed, anyway.

But the garden itself was turning into a crisis, and the stress of it was getting to them. Rachael still wrestled with frequent bouts of sadness. She felt like half a person. She would occasionally stay in bed for long periods. Tushar would urge her to get up, get going, promising her that work would help, work was empowering, and Lord knew there was work to be done.

A certain cyclical pattern, almost diurnal, had come to define their relationship. Most days would begin all lovey-dovey, but as the hours wore on, as Rachael would commute from Pleasure Point to the Summit, leaving Tushar behind to work from home in his two roles as CEO of AtreNet and founder of a cannabis start-up, strife would elbow its way in. Disagreements would blossom into shouting matches. The arguments were always about the business. And then every night back at home they'd make up in the typical way. And then they'd awaken the next morning and the cycle would begin again. . . .

Around this time, Tushar wrote Rachael a kind of poem. He loved poetry and would send her poetic notes from time to time. Like e. e. cummings, he wrote in the lower case:

so many circles.
it's easy to lose track, here there and everywhere.
each one of them has a soul, some special meaning connected between
loved ones. dear rach cherishes them all so well.
and while the earth spins seemingly out of control, she holds on tight,
with grace and consideration.
my sweetheart is the center of my universe. i'm blessed that she holds
on tight for me, and everyone.

After seven months, the crop was almost ready for harvest. Rachael had hired her old Vermont friend and farmhand Hank to assist her. Hank moved onto the Summit property, living in a camping trailer. The plan had been to grow the crop from seed—seed to sale, like she'd drawn up on the whiteboard at the Los Gatos house, what seemed like a million years ago. They'd converted Tushar's dining cart back into a greenhouse and parked it on the property. As the sprouts were coming in thick and fast, Hank pissed off a neighbor by speeding down a shared driveway. The neighbor confronted Rachael and told her he knew what was going on over there, and he wasn't going to stand for it. He threatened to take pictures and alert the authorities. When Rachael told Tushar what had happened, she saw how fear produced fury in him. Tushar immediately called Hank and told him to get the fuck off the property, and that was it for Hank. Rachael was down a seasoned farmhand and friend. Luckily the neighbor never followed up on his threat.

Then Tushar's sensei, while sparring with him one day, kicked out Tushar's knee and tore his ACL. He had to have surgery and was hobbling around on crutches for weeks, physical therapy, no surfing. Grouchy, conspiracy minded, Tushar was convinced that the sensei had never liked him, had maybe done this to him on purpose.

Also around this time Rachael brought a group of Emerald Triangle friends to the table. They were growers and dealers from the 215 era who were also trying to go legit by launching a licensed cultivation company—Monterey Tilth was the name they were using—in the Salinas Valley greenhouse district. The deal they were proposing would have provided the Fern Street lab with all the biomass it would ever need. The Tilth guys had spent time in state prison on marijuana-trafficking charges, but that was actually a good thing because it qualified them for certain rebates and tax breaks. California's cannabis-equity program extended these assists to weed companies founded by people deemed to have suffered injustice during the drug wars. The agreement called for one of the Tilth ex-cons, a gentle-vibes sweetheart, to be the CEO of the combined entity. "There's so much potential to excel in today's markets. There's limitless growth potential," Tushar wrote exuberantly in an email to the Tilth guys. But then Tushar got cold feet. He shifted the financial terms in his favor and stipulated that he would be the CEO. The Tilth guys pulled out, and the deal collapsed. "But, hey, I'm open to being corrected," Tushar wrote in a long email (subject line: "mea culpa") in the aftermath.

> Because in the end, we all say it's all about life, right? Honestly
> I'm still trying to figure that one out . . .
> Wishing you all the best, always.
> Tushar (and yes, my friends sometimes call me Too Far ;-)

So once again, it was just Tushar and Rachael. They had in fact scored a few successes. The City of Santa Cruz had approved 211 Fern Street for its use permit, and Tushar had applications pending for the requisite state licenses. They'd found an extraction expert to replace Evan Scott. Tushar had met the new guy even before the breakup, at a gathering for Bay Area cannabis entrepreneurs in Berkeley. The guy's name was Brian Kenny. Tall and extremely fit, he was a software programmer. Cannabis was a side project for him. Or maybe vice versa; tech was his side hustle, a way to keep himself afloat as he pursued his own entrepreneurial dreams in weed. He had managed to combine the two, writing a piece of data-analytics software that scraped market information from the growing number of strain-review and dispensary-finder websites. Kenny called the software Firewalker. Always attracted to intelligence and smart conversation, Tushar latched right on to Kenny. By July, Tushar, Rachael, and Kenny were "scrumming" on a daily basis, Kenny and Tushar talking extraction equipment and lab setups, Kenny advising Rachael on cannabis-harvesting issues, since he had experience in cultivation, as well.

Meanwhile, Tushar had his eye on an oceanside home at 3034 Pleasure Point Drive. The location was irresistible, positioned right next to the best surf breaks on the east side, including Sewers. (Funnily enough, it was right across the street from the Point Market and Evan's old trap office.) The house looked as if it were built into the cliff. It had its own staircase leading down to the surf. From its deck and back windows, there were insane views of Monterey Bay and, beyond it, the northern peaks of Big Sur's mountain range, the Santa Lucias, hovered at the horizon. Strategically, Tushar had befriended the owner of the house, a retired cop whose health was breaking down, whose children were not around, and who'd found himself in financial trouble. Tushar would chauffeur the eighty-two-year-old to his regular dialysis treatments, hang out with him, bring him groceries. Then, just before the house was set to go into foreclosure, Tushar swept in and made the guy an offer. He paid off his mortgage and gave him a few hundred grand in exchange for the deed, $3.5 million all in for Tushar. Although the place needed a lot of work, that price was a steal for oceanside anything. Tushar had won again. But the cash outlay stretched him further financially—he had to borrow a million dollars from a local bank to complete the deal—and that, too, multiplied the stressors. . . .

On a late July morning, Tushar broke from the pattern of early tenderness. He was worried. He was in his office in the garage at the house on Thirty-Eighth Avenue, trying to work his way out of the problem. They were *driving off a cliff*, he said! They were smarter than this!

Rachael was now working extra-long days. With Hank gone, she'd hired two Vermont boys in their twenties, brothers, friends of a friend from South Pomfret. The boys had been traveling around the country and wanted to earn a few bucks working a cool summer job. The Summit property's caretaker under the previous owner had also agreed, after Hank's firing, to continue in that role, which came as a relief to Rachael. Ernesto* was a soft-spoken man in his forties, and he knew the land intimately.

July is a treacherous month in cannabis cultivation. As usual, Rachael planned to bring two crops to harvests. For the first, she was using a technique called light dep, short for light depravation. For this purpose, she'd built six hoop houses, the tunnellike structures you see at garden centers that consist of a series of rods arched into semicircles. By pulling opaque tarps over the arches as a roof, you blanket the structure and block out the sun. Blocking out the sun for twelve hours a day mimics the equinox and fools the cannabis into thinking it's autumn and, per the instructions encoded in its DNA, time to flower. Light dep accelerated the vegetal life cycle, shortening the period it took for cannabis plants to reach the optimum stage of profuse, potent, THC-charged maturation.

The first crop was ready for harvest by mid-July, which meant Rachael had to cut those flowers down and quickly plant the second crop, which would be straight-up outdoor weed, ready for harvest in October. Not only that, she was using organic farming methods—no chemical pesticides, no

---

* Not his real name.

artificial fertilizers, no grow pots—which only increased her workload, made everything more time-consuming.

On top of that, she wanted to freeze most of the July crop to create a big batch of fresh frozen. (Tushar knew all about fresh frozen.) This was a dramatic change of plan, but she felt she had no choice. The reason she felt she had no choice was that the plants weren't finishing right—they were yielding smallish popcorn-size buds, so-called popcorn nuggets. When cannabis plants yielded popcorn nuggets, it often meant the specimens had been stressed in some way as seedlings—always a risk when buying clones from a third party. The reasons she'd had to buy clones from a third party—a Santa Cruz black market girl grower she'd met through a friend—was because they'd had to fire Hank. With Hank no longer around to babysit the sprouts in their nursery, she'd had to forsake her whole seed-to-sale plan. So she bought clones, more than a thousand, from the clone girl. Popcorn buds like these would have to be sold at a discount. Better, Rachael thought, to pivot, and flash freeze the light-dep harvest, and make it into fresh-frozen biomass, out of which the highly desirable live-resin hash oil could then be conjured. This meant she had to begin the process as soon as the stalks were cut down, which required that she flash freeze the biomass right there at the property. From a supplier down in Watsonville, she bought a load of dry ice pellets and hauled them to the Summit in one of Tushar's pickup trucks. From Home Depot, she bought Styrofoam coolers and black plastic bins with yellow lids for the dry ice. Then she and her Vermont helpers placed the weed on top of the steaming carbon dioxide and shut the lids: frozen biomass in no time. But soon she realized that the bins and coolers weren't big enough for the sheer quantity of cannabis she had grown. So she bought kiddie pools and filled the kiddie pools with the dry ice. From Sears, she bought three top-loading chest freezers, eight feet long and seven hundred dollars a pop, and had them delivered to the Thirty-Eighth Avenue house. Meanwhile, a summer heat wave was pushing temps toward one hundred degrees Fahrenheit, straining the whole flash-freezing operation. There was no flash, really. Fortunately, the weed did eventually freeze. This was farming: Shit happened, and you dealt with that shit as best you could. Rachael was making it happen. She was being nimble, entrepreneurial, meeting challenges, clearing hurdles. . . .

On top of all of this, Shaku had come to Santa Cruz for her annual summer visit. Rachael, proud, wanting to impress Tushar's mother, decided to invite Shaku to see the pot farm. At the outdoor kitchen Rachael and Ernesto had built at the edge of the meadow, Rachael prepared a lunch they all ate at a picnic table—thick pink salmon fillets, a colorful salad. She took Shaku on a tour, showed her the beautifully done kitchen, the outdoor shower, the FedEx truck Tushar had converted into a portable office space—their Summit headquarters. She walked Shaku slowly down the alleys between the cannabis plants, now seven feet high and dense as hedgerows. In her standard workwear—jeans, a Benevolence Bound T-shirt, a pair of Merrell hiking sneakers—Rachael towered over tiny Shaku, who'd come to the farm wearing a sleeveless blouse, golden bangles, and a silk scarf of radiant fuchsia. Tushar told Rachael that he'd finally clued his mother in to their plans to build a cannabis company together. Still, they made sure to stress that this was Rachael's cannabis farm, definitely not Tushar's. It was all pleasant and enjoyable on the surface, but the stress of a Shaku visit swam beneath the surface in silent, baleful turnings.

At the Summit a few days later, Tushar finally erected the towering tepee he'd bought many years earlier, outfitting it with rugs, a bed, a woodburning stove, and Christmas lights plugged into a generator. Raising the structure was a whole elaborate process, and he did it with the help of the Vermont brothers, gently instructing them while discoursing all the while on an obscure work of anthropology, saying, *You know how I learned about this? There was a couple, the Laubins, Reginald and Gladys Laubin . . . and they dedicated their life to studying the Native American tepee, and they wrote a book called* The Indian Tipi, *and it's unbelievable. . . . Before there were horses in this country, tepees were originally really small . . . way smaller than this. . . . They had to be dragged around by dogs*, and Rachael, who recorded the whole thing on video, awoke again to why she loved him—his quirky enthusiasms, his intelligence—and why, also, she was so frustrated by him, since this was not the first time he'd shown up at the Summit and assigned her workers a task totally unrelated to the harvesting of her six-figure crop.

Tushar could also be a patronizing asshole, Rachael was seeing, prone to mansplaining. He was insistent that Rachael properly account for expenses. He wanted her to think strategically—and in his language—about balance sheets, liabilities, cash conversions. He saw her resistance to it as a reflection of bad black market practices. *Legal businesses speak a financial language, and learning it will really help you*, he told her. When she finally produced a profit and loss spreadsheet for him, the sum in the gross-revenue cell came to $576,836—way short of the eight hundred thousand dollars that she'd projected hitting months earlier, before planting. Her initial financial projections, it turned out, were a fantasy.

Publicly Tushar was supportive of her and her hustle, especially getting the biomass off the vine. In private, though, he was alternately freaked out and pissed off. How long could she go on like this, winging it? he wanted to know. Running around like a headless chicken. Maybe she wasn't as competent a grower as he'd once believed, as she'd made herself out to be.

Your ego blinded us both to the truth, he said. He accused her of making stupid business decisions.

You want me to just quit, don't you? Rachael said.

No, Tushar replied. *I want you to wake up!*

Every evening that July, Rachael would come home to the Thirty-Eighth Avenue house, stinking of sweat and dirt and ganja resin. She would shower and collapse into bed and, some nights, weep into her pillow.

29. Trinity

Not long after graduating from high school, Rachael started dating her pot dealer. The guy was the town prince. Everybody knew him; everybody loved him. He sold weed to all the partying teenagers of the greater Woodstock-Pomfret-Killington region. Vermont had a robust tradition of cannabis cultivation, with its rolling forested natural beauty, its outdoorsy populace, its jam bands and hippies. Because of the short summers, Vermont's weed growers had acquired a vaunted reputation specifically for their indoor flower, grown in basements, garages, and barns.

Rachael first inhaled at age thirteen. She was an adventure seeker, and so were her friends. Teenage life in rural Vermont was conducted largely out of doors, especially in summer. In high school, she and her friends threw parties deep in the woods, parties in the abutments under covered bridges. They tubed in rowdy flotillas down slow-moving rivers. There were rope swings and swimming holes. They went on days-long camping trips. Staring at the sky and contemplating the big Vermont nature, they tripped on acid and other things. In winter, they skied and snowboarded at Suicide Six, where some people claim snowboarding was invented in the early eighties, its slopes visible from the South Pomfret grange. A kind of small-town party life prevailed, healthy in some ways, but also beer and weed fueled.

For her junior year of high school, Rachael was going to New Zealand as a foreign-exchange student. Before she left, Cynthia expressed concern about her drug use. It was just the two of them in the house now, all of Rachael's five siblings grown and gone. Cynthia thought weed made Rachael look stupid. Bloodshot and droopy eyed. *You look dumb when you're high.* She worried about what marijuana did to a still-developing brain. Rachael countered that she was a straight-A student. She didn't want to lie to her mother, but she wasn't going to stop using weed, either. *I can either lie to you, or you can try this joint and learn that it's not so bad, and then you never have to try it again, but just get off my back so I don't have to lie to you anymore.* Then she went to New Zealand. When she returned the following year, Rachael persuaded her mother to try a few puffs from a joint—not with Rachael, that would've been weird, but with one of Cynthia's progressive, aging hippie friends. A day later, Cynthia knocked on the door of Rachael's bedroom. In her mother's hand was an illustration in Cynthia's signature style—part Victorian botanical, part psychedelia—of a cannabis plant. It would become the central brand image for Rachael's nascent cannabis enterprise, Benevolence Bound.

From her dealer boyfriend, Rachael learned the fundamentals of underground dope sales. She was eighteen years old, class of 2004. She grew weed in a sunny spot in the woods behind the South Pomfret house. She started driving her boyfriend's weed to Boston, where her oldest brother, a kind of itinerant artist and aspiring filmmaker, dealt weed on the side. It was easy money, transporting the weed. Her boyfriend became her brother's supplier. Her love of horses persuaded her to apply to Centenary University in western New Jersey, an expensive private college known for its equestrian programs. This was a turning point. The dealer boyfriend, now an ex-boyfriend, gave her some big jars of his premium flower, which sold fast to the children of the horsey set. The margins were fantastic—the horsey kids were willing to pay twenty dollars a gram for weed she could buy in Vermont for less than five dollars. After one semester, she did not see a future for herself in horses, so she dropped out, eventually making her way to Burlington, and then the University of Vermont, where, finally, in 2012, she obtained her degree—BS in environmental studies from the university's College of Agriculture and Life Sciences. Weed dealing paid for the majority of her schooling.

That's when she decided to leave the drug trade behind. Time to grow up, go square. She even quit smoking weed. A friend from high school had moved to Portland, Oregon, a prime place to find a job related to environmental science, she thought, but in the meantime have a good time exploring Portlandia. She got a job bartending. She wound up renting a room in a house filled with twentysomething graduates of Reed College and started smoking again. One of her roommates, Ashley,* whom everyone called Ash, turned out to be a dealer. Rachael joined Ash as she delivered three pounds to a guy who gave her something like three thousand dollars cash. Surprised, Rachael asked, *You're selling pounds for a thousand each?* In these parts, Ash replied, that was the going rate. *Not where I'm from!* Rachael said. In Vermont the wholesale price was double that. Buy low, sell high . . . now *here* was a business idea.

In early fall of 2013, Ash invited Rachael to join a group from Portland heading down to a remote place, a pot farm in the legendary Emerald Triangle, in the least known of its three counties: Trinity. They would camp on-site in the middle of a wilderness of redwood and madrone. They would trim bud. They would party like hippies in 1969. Paid in weed in return for their labor, they would return to Portland with product to sell. During her ten days as a trimmigrant, Rachael hit it off with the farm's owner, an older woman who, it turned out, was a venerable Portland personality, the publisher of one of the city's alternative weekly newspapers. She also owned this California pot farm, a registered collective with a roster of "patients." The publisher was a city person, though, definitely not a farmer of anything. Each season, she hired a grower to cultivate weed on her land. She had forty acres, though only a tiny fraction

* Not her real name.

was given over to cannabis. Weed growers were often like tenant farmers. They'd split the crop yield with the landowner. But the publisher was frustrated with the growers she'd had. Always men, they stole from her—lying about their yields and skimming off the top. *I don't want to work with men anymore*, she said. Opportunity banging on the front door of Rachael's mind, she answered. She told the publisher about her degree in environmental studies, in permaculture, about her youth in Vermont surrounded by hills and barns and crops of weed on the hills and in the barns. She told the publisher about her weed-dealing past. She was hired.

In the spring of 2014, Rachael, now twenty-seven, left Portland and took up residence on the publishers's forty acres. Their deal was that Rachael would pay for all costs associated with the cultivation. On the surface that sounded like a terrible deal, but to Rachael it would be a great deal if she could run the farm efficiently and maximize its yield. She was energetic, optimistic, enterprising, a problem solver! She got to work. The land was raw except for a windowless 256-square-foot cabin with no running water or power. It sat on steep terrain near the top of Hennessy Peak, elevation thirty-six hundred feet. The closest town was a forty-five-minute drive away: Burnt Ranch, little more than a crossroads. Rachael lived in the cabin alone. And she alone would perform almost all of the labor during that growing season, her only company a dog. The publisher, terrified of bears, would not allow Rachael to live in the cabin without a dog, so she let her borrow one of her own, a one-year-old husky/cattle dog mix who didn't answer to the name the publisher had given him. So Rachael renamed him Hashtag, which he did answer to. The property didn't have even an outhouse. She shit in holes she dug herself. She cooked her meals in an outdoor kitchen with a propane grill. She locked her food and garbage in bear-proof bins, but nonetheless she'd regularly awaken in the mornings to find the kitchen in disarray. Hashtag was not doing his job. One night she heard sounds outside, sounds of a furtive breaking and entering. She opened the cabin door and there it was, a heaving raunchy hummock of fur, slick and sable, maybe ten yards away, nosing around in the kitchen, mid-ransack. She looked down at Hashtag, but Hashtag was just standing there, panting, calmly observing the bear as if on a visit to a zoo. Rachael decided maybe she needed to teach Hashtag how to respond to the bear, to all bears. She knew bears could be scared away by loud sounds. So she beat on a pan with a big metal spoon and started to bark. Loudly, to bark. And then, filled with fear, she forced herself to charge at the bear while barking and banging, and Hashtag joined her, barking and howling and himself now charging toward the beast, who turned and exploded through the kitchen structures galloping away into the forest, garlanded with shelving and towels and clothes and cookware. After that Hashtag barked at bears.

Bears weren't the only threat. The slopes of Hennessy Peak were covered in pot farms. As it was throughout the Emerald Triangle, almost every hill, every ridge, comprised its own community of weed plantations. She knew from her ten days as a trimmigrant the year before that she'd be living in the middle of the woods surrounded by stoner dudes. And despite all the do-gooder talk about medical weed and patient rosters, most of the stuff was being sold out of state into the recreational black market. It was an industry that attracted rogues. Already the Emerald Triangle was famous for its desperate missing-persons posters. She knew she wasn't safe living alone in this place. So when she first arrived on the hill, she threw a party and invited all her neighbors. It was a cookout—a big slab of beef, cold beer. She wanted everyone on Hennessy Peak to know her, and she wanted to know everyone on the peak, wanted to look people in the eye and decide for herself whom she had to be careful with, who would help her feel safe. In the former category at the party were two guys she never wanted to see again, jittery, tweaked out, cracking crude jokes. In the latter category, she met the guys who would, four years later, try and fail to partner with Tushar. The Tilth guys were a high school friend group, all about Rachael's age, late twenties, who also lived at their farm site. They became fast friends.

Rachael planted her garden on just one-eighth of an acre, on two terraces carved out of a thirty-degree slope. The terraces had no real irrigation system. She had to water the plants with buckets filled from a hose fed by gravity from a tank at the top of the hill. The tank, in turn, was fed by a well with a pump run by a generator below the property, the whole system shared by several neighbors, all pot growers. Once during her turn for its use, the pump malfunctioned, and she had to jury-rig the thing with spare parts harvested from an old broken pump in a shed on the property. She got it to work! She did a little jig, surprised by her own ingenuity, until the two pipes she'd married together sprung loose, water gushing out, flooding the gravel driveway of her biker-gang neighbors. They were cool about it, friendly hirsute Harley-driving granddads, members of the local Fog Dogs club. She got buff hauling buckets and compost (she was an organic grower, of course). Despite these new friendships, she spent most of her time in monk-like solitude, developing a close relationship with Hashtag. At times she felt like she was losing her mind. The publisher wasn't helping. She'd hector Rachael in phone calls and periodic visits, complaining that she wasn't growing enough weed, wasn't doing it right. Each evening as the sun set, Rachael climbed the hill to the summit of Hennessy Peak, the only place she could find a signal, sat under a big madrone tree, and called her mother in Vermont. Sometimes she cried. But Cynthia would say something calming and wise, and she'd hike back down the hill feeling better. Whatever the publisher's complaints, the crop yielded well—about 150 pounds. Friends from Portland came down to help trim. Rachael sent her half in vacuum-sealed batches to Vermont through the US Postal Service, that venerable pot-smuggling institution, most of it directly to Cynthia's South Pomfret door. Rachael had spent more than she thought she would, but the interstate trade was lucrative. After her first season, her take-home profit was $150,000.

Back in Portland, however, the publisher wasn't happy. The accusations she'd leveled at her previous growers should have served as a warning because now she was leveling them at Rachael. Despite all the girl-power talk, the publisher refused to believe that Rachael hadn't also skimmed. They agreed to part ways. Hashtag stayed with Rachael.

With the publisher out of her life, Rachael definitely wanted to do it again. She had, after all, made far more money that year than she ever had before. She figured she'd remain in the Burnt Ranch–Hennessy Peak area, but she didn't want to live on a hill alone again, so she moved out of Portland for good and rented an apartment in Arcata, on the coast in Humboldt County. From Arcata, it was about an hour's commute to Burnt Ranch, not bad. Better than shitting in the woods with bears. To find a new landowner to partner with, she hung out during the day at a honky-tonk dive bar that served as the area's unofficial community center. The first two people she met she did deals with. She had come to believe in the power of manifestation, and here it was happening to her again, the universe answering her call in the form of two bar regulars: a woman in her fifties named Terry who owned a smallish parcel on the banks of a creek that fed the Trinity River, and a man, also in his fifties, who went by the moniker Rasta John. Terry was a charismatic former singer and was herself extremely handy. She could easily have grown weed on her own, but didn't want to be "married to the plant," or "married to the tarp," didn't want to commit to the massive amount of physical labor that commercial weed growing required. Rasta John, a bald white guy from Atlanta, owned seven acres across a canyon from Rachael's former hermitage on Hennessy Peak. People had started calling him Rasta John because he'd spent time in a Jamaican prison, for what no one really knew.

By spring of 2015, Rachael had hired farmhands to do most of the heavy labor while she oversaw the planting, commuting almost daily from Arcata. One of the hands she'd hired was Hank. Even though Racheal no longer lived on the hill, certain dangers remained. Rasta John's acreage abutted the immense wilderness of Shasta-Trinity National Forest. One of the properties near Rasta John's was a weed farm operated, it was said, by a man affiliated with the Mexican Mafia prison gang, reputed ally of certain cartels, including La Familia Michoacana. In the fall, during harvest, Rasta John invited Rachael to meet the neighbor, have a look at his operation. It was crazy over there, Rasta said. The trimmers were all women . . . and when they trimmed, they were . . . topless! According to local rumor, the trimmers belonged to a pimp. Which, Rachael surmised, could only mean that these woman had been trafficked. Rachael didn't want to know more.

It was a bumper season. At both her spots, Rachael used a combination of light dep and full outdoor, which resulted in two harvests per spot, four in all. That October, between the two properties, the plants yielded around three hundred pounds—worth more than six hundred thousand dollars wholesale based on East Coast prices. Again, Rachael sold the flower in Vermont and Massachusetts, via her brother and other connections, including a young, charming dealer who specialized in the dense college-campus weed markets of Boston and environs. Everyone called him Push. He was a local hip-hop impresario, had his own record label, his own stable of artists. Push and Rachael had met in Vermont years ago, before she'd moved to Portland, when he was visiting a friend's vacation home outside South Pomfret. Push was the kind of magnetic operator who could float seamlessly between the status extremes of the Boston streets and the boarding school set. He was the rich kids' pot dealer, their edgy hang.

Push gladly and profitably moved much of Rachael's Trinity weight. But by 2015, even he couldn't quite handle all of Rachael's supply, which now included product grown by other Trinity cultivators. In 2015, she cleared a personal profit of more than three hundred thousand dollars. She created a California LLC called Lynch Landscaping and filed returns and paid taxes. The next year was looking even better.

She traveled around the country, doing deals. By now, she was flipping boxes, a broker as well as a cultivator. She did a deal in a vast casino parking lot in Las Vegas. She liked to route herself through LAS whenever she flew back to the East Coast. Invariably carrying large sums of cash to bring back to her South Pomfret trap queen, she knew that traveling through Vegas with a lot of cash would not raise any suspicions. She met Rasta John in Atlanta to pay him out. He demanded she join him at a strip club, where they bought stacks of one-dollar bills and popped the bands and made it rain.

But that was the end of the fun. At the start of the 2016 growing season, Cynthia fell ill. Traveling back and forth from Vermont, Rachael couldn't give her full attention to the planting and left things in the hands of her on-site growers. Hank ran the farm on Terry's land and did just fine, but Rachael had had to hire another hand—also a Vermont transplant—to oversee Rasta John's grow, and that was a total fail. Rasta told Rachael they had to renegotiate their deal. She could keep the light-dep harvest, but he was taking the entire outdoor field as his own—70 percent of the total number of plants Rachael had already paid to cultivate. What could she do, sue him? Weird shit was happening in the Triangle. A girlfriend was roofied and nearly abducted. Rasta John's reneging, the cartel grow, the topless trimmers, the attempted kidnapping. . . . As Cynthia's condition deteriorated, Rachael knew she needed to get out.

Recreational legalization was coming. She'd had an entrepreneurial vision of doing good in the world but also banking coin like she had the last few years. She was Benevolence Bound. She'd traveled the California coast from San Diego to San Francisco, seen nearly every major coastal town. As the chemo treatments slogged on, as Cynthia's blood work made its dire prognosis, Rachael formed a plan. Spend time with her mother, quality time, in a place easy for Cynthia to enjoy. Somewhere sunny and pleasant. Rachael really liked Santa Barbara, but Santa Cruz, somehow, spoke louder to her. Hunting for apartments online, she logged on to Airbnb, zoomed in on Pleasure Point . . . clicked on a posting. . . . The place looked nice, near the water. . . . She contacted the host . . . Tushar Atre was his name. . . . He was asking forty-two hundred dollars a month. . . . Four twenty, ha! How could she resist?

30. The Autopsy

October 7, 2019

Detective Miyoshi spent who knows how many hours reviewing the video recordings, time stamp 3:01 a.m. to 3:04 a.m. Three minutes. Three fraught and decisive minutes on the pavement of Pleasure Point Drive. Rewinding, watching again, rewinding, watching again.

By now, he'd seen the results of the autopsy. Dr. Stephany Fiore, Santa Cruz County's chief forensic pathologist, had performed the examination. The victim had suffered an entrance wound from a rifle round fired into the back of the skull—the immediate cause of death—and also a "perforating rifle wound" to the shoulder, and "two perforating gunshot wounds to the cheek." Atre had been shot four times.

Additionally, the victim had suffered five "sharp force injuries" to the head and neck, and one to the chest, and one to the abdomen above the navel. Atre had been stabbed seven times.

The three minutes of video footage that Miyoshi kept reviewing included the moment when Atre was tackled to the ground after making his escape. He hits the pavement hard, and a dark pool appears on the pavement where his head hit, suggesting that the victim may have lost consciousness. Fiore's examination also showed "blunt force injuries to the face, right elbow, the lateral right hip and the lower leg and left knee," consistent with a violent fall. In the grainy, ghostly footage, the perp who tackled Atre stays crouched over him and appears to strike at Atre's torso multiple times with his right hand or fist. Is it a punching motion? Or a jabbing motion? Then the perp stands and walks urgently back toward the house just as another perp jogs toward Atre. This second perp then also crouches over the body and strikes at Atre with his hand or his fist several times more. In the footage, the dark pool underneath Atre appears to expand.

In time, Miyoshi would come to believe that at least one but probably both perps were carrying knives. And they weren't punching Atre. They were stabbing him.

31. Dabs

Tushar was high.

So was Brian Kenny. Not couch-lock high but approaching it.

They were at Brian's house, and they'd just smoked a joint sprinkled with bits of a dab Brian himself had extracted from biomass grown by Rachael at the Summit. He had elected not to smoke the dab from his dab rig, his favorite method of ingestion, which resembled a complicated water bong. He thought it might be too much for Tushar. Like bongs themselves, dab rigs could be ornate, sculptural. Some were shaped into whimsical animal forms, giraffes or elephants or dinosaurs, or balloon dogs that looked exactly like mini Jeff Koonses. Others had beaker-shaped glass filtration chambers, spherical glass reservoir chambers, stoppers, percolators, gaskets—like laboratory equipment designed for some abstruse purpose, which was probably the point.

The sampling of the extract was Tushar's idea. Just a few days earlier, Brian had visited the pot farm that Rachael was managing near the Summit. It was his second visit to the place. He didn't like going there. Didn't want to be there if, as unlikely as it may be, the sheriff decided to raid the unlicensed grow on the day he'd come for a visit. When he arrived, Rachael and some helpers were harvesting light-dep weed from hoop houses in the middle of a big meadow and freezing the stuff onsite with dry ice. She looked almost glamorous in her jeans and V-neck

T-shirt and straw sun hat, her thick chestnut hair tied back in a ponytail. She engaged easily with her workers, laughing with them, encouraging them, but she appeared also to be struggling with the whole fresh-frozen process. Brian, also an experienced grower, offered some pointers, and Rachael gave him a few frozen tops—stalks budded with cannabis colas—from which he would later extrude a batch of hash. Tushar was treating this as an experiment, a proof of concept, in which Brian would make a "prototype" extract. If they could conjure a quality product from Rachael's cannabis, that would be a great first step on their journey toward building a premier extracts company. Brian employed a traditional method that did not require solvents of any kind, much less explosive ones. Instead, it involved ice water and pressing the resinous mass through sieves and then squishing it between the plates of a food-grade hot press machine. This produced a type of hashish called rosin, seemingly named after the hunks of amber pine tree extract used to rosin violin bows. In the hash context, however, it was more of a paste. "Frosin," Brian called it, half joking, a contraction of *fresh-frozen rosin*. Tushar loved that. Always vital to create new product "categories," he said. To Brian, this whole thing felt like an audition. Tushar was vetting him to see if he was as good an extractor as he said he was.

They'd met nine months earlier, in the fall of 2017, at a meetup, that Silicon Valley institution in which entrepreneurs gather socially to talk shop and network. This one—a cannabis meetup in Berkeley—was hosted by an Oakland outfit called Holy Water Extracts, a group of traditional market producers who wanted to go legit. The Holy Water guys had the expertise; they were seeking a backer. Someone like Tushar. And Tushar was looking for reliable people who knew how to extract. That's where he found Brian Kenny.

Brian Kenny had spent most of his life within a two-mile radius of the Sunset District of San Francisco. His passions were paradigmatically Bay Area: computers, music, weed. After high school, he studied computer science at San Francisco State and played guitar in a death metal band. They called themselves Sol Asunder. He had hair down nearly to his waist. Not wishing to pay for his weed, he learned how to grow it. Soon a friend introduced him to hash extraction, specifically open blasting, using propane on the balcony of the friend's apartment in South San Francisco. Not a great idea. The same guy would later set himself on fire while extracting with hydrocarbons inside a hotel room in Mendocino County.

After a Sol Asunder show one night at the San Francisco bar Zeitgeist, this good-looking woman came up to Brian Kenny. They had already been chatting on MySpace. She was in the music industry, a promoter. One thing led to another. She got pregnant (twins), she and Brian got married, he took a job as a software engineer, he quit the band. He grew backyard weed and made small amounts of hashish using nonvolatile methods. By 2015, however, seeing legalization coming, he decided it was time to take his shot, to become an entrepreneur in this fast-growing new industry, to set his family up. So he quit his job in tech to make a play in legal weed.

A friend in the metal scene told him about these guys in Oregon who taught classes in hydrocarbon extraction. He took the course. He networked. He met and partied with Boris Kogon in Las Vegas at MJBiz, the giant cannabis-business conference held annually there. Kenny himself was a human incubator of Mary Jane–biz ideas. He invented a filtration gizmo that he thought could radically alter the hash-oil-distillation process. He and friends held hacker weekends in their Bay Area basements and garages, where they tried to dream up weed innovations. Bringing his software skills to bear, he wrote the code for an application that could glean weed-market analytical insights from data scraped online. He was calling it Firewalker. He had big dreams. He felt he was smarter, had better ideas, knew more about the real business world than all these trap-lab Wookiees. One thing he knew for sure: Most hash oil made in trap labs sucked. Tushar had this gunk he said he'd gotten from some black market spot he'd been financing the previous year. Appalling stuff. Brian knew he could do better.

Like Tushar, Brian wanted to bring cannabis out from the grunge of the black market. His desire sprang from a personal, emotional place. In a way, he was following in his father's footsteps. In another way, he wanted to do whatever it took *not* to follow in the footsteps of his father, David Kenny, who was expelled from high school in the early sixties for dealing drugs, who ran away from home, who eventually took up residence in Haight-Ashbury, who made a name for himself dealing LSD, who somehow acquired the absurd street name Happy Harpo the Dippy Hippie, who had four children by four different mothers, who went into business with a group of Hells Angels on a series of pot farms in Napa Valley, who would sometimes help his three-year-old son (Brian) fire .357 Magnum rounds at targets on the Napa property, who decided to fell an enormous centuries-old oak tree that was casting too much shade on his million-dollar crop, and who, with the help of some stoner partners, fucked up the chopping down of said mighty tree, which fell the wrong way and obliterated something like 80 percent of the Hells Angels–financed crop, which had also recently attracted the attention of the Napa County Sheriff's Office, the Campaign Against Marijuana Planting—CAMP—and the DEA, at which time David Kenny promptly emptied the family bank account and fled to Singapore—leaving his family behind. David Kenny reappeared in San Francisco in 1989, when Brian was in the fifth grade, and attempted to reestablish a relationship with his son, a move that was swiftly halted by Brian's mother, now remarried and still paying off the onerous tax bills that David Kenny had saddled her with. David eventually got sober and tried to go straight, but he died broke and alone, his health in disarray, at the age of sixty-two. Brian's father had been a complete failure. His story was a "miserable story." Long ago, Brian had decided to use his father's story—his career, his life—as an "anti-template."

So when Brian went to the meetup at the restaurant in Berkeley, Tushar Atre seemed like the opposite of David "Happy Harpo the Dippy

Hippie" Kenny. Competent, professional, an experienced entrepreneur, Tushar was also on the verge of having something else Brian coveted: a Type 7 license, California's designation for a cannabis-oil-manufacturing facility that used volatile hydrocarbons in its processes. As much as Brian had a soft spot for home-kitchen solventless extraction, he knew that hydrocarbons resulted in a much more potent product, and it was the only efficient way to produce concentrates at scale. A few months after the meetup, Tushar invited Brian down to Santa Cruz, wined and dined him, took him on a tour of his properties, culminating in the gem: a still-empty 211 Fern Street, where, Tushar said, Brian would have free rein to design the state-of-the-art extraction lab of his dreams.

They visited the burly bearded equipment supplier Elliot Kremerman at his unmarked store. They took some rudimentary gear—nylon filters, steel mesh, buckets, a hot press—to the garage at the Thirty-Eighth Avenue house. Using the gear and a sample of Rachael's biomass, Brian created this pretty kick-ass rosin, the THC from which was now going into their lungs . . . and traversing the blood-brain barrier . . . and unleashing its cascades . . . and now it was after midnight at Brian's house in Richmond, and Brian was walking a heavy-lidded Tushar down the driveway and pouring him into the Uber idling outside. . . .

The next morning Tushar was up bright and early, texting Brian, raving about the dab, the experience, the trip, wow. "I saw colors and patterns that I've never seen," Tushar wrote. "There was no sense of tension."

Brian had to agree—the hits on the dab "were like doing lines of powdered gobstoppers at Wonka's afterparty."

"You're such a learned and wise wizard," Tushar replied. "It's like a delicate treasure that needs to be handled very carefully. . . . I'm clear-headed and well rested this morning. . . . It's amazing . . . precious, like the ring . . . must be kept in trusted hands. . . . You are the young Gandalf."

Then Tushar said he had to go. He and Rachael were meeting a guy named Bomi Joseph—a doctor? an inventor?—for Sunday brunch.

32. Forty-Ninth

Rachael and Tushar had been getting high together since they met. Infrequently at first, then more often. Despite the story he had told of his bike accident in NYC many years earlier, and the advice from the priest to ameliorate his pain with weed, despite all his talk of smoking with friends, of smoking the weed he grew himself in his backyard, Tushar, to Rachael, seemed like a novice. He seemed unsettled, even scared, at the idea of being high, of appearing witless around other people, of losing control in front of them. As far as Rachael knew, he didn't feel anxious when high. He was, however, prone to a kind of prehigh anxiety—a meta-anxiety about the anxiety that the plant's cannabinoids might induce in him. It was good, then, that Rachael had a powerful tolerance. She could guide him, give him advice. *If your mind spirals*, she explained, *you can choose to ignore the spiral. Choose not to give it your attention. It's your mind. Whether you experience heaven or hell, it's your mind that creates them. Turn off your mind.*

Gradually Tushar's tolerance grew, and so it wasn't a total surprise for her to learn that he had smoked a dab with Brian Kenny the night before. When he awoke the next morning he seemed like a new man, refreshed, calm, sensitive, absolved.

But then Rachael and Tushar went to brunch with Dr. Bomi Joseph and his girlfriend at Café Sparrow, a Tushar fave, and the fine feelings vaporized. These two older men were discussing a business deal and ignoring her, as though she were Tushar's bimbo. Eager for an injection of capital that would ease their overstretched finances, Tushar spoke of Bomi as another possible partner. Tushar liked to say that freedom didn't result from having a lot of assets, or a giant balance sheet, or a brilliant business idea. What gave you freedom was cash flow, and right now they had a *cash flow* problem. Bomi Joseph had visited the Summit property several times, after which they all headed to the vineyard down the road to sample the pinot noirs. Wouldn't it be great if Bomi grew his Kriya hops right here at the Summit? Wouldn't it be great if they extracted the essential CBD oils from those miracle plants at the Fern Street lab, using special equipment that Bomi would install?

Tushar described Bomi as a good person trying do good in the world, but Rachael wasn't so sure. Her initial enthusiasm for the man had cooled since Cynthia's death. Bomi didn't respect her, she thought; maybe he didn't respect women in general. And Tushar, too, seemed to lose respect for her whenever he was with Bomi. She once saw Tushar roll his eyes at something she said. Bomi felt threatened by Rachael, Tushar told her privately. Like Tushar, Bomi scorned the black market weed business, of which Rachael was an alumna.

"You (and I) are from the normal ethical corporate world," Bomi later texted Tushar. "Our world is based on trust and honesty. The weed world is the wild Wild West. It's grab it quick. Shoot the other guy first. . . . Trust no one. Paranoia. The two worlds can't coexist. I was honestly baffled by [Rachael] for a while. It's easy for me to walk away."

Tushar pushed back: "Not everyone in that world is warped. There are morally good people. The problem is the milieu."

IN LATE JULY, without telling Rachael beforehand, Tushar fired the farmhand Ernesto, the legacy caretaker of the Summit property. Ernesto had been living in a tent on the meadow near the cannabis crop for several months, working all the time, hardly ever leaving the land. Ernesto had helped Rachael build the hoop houses, helped her put the clones in the ground. Rachael and Tushar had told him that this was a legal cannabis grow, with proper permits, but Ernesto came to believe that this was not true. He didn't really care. He stood to make a thirty-thousand-dollar bonus if he stuck with her through the whole season, in addition to his monthly salary of forty-five hundred dollars. Out of lumber milled from fallen redwood trees on the property, Ernesto had recently built an outdoor shower and kitchen. Then one day two weeks earlier, he'd showered, gotten all nice and clean, and driven down to San Jose for dinner and a drink, a little breather from the relentless outdoor toil. Next thing you know, a drunk guy at the bar got in Ernesto's face and sucker punched him in the mouth. He called Rachael the next morning, shaken, and told her he needed some time off to recuperate at his home in San Jose. This wasn't great timing. The light-dep harvest had to start right away. Same with the freezing process. But what could she do? She said OK, but she really needed him back on site ASAP. . . .

Tushar had a different reaction. Inside the FedEx truck, Tushar met with Ernesto alone. Rachael was paying him a generous wage, Tushar said, but the weed crop was looking pretty shitty. The pot farm had entered its most labor-intensive period. What a terrible mistake Ernesto had made, fucking off to San Jose, getting plastered, and starting a goddamn bar fight exactly when Rachael needed him most! Tushar got in his face but didn't punch him in the mouth. *Ernesto, you fuckup*, he said, *you're fired*.

Now Rachael really needed help: manpower, womanpower, any of it, all of it. And then, once again, she manifested. And, again, the universe responded. A guy she'd employed as a trimmer for two seasons in Trinity County called her up out of the blue, looking for work. Habib* was his name, a skinny Jack Sparrowish dude with a fuzzy goatee and his hair made into thin dreadlock strands. He spoke in an exuberantly Italian

* Not his real name.

accent but was originally from Morocco. His true passion was tattoo art, but in Trinity, Habib had shown himself to be a hardworking, street-smart guy. "Management material," Rachael called him. She also knew that Habib, who spoke several languages, including Spanish, was adept at recruiting trimmigrants who were actual immigrants—a large, reliable labor pool.

And so Habib recruited people to work on the Summit farm. The biggest job right now, in late July, early August, was to continue cutting down the mature plants and freezing them with dry ice. Then Rachael and Habib would haul it all down to the Thirty-Eighth Avenue house and transfer it into the Sears meat freezers.

Tushar's forty-ninth birthday rolled around, August 1, 2018. As usual, he threw a party—this time a combined birthday and house-warming party to show off his newly renovated oceanfront home on Pleasure Point Drive. Rachael and Tushar presented as an emerging Santa Cruz power couple—happy, attractive, healthy, talented. She looked preppy chic in a gray skirt, a trim blue blazer, and pearls, while Tushar was surfer hip in flip-flops, black jeans, and one of his black "Sea Shepherd" T-shirts. (Everyone knew that Tushar loved Sea Shepherd, the group that sailed around the world attacking the ships of illicit whale and dolphin hunters because, as everyone also knew, he loved the idea of vigilante justice.) At the party, they grilled fish, a bluegrass band played, and throughout the evening Rachael and Tushar posed arm in arm, smiling, snapping photos of themselves and friends in front of the dramatic backdrop: the rocky cliff, the pounding waves, the blue sea, the pale-green mountains beyond the sea, and a setting sun that turned the sky bloodred.

AT THE THIRTY-EIGHTH AVENUE HOUSE, the ice chests were jammed to the brink with hundreds of pounds of frozen weed. There were immediate problems. The power at the house kept going out. Not good. Also, they had more material than even these huge, twenty-five-cubic-foot freezers could handle, so they had to drive the overflow frozen weed down the street and around the corner to the oceanfront house on Pleasure Point Drive and stuff it into the kitchen freezer there, carrying icy bags of cannabis in both hands, walking them from the truck parked at the curb through the front door, the bags turning white and crystalline when they hit the warm outside air. Tushar freaked out—did any of the neighbors see them?—and vented his frustration with this whole wretched turn of events. The mediocre harvest, the popcorn nuggets, the increasing probability that Rachael would fail to earn back her original nut plus the $250,000 needed for the balloon payment. Why had they taken on all this risk in the stupid fucking black market—of being raided by law enforcement and charged with felonies, to say nothing of the financial risk—if they weren't going to make a shitload of profit? Indeed, all of this was made worse because Rachael refused to heed his sober, MBA-level advice. If he had any hair, he'd be pulling it out! She was making moronic decisions. He actually called her a moron. He accused her of taking the lazy way out, like all the other stoner dipshits and weed rats he'd met since getting into this goddamn business. She was lazy. Sleeping late, sobbing all the time, and blaming her behavior on her grief. . . . *Give me a break*, he said. *Stop using your emotional drama as a smoke screen. Pitch in, get to work, and help me instead of focusing on yourself!*

Was he serious? Rachael was working her fucking ass off. Working to rescue the farm and the whole endeavor by pivoting to fresh frozen so they could earn enough money to make the balloon payment that was due in December and save the Summit property that Tushar had already put a million dollars into, something he brought up constantly, his one mil at risk. . . . Tushar was ignoring all the money she'd invested in the farm, now approaching three hundred thousand dollars. Tushar didn't care about love; he cared only about his money. *Love means shit to you over business*, she said.

She had him all wrong, he said; he was only trying to help her succeed, guide her through this difficult transition from black market drug dealing to proper, legal entrepreneurship. . . .

He said, *You see me as something other than what I am!*

Rachael reminded him that live resin was a hot market. And live resin turned into distillate for vape pens was even hotter—in 2018, arguably the hottest product category in cannabis. By Rachael's calculations, oil extracted from the quantity of nuggets she'd frozen could fetch as much as $716,000 if it were put into vape cartridges and sold in that form.

Look, she said, *I don't want this frozen shit sitting around in the middle of Pleasure Point either. But this is what farmers do. You have to put the health of the crop, the yield, above everything. The crop comes first!*

But Tushar would not, could not, listen to her. He wanted the weed gone from the premises. Immediately, ASAP, all of it, gone.

Was he serious? Why?

Because, he said, *this is my mother's house!*

Wait a second. The shocks kept on coming. His mother's house?

Yes, yes, Tushar said. Shaku owned the goddamn place, not him! And so the weed had to go!

She stared at him blankly. She was stunned. Who *was* this guy? This middle-aged mama's boy. But it was worse than that. If he had lied about a thing like that, what else was he hiding from her?

A few nights later, in the wee hours, Rachael awoke suddenly. The lights in the bedroom were ablaze. Tushar was sitting cross-legged on the floor beside the bed, staring up at her with his uncanny green eyes. Despite the meditative pose, he seemed almost sightless with rage.

Where is the money?! he said. *Give me your money!* They needed to make the balloon payment, and he wanted the money she'd promised him *now*. He threatened to unplug the freezers, which would ruin the only remaining asset of hers that had any value, the very thing that would allow them to make the balloon payment! He was out of his mind.

Rachael willed herself to be calm. *There's nothing either of us can do about any of this right now*, she told him. But later she succumbed to another crying jag, feeling vulnerable, broke, alone. She felt like she was being chased by a lion, Tushar the lion, the apex predator, the monster . . . and she'd do anything to escape from it, from him. . . .

Habib had this friend. Kyle was his name, a self-styled DJ with tattoos all over his body. Along his right jawline in blue-green cursive were the words *Pretty Boy*—Habib's handiwork, in fact. Kyle also had gold-capped teeth and sometimes spoke in a hip-hop patois; he hailed from semi-rural Oregon. According to Habib, Kyle was also a weed broker, fairly well-known in the Santa Cruz cannabis ecosystem. Santa Cruz was an important brokering hub in the state and national and even international weed trades. If you didn't want to travel to gnarly, dangerous, backwoods Humboldt, Santa Cruz was far easier to get into and out of. Every year at the conclusion of harvest season, it seemed like half the hotel rooms in town were rented out for the purposes of consummating bulk wholesale drug deals.

Not long after Tushar had awoken Rachael in his cross-legged fugue state, Kyle and Habib were hanging out at the Summit property. Rachael was there, working hard. The second crop of strictly outdoor cannabis was on its way toward October maturation, and it required tending. She told Kyle and Habib that she needed to move the frozen weed out of Tushar's house and needed to find an extractor fast, one who wouldn't screw her over. From a grower's perspective, the extractor held all the cards. There were many ways for a lab to skim. Most commonly, they just lied to the grower about the yields they were achieving from the grower's biomass, told the grower it was lower than it really was, and held back the difference. Rachael didn't want that.

Reclining in a lawn chair at the Summit, his eyes masked by a pair of enormous sunglasses, Kyle piped up. He could process Rachael's fresh-frozen weed. Habib nodded in agreement. Kyle came from a long line of growers and dealers in Oregon. His mother, in fact, was an OG cultivator, an old hippie who'd been growing in the hills outside Eugene—home of the University of Oregon, major campus weed market! Kyle offered to take all that fresh frozen off Rachael's hands and give her a better deal than any other extractor would or could—a friends-and-family rate. Kyle's dad had a metal-fabrication shop in the woods outside Eugene. Habib nodded. It was like a compound. Multiple buildings. Isolated. Perfect spot, he told Rachael, for a small hydrocarbon closed-loop system—if you kept it far away from the sparks! Kyle knew people who had the equipment they needed and had friends who could operate it. Habib nodded. This way, Rachael didn't need to worry about stranger-danger extractors screwing her over. Plus, Kyle said, his OG mom loved to help other women in weed. She would love Rachael, and Rachael would love her. Rachael was warming to the idea, thinking this could be the answer. . . . Get the weed out of Tushar's mother's house, get it away from the lion . . . and turn it into oil in a secure environment up at Kyle's family's compound. . . .

And yet, Rachael didn't fully trust this dude, despite Habib's endorsement. So, as a due diligence test, she gave Kyle a task. Rachael had earlier instructed her crew of trimmers to pick through and find the best and biggest buds for sale as standard smokable flower. If Kyle was a player like he said he was, he could help her sell this small amount of weed, right? And soon Rachael was talking to one of Kyle's connections, a guy from Oakland who said he could move any amount of weight she wanted. And the guy did move what she wanted, and did it fast, and paid up quickly, forty grand in cash when Rachael delivered it to some industrial building near the Oakland waterfront.

Had she successfully manifested again? *OK*, she told Kyle. *Deal.* There would be no contract of course, just a handshake, and the next thing she knew she, Habib, and Kyle were at the Thirty-Eighth Avenue house, carefully weighing out all the frozen weed—717.31 pounds—unplugging the freezers, packing them with dry ice, and loading the huge things directly into a U-Haul box truck, which drove away, pointing north, toward Oregon.

The driver of the U-Haul was Rachael's father, Bruce Warren Lynch, of Boston, Massachusetts, Cynthia's first and only husband. Over the years Bruce had tried, more or less, to stay in Rachael's life. As luck would have it, he had chosen this very moment in August to pay a visit to his daughter in Santa Cruz—the precise moment when the deal with Kyle was struck—and Bruce was like, *Fuck it, I'm coming along!* Bruce was always game. Bruce knew all about Rachael's career. He himself was a raffish product of East Coast privilege, boarding schools, Bowdoin College, all of which, in Rachael's view, made Bruce believe he could always, and with elegance, dance his way out of trouble. He looked like a member of a WASP country club, in Brooks Brothers and boat shoes, but he also enjoyed smoking pot. Copious amounts of pot. So Bruce Lynch was in the U-Haul, along with a friend of his from Boston, a guy named Ron. Bruce and Ron were both in their late sixties, hauling more than half a million dollars' worth of a Schedule I narcotic across an interstate border. Rachael knew from experience that the person with the money—in this case, her—should not drive the vehicle with the contraband. Should the worst-case scenario unfold, she could bail them out, but they wouldn't be able to bail her out. And so in the white BMW SUV that Rachael had owned since her days in Trinity County, she and Kyle followed the U-Haul to Oregon.

Ten or so hours later, they pulled up to Kyle's dad's metal-fab shop in the foothills of the Oregon Coast Range, thirty-five miles west of Eugene. Machines that looked like car lifts to Rachael, maybe lathes or something, were positioned around the smooth concrete floor, but the space was big enough that it seemed pretty empty. Perfect spot for a trap lab. Could easily put an explosion-proof room in one of the corners. They'd get started on that right away. Kyle introduced his father, a short man, bald, terse. *Just put 'em over there*, he grumbled. And they did. The plan was for Habib to relocate temporarily to Eugene and babysit the extraction process, serving as Rachael's eyes and ears, a security measure.

Still, Rachael had a feeling, a slight nausea that she chalked up to the normal trepidation that came with placing a valuable asset in another person's hands. As she and her elder coconspirators walked back to the U-Haul and the BMW, Kyle's father locked the gate behind them.

33. The Reward

October 23, 2019

> **Unnamed private parties are offering a $25,000 award for tips related to the Oct. 1 kidnapping and fatal shooting of tech entrepreneur Tushar Atre.**
>
> **The Santa Cruz County Sheriff's Office has confirmed the validity of the offered reward, which will be available through Nov. 30 for anyone assisting the department in the arrest and conviction of the suspect or suspects involved.**
>
> **"Several people were involved in this murder and someone out there knows who they are," Sheriff Jim Hart stated in a released statement. "That is a terrible secret to keep."**
>
> —***Santa Cruz Sentinel,*** **October 23, 2019**

As the November deadline approached without any viable tips, as the months dragged on with no arrests, the reward was increased to $150,000, and then again to $200,000. The sheriff's office would soon come to learn that Tushar Atre had a fiercely loyal friend group. These were the "unnamed private parties" funding the reward, and they were a cross section of Silicon Valley. A "digital business coach" and VC. An app builder and VC. A "legendary" marketing guru and VC who had retired at thirty-eight. A software engineer turned "strategic material impact leader with a history of building successful companies" and VC. Almost all of them surfed. Almost all of them had gotten into surfing because of Atre's relentless influence. Several were bachelors or childless. They were healthy and strapping and handsome, of the "live hard, play hard . . . Masters of the Universe" school, as one longtime AtreNet employee described them. "He loved those guys, and they loved him." Tushar was also such a supernova of adventurous energy that his death seemed to create this sucking void at the core of his friends' lives. He was an agent of chaos, but in a good way. He was the one who conjured the fun, who made everything happen. The surf trips to Mexico, Hawaii, Australia. The nightlife excursions into San Francisco. What would the friend group do without him? He was their guiding spirit, and now he was gone.

The intensity of their friendship with him meant they considered themselves part of the Atre family. "A brother from another mother" is how one of them liked to describe his relationship with Tushar. And so the friends believed their most important job was consoling the inconsolable: Atre's elderly parents and his sister. How do you make sense of something like this? A son snatched away from a mother and father who were in the twilight of their lives. How do you begin to grieve?

The world was not just. In addition to crushing sadness, the friend group felt enraged. The Atre family had enlisted the loyal friend group to deal with the sale or unwinding of Interstitial (d/b/a Cruz Science). Tushar's dear mother Shaku, in her late seventies, was named executor of Tushar's estate; she couldn't do that job alone. So her son's friends stepped up. No one outside Tushar's circle could fully grasp the madness and utter villainy they had to deal with in the wake of the murder. People were coming out of the woodwork to make absurd claims on the estate. Crazy people. Some of the suspect people coming out of the woodwork were also making allegations about Tushar's business practices in cannabis. Allegations of fraud, of black market activity. His friends knew, of course, about Tushar's weed start-up. Some of them had wanted to invest in it. They also knew, or thought they knew, that Tushar hated the black market, wanted to conquer that world and bury it. But when the friends started the hard job of going through Tushar's belongings at 3034 Pleasure Point Drive—alternately sorting through his valuables but also looking for clues as to who might have wanted him dead—they learned about the gallons of hash oil in the house and the bags of marijuana jammed in the freezer. None of that stuff was legal product. Tushar liked to dance on the edge, that was for sure. In the swells, or out on the town, that's why he was so much fun. So maybe it wasn't outlandish to think that Tushar was involved in something dark, something he'd kept secret even from them?

34. Fire

Nick Montoya had scars all over his body, his face. Though he was just in his early thirties, he spoke slowly, moved slowly. In 2015, he'd been engulfed by flames in a hydrocarbon extraction lab in Albuquerque, New Mexico.

Even after the accident Montoya stayed on in the business. He had come to California from his native New Mexico in 2017, bringing with him a diverse network of contacts in the cannabis world. Brian Kenny thought he could bring a lot to Interstitial Systems, especially on the sales-and-distribution side of things. Montoya knew extractors who were already producing millions of dollars a month worth of crude oil, millions of dollars of distillate. Unlicensed oil and unlicensed distillate, yes, it was true. But these weren't just trap labs; they were industrial-size trap labs. And not for long. These were big, serious players who were applying for cannabis manufacturing licenses from the State of California, and they had more biomass supply than even they could handle. Once everyone was fully licensed, once Fern Street was up and running, Interstitial could take some of the overflow business from those big players and generate immediate cash flow for their start-up. Now Brian Kenny was talking Tushar's language.

That's why Brian wanted Tushar to meet Montoya, who had his own little sales pitch. No one was more dedicated to this plant, and to the business of this plant, than Nick Montoya. After all, he'd sacrificed his body for it. Even with his injuries, or maybe in part because of them, Montoya had a certain charisma, a certain authenticity. To say Brian felt sorry for him wasn't right. The guy had faced trauma and adversity and bounced back. He respected Nick Montoya.

They'd first met maybe a year earlier, not long after Brian had invented a device, a hash-oil-filtration system, which consisted of a centrifuge and a special filter plate. The device was designed to separate hash oil into solids in one chamber and liquids in another, the solids taking the form of a powder, a super-pure, 95 percent to 98 percent THCA powder. White as high-altitude snow, it looked like refined sugar. It looked—a little alarmingly—like refined cocaine. THCA, the acid form of THC, could be used for any number of applications, including, Brian believed, as the main ingredient in an exceptionally high-quality vape pen. When the powder collected for the first time at one end of a syringe Brian had affixed to an eighty-dollar blood centrifuge he'd sent whirling in high-velocity orbits—his first prototype—he started jumping around with his hands in the air. This was his eureka moment. This was his flash of genius. He felt like he had a multimillion-dollar idea.

Now all he had to do was launch a business. To do so, he needed help and money. He needed a partner, someone adept at sales, someone with connections, and he needed an investor. He met both on the same day, at another cannabis-industry meetup, this one inside a nondescript tract house in a suburban development on the outskirts of Sacramento, where the sprawl ended and the flat Central Valley agriculture began. A group of men in their thirties and forties had gathered inside the house. To each other, they spoke a dense Asian language. To the white blokes in the room, they spoke in accented English. Brian didn't know any of their names. In front of out-group people, they addressed each other only as Uncle or Nephew or Cousin. They looked Vietnamese, but they did not identify as Vietnamese. They were Hmong people, an ethnic group indigenous to the jungled mountains of Southeast Asia, where they'd grown opium for centuries and helped the CIA fight its secret, illicit conflict in Laos during the Vietnam War. After waves of postwar migration and resettlement in the United States, largely in California, many Hmong people had made their way as field workers to the vast farms of the Central Valley and then, afterward, to the Emerald Triangle and other remote Northern California counties, as owners and operators of secret marijuana plantations. Brian never did get their real names. In settings such as this, he knew, best to not ask too many questions.

Now Brian and a handful of others were gathering in the West Sacramento house of a big Hmong pot cultivator, or family of cultivators. As far as Brian could tell, their business model was volume: quantity, not quality. And like everyone else in weed, the Hmong wanted not only to go legal, but to integrate vertically. They wanted to expand beyond cultivation and into the extraction business. The meetup was meant to explore those moves with potential partners.

Brian's invitation had come through his wife, who'd emigrated from Poland to San Francisco while in her teens, had immersed herself in the city's music scene, specifically its death metal scene, and had eventually worked as a promoter of concerts, specifically death metal concerts. When Sol Asunder appeared on the bill of one of her shows, the rest was history. Twins, marriage, domesticity. Not exactly a rock 'n' roll life. But Brian Kenny, the tall, handsome musician and software whiz, was also an amateur grower of superb weed. Still working as a concert promoter, Brian's wife began taking small portions of his homegrown stuff and selling it people in the metal scene. Then slightly larger amounts. Then not-so-slightly larger amounts. Tapping deeper into her music network, she found other, more substantial sources of weed. She scaled up. Soon enough, she'd made a name for herself in the Bay Area's bulk black market cannabis trade. Then came the day that Brian arrived home to find forty pounds of wet, newly harvested flower lying on newspapers all over the master bedroom. You could smell it from the sidewalk outside the house. She had a huge pot deal going down. This was close to the end of their relationship. Eventually they divorced. But not before she told her entrepreneur husband all about one of her biggest pot sources, these Hmong cultivators, based in Sacramento but with grows all over the state, who were planning to go legit. They had a lot of money. Brian should meet them.

Nick Montoya was another guest of the Hmong that day. Also present was a guy from mainland China now living in Singapore. He was young, in his twenties, and, it turned out, exceedingly, maybe obscenely, rich. He said his father was a high-level PRC government official, and the young guy was here in California to scout for cannabis investment opportunities. All three guys got along well. They politely declined any kind of deal with the Hmong, and before they knew it, Brian and Montoya had an LLC and almost two hundred thousand dollars of the rich kid's cash in a bank account. They were calling their company Kasai Labs. Brian Kenny's idea. *Kasai* is Japanese for "fire." Count the meanings: slang for excellent dope. What you needed to convert THCA to delta-9-THC. And what had happened to Montoya.

As they got to know each other, Montoya divulged a little more of his background. He had been around the block in New Mexico. He knew all about the perils of the weed trade. He had one scar from the entry wound of a bullet he'd taken in his stomach and another on his elbow. Acquired, Brian remembers Nick saying, in gunfights while defending an extraction lab against an invasion of armed thieves. Again he'd sacrificed his body for this business. (To another person who Nick knew in Santa Cruz, his stories of the weed trade in New Mexico were reminiscent of *Breaking Bad*, except with hash labs, not meth labs.) In part because of these violent encounters, Montoya had left New Mexico and come to California, the most important cannabis market in the world. Once here, he'd hooked up with a few extraction outfits that had notoriously huge production capacity in Oakland, Sacramento, Santa Rosa, Modesto. The owners of these operations were all applying for their California manufacturing and distribution licenses, preparing to go legit.

That's where Nick Montoya was in his life when Brian Kenny told him about another start-up opportunity, totally on the up and up, a legal extraction facility in Santa Cruz founded by a Silicon Valley entrepreneur, Tushar Atre. When Brian introduced the concept of Nick Montoya to Tushar, he emphasized that Montoya wanted nothing more than to push the industry into the light, just as Tushar did.

And so on Halloween, Tushar and Rachael took Brian and Montoya on a little tour of Santa Cruz. They met at the Thirty-Eighth Avenue house, then headed over to look at Fern Street, where workers were just then framing out the various lab spaces and explosion-proof rooms and storage vaults—the extraction lab that Brian had been hard at work designing, the lab of his dreams.

The next day, the Day of the Dead, Tushar and Rachael invited Montoya to dinner. Brian couldn't make it, but Montoya accepted. He was interested in joining Interstitial, and Tushar was almost sold on the idea.

35. Harvest

The harvest season for outdoor weed arrives in October, a time of unrelenting toil. Ever since the dawn of California pot agriculture in the 1960s, word got out to the rest of the country about the underground industry's demand for labor during harvest season. Starting as early as August, then, the migrants—the trimmigrants—would come. To the Emerald Triangle and the Sierra Foothills, to Sonoma, Marin County, Santa Cruz, and Big Sur, all the way down the spine of the coastal ranges through Santa Barbara, hopping over L.A. to Laguna Canyon, the unwashed, dropped-out, dreadlocked, Deadhead, patchouli-stink, jam-band-listening flocks would come. They hailed from all over the country and world. From South America, Europe, Australia. Young Israelis seemed especially drawn to the California cannabis fields. The trimmigrants would form encampments on the farms, living in tents—trim scenes, they were called, but they were also party scenes. When the harvest was complete, it became traditional for each farm, or each community of neighboring farms, to throw a harvest party. These evolved into days-long celebrations in which everyone would sample one another's product. The big one in Humboldt eventually developed into the Emerald Cup, the pot industry's version of the James Beard Awards. In Big Sur, where the weed-growing community had long been aggressively, righteously insular, the harvest parties were legendary. On the final day of the party, they would build a monumental bonfire and throw one of their giant mother plants into the flames, a ritual sacrifice to the higher registers of cosmological vibe. There were rumors of bacchanals, of acres of naked, beautiful young people cavorting in the Big Sur woods. The harvest celebrations almost always coincided with Halloween and the Day of the Dead.

During her Trinity years, Rachael had thrown a harvest party each season. She had dreamed of creating a vibrant social scene at the Summit property, hosting dinner parties throughout the year and a big harvest bash at the end of October. But there would be no such celebrations in 2018. There was too much work, too much stress, too much at stake. By late October, Rachael's outdoor, full-sun crop had reached maturation. She and her crew were pulling thirteen-hour days, harvesting two hundred pounds of cannabis flower, trimming the flower, hanging it to cure in one of the two shipping containers that now sat at the edge of the meadow. She needed this to be a high-quality harvest so she could sell it at top dollar and earn enough to make the balloon payment and prove Tushar wrong. Meanwhile, she still hadn't received the highly valuable live resin that was being extracted in Oregon. Fucking Habib and Kyle had shown up unannounced in Santa Cruz. Where was her oil? They didn't have clear answers. It was in process, they said. Don't worry. And also Kyle needed a car. Could Kyle borrow Rachael's car to do some important weed-related business thing? This was crazy. It was hard to think, but she needed Kyle on her side because fucking Kyle had all her fresh frozen, so she let him borrow her BMW.

Then on Halloween itself Rachael had to come down from the mountain for a meeting with Tushar, Brian Kenny, and a guy Brian knew. Another consultant? Someone who might be joining the Interstitial team? They convened at the house on Thirty-Eighth and went to Fern Street, where Tushar showed the newcomer around. The next day, the three of them went to dinner at a restaurant near the Santa Cruz Harbor. Rachael thought Nick Montoya was interesting, knowledgeable, but she was also skeptical. Didn't he get blown up?

On the other hand, she was hardly paying attention. Just under the surface of this pleasant evening, with the clang of sailboat rigging carried on the ocean breeze, tension was roiling. The foundering deal with Kyle had Tushar on edge. More black market buffoonery. And although Rachael had finally put together financial projections using accounting software, something Tushar had been after her to do for months, her P&L statements were a confusion. Her calculations were, in fact, wrong, like mathematically wrong, off by a factor of five. If the farm was going to miss its projections so dramatically, the reward was not worth the risk, Tushar asserted, and the risk, as he saw it, was primarily his. Her ego wouldn't allow her to take advice from her white market boyfriend even though that's where the weed business was headed. The black market would eventually disappear, he told her, surpassed by white market guys like him. How stupid was it of her to have sent her entire precious net worth, in a truck driven by her dad, for Christ's sake, to some weed rat trailer trash in bumfuck Oregon? She'd wasted a whole year on that kind of shit instead of focusing her efforts on obtaining building permits for the sixty acres, as Tushar had advised her to do, which would have hugely increased its value. She'd wasted a year by not working to get the property zoned for commercial agriculture so they could obtain a cultivation license. She'd fucked up what should have been a beautiful thing. Later, when Rachael made about forty thousand dollars from the sale of a portion of the harvest through her black market connections, she used much of it to pay out her crew of trimmers. When Tushar found out about that, he was furious. Why would she do that? *Fuck the servants*, he said. *That money should have gone toward the balloon payment!* He told her she was an apologist for people who didn't have their shit together, the patron saint of degenerates. It was as though he saw her as a wild specimen from this primitive tribe of black marketeers. Beautiful but untamable.

•

TUSHAR HIRED THE GUY OFF CRAIGSLIST. Adam Jones, who'd been living in the woods somewhere in the Colorado Rockies, was a tree trimmer by trade, and that's what Tushar had brought him in to do. Trim some of the big trees on the Summit property, dig some ditches, grade some roads. Jones would live on-site rent free, in the big tepee, which suited him just fine. He was a bearded mountain man, wiry and scrappy, a former boxer, with thirty-four amateur bouts to his name, not to mention one unsanctioned underground match in the back room of a bar on the outskirts of Texarkana. Tushar latched on to this, and he and Jones bonded, ever so slightly, over their shared pugilistic interests. Otherwise they had zilch in common, urbane Tushar and Jones, an itinerant Oklahoman who'd dropped out of high school.

In late September, Tushar picked up Jones and his dog and his bag of axes and chain saws from the Greyhound bus terminal in San Jose. Jones was broke. He looked as though he'd made his way to California not on a bus but a boxcar on a freight train. The bus from Denver had made a pit stop in Las Vegas, where he'd gotten off and promptly lost his bankroll at the poker tables. But Tushar liked that Jones had a deep, sonorous voice, and a philosophical, soulful bent. He used the word *soul* a lot. Tushar told Rachael that Jones seemed nice. Uneducated, but nice.

Jones learned it was a weed farm he'd be working on only after he arrived, but he didn't care about that. He just asked if there was any spare stuff he could smoke. Tushar reminded him of the terms of his hiring: He'd be paid piecemeal, by the job. The rates Tushar proposed were low, but Jones didn't mind that either because the property was awesome, a paradise. His dog could run free. And of course there were the trees—a dense forest of huge, beautiful redwood specimens, which Jones had never seen before. It's what drew him to the job in the first place; he was a tree guy, and he wanted to climb them and behold them up close.

Jones told Tushar that he had the uncanny feeling of having been here before, on this very property. Even the tepee was familiar. It was like he'd dreamed long ago of this place.

•

By mid-November, Rachael and her crew had just about finished the trimming and curing of the outdoor crop, and were starting the process of weighing it out and stuffing the buds into plastic bags. Like most cultivators, she used a specific kind of plastic bag, the turkey bag, so-called because pot farmers had long ago learned to repurpose these things from their typical function: the roasting of holiday birds. Each turkey bag held a pound of weed. The bags then went into tote bins, which were stacked inside one of the shipping containers at the Summit. The weed would stay there until Rachael could begin sending it to her primary movers of weight back East, including Push.

In the middle of one of these busy days, Adam Jones climbed onto the Bobcat front-end loader that Rachael had purchased at the start of the growing season. Jones parked the machine in what he believed to be a strategic location, in the middle of the road that led from the meadow to the main driveway. He climbed down off the Bobcat, removed the key from the ignition, and made a phone call to Tushar. Did Tushar and Rachael want to bring their illegal weed to market? Well, then, Tushar had better pay a non-poverty-level fee for the next job Jones was scheduled to perform (the digging of a quarter-mile-long ditch).

Jones was pissed. He wanted his money. There were always delays in Tushar paying him for these pretty arduous jobs. Tushar would say, *Start the next job and then I'll pay you for the last one*. Just days earlier, Rachael had begged Tushar to please settle up with this guy. Tushar's control freak way of dealing with employees made them all just want to quit. She said, *This will come back to haunt us*.

And now it had.

On the phone with Jones, Tushar told him, *You've just made a very bad decision*. But then, instead of helping Rachael deal with this shit, Tushar told her, *It looks like you've got a big problem*. Then he fled. He drove to the airport and got on a plane to New York for a little impromptu visit.

Better, he said, *if I'm not around*. As he was leaving, he gave her some advice: *Don't pay Jones. Just get rid of him*. Rachael outwardly played it cool. *Sure, OK*. But inside, she was furious. Who knew what this guy Jones with his axes and chain saws was capable of? Then she thought, maybe she could use Tushar's absence to her advantage. Her biggest problem was that her crew still hadn't finished trimming all the weed. It could take a few more days to get it all done. But she had an idea. She approached Jones outside the tepee in the early afternoon and calmly, nicely, asked him to lunch. Since Kyle still had Rachael's BMW, Tushar had given her one of his Toyota pickups. With Jones in the passenger seat, she drove them to a restaurant off Route 17. *Tushar's out of town*, she said. *When he's back, I'll make sure he pays you better. Until then, let's just chill*. Jones agreed. She was kind to him. She asked him questions about himself. He relaxed. He drank a beer and then another. He told her all about his hardscrabble life. He seemed smitten. It was possible he was falling in love with her.

What Jones didn't know was that there was a rear entrance to the Summit property, hidden at the tree line at the back of the meadow, right behind the shipping containers. Rachael had instructed her crew: Keep trimming; don't stop. Then, each day for the next two days, she took Jones out to lunch. Late at night for the next two nights, while Jones slept in the tepee, she drove onto the property via the back entrance, removed the turkey bags from the bins, and drove them back to town. On the third day, when all the weed had been moved, she brought Jones back from the restaurant to the property and broke the news to him. *OK, Adam*, she said. *The weed's gone. It's over*. He looked shocked. Then he laughed and shook his head. *You're so smart*, he said. *And I'm so stupid*.

THEY SHOULD NEVER have gone into business together. Had they just been lovers, she would still have her life savings, and he wouldn't be burdened with the Summit's debt. Everyone knew that mixing love and business was insane, yet they had idiotically plowed ahead anyway.

Tushar accused her of using him, of fleecing him. He called her a thief. Now that she'd removed the last of her weed from the Summit, he was sure she was going to leave him. He was screwed, he said, because he loved her no matter what.

Wrong, Rachael said. He was the one who had all the leverage over her. He had maneuvered himself into the power position. If she wanted to recover her life savings, she had no choice but to stay with him and keep working. Their relationship was pitted with sunk costs, emotional, financial. He reminded her that he'd spent a million dollars on the down payment for the Summit to further her career.

Or to trap me, she replied.

In desperation, Rachael sought out the guidance of a psychic. She'd had readings before, usually in the company of her mother. And although she identified as more of a skeptic than a believer, she was seeking some kind of contact, any contact, with Cynthia's essence. A friend recommended a woman who lived in Marin County, who only saw clients through referrals. The woman was strikingly beautiful and spoke with a heavy accent, possibly Russian. In a dim calm room full of murmuring water features and crystal prisms broadcasting tiny rainbows onto nearby surfaces, the woman turned over tarot cards. She spoke of Cynthia, of Rachael's childhood, of the possibility of an ultimately sweet and fulfilling future for Rachael. Then the woman stopped, and a look of worry came over her face. She was seeing a number . . . the number one. . . . It was red in color. . . . It was pulsing above Rachael's head. *Do you have a boyfriend?* the woman asked. Rachael nodded. *This is a warning*, the woman said. *Your boyfriend is in danger; he has made someone—some group—angry. Something is coming. It is already set. And you are not supposed to be there when it comes*. The psychic said she normally didn't give advice like this, but the feelings were powerful. A spirit or spirits, a female spirit or spirits, were going through a lot of trouble, using a lot of energy, to transmit this message. She was direct with Rachael: *You need to not be there. You need to get away!*

That night, back in Santa Cruz, Rachael was a little shaken but also didn't exactly believe what she'd heard. She described the whole scene to Tushar. Surprisingly, he did not dismiss the reader as a charlatan. He took her words not as a literal forewarning but as a metaphor, a piece of psychological insight. He agreed with this woman—he did need to change, did need to stop pissing people off so much.

Rachael was reassured by Tushar's self-awareness and his smart interpretation. Amid the chaos of the events that were to come, she almost forgot all about the psychic's warning.

36. The Trimmer

Late October 2019

Victim's (ex-)girlfriend had mentioned Adam Jones during their initial sit-down with her. Rachael Lynch had urged detectives to look into the guy. And they did, quickly verifying that, indeed, Atre had made a series of 911 calls the previous December that had resulted in an investigation by the SCSO's Daniel Robbins. Atre had accused Adam Jones of stealing a truck and then running him over with it.

Jones had come from Oklahoma by way of Arkansas by way of Colorado, and had an outstanding DUI charge for which there was a warrant out for his arrest in Colorado. Jones had lived on the Summit property for four months, late September through early January 2019, then disappeared, and hadn't been seen in Santa Cruz County since.

Steve Carney can't remember just how or why he was brought into the loop of this part of the homicide probe—but when he learned about Adam Jones, his mind flashed. Holy shit, he knew this guy!

In November 2018, Carney had received a random call on his work phone, and the voice on the other end was like a stoned foghorn. The guy had a tip. He said he was working for a man who owned property in the Santa Cruz Mountains and was growing a big crop of illegal weed.

Carney got phone calls like this all the time. Mostly he just let the person talk, then gently tried to extract the pertinent information. *What's your name? How do you know what you say you know? How much weed?* And, most important: *Where?* Carney needed an address.

The guy said his name was Adam Jones.

He wouldn't give Carney the name of the owner of the property, or its location, though. Just said he was "somewhere in the mountains. I'm not gonna tell you where." Jones had a question for Carney, too: If he ratted out the landlord, "what kind of trouble would that get somebody in?"

This was the first of at least two phone conversations between Jones and Carney. They began to bargain. If Carney could do something for Jones, maybe that would make it easier for him to help Carney. Carney could talk to the Colorado prosecutor, say, and try to resolve Jones's outstanding warrant. . . . But Jones still wouldn't disclose the precise location of the property other than to say it was in the area of the Summit. . . . So Carney sent the Santa Cruz County aircraft to surveil the area, to see if his team could spot the black market pot farm from above, but they couldn't find anything; the area was just too huge and the info not specific enough.

In the end, Adam Jones "fell off the radar," and Carney moved on. He had plenty of other stuff to take care of, and he didn't hear or even think about the name Adam Jones until the murder of Tushar Atre, almost a year later.

37. Venture Capital

Buckeye RV, "America's RV dealer," the largest retailer of motor homes and travel trailers by volume in the Ohio River Valley, occupied twenty-five acres of pavement off Interstate 71 between Cincinnati and Columbus. Fleets of six-figure Forest Rivers, armadas of forty-five-foot East to Wests, squadrons of two-bed, two-bath Keystones were arrayed on the lot nearly to the horizon like some tremendous gathering of aerophobic retirees. During the atmospherically volatile months of late spring and early summer, funnel clouds sometimes threatened the vastnesses of Buckeye RV, America's RV dealer, sending its owner and chief executive, Jeff Walker Sr., into a fit of pique involving insurance adjusters and insurance claims and deductibles and force majeure. He was a portly man who wore his sandy hair in a near mullet. He spoke in a football coach's twang. He was the kind of guy who didn't have a mustache but later after meeting him you could swear that he did.

Jeff Walker Sr. kept an enviable wine cellar. He and Mrs. Walker wintered down on the Gulf of Mexico amid the golf retreats of Collier County, Florida. The Walkers were proud alumni of Miami University of Ohio, sometimes called the Harvard of Ohio but more often the Mother of Fraternities since so many were first organized there. The Walkers' sons and a nephew, John Gilbert Heekin III, aka Jack, had also attended Miami University, in the 2000s and 2010s. The leafy college town of Oxford,

Ohio, boasted a robust and all-encompassing Greek party scene. As on countless other American college campuses, the frat culture of Miami was populated by boys of a certain hard-partying, bong-hitting, business-majoring variety. The amount of cannabis consumed by Miami's frat row, in other words, made Oxford, Ohio, a major Midwestern pot market. After graduation, in 2015, Heekin launched a weed venture capital fund. "With a long-time passion in the Cannabis industry, Heekin believes the medicinal uses of both Hemp and Marijuana are and will continue to experience extraordinary growth," Heekin's LinkedIn page at one point proclaimed. His fund would focus on extraction labs in legalized jurisdictions around the country. To raise capital for the fund, Heekin tapped the Miami University alumni network, including his uncle Jeff Walker Sr., owner of Buckeye RV, America's RV dealer.

They called the fund OWC Ventures, which stood for OpenRoads Wealth Capital. Walker Sr. was one of the lead investors and agreed to lend his entrepreneurial experience to the fund, taking a managerial position as OWC's copresident alongside Heekin. A corner of the vast Buckeye RV campus became the headquarters of OWC. With views through the plateglass windows of luxury coaches and destination trailers, Heekin got to work scouring the country for weed start-ups when one of his college pals came to him with a tip. The pal's uncle was involved in a young cannabis company in Santa Cruz, California. California: golden land of cannabis legend, of cannabis opportunity and scale. Heekin got in touch with the uncle.

Brian Kelly was his name. A Cincinnati native, he was the type of Silicon Valley executive that start-ups recruited when they needed to raise money—a hired gun for the big game hunting of multimillion-dollar venture capital investment. Kelly met Tushar Atre when AtreNet had built a website for the software start-up Kelly was running at the time, ten-plus years ago. Then Kelly went through a divorce and sank into a funk, and

Tushar invited him down to Santa Cruz for weekends and basically forced him to learn to surf, and Kelly, then in his forties, did learn—*It's never too late!* Tushar always said—and the two became close friends.

In the spring of 2018, Tushar invited Kelly into his cannabis start-up. He'd finally gotten this thing to the stage where he needed outside funding. Tushar described the opportunity: wide profit margins, an exploding market, the end of prohibition, the dawn of a new industry. The chance to come in and dominate a market heretofore controlled by stoners and former drug dealers.

WHEN THE OTHER BRIAN—Brian Kenny—heard from Tushar that one of his Silicon Valley pals with a similar name was coming aboard, he was all for it, despite the confusion that would surely result. And indeed pretty much everyone mixed them up all the time so that the pair came to be known collectively as the Brians, or the BKs.

The first task Brian Kelly took on was the wholesale revision of the business proposal that Tushar and others had earlier put together. Kelly knew the winning recipe. The story they were telling needed to be tighter, more compelling, the financial projections more detailed. With Tushar, he created a new pitch deck. Into the revised financial projections, they baked assumptions that were based in some large part on the big extraction deals they felt Nick Montoya could score for Interstitial. Montoya knew Victor Suarez, the force of nature behind a popular vape brand called Loud and Clear, and another guy, a highly liquid mover and shaker out of Modesto. Montoya knew the Hmong people, major weed growers looking to enter the legal-weed business. He bragged about being able to move hundreds of barrels of hash oil at a time through his network of connections.

As they were putting together the new proposal, Tushar invited Montoya to stay in one of the apartment units at the Thirty-Eighth Avenue house. Montoya told Brian Kenny that his intention was to conduct a little due diligence on Tushar Atre.

Tushar, for his part, was still unsure about Montoya. Tushar was somewhat repulsed by Montoya's injuries and his sloth-like way, even if his scars and his slowness were the result of a near-fatal accident. Tushar also sort of disliked that this guy had even been in an accident—didn't that indicate a lack of prudence, of competence? So the due diligence was mutual.

In the pitch deck created by Kelly for the initial presentation to OWC's Heekin and Walker, the start-up was called Fern Labs. On the page with the headline "Cannabis Experts + Silicon Valley Executives," the executive team consisted of four people: Tushar Atre, GM and chairman; Brian Kenny, head of manufacturing ops; Brian Kelly, CEO; and Nick Montoya, head of distribution ops. Fern Labs had ambitious goals. According to the financial projections in the pitch, the company's revenue in its first twelve months of operation would reach ninety-eight million dollars. Its profit? Fifty-four million.

Brian Kelly presented all this information in felicitous MBA language while clicking through a concise slideshow on a videoconference call in December 2018. Heekin and Walker listened from their office on the Buckeye RV lot. They were intrigued.

IT WAS AROUND THIS TIME that Brian Kenny first started seeing what he would later call "the red flags." Things about Tushar that made him uneasy. When he tries to remember the very earliest red flag, he first recalls a seemingly trivial incident. He and Tushar showed up at a popular Santa Cruz restaurant one night without a reservation. Tushar said to Brian, *Watch this.* He strode up to the hostess and insisted that she bring out a new table and set it up for them in a corner of the dining room near the kitchen. He would not let it go—he appeared to be getting a rush out of making the hostess uncomfortable—until finally Brian took Tushar by the elbow and got him out of there. Brian was embarrassed to be seen with a guy who acted like this. Red flag.

Another time, Tushar, in a rare confessional mode, told him that when he first started AtreNet, he had to create almost an alter ego. Had to force himself to be a dynamic charmer to his clients on the one hand and an exacting boss to his employees on the other. None of it came naturally to him. But he got better at it and better at it until he eventually became the alter ego, got trapped inside it, and the line between who he really was and who he pretended to be had dissolved completely. Red flag?

A week before Christmas, Tushar and the two Brians got on a conference call with Heekin and Walker. Turning on the charm, activating his prodigious skills as a salesman, Tushar took pains to describe the Fern Labs team, including Nick Montoya, as a family. He showed OWC blueprints for the Fern Street interior, for the design of the lab, and made bold predictions: The Fern extraction facility would begin operation in March 2019, reach full capacity by June, and be ready for expansion by October. Brian Kenny recalls being made queasy by these aggressive predictions. Red flag.

Nick Montoya did not participate in that conference call. By then, his trial period living at the Thirty-Eighth Avenue house had expired. According to what Brian Kenny remembers, it only lasted a week, each party coming out of the experience disliking the other. Tushar told Brian Kenny he was no longer interested in having Montoya on the team. They'd have to tell OWC that he was no longer with the start-up—no big deal. Montoya, for his part, told Brian Kenny that he had a bad feeling about Tushar. He summed it up in two words: "psychopathic tendencies." Montoya had overheard Tushar berating people who worked for him. *Tushar's no good, man*, he said. *A loose cannon*. Montoya wanted to steer clear of the guy, and he counseled Brian to do the same.

Red flag.

38. A Proposal

Rachael refused to spend Thanksgiving with him. Or Christmas. She went back to Vermont for both holidays, and even when she returned to Santa Cruz she refused to see him. She camped at the Summit; she couch surfed with friends. Once or twice she stayed at a hotel in Santa Cruz—rooms that Tushar, despite all of this, gladly paid for. Their relationship was strange, had always been strange. She justified letting him pay for the hotel by telling herself—and him—that all her money was gone because of him. His abandonment of her during the Adam Jones crisis had broken her spirit.

While in Vermont she hatched an idea. Massachusetts, too, had recently legalized recreational weed. Her brother was thinking about opening a dispensary in the town where he lived. What if she left Santa Cruz, moved back East, and launched her own licensed cannabis-cultivation company in Massachusetts? On her own, free from Tushar.

To the outside world it looked as though they'd broken up, but even Rachael couldn't say for sure. Part of her wanted to leave him for good, but she wasn't ready to do it. What was holding her back? Love? Yes, she told herself, she loved this man, this asshole, her feelings complexly mixed up with her mom's last months on Earth, in Tushar's house, Tushar caring for her, all of it encapsulated in that photo of them at the shrine at the

Medicine Buddha. . . . And she also still felt an urge to protect him. From himself. From the world.

Tushar, for his part, wouldn't let her go. He wrote her love poems. He sent her gifts. He apologized and apologized again. He was changing, he assured her. The Adam Jones incident, he said, had shocked him into realizing that he needed to change once and for all. And so he would. He would prove it to her. As if to begin the process, he publicly announced it. He wrote an email to a friend, with a copy to Rachael: "I'm committed to a sea change with Rachael. She's the most important person to me and I love her so much. I've been terrible in the way I treat her. . . . We're dealing with major issues, and we are not in the clear by any means, but I'm completely committed to the shift."

Two days after Christmas, Tushar called her. She was on her way to Logan airport to catch a flight back to California. He was frantic, injured, in pain. He'd been run over by Adam Jones at the Summit with his own damn truck.

Tushar had an Old Testament sense of justice. In the aftermath of the weed-hostage incident, still angry at Jones for trying to extort him, he came up with a crazy scheme to entrap him and then call the cops to have him arrested. But the trap would take a few days to spring. In the meanwhile, Tushar couldn't resist having Jones do just a little more work for him at the Summit—the guy was there, he was cheap, why not? And then on this very morning, Tushar had gone to the property to check on Jones's work and saw that the guy had been using the property vehicle, Tushar's 1999 Toyota Tacoma, without his permission. In the area near the tepee, Tushar and Jones made eye contact from a short distance, the Toyota parked between them. Immediately, they both took off in a sprint toward the truck, but Jones beat him there, jumped into the cab, and slammed on the gas just as Tushar put his arm through the window, trying to snatch the keys out of the ignition. Jones gunned it, and Tushar slid to the ground, and the rear tire thumped over his thigh, close to his groin.

Jones didn't stop, he fled, and now he was gone. Hit-and-run. Rachael told Tushar to call the police and report the truck stolen and then go to the hospital! And Tushar did as he was told, calling 911, reporting the incident, and soon he was giving a statement to sheriff's deputies from a hospital bed. The Santa Cruz County Sheriff's Office promptly opened an investigation.

Luckily his leg wasn't seriously injured, but Tushar wasn't done with Adam Jones, no way. With Jones still nowhere to be found, Tushar called his cell number, and the fucking guy answered! In a smooth and controlled voice, Tushar said, *Hey, man, let's try this again. Let's get this back on track*. Tushar had some huge redwood logs he wanted milled. There was a planer at the Summit—would Jones tackle that job? Incredibly, Jones agreed! Agreed to meet Tushar at the Summit on the afternoon of January 9, 2019.

When Jones showed up at the appointed hour, Tushar, of course, wasn't there. All part of the plan. And when Jones got in touch with Tushar to see what was going on, Tushar told him sorry, man, he was running a little late, but don't worry, he'd be there in twenty. And then Tushar called the police.

He'd also asked Rachael, who by now was back in Santa Cruz, to go to the property with Habib and, no matter what, to keep Jones there. When Rachael arrived, she didn't speak to Jones—she let Habib do all the talking—and she walked up to the meadow. The hoop houses were just as she'd left them, empty of weed. Only the stumps of cannabis bushes remained.

Back near the tepee, Jones believed he saw Rachael throw him a look, a look of warning. *What the fuck, man*, Jones thought. So he jumped behind the wheel of the Tacoma and pulled out onto Soquel San Jose Road and sped south toward the ocean, and before he got a mile from the property, he saw a big Dodge pickup truck with monster tires, which Jones recognized as part of Tushar's ragtag fleet of work vehicles, heading straight toward him. Waving out of the Dodge's driver's side window was this arm, Tushar's arm, frantically waving and pointing at Jones. With horror, Jones realized that Tushar was signaling to a posse of Ford Interceptors bearing down the highway behind the Dodge—"four cop cars," Jones recalled, or "ten cop cars" or, anyway, a "bunch of cop cars"—Tushar leading the posse like a vigilante honcho. Jones made a hard right onto the next road he came to, flooring it till he reached a big, gated mansion with a sign: "Do not park here." But he parked there, and he got out of the truck, and he walked into the woods with his backpack and his dog. He could hear the Interceptors swarming around the Tacoma, so he kept on trekking and bushwhacking into the woods until he came upon a commune of woodworkers who lived deep in the forest and scraped together four hundred dollars, which he used to buy a bus ticket to Arkansas, where he had kin, and where he has remained ever since that day despite keen interest, for a time, from detectives of the Santa Cruz County Sheriff's Office in discovering his whereabouts, and hearing his story, and learning about that story's intersection with Tushar Atre and his girlfriend Rachael Lynch.

AFTER THE JONES INCIDENT, Rachael and Tushar had patched things up enough that they finally moved in to the house at 3034 Pleasure Point Drive—together. Tushar gave her a present with a note. It read:

dear rachael,
when you are
comfortable,
everything is
easier.
love, tushar.

She had once said in passing how great it would be to have a bathtub overlooking the sea, and now Tushar had one installed in the master suite, right in front of the oceanside windows. He was ready to do anything, he said, to make her happy. "Christmas was a rebirth of sorts," he wrote to her. "A chance to embrace each other and the universal togetherness." Still, Rachael sensed that Tushar was withholding information from her about the Interstitial start-up. She felt she was drifting away from its workings. He hinted cryptically that he was working on something big, very big. Finally, weeks after her return, he told her: He had found an investor, a cannabis venture capital fund out of Ohio, of all places, that was interested in buying a chunk of Interstitial. Negotiations had begun! This could solve all their problems, he said, could change their lives forever.

The clock, though, was ticking down on the deadline for their first balloon payment on the Summit purchase deal. Tushar had persuaded their creditor to let them delay the due date until February 10. If they missed it, they would owe a twenty-thousand-dollar penalty.

By now Rachael was supposed to have the cash from the Oregon fresh-frozen deal with Kyle. He'd finally returned the BMW but now he was ghosting her. And Habib was no help. He'd botched his babysitting job in Oregon, returning to Santa Cruz before the processing was finished. Where the fuck was Kyle? And where was the seven hundred thousand dollars' worth of oil?

One afternoon at the Pleasure Point house, Tushar and Rachael had it out. *This is what happens when you trust weed rats*, Tushar told her. He was reentering panic mode. They were going to lose the property! Rachael pleaded with him. *Why can't you just pay the $250,000? You're the millionaire!* Tushar said it wasn't that simple; he was cash-strapped—he'd bought all these goddamn buildings for the weed business, he'd bought the Pleasure Point house and owed another one million dollars on that to the Santa Cruz County Bank, he was funding the Interstitial start-up, and he couldn't take any more money from AtreNet. . . . *OK*, Rachael said, *then fuck it, let's just sell the Summit property right now. Let's find a buyer!* Tushar for a moment considered the idea, but no, he couldn't do it—the farm was a symbol, a symbol of them, their dreams, their love. Rachael said, *If* *you really loved me, you'd stop yelling at me! You'd give me my fair share of Interstitial.* She was the one who'd given him the whole idea for a cannabis start-up to begin with! They had an agreement, made that day in front of the whiteboard at the Los Gatos house: They were partners. She told him she wanted 2 percent of Interstitial or she was gone. *Put me on the cap table as part of the founders' team or I'm gone*, she said. Tushar told her he couldn't do that—she didn't understand how equity structures worked. He couldn't just make her a stakeholder right now, in the middle of his negotiation with the VC investor! Plus, he would never add someone to the cap table that he couldn't communicate with—and he certainly couldn't communicate with her these days!

As they argued, they moved through the beautiful rooms of the house. From the sunny entry area with its surfboard artwork and acoustic guitars hanging on the walls, through the open kitchen and into the living room with its vaulted ceiling beamed in redwood timbers, and out through the glass doors to the deck overlooking the thundering sea, they argued, Rachael one step ahead as though trying to escape him, Tushar stalking her right behind, saying: It was *she* who'd been stringing *him* along, lying about loving him for her own ulterior motives—

It was clear to her now. He was cutting her out of the Interstitial deal—finally admitting it to her face. Rachael had a sailor's mouth; she'd grown up among boys in the Vermont woods. He was a pussy, she said. He didn't have the fucking balls to tell his Silicon Valley tech bros the truth, that she was his original partner. *You made a deal with me. Fuck you. I'm gone.*

And Tushar said that yes, yes, they did have an agreement! Rachael had agreed to pay the $250,000 balloon payment! It didn't matter that some dirtbag had apparently stolen her product; she was the one who was failing to honor their agreement—and now she was ditching him? *I'll fucking sue you*, he said.

And Rachael laughed. *Sue me?* she said. *For what?* She had nothing left; she was broke.

She walked toward the bedroom to pack her bags, Tushar marching after her, and then he said it. It must have popped into his mind as the thing he knew would cut her the deepest.

You give up on everything, he said. *You fuck up everything. You even fucked up caring for Cynthia at the end. She suffered because of you. You killed her.*

Rachael, standing just inside the bedroom doorway, turned and watched as Tushar approached. Just as he came to the threshold, she slammed the door as hard as she could. His nose exploded. There was blood everywhere. He put his hands to his face. He howled, *You broke my nose!* The shock of the strike, the pain of it, seemed to jolt him out of his rage. He was contrite. *I deserve it. I deserve it*, he said through tears. Rachael was in the living room now, sitting on a couch, and he came to her, got down on the floor, and put his head in her lap. She spoke to him tenderly, stroking his head.

It should have been over, this scene, at that point. But as with many of the smaller stories that constitute this larger story, there was a further turn of the screw. Tushar sprung to his feet. He announced that he was going to do what he should have done a long time ago.

And then he was gone from the house, tearing off down the street in one of his vintage cars. When he returned, more than an hour later, Rachael was lying in bed. He walked into their bedroom, carrying an eggshell blue shopping bag. He got down on one knee. He pulled a small blue box from the bag, which contained an even smaller hinged velvet box, which he opened to reveal a dazzling two-carat diamond ring.

Will you marry me?

It would solve everything, he said. In the eyes of the law, she would instantly own half of his assets, half of the businesses. All that she had been asking for and more. *Let's not wait any longer*, he said. *Let's go down to city hall and make it happen now, tomorrow, whenever you want. . . .*

But already she was shaking her head.

No, Tushar was her answer. *Not like this.*

She wanted a fairy-tale proposal. Romance and whimsy and joy. Not something he'd literally dashed off to do. He wasn't doing this because he cared about her feelings, she said. What he cared about was winning, winning what he wanted, which, at that moment, was her.

Tushar groaned.

But it also wasn't a rejection! she added quickly. She wasn't saying no to him forever. Just not now, not like this.

She would later come to regret this decision.

39. The Investor

October 2019

Jack Heekin arrived in Santa Cruz from Cincinnati to deal with the fallout from the murder of the CEO of the company he'd sunk millions of dollars into six months earlier. It must have been a nerve-racking moment for the young pot venture capitalist. He tried to gain access to 211 Fern Street to have a look around. He spoke with the compliance manager, Atre's final hire, and then rehired her to help manage the business that, now, wasn't a business at all but a crime scene. The relationship between OWC and Atre's family and his loyal friend group, who were administering the victim's estate, had quickly deteriorated. Heekin and his partner, Jeff Walker Sr., had denied the estate's representatives access to the lab. Heekin had sent a letter to the estate alleging that Atre had secretly engaged in the sale of black market product without OWC's knowledge. The estate's representatives had reacted to that with hostility, ordering Heekin to cease and desist from making these "defamatory remarks."

Detective Miyoshi interviewed Heekin. At this point Miyoshi was trying to better understand the Cruz Science/Interstitial company's business—what Tushar Atre had been up to, what the financial stakes were, who had whose money and why. During the interview, Heekin reported that he'd discovered something alarming. He had access to certain "transaction logs" regarding Atre's use of capital. Anytime Atre wanted to spend more than twenty-five thousand dollars, he was required to consult with OWC about the expenditure. But, for no discernible purpose, Heekin said, Tushar had withdrawn a quarter of a million dollars from the company's account. And the money was nowhere to be found.

40. A Deal

By late February 2019, Brian Kenny was commuting a few times a week from his house in Richmond to Fern Street in Santa Cruz, a three-hour drive because traffic sucked. One day, he arrived to find Tushar's nose grotesquely swollen. Tushar explained matter-of-factly that he and Rachael had had a fight the night before. *TMI, dude*, Brian thought. *Just say you ran into a door.* Tushar must have done or said something nasty to provoke that kind of reaction. Anyway: red flag.

In the months of January and February 2019, Tushar and the Brians were in the middle of protracted negotiations with the weed venture capitalists of southwest Ohio. Tushar and his team had initially asked for an investment of five million dollars. After trading numbers over the course of a few weeks, OWC eventually countered with $4.25 million for 42.5 percent, a ten-million-dollar valuation for what was, essentially, a prerevenue hashish company. When the parties electronically signed a letter of intent on January 4, Tushar roared with satisfaction. "I'm a lion!" he wrote in an email to Rachael.

Soon after, Walker and Heekin flew to Santa Cruz to visit the lab for the first time. In a conference room inside 211 Fern Street, the manufacturing floor still innocent of actual extraction machines, the group convened over a spread of wine and cheese, pâté and cannabis-infused olive oil: Heekin, Walker, Tushar, the Brians. Of course Tushar charmed them. His choice of a local pinot noir—from the world-renowned Rhys Vineyards—impressed oenophile Walker. Brian Kenny displayed his deep extraction knowledge, wowing the Ohioans. Outside, the weather had turned inclement. One of those atmospheric river storms of the wintertime north Pacific, a Pineapple Express, was lashing the California coast. Later, as the storm raged, the group went to dinner at a high-end Italian restaurant, though Tushar had to leave a little early, something to do with his girlfriend. . . .

What followed this celebratory moment were nearly two months of intense and at times contentious negotiation over the terms of the operating agreement. At one point, Tushar pissed off the OWC guys by demanding more board seats under his control than they'd originally agreed to. Then he added another request on the term sheet. He told OWC that he'd personally made a loan to Interstitial in the amount of $250,000. It was on the company's balance sheet. The loan was meant to cover certain start-up costs, including licensing application fees and the initial construction expenses at Fern Street. He produced a promissory note, signed and dated January 1, 2019. Out of the capital that the Ohioans had agreed to invest in the start-up, Tushar now wanted to repay himself that $250,000.

To say this was atypical was an understatement. Ordinarily, VCs want their capital spent on building the business, not on paying down debt. It was expected—almost mandatory—for founders to invest their own money in their start-ups; VCs wanted to see that founders had skin in the game. Kelly was surprised that OWC agreed to Tushar's request where more seasoned VCs would have refused it or even killed the deal completely. What kind of founder would try to wring cash like that out of his infant business? Even weirder, neither Kenny nor Kelly could remember Tushar loaning $250,000 to Interstitial at all. Red flag.

As the end of February approached without a deal, Tushar grew more agitated, more demanding. When a close childhood friend of Brian Kelly's died unexpectedly, Kelly flew immediately to Cincinnati; he was serving as a pallbearer in the funeral. But negotiations with OWC had reached a critical juncture, and Tushar burned with rage. He needed all hands on deck. This should have been a one-day trip! What was Brian Kelly thinking? Where were his priorities? Tushar had once spoken of a kind of business mantra he'd learned from his mother, Shaku: Whatever task you're trying to accomplish must be the most important thing in the world. Nothing else can matter. No one else can matter. Here was Tushar putting his mother's wisdom into practice.

Finally, on February 22, the agreement was ready for signature, but not before a flurry of phone calls over a handful of small details threatened to postpone the deal's consummation again, and Tushar reentered a state of rage panic. It was as if he needed the OWC money now, today, *this very second*. As if any further delay would make the difference between life or death.

41. Weed and Thieves

He was just now coming down "off the mountain," he said. He'd been on an ayahuasca retreat. That was his excuse. That's why he'd been unable to respond.

Fucking Kyle.

Finally in March 2019—seven months after she'd dropped off the freezers in Oregon—he was returning her calls. Rachael had concluded long ago that Kyle was a thief who'd stolen not only her fresh frozen—all 325.368 kilograms of it—but what amounted to her entire career in weed. She had put her life savings into those Sears freezers. The yield should have been enough to turn her initial three-hundred-thousand-dollar investment in the Summit pot farm into a cool half million, plus equity in a sixty-acre parcel smack in the middle of some of the most expensive real estate on Earth. Now, she had nothing. There was only one thing to do. Confront that fucker face-to-face. She would go to Oregon. She would rescue her net worth—or try to.

She asked Habib to go with her. Though she didn't fully trust him, she was desperate. She needed a wingman, and Tushar was useless; he was staying behind in Santa Cruz. She had this wild tone in her voice, trying to convince Habib to go with her. *We need to leave now*, she said. *Tonight!* The idea of confronting Kyle and his family made Habib nervous. He tried to talk her out of it. *Please just let it go*, he said. But she couldn't let it go.

Habib felt almost guilted into agreeing. He was the one, after all, who'd introduced her to Kyle.

They traveled by train, the Amtrak Coast Starlight, almost seventeen hours overnight from San Jose to Eugene, and now they were idling in a rental outside Kyle's dad's fabrication shop. It was dusk, the Oregon light quickly fading, the dark, wet forest closing in. It was now or never.

On the phone, Kyle, sounding chipper and accommodating, had told Rachael that he and his family had been able to produce five liters or so of hash oil—a fraction of what the yield should have been. But he made it seem as though the rest of her raw biomass was still sitting there in the freezers. She and Habib could just grab that and the jars of oil from the shop and haul them away. Too good to be true? Habib certainly thought so. But Rachael said fuck it. She had nothing left to lose.

Habib, who knew Kyle's family fairly well, had called ahead to say they were coming. Now a dude emerged from the main building and strode toward the gate. This, Rachael believed, was Kyle's brother. He and Habib slapped hands and bro hugged, and everything was cool until the brother told them Kyle wasn't around. Neither was their dad. And then he said, still friendly, still smiling, that she and Habib couldn't come in. Rachael pressed him: *I want my weed. Where's my weed?* But the brother wouldn't relent, and his smile evaporated. *You guys need to go.* Habib nervously directed Rachael back to the car, and the brother walked back to the shop, but Rachael refused to drive away. *I'm not going anywhere till I get my fucking weed*, she said. So they idled there for five minutes, ten, Habib growing more agitated, freaking out now, shaking his head, whispering, *Rachael, I do not think we should be doing this. We are pissing them off, I can tell. We are really pissing them off.* More minutes passed, Rachael refusing to budge. Then a big, burly dude emerged from the shop—not Kyle's brother, someone else—and walked up to the driveway with urgency in his gait and got into one of the many trucks parked on the grounds of the compound. Rachael hit the gas and sped away, but when she glanced in the rearview mirror she saw the truck behind her, accelerating, zooming right up on her ass, inches from the tailgate, high beams blinking on and off, the guy swerving maniacally across the yellow line and into the oncoming lane, trying to overtake her. . . .

What Rachael didn't know was that Kyle's father had a rap sheet that included multiple arrests, including for the operation of not a hash lab but a meth lab. With this knowledge, she may have acted differently. As it was, without this knowledge, she thought, *I'm not going to let this asshole ram my rental car! Let's just see what he has to say*. And so at the nearest carve out, she pulled over, and the truck followed, stopping right behind. Rachael and Habib twisted around in their seats to watch the burly guy get out of his truck, start walking toward them, and reach behind his back to his belt, and when he brought that hand around again he was clutching something, and Habib was yelling now, breathless, hyperventilating almost—*Gun! Gun!*—and she mashed down hard on the accelerator, tires spinning. In her rearview she saw the guy scrambling back toward his truck, but she was roaring down the highway now, and then she yanked the wheel and turned onto an intersecting road, fishtailing almost, and the guy never caught up. They'd escaped.

On the way back to Santa Cruz—they drove instead of taking the train—Rachael cried. It was obvious to her that Kyle had fucked her over from the start. Habib again tried to tell her it was over. The weed was gone. Time to move on. It was no consolation, but extractor-cultivator deals went sour like this all the time even in the legal cannabis industry. A licensed grower would sign a contract with a licensed extraction lab, deliver the biomass, and never see a penny, never see the biomass again. Outright theft. The county courts were replete with the resulting litigation.

Back at home, Tushar said, *What are we going to do now?*

What are we *going to do?* Rachael asked. What kind of jerk lets his girlfriend go bang on a strange door six hundred miles away, in the middle of nowhere, alone? She was the one who was fucked, not him. Her net worth had been zeroed out, not his. Rachael was going to send a letter to Kyle's mother, detailing what had happened, a narrative of the theft as well as an appeal to her decency. Get Kyle to return the oil or the frozen weed, even just a fraction of it. Tushar had an idea: They could print, like, fifteen thousand copies of the theft story, make flyers, and drop them from an airplane above Kyle's family's neighborhood, like some Cold War psyop over East Berlin! Let their community know what Kyle and his people had done! Rachael couldn't believe it. *Are you serious?* she said.

Rachael, in any case, wasn't done. Unprompted, Kyle got in touch with her and told her she'd run off too soon last time! He did have her stuff, her oil. Rachael did not believe this. Nonetheless, four days after returning to Santa Cruz, she got on a flight back to Eugene, alone, possessed with the idea of confronting Kyle and those fuckers at the compound, forcing them to tell her what they'd done with her hundreds of thousands of dollars' worth of product. Tushar begged her not to go. It was way too dangerous. But he seemed to understand that he was incapable of convincing her not to—plus he was tied up at the lab. The first extraction machine had arrived, a hydrocarbon closed-loop system, hand built by a welding master turned hash-oil-equipment manufacturer in Washington. (Not Boris Kogon. Never again Boris. This system was made by Boris's rival, a guy named Carl.) So Tushar's mind was not fully locked in. . . . He had so much work to do. But then he had second thoughts. . . . Fuck, he was going to lose her for good! She might get killed! So quickly he booked a flight and rushed to the San Jose airport and got on a plane that took off right after Rachael's. In Eugene, Tushar pleaded with her again. *Please don't go to that freaky compound in the woods. Enough*, he said. *It's over*. They argued all night and into the next day. Then Kyle got in touch again. He told Rachael to go to a certain roadside diner outside Eugene. There was a shed out back, he said. And inside this shed, Kyle had stashed her stuff, her oil. She could pick it up there. *Totally ridiculous*, Tushar said. But they went anyway and walked around the restaurant to this dingy hovel behind it, and they looked at each other and they opened the doors, and there in the shadows were two measly mason jars of a wan yellow fluid.

Back in Santa Cruz, they sent the jars to a prominent local cannabis-testing facility.

The results soon came back. Zero percent THC.

Whatever this was, the lab technician told them, it wasn't cannabis.

42. The Caretaker

November 1, 2019

His name was John Lapine, and he'd been hired by the victim around April 2019 as a handyman and caretaker for the Summit property. He spent a lot of time up there, commuting from the Thirty-Eighth Avenue house in Pleasure Point, owned by the Atre family as an investment rental property, where he lived in a tiny unit on the first floor.

Eager to help, Lapine had phoned the sheriff's office as soon as he'd found out that Atre had likely been kidnapped. According to Lapine, Atre's former girlfriend Rachael Lynch had informed him of the kidnapping. Lapine told dispatch that he wanted to "provide" the SCSO "with some information." That information turned out to be . . . weird. Lapine said that he'd received a text message from Atre's phone at 7:45 on the morning of October 1, at which time Atre was already deceased. The text message itself was blank, but it contained a forwarded file. Lapine tried to open the file, but it wouldn't open. Then he replied to the text—this was all before he heard the terrible news from Ms. Lynch—writing, "Hey man I can't open this." There was no reply. Lapine eventually gave his phone to the sheriff's office, but they couldn't open the file, either.

On November 1, Lapine went to SCSO headquarters and provided a DNA sample and fingerprints for elimination purposes. Many people interviewed by detectives were doing the same around this time. After CSI had finished processing Lapine, Miyoshi asked him if there was anyone else . . . anyone else he could think of at all . . . who worked at the Summit property when Lapine was there? Someone who'd spent enough time up there to know their way around?

Lapine replied yes—two guys, actually. They were only around for a couple of weeks. Brothers or something, who had come up from Southern California. Lapine thought they might have been "army guys." They'd started working at the lab on Fern Street but then spent most of their time laboring outside with Lapine at the Summit.

43. Betrayal

One day in March 2019, Brian Kenny checked the balance on one of his bank accounts online, expecting to see around $180,000—what remained of the working capital invested by the mysterious Chinese rich kid living in Singapore, who was investing his father's fortune in an array of Western ventures, including cannabis ventures, including Brian Kenny's centrifuge contraption venture—and instead saw a balance of zero.

All the blood in his body seemed to drain to his feet. He clicked frantically on various links. What had happened soon became obvious. Only one other person had access to the account: his partner in the centrifuge enterprise, Nick Montoya. He felt sick. He called him, and, miraculously, Montoya answered. Yes, Montoya said. He had taken the money. Why the fuck would he take the money? *I just needed the money* is all Montoya would say. He assured Brian that he would pay it all back soon, that Brian and the Singapore investor would be made whole.

Brian thought about calling the police. He was on the verge of dialing the number for the SFPD fraud unit but then stopped himself.

He wanted to give Montoya the chance to pay the money back. That was part of it, at least. But the other part, the deeper part, was that Brian Kenny was afraid of Nick Montoya.

•

MONTOYA'S BETRAYAL WAS DEVASTATING. It ruined the centrifuge enterprise. So Brian had little choice but to pour all his energy and aspiration into his other partnership, Interstitial. Things there were starting to look up. With the infusion of cash from OWC, Brian was working hard on building the lab of his dreams at 211 Fern Street. He spent about eighty thousand dollars of Interstitial's fresh capital on a closed-loop extraction system made by a company called Iron Fist. The Iron Fist system had four five-foot-tall stainless steel columns, gleaming cylinders connected by pipes with beautiful welded joints.

Brian also began to assemble an A-team of staffers who would assist him in operating the lab. He sought talent from the hard sciences. He brought in a brilliant young chemist who'd studied at Washington University in St. Louis, who'd conducted research at the renowned medical school there, and had experience in the isolation of novel cannabinoids. The chemist, in turn, recruited a friend who had a PhD in organic chemistry, and another acquaintance, a nuclear engineer, Neil Ide, who'd worked on reactors on submarines in the US Navy. The area inside the Fern Street building was tight—thirty-six hundred square feet. When it was finished it would be Tetris'd with equipment, every square centimeter efficiently used, nothing extraneous. Even before Ide came aboard, they took to calling it "the submarine."

Tushar had kept Brian Kenny somewhat in the dark during the last leg of the negotiations with OWC. Brian didn't really have much of a window into the final draft of the operating agreement, which Tushar had called "a work of art." He had promised the Brians sweat equity in Interstitial: 10 percent each. Then came the day, in March, when Tushar announced without warning that Brian Kelly was no longer CEO, that he and the company were parting ways. *Brian Kelly won't be going on this journey with us*, Tushar said. Kenny assumed the separation had to do Tushar's notion that Kelly was insufficiently dedicated to the project. But it seemed like a crazy decision, and it basically put everyone on notice: The guy who'd just raised $4.25 million for Tushar had been summarily jettisoned.

Not long after, Tushar asked Kenny, *What would you think about taking on distribution?* Kenny was an extraction expert, an innovator, not a salesman. This was not what he signed up for, making cold calls on behalf of Tushar Atre. Here was the ultimate red flag. He knew this meant that Tushar's promise of 10 percent equity was a fiction. Ever since the ink had dried on the OWC deal, Kenny had been tactfully inquiring about the paperwork that would make him a stakeholder in the start-up. Tushar always had some excuse or ignored the question completely. *Fuck all of this*, Kenny thought to himself. *Cash me out. I'm done.*

Betrayed by Nick Montoya, betrayed by Tushar Atre. It wouldn't be long before Brian Kenny abandoned the cannabis business completely, his dream in ruins. Like his father, he had failed in weed. Other than what Tushar paid him, he never made a cent from cannabis. "I just tapped out and asked for mercy," he would say later, and he went back to writing code from his apartment in the Sunset District.

44. Cannabis Karma

Rachael told him she was leaving. She'd been thinking about it since December. She was moving to Massachusetts. Tushar had abandoned her too many times, she said. In Santa Cruz, she was "stuck." Tushar kept promising to make her a partner in Interstitial—not with straightforward equity on the cap table, but through a convoluted scheme involving a shell company. He kept promising to put her name on the title of the Summit property. But he had yet to do either of those things. She was broke. She was dependent on him financially. If he felt that she was an impediment—a black market impediment—to his success in legal cannabis, then she would launch a legal start-up of her own, would get Benevolence Bound back on track after its derailment in Santa Cruz. All her people were in New England. Her brother was moving forward on his plans for a Boston-area dispensary. She would brand her cannabis start-up with Cynthia's art. Brother and sister could vertically integrate. She told Tushar that she'd made up her mind: She would spend the summer in Massachusetts studying the situation on the ground. Nothing he could say would stop her.

And yet she couldn't bring herself to actually break up with him. *It's just for the summer*, she said. And if Tushar came around, and made her an Interstitial partner, her Massachusetts cannabis start-up could one day merge with his California one! But he was distraught. He didn't believe her. She was dumping him! This was infuriating. She was infuriating. The way he saw it, she was running away from problems that she had created. He alternated between anger and remorse and a third register, self-pity. *I am under tremendous pressure at the lab*, he said. The people there were dragging him down. He was losing his sanity. It was too much to handle. He was just stumbling around, couldn't she see that?

He told her, *I need you now more than ever!*

As the day of her departure drew closer, he was begging her not to leave. He brought up Cynthia on her deathbed. Remember? They'd just returned from Paris and were standing vigil in the South Pomfret house when Cynthia called Tushar into her bedroom? Yes, she remembered. Tushar hadn't told Rachael the full story of what Cynthia had said to him: *Promise you'll take care of my daughter. Promise to keep her safe*. And Tushar had agreed. And now, Tushar said, his voice husky with emotion, Rachael could not leave Santa Cruz because he would be breaking his promise to Cynthia! Now Rachael was crying, too, but also wondering why he hadn't told her this before. In the end, she persisted with her plan, and Tushar finally said he was OK with it. Because even if she did leave, he would still keep his promise to Cynthia.

By mid-April, Rachael was just about packed and ready to go. She was taking Hashtag and her cat, Juno, with her. This also saddened Tushar, who had grown attached to Rachael's pets. They were like a little family. She had left a few things at the Thirty-Eighth Avenue house, and when she went back to retrieve them, she saw the guy with the burn scars again. . . . What was his name? Nick? Nick Montoya? She didn't think much of it. Interstitial lab workers and team members and Tushar's personal assistants were constantly coming and going, hired and fired or quitting, fed up by Tushar's treatment of them. Similar to how she was fed up with him, but also different. And she would warn him, had explained to him about the karma of cannabis. The way you treated the plant and its people would decide your fate. Just recently she'd gotten angry with him and said, *Too bad you'll learn too late that cannabis comes with karma, and that you're not paying your dues. . . .* But apparently the guy with the scars was working with Tushar again, so maybe Tushar was treating him right? Maybe it was a sign that Tushar was in fact changing.

On the morning she left, she fought back tears as they embraced outside the Pleasure Point house. *It's just for the summer*, she told him again. She was going to spend time with her family, file for a cannabis-cultivation license, get unstuck. She drove away, and in the rearview mirror saw Tushar in the driveway, dejected, heading back to the house.

45. The Memorial

November 16, 2019

They gathered at dawn at Land of the Medicine Buddha. Family and closest friends: Atre's mother and father; his sister and her husband and children; the core people from his loyal friend group. A few sheriff's deputies stalked the periphery. The family had requested an SCSO presence. Rachael Lynch. She arrived late and in a rush, having only just learned that the event was taking place. Heads turned and eyebrows lifted as she approached. She wore a dress, the one Atre had bought for her in Paris two years before—a long-sleeve knit number, white at the shoulders, black the rest of the way, that hugged her figure and ended above the knees. Not exactly funereal. Completing the unorthodox look, she wore sandals and a pair of old wool hiking socks—Atre's old wool hiking socks—pulled up over her calves, an homage to his signature style. His friends at the ceremony loved that part and told her so. *Legendary*, one of them said.

Rachael Lynch was, at this point, still in the good graces of the Atre family, but tensions were mounting. The family and much of the friend group would soon come to believe, if they didn't already believe, that she was involved in the murder, was perhaps even the mastermind of it.

The weather on this morning was gray and misty, the marine-layer fog sending down ragged pieces of itself to glide among the redwoods like phantoms. The friends and family formed a loose circle next to the shrine of Ksitigarbha, the Buddhist protector of the hungry ghosts. Several mourners spoke, remembering the tragically shortened life of Tushar Atre. Rachael Lynch read a poem.

That the memorial was held at the Medicine Buddha would come to disturb her. This was where Atre had taken Lynch's terminally ill mother on that January day not three years before, full of hope that turned out to be empty. And now she was gone, and he was gone, and this place was being invaded by people who didn't have a clue what had gone on here. It was as though this sacrosanct spot had been appropriated by outsiders.

Later in the morning, a ceremonial paddle out took place, more than sixty surfers in wet suits shuttling out to sea on their boards off Capitola Beach—the surf in front of Atre's house was too rough on this day. They formed another circle and sat on their boards and went around the circle, friends sharing memories and shaking their heads in grief and holding back tears and not holding them back. Lynch had borrowed a board and had paddled out, too. Atre's body had been cremated, and one of his friends poured the ashes, or some of them, into Monterey Bay, the water turning milky where the dust entered. Later still, in the evening, an even larger group would gather on the beach around a bonfire. A mural of a sperm whale, the work of a local artist, which had hung at Atre's house, was broken apart and ritually fed into the flames, a kind of funeral pyre. A fine, ghostly rain was still falling, dampening the air, and the people who knew him couldn't help but point out that *tushar* in Hindi meant "mist."

But Atre himself had a somewhat different interpretation of his name, Lynch recalled. In Hindi, Tushar once told her, there were many specific terms for different kinds of mist. His name wasn't the name that referred to the standard vapors of fogs or clouds. His name was the name of the nebulized water that billowed at the bottoms of waterfalls. It was the mist produced by collision, by disruption, by interference. He put his thumb over the mouth of a garden hose as it gushed, and a plume of cooling spray occupied the air with its multimillion droplets. *That*, Tushar said, *is tushar*.

46. A New Lease

It was a bad idea, and she told him so. Rachael was staying with one of her sisters in Salem, Massachusetts, as she looked for the best location to buy land for her cannabis farm. She and Tushar had been in daily, sometimes hourly, communication since she'd left Santa Cruz. And one day not long after settling in Salem, he told her about his new plan for the Summit.

Horrible idea, she said.

What he wanted to do was lease the property to "a group" for a short period of time. Tushar described it as a "trim scene." He was vague on the details. This group would come to the Summit and "process cannabis material" there, or sort through and package biomass there, getting it ready for extraction. In return, the group would pay Tushar a nice sum. Rachael understood all of this to mean that the group was a black market group—or a licensed operator unafraid of engaging in black market business, with its wider profit margins. She understood it to mean that the group had a bunch of freshly harvested black market flower, and they needed a secret place to trim the flower and prepare the trimmings for extraction. This biomass, Tushar seemed to be saying, would then be transported down to Fern Street, where he and his crew were just then installing the Iron Fist closed-loop extraction system.

This made no sense to Rachael. It was another example of Tushar's divided mind when it came to the black market. Hating it, excoriating Rachael for participating in it, and then himself participating in it! Tushar said he would run his trim scene in a sane way, unlike Rachael. There would be no naked hippies running around, communing with nature. It was a way to recover at least a little money from the property they'd both sunk so much into. She pushed back. She was afraid he'd treat the group's workers like shit. And black market trimmers, when they felt they weren't being treated right, figured out ways to make things right. *You'd better buy them pizza*, she warned him. *You'd better make them happy!*

Around this time, in April 2019, Tushar told Rachael that he was considering another new partnership, this time with a fellow tech veteran trying to make his way in legalized weed named Latif Horst. Latif had recently obtained a so-called microbusiness license, which allowed for a small cultivation and a small amount of nonvolatile extraction. With this license, Latif could take basic hash oil and distill it into the purer substance whose most lucrative end market was vape cartridges. Latif had a small distillation lab right around the corner from 211 Fern Street, not a hundred yards away, and he'd made something of a name for himself in Santa Cruz. He was a Brit—or he had a British accent, anyway. He'd grown up in England, had gone to school there, though his parents were Americans—were, in fact, from Santa Cruz. The Horst clan was well-known in the Soquel area of the Santa Cruz Mountains, where they'd owned a forested parcel for many decades. Latif had come back to California from the United Kingdom as a rising sales executive working for the tech giant Cisco Systems. But the call of cannabis legalization had been strong, and Latif decided to take the entrepreneurial plunge.

Rachael remembers meeting Latif a few months earlier, at a restaurant in Pleasure Point. She and Tushar were having dinner with Latif and his father, Joshua Horst, an older man whose long gray mane of hair, carefree demeanor, and references to his walnut farm in the foothills of the Sierra Nevada suggested a back-to-the-land hippie of the original generation. Also dining with them that night, counteracting Joshua's good vibes, was a handsome man whose name Rachael couldn't remember. He was in his forties, very tall, like six eight or something, and had ignored her so aggressively that he made her feel both insulted and uneasy. Later, Tushar invited Latif and the tall guy over to the oceanfront house to hang out. And later still, Tushar told Rachael that Latif was trying to convince him to rent the Thirty-Eighth Avenue house to him, the whole building, not as a place to live, but as a business and party property, a place to entertain clients of Latif's successful and award-winning cannabis brand. Latif, by all accounts, was rolling in profit at this point. But Tushar didn't want to let Latif occupy Shaku's house, no way. Latif, Tushar told Rachael, was involved in other kinds of business that Tushar didn't want anything to do with.

And yet here was Tushar talking about a joint venture with Latif and his weed company! The name of the entity that held Latif's California state cannabis license was called HC Ventures. But its d/b/a, the name everyone knew the company by, the name everyone recognized, was different. It bore a very famous name, one of the most famous names in cannabis in the world. The Herer Group.

47. The Gofer

November 2, 2019

John Lapine, the caretaker/jack-of-all-trades who'd worked at the victim's Summit property, told detectives they should talk to someone named Sam Borghese. Detectives already knew Sam Borghese. A recent graduate of the University of California, Santa Cruz, Borghese had been until recently an employee of the victim, described by several other Atre staff members as the victim's "gofer." Atre employed any number of gofers and personal assistants and office managers. Went through them rapidly. This one lady, for example, had quite a long rap sheet: meth possession, breaking and entering, fencing stolen goods. She was definitely a person of interest. But so were a lot of people. A month into the investigation, only a few had been completely ruled out.

Borghese was no longer living in Santa Cruz. He'd moved back to Los Angeles, his hometown, and was now enrolled in the graduate economics program at UCLA. He'd left Santa Cruz about a month before the murder. Detectives had already spoken to him and learned that in the fall of 2018 he'd rented a room at a residential property owned by Atre in Felton, just north of Santa Cruz. When Borghese discovered that his landlord was in the tech industry, he saw a networking opportunity. Atre had hired him as an assistant, had him doing all sorts of odd jobs, including helping procure a thousand marijuana plants for the unlicensed property at the Summit.

At the time of his first interview, Borghese had asked the detectives, *Can I get in trouble for this?* And the detectives had said, *We don't care about the weed.*

Now Miyoshi was calling Borghese again, on Lapine's suggestion, wanting to know more about these two "army guys." Borghese had hired them, two kids from somewhere down South, early twenties, maybe younger. They worked at the lab at Fern Street for a minute, Borghese said, grunt workers who stuffed weed into the machines, and then the boss sent them to work up at the Summit. The two "army guys" helped get the small farm started and then, after only a few weeks on the job, they had a dispute with Atre and quit. Borghese gave Miyoshi their phone numbers and their names: Kaleb Charters and Nick Lindsay.

The detectives asked Borghese, *Who do you think did it?* And Borghese replied, *Could be a hundred people.*

48. Jack Herer

Dan Herer can pinpoint the exact moment he learned that this stuff called weed existed. He was ten years old, 1972. He and his brother were visiting their recently divorced father at his apartment in the Sherman Oaks neighborhood of Los Angeles. *Hey, guys, I've got a job for you!* their dad said. *See all these cardboard boxes over here?* They were crowding the living room, each one filled with dozens of copies of the same book, a paperback with their father's name, Jack Herer, on the cover. Jack Herer (pronounced like *terror*) was an unconventional bear of a person, with a thrilling and skillful propensity for foul language. He explained to the boys that a mistake had been made. All published works in the United States are supposed to have a copyright page. But his printer had screwed up and forgotten to include the copyright page! So, to fix the mistake, they were going to take these rubber stamps here, and these wet ink pads, and they were going to *stamp* the copyright information into every copy of the book. There were thousands of them. For hours upon hours the boys were consumed by the repetitive act of stamping all these freaking books, one after the other, like some countercultural sweatshop. The book was called *G.R.A.S.S.: Great Revolutionary American Standard System*, subtitled *The Official Guide for Assessing the Quality of Marijuana on the 1 to 10 Scale*. Later, Dan Herer would come to understand that the book was something like a how-to manual for newbie pot consumers in

1970s America—how to find and buy the best stuff at decent prices without getting cheated (or busted!)—during the time of total prohibition. In that moment, though, Jack Herer did not explain any of this to the boys. They didn't even know what *grass* or *marijuana* meant.

The story of Jack Herer's conversion is well-known. Raised in Buffalo in the 1940s, he patriotically enlisted at age seventeen, serving in the military police. After his stint, he migrated like millions of others to postwar California, where, with his young wife and young children, he pursued an upstanding middle-class life, a conservative Republican who idolized Barry Goldwater and despised the growing counterculture. And yet Jack had beatnik tendencies himself. In L.A. in the 1960s, he worked as a commercial artist who made murals and painted signs for small businesses across the city. He repaired neon in Chinatown. He met a young woman with flowers in her hair. When he smoked weed for the first time with the young hippie woman—the year was 1969—nothing happened. Nor the second time. But then, on the third try, a feeling came over him that was not merely profound. It was as though, like an ant in the rainforest, he'd inhaled a spore that lodged in his brain and seized command of his existence. He got divorced. Obsessed, he researched and wrote *G.R.A.S.S.* He grew increasingly outraged that weed was subject to prohibition at all. He jettisoned sign making and became a full-time cannabis-legalization activist. He joined the first recreational-legalization movement in the United States, which sought to let the citizenry decide whether pot should be unlawful or not—Proposition 19, which failed at the ballot box in 1972. To fund his activism, he launched businesses. For example, he invented secret weed-stash containers—cans of WD-40, shaving cream, or antiperspirant—the ones with false bottoms that revealed secret compartments for weed. He had a whole line of these things! He sold them to head shops across the country and put his sons to work, hand making them in his Sherman Oaks apartment and even at their mother's home, where the boys lived. Their mother knew the only way Jack could make his alimony payments was if he kept selling these goddamn things. Jack would buy the vessels in bulk from a wholesaler—actual cans of actual WD-40, Barbasol, Ultra Ban. He'd contrived a method for creating the reservoir while also maintaining the functionality of the original product. If the pigs showed up, just be like, *Hey, man, this is just my deodorant, man!* Dan and his brother, home from school, would knock out a few dozen units before moving on to their homework. Another of Jack's innovations was a telescoping metal straw for the inhalation of cocaine. No need to snort your pink Bolivian through an unsanitary rolled-up hundred-dollar bill! Use our clean, clever, discreet Johnny's Snowflake straw instead! That was the actual name Jack came up with for his cocaine-paraphernalia brand: Johnny's Snowflake. He ran ads on KROQ, the legendary L.A. radio station—coded, of course, but an obvious dog whistle to the (many, many) cocaine consumers in the greater Los Angeles area circa 1979. Dan and his brother worked for Johnny's Snowflake, and, as they got older, they also managed Jack's renowned head shop in the San Fernando Valley, called High Country. The cops hated that place. Raided it every few months.

Every penny Jack squeezed from these ventures went toward the cannabis legalization movement. He had a stall at Venice Beach where he'd go to register voters and proselytize for legal weed and his yearly effort to get a legalization proposition onto the ballot. Put it to the voters! He helped organized an encampment outside the federal building in West Los Angeles in November 1981, a protest against the nation's cannabis laws and the nascent presidency of the drug warrior Ronald Reagan, who, as it happened, lived around the corner from this federal building. According to legend, Reagan was being driven past the building on his way to a barbershop while on a visit to his hometown when he saw the protest and asked his driver to pull over. Reagan had glimpsed the flags and banners that Jack Herer and his acolytes were waving, the ones with the big marijuana leaves on fields of white, flags that prompted Reagan to ask—again, according to legend—"Why are all these Canadians so upset?"—Reagan evidently having confused the cannabis leaf (never mind the color) with the maple leaf. A day or so later, the LAPD cleared the encampment. A cop poked Jack Herer in the chest. He was under arrest. *On what charge?* Sedition. *Sedition?* Yeah, the cop said, Jack and his deadbeat friends had violated the sedition laws because they were on federal property after dark during a time of war. *But we're not at war*, Jack said. And the cop poked him again and said: *We're at war with you*. Jack refused to pay the five-dollar fine on principle, refused to plead guilty, lost at trial, lost the appeal, and was sentenced to fifteen days in federal prison at Terminal Island, off Long Beach. In his cell, he started to work on a book about the ancient history of cannabis cultivation and the efforts of big government and big business to criminalize and suppress widespread legal access to this magnificent plant and its myriad beneficent molecules. He called the book *The Emperor Wears No Clothes*, which went on to become a seminal text in the pot-legalization and anti-drug-war movements.

Jack Herer collapsed from a heart attack backstage at a cannabis-decriminalization event in Portland, Oregon, in 2009, and died seven months later. By then, Dan was working as a set builder for the Hollywood carpenters' union, Local 44. He had health insurance, a retirement plan, was married, and lived in a nice house in Woodland Hills. Then one night in 2013, he was startled awake in his bed. Crouched over him was his father—his hairy, burly father—who grabbed him by the front of his T-shirt and lifted him from the mattress and shook him. He put his face into his son's face. Through gritted teeth, his father said, *When are you going to* say *something?* Dan could feel the spray of Jack's spittle on his skin. Then Jack shoved him hard in the chest and was gone. Dan looked over at his wife. She was asleep.

If you ask Dan Herer today about the vision he experienced of his father—he will stop you. He will testily correct you. "It was not a vision," he will say. "If I grabbed you by your shirt right now and shook you, would that be a 'vision'? It wasn't a vision. This was definitely him. Not just some dream."

Dan felt he had no choice. He quit his job in Hollywood and became, like his father, a cannabis activist. He started a foundation, the Jack Herer

Foundation, with a mission to educate people on the deep history and power of the plant. And, following Jack's example, he started a business with the idea of using its profits to finance the foundation.

At first he started a hemp company, Herer Hemp Industries, but pretty soon it became obvious to him that the real basis of the business had to be the world-famous Jack Herer cannabis strain. In the nineties, a secretive cannabis breeder in Amsterdam created a new strain by hybridizing the genetics of perhaps the three most famous California cultivars of all time: Northern Lights, Dave Watson's Skunk, and the Haze Brothers' Haze—the last two, of course, developed in Santa Cruz. The breeder worked for Sensi Seeds, the renowned Amsterdam cannabis-seed company, whose founder, Ben Dronkers, an idealistic Dutch hippie and strain hunter, was a friend of Jack Herer. Dronkers named the new strain in honor of his friend. When Jack Herer bud became a global blockbuster, it made Sensi Seeds a lot of money. Dronkers and Jack had made a gentleman's agreement, and Jack received a small percentage of the profit from his namesake cannabis variety. After Jack's death, however, the payments ceased. Dan Herer thought he would start there. He booked a flight to Amsterdam. In the Sensi Seeds offices, Dan met with Dronkers's sons, who now ran the company. Dan was seeking not only back payments but also the formation of a partnership that would launch the Jack Herer cannabis brand in the United States. Dronkers's son Che refused. *Why would we do that?* Che Dronkers told Dan. *We own your father.*

The Dronkers brothers had no interest in entering the US market. Too much of a mess, they said. They would continue to sell their seeds from Amsterdam, but Dan was free to do whatever he wanted with the Jack genetics in the United States.

Back in California, Dan faced an array of challenges, none more vexing than the question of intellectual property in weed. A large number of cannabis producers in the United States were growing and selling the Jack Herer strain, using Jack's name and likeness as if it were all open-source. Because cannabis strains with THC in them were still federally illegal, they were essentially open-source: ineligible for the IP protections afforded by the United States Patent and Trademark Office. Whether the courts could offer any protection was a somewhat different question. In California, Jack Herer flower was being sold in dispensaries all over the state. His father was not the inventor of the strain, of course. So Dan Herer didn't have a problem with individual people buying Jack seeds and growing Jack weed for their own use. What irked him was when large-scale corporate businesses in the legal market sold Jack Herer–branded flower for profit by using his father's unmistakable image—the unruly beard, the wild hair, the hawkish nose, the mischievous gleam in his eyes. He hired a lawyer who started writing letters. When California established a way to trademark cannabis brands in the state, Dan traveled to Sacramento so he could register Jack Herer in person on the first day the state began accepting applications. He was second in line.

Another thing Dan Herer needed was a partner. Despite his legacy, he knew very little about the business of selling weed. Through a friend, he was introduced to a guy from Santa Cruz who did seem to have such knowledge. Dan, who arranged to meet the Santa Cruz guy at a cannabis conference in Oakland, would come to "love and trust him like a brother." Within months they'd formed a partnership, and soon Dan Herer was commuting from the San Fernando Valley to Latif Horst's family compound in the mountains, nestled among the redwoods halfway up the Soquel-San Jose Road.

They agreed that the company's core product should be vape pens. Vapes were relatively easy to make and very popular—plus Latif had experience selling them. Latif had a demanding day job as a sales executive at Cisco Systems, but his side hustle was weed. He had a vape brand, which he'd launched in 2016, called Dr. Delights. He'd also operated, briefly, a local weed-delivery service.

Soon Dan and Latif were staffing up and developing the Jack Herer vape. This was tricky because distillate did not retain the smell and taste of the bud it came from. To create a vape cart that bore the same flavor profile as the original Jack Herer flower, you had to add back into the distillate certain molecular compounds called terpenes that were almost completely removed during the extraction-and-distillation process. To achieve the right Jack aroma and flavor, to ensure that their vape carts mimicked precisely the experience of smoking Jack bud, took much trial and error. This was to say nothing of the complex ways in which terpenes are believed to alter how cannabinoids interact with the brain to produce different psychotropic experiences. Aroma, taste, feeling. It was akin to a perfumer creating a scent, except in three dimensions. They had to experiment with a whole palette of terpenes. Formulation, it was called. They hired an expert whose specialty was just that.

Latif oversaw this part of the business, while Dan, son of the famous activist, was the brand's public face, headlining at cannabis festivals and conferences, always onstage. One of Latif's other main jobs was to supervise the sourcing of the biomass. Latif had a guy for this, too, a local cultivator. From Dan's perspective, they seemed to go way back—or at least they'd been doing business together before Dan ever met Latif. Latif's guy was a grower of magnitude in Santa Cruz. Also literally, physically, *of magnitude*. Dan Herer was a short portly fellow. To look Josh Rich in the eyes, he had to crane his neck and peer into the sky. Josh Rich was six six at least, NBA small-forward tall. In proportion and physiognomy and even in the tone of his voice he resembled the actor Vince Vaughn. People called him Big J. Dan did not know him as Big J—he knew him as Josh—and they got along swimmingly right off the bat. Dan found him smart, determined—spiritual, even. "A complex individual" is how Dan would later describe him.

When the Jack Herer brand finally launched, success seemed preordained. Retailers were eager to stock Jack, especially after their vape-pen formulation—all their hard work had paid off—won first place in the distillate category at the 2018 Emerald Cup. Sales were strong. Cash flowed in torrents through the company. Actual cash. Duffel bags of it. "At the beginning, there was just a ridiculous amount of cash," remembers one Horst associate. "But just because you've got cash flow doesn't mean you've got *good* cash flow. People just take the money and spend it."

In 2018, Latif and Dan rented space in a building in a light-industrial section of Santa Cruz. They'd teamed up with a distiller who had a PhD in chemistry from the University of California, Davis, but they sourced their crude oil from third party labs (one employee recalls the oil being delivered in buckets), so quality control was an ever-present issue. Dan demanded that they keep improving the terpene profile of their vapes, keep inching it closer to the beautiful experience of smoking a joint full of original Jack with its regal triumvirate of California genetic precursors. And so this space in the industrial section of Santa Cruz would be their new distillation lab. They would not do volatile extraction—that license was too difficult and expensive to obtain. Instead, they would just create the distillate that would go into the vape carts. Almost immediately there were problems. The City of Santa Cruz had its own set of requirements for operating a cannabis-manufacturing facility. After prolonged discussion, the city was demanding that extensive renovations be made to the building—including a larger parking lot and improved ADA access. More parking? This wasn't a retail outlet! This was total bollocks! The changes the city required would cost as much as a million dollars, probably more than the whole property was worth. They realized they'd rented the wrong building. Despite the influx of cash, the company's profit margins were frighteningly thin due to the exorbitant state and local taxes and fees. And now, without a local permit to conduct distillation, they would not be able to obtain their permanent California cannabis license.

This was a crisis, but Dan wasn't deterred. He knew he had to keep "taking it on the chin." He knew that "if you're not tough and willing to push through no matter what," the cannabis business wasn't for you. He couldn't help but think, in the conspiratorial vein of his father, that big business was playing some kind of sinister long game. Big Pharma, Big Tobacco, Big Ag, waiting cunningly to move into weed. That's how these fuckers worked, big business in cahoots with government to crush the mom-and-pops, the small legacy growers who'd braved decades of drug warring, risking their liberty and sometimes their lives to produce this spiritual substance. Big business was just biding its time, waiting for the small legacy operators to go bankrupt. Then, when prices collapsed, the corporate vultures would swoop in. Dan Herer would be goddamned if he was going to let that happen. Despite all the headaches and frustrations, he knew one thing: He wouldn't disappoint his father. He would keep fighting no matter what.

Latif had an idea. As always, he knew a guy. A guy with a Type 7 volatile-extraction license in a building just around the around corner from their rented space! He proposed they form a kind of joint venture with the neighbor. Move all the Herer equipment over to this other building and operate under the license of the company that owned the building, Interstitial something. *Fuck it*, Latif told Dan, *we can get rid of the cost of trying to operate a facility ourselves*. Latif crunched the numbers. This would work. The Herer Group agreed to pay Tushar Atre's lab close to the market rate: twenty dollars for every pound of Jack Herer biomass that Cruz Science converted into crude oil, and seventy-five cents for every gram of distillate produced for the Jack Herer vape carts.

When Dan toured 211 Fern Street in the summer of 2019, the facility was still being fine-tuned, but it was impressive. Compact, spotless, just waiting for someone to flip the switch. Walking through the space, he glanced into one of the offices and saw a busy Tushar Atre talking on his cell phone. Dan Herer can't remember if he shook hands with Tushar that day or any day. Can't remember if he ever exchanged words with him. But soon Dan Herer—and by extension Jack Herer—would be partners with Tushar Atre, too.

49. The Brit

November 2019

In the first month of the investigation, Miyoshi and the other detectives tried to interview just about every person in cannabis in Santa Cruz who'd ever done business with Tushar Atre. High on that list of people was Latif Horst, mid- to late-forties, shaved head, gap in his front teeth, British accent.

Miyoshi already knew from other Cruz Science workers that Horst and the victim had been involved in some kind of dispute, that some kind of "incident," as it would later be described in a court hearing, had occurred between them. When Miyoshi got in touch, he was a little hard on Horst, made sure the guy knew he was a suspect.

It turned out Horst had a story to tell. It wasn't an "incident," Horst replied. More like a *contentious discussion*. More like a *negotiation*. What had happened, Horst said, was that Atre had surprised him one afternoon by changing the terms of their agreement: The cut that Cruz Science was taking for its services would be increasing, Atre told Horst, from twenty dollars to thirty-five dollars a pound, a 75 percent hike. Atre had the leverage. If the soon-to-be-unlicensed Herer Group wanted to continue to operate, they'd have to pay Atre what he wanted.

When did this conversation take place? Miyoshi wanted to know.

September thirtieth, Horst said.

September thirtieth?

The "incident" had occurred on the literal eve of Atre's killing.

50. Fiftieth

At first she couldn't believe it. Tushar was going to grow weed at the Summit. He would do it himself. Or, rather, oversee it himself. He would hire a few people to help. And, of course, he had Rachael. He could rely on her deep cannabis-cultivation knowledge, right? It was something he almost had to do. Commune with the karmic cannabis plant that had become the source of his—their!—business. And with the yield from the harvest, they could earn back what Kyle had stolen.

It was July, late in the season to be starting an outdoor crop. To Rachael's mind, his sudden interest in cannabis horticulture was a pretty transparent ploy. He was planting at the Summit in the hope of enticing her to come back home and rejoin him in Santa Cruz as his partner. His partner? Had he put her name on the title of the Summit property yet? she asked. His answer was the same: He was working on it. She had to trust him. *I promise to do everything I can to make it all better*, he said. *The cannabis business is meaningless to me without you.*

He had an idea for how to grow legally, even though they'd never applied for a commercial-cultivation license from the state. His friend Sam LoForti, Santa Cruz County's cannabis licensing manager, had given him the idea. Like a handful of other counties, Santa Cruz had launched a program under which an "established agricultural research institution" could grow "industrial hemp for purposes of research." The application that Tushar would later submit to Santa Cruz County contained impressive language: "We are facilitating the discovery of new hemp technologies through an agricultural research center founded on robust scientific principles." On the cover of a brochure Tushar would later produce, Rachael was identified as "executive director." Tushar even had a catchy name for the scientific entity that would conduct studies at the Summit property: the Monterey Bay Agricultural Research Institute—MBARI.

That growing psychoactive cannabis, which Tushar had every intention of doing, under a "hemp" "research" permit might be fraudulent and perhaps even against the law didn't bother Rachael. Or even really occur to her. What did bother her was that she still wasn't on the fucking title! Which Tushar kept telling her he was actually, legitimately striving to fix.

For Tushar's fiftieth birthday on August 1, 2019, he and Rachael met up in New York City, where they stayed with his parents, who now had an apartment in the West Village. Shaku prepared a big birthday dinner—naan, curries, many different dishes, delicious. Tushar's sister and children joined, and to entertain them he brought out a surprise: a drone! Who knows where he got this thing. But he went to the balcony and turned it on and flew it out into the hot summer-night NYC roofscape . . . swooping it and banking it and buzzing the water towers and the windows of adjacent residential buildings, roaming the thick airspace near the Hudson, helicopters up there, seaplanes, NYPD all around! The kids were thrilled, Tushar's sister was not, and all the while Shaku was shaking her head, going *ay-yai-yai*, the fun, mischievous uncle causing a ruckus again.

Tushar wanted Rachael back in Santa Cruz, but he drove with her to Salem and went with her to look at possible properties—giving her advice in one of his areas of expertise, real estate deals. She had set her sights on the Berkshires in western Massachusetts.

Because he was late starting on a crop, Tushar needed seedlings, clones, so he sourced and bought more than a hundred of them. Arrayed in their black plastic pots under one of the hoop houses at the Summit, they could have been tomato plants. With the help of his farmhands, Tushar put them in the ground, but he soon judged that they weren't enough. He needed more. A lot more. He found a cannabis nursery in Humboldt that was offering late-season bargains and cut a deal for a thousand clones. He put Rachael on video calls from the Summit, and she advised him from afar. *Don't worry about that insect. But that's powdery mildew! Here's how to combat it.* He was confused on the proper way to prune young cannabis plants. She explained how. Cut away all the junk at the bottom of the stalks, "clear up the skirt," "make the legs visible." *Don't overthink it*, she told him. *Guaranteed you're thinking too much.*

Tushar was happy at the Summit, happier there then anywhere except on a surfboard, maybe—working outside, getting dirty, making progress, creating this garden. He texted Bomi Joseph: "I feel so good working up here . . . sweating like a pig happy as a pig in shit." Bomi replied: "That place needs to be a health retreat. A meditative workout area. A lodge," and suggested that the two friends hang out at the property again sometime soon.

Tushar told Rachael that he'd changed, that he was "reborn." Working at the Summit was part of his transformation, but he wondered if Rachael would ever come back. "I'm sad to realize that the damage I caused just might be too much," he wrote. Other days he was optimistic: "Remember when the sky was the limit?" he wrote. "It still is."

Rachael did feel he was changing. He had started using the property in Felton partly as employee housing—the original plan for that building. The tenants invited him over to celebrate his birthday, and he played beer pong with them. This was a breakthrough. In the past Tushar would never have stooped to socialize with the help like this. He even had a pretty good time. He told her he was working with his lawyer and CPA, preparing the documents to make her his business partner. *It's the stupidest thing I ever did in my life*, he said, *letting everything drag on so long.*

Tushar did not mention what happened with the group he'd leased the Summit to, the group that wanted to package weed there, the deal she'd been so against. But presumably they'd finished their work, whatever it was, and that was that.

51. The Pod

November 2019

Armed robbery has always been a risk in the weed business. But in the twelve or so months leading up to the Atre home invasion and killing, a spate of heists had afflicted Santa Cruz and Monterey counties. Licensed companies as well as black market operators were hit. Retail stores, distribution hubs, farms. Crews from Los Angeles or Oakland or both were said to be driving into the hills and pulling off heists. From Steve Carney, Miyoshi and his team of detectives had learned about the passel of Big J biomass sitting in Atre's Fern Street lab. And from Carney, detectives had also learned more details about the armed robbery down in Watsonville: A business partner of Big J's had a large indoor grow in a converted airplane hangar down there, and men in ski masks with guns had evidently broken in one night, making off with a load of product. This partner had recently fallen out acrimoniously with Big J. The two *hated* each other. As with all such disputes in weed, each side thought the other side was defrauding them. Was Big J capable of sending in a heavy crew to take back what he thought he was owed?

It had been a tough year for Big J and his whole organization. In November 2018, a service drop from a utility pole had flashed and sparked, igniting nearby underbrush; too much power was being drawn through the line to its destination: a greenhouse on a property in the hills above Soquel. Big J controlled many pot farms. But this complex of properties in many ways represented his showcase pot farms, primo land situated high on an escarpment, with views that stretched south to the blue continuum of Monterey Bay and the open Pacific. There were soaring redwoods, many outbuildings, and rows of cannabis. CAL FIRE responded, and the blaze was quickly extinguished. But then, of course, Steve Carney responded. Inside the greenhouse were more than seventeen hundred cannabis plants. Each day the property had been drawing 580 kilowatts of electricity, more than ten times what an average residence uses. The site was unlicensed, a black market grow, and the fire sparked Carney's interest in exploring the complicated business affairs of Big J.

Joshua Rich grew up in a spiritual community that his parents had belonged to in Southern California in the 1970s. Calvary Chapel was one of the handful of nondenominational churches that were part of what came to be known as the Jesus freak movement, defined by hippie Christians who lived in communes, hosted rock shows, smoked weed, tripped on psychedelics, and praised the Lord. Everyone had Jesus-length hair, including Lonnie Frisbee, one of Calvary Chapel's leading figures, who'd become a believer after taking acid near Joshua Tree National Park, who thought of himself as a prophet, a Christian guru. He preached on the beach and baptized young hippies by the hundreds in the rolling Pacific surf. Peter Rich, Big J's father, also found Christ in a vision while tripping on acid. In 1978, with a small group of other Calvary acolytes, Big J's father moved the family to the Santa Cruz Mountains and became the pastor of the Calvary Chapel of San Lorenzo Valley.

Initially, Big J rebelled against his parents' hippieness. They didn't believe in property ownership, were anti-capitalist. This did not describe Big J. By the time he graduated from high school—San Lorenzo Valley High, class of 1990—he was working in construction, but at some point he started dealing weed. According to several people who have known Big J for many years, he got his start in the same way that many other young Americans in the weed business in the nineties got their start: by buying weed grown indoors in British Columbia—the legendary so-called beasters weed—and selling it in the United States. In the nineties, California pot was still largely grown outdoors, subject to climate variables and the seasons. In Canada, where the criminal justice system tended to treat the cultivation of cannabis with leniency, a group of advanced cannabis farmers pioneered large-scale indoor cultivation. By growing indoors, you could control the climate and harvest all year long. Beasters were considered of middling grade, but the reliability of the supply twelve months a year made up for the relative lack of quality. Big J was a beasters broker. He and others like him turned Santa Cruz, already a hot spot for drug smuggling and outdoor pot cultivation, into a distribution hub for beasters. When Big J was busted in 2002 at the age of thirty, he was caught with what was likely a portion of a load smuggled from Canada. He made the twenty-five-thousand-dollar bail and pleaded guilty to one of the two charges against him. He served no jail time.

He probably started growing weed commercially around the same time, in the region of Boulder Creek. He staked small indoor grows there and throughout Santa Cruz. He bought the showcase property in Soquel in 2007. By that point, he'd expanded into Mendocino County, in the Emerald Triangle, carving out several farms in the deep wilderness east of Covelo, a place notorious for its general outlawry. He was once chased by cops in helicopters. Then, in September 2008, another aircraft flew low over acreage on which Big J had bankrolled a pot farm, and agents of law enforcement, including the DEA, raided it. Two underlings from Santa Cruz were caught and charged, but they didn't rat out Big J. In Mendocino, Big J was learning to work the political and regulatory levers. Having registered as a patient collective, he obtained, in 2010, a cannabis-cultivation permit from Mendocino County, the first jurisdiction in the nation ever to issue such legal authorizations.

But Big J's headquarters were always in Santa Cruz, in a stately Victorian home. The house had turrets and balconies and multiple garages. It had a green fairway-trim lawn and a white picket fence. It looked like the home of an affluent judge, a retired rear admiral. Here every workday morning Big J would preside over his famous Buddy Breakfasts. That was another of his nicknames—Buddy or Big Buddy—and his group came to be known by some as the Buddy Crew. He would answer the door at eight in the morning in his bathrobe, a mug of coffee in his hand, and embrace each member of the crew as they arrived for his operation's morning meeting. Big J was a hugger, that was "his energy," said one former associate, and "his energy follows him." Then he would dole out cash to cover bills and assign everyone their tasks for the day. Finishing the build-out of an indoor grow here, cutting clones from mother plants there, nutrients needed at this property, a water pump requiring maintenance at that one, finishing a harvest, drying and curing, selling and buying, troubleshooting, problem-solving, a storm of activity each day in Big J's loose confederation in which he essentially financed farms operated by others and oversaw sales and took a percentage of the profit. But Big J wasn't just a delegator. He got his hands dirty, pitched in with the grunt work whenever he could. He didn't need to be doing that. This was peak 215, in the years between 2009 and 2015. Prices for high-quality herb were reaching four thousand dollars a pound wholesale. The number of people working for Big J, in one way or another, directly and indirectly, had, according to estimates from members of the Buddy Crew, surpassed a thousand. Many of the lower-level workers wouldn't even have known they were working on a Big J–backed grow. His business seemed to touch almost everyone in weed in Santa Cruz. "He's the ghost in the machine," said one of his trading partners. "He's the golden Buddha," said a former Buddy Crew member. According to another person who worked with the crew, there were "tales being told" that Big J's operation was booking $250,000 in profit a week, which equates to thirteen million dollars a year. Big J himself has said that a lot of what you hear about him in the community is "folklore" and "totally fabricated." A former top associate of Big J's who worked with him during these peak times said those profit figures sound too high. It's hard to know, the associate said, what the real figures were—impossible, even. Things were not exactly well organized. Still, tidbits in the public record indicate that Big J had achieved a certain scale. In May 2016, Big J paid $1.45 million in cash for two large warehouse structures outside King City, in central Monterey County. He and his entourage arrived at the closing with a box containing all $1.45 mil in ten-thousand-dollar bundles. Around the same time, Big J bought still another property, a greenhouse complex outside Salinas, "in typical Big J style," said the seller in this deal, a rival Santa Cruz weed baron, by which the rival meant that Big J had paid him with cash in a bag.

Cash flow, in other words, was not a Big J problem.

According to many veterans of the weed trade, generating the kind of cash flow that could even approach a profit of a quarter million dollars a week would not be possible if you were selling weed only in California, even during the 215 peak. That much cash could only be generated from the sale of weed out of state or out of the country. That's where the highest prices and biggest profits have always been. Interstate and international commerce in weed on a large scale wasn't just common among California producers. It was—and is—an industry unto itself. How does the weed get out of the state? If you're dealing at the biggest commercial scale, you may have connections at maritime ports so that bales of pot hidden in containers are carried on cargo ships that transit the Panama Canal. You engage trucking companies and freight-brokerage companies that exist solely for the interstate and international trafficking of weed. A West Coast trucking concern that specializes in shipping large devices for a specific high-tech industry also has an illicit side business carrying black market weed in its tractor trailers. An underground freight-brokerage firm based in Utah ships weed around the world. In 2012, one of Big J's top subordinates was arrested after walking into a trap house in Sonoma County with ninety thousand dollars in cash in his backpack, tasked with shopping for certain weed strains on behalf of buyers in New York. Accused of being part of a ring that was allegedly smuggling weed from California to the East Coast, the subordinate gave up nothing. The charges against him were eventually dropped, but the police seized the cash.

Not long before the November 2016 vote on Prop 64, Big J told a colleague that he could retire, walk away; he had enough money for himself, his kids, his kids' kids. But he wouldn't. He was going to go as hard as possible. "God put me here to do this," Big J said.

And Big J did go hard. He leased a building in Soquel that had once belonged to a tech millionaire who'd designed it as his man cave. The floor was black-and-white checkerboard. It had a bar, a DJ booth, a stripper pole. Big J converted the building into his headquarters and his party temple. He threw rave-like soirees there, DJs spinning in the booth, dancers slithering on the pole, and psychotropic substances going down the hatches of the partygoers on the floor. (The Herer Group had its launch party there.) He hung out on Necker Island with Richard Branson. He hobnobbed with local politicians. He came out of the shadows to help influence cannabis policy on both the local and state levels. He participated in the markups of Proposition 64. Legalization had arrived. Now was the time. Carpe diem. Big J bought properties, applied for licenses, formed partnerships, and blew up partnerships. Some say Big J behaved ruthlessly. Others say he was led by the knowledge that "psychotropic plants are highly spiritually charged substances" and "the only hope for humankind." The grow in Watsonville operated by one of his former partners got robbed. But the thieves turned out to be Hells Angels most likely, *not* Big J! As legalization in California took hold, Big J stacked California state cannabis-business licenses—cultivation, distribution. He expanded his empire into New Mexico, opening eight hundred thousand square feet of growing space in Las Cruces, not far from El Paso, from the Mexican border, from Ciudad Juárez. He played a role in forming New Mexico's cannabis regulations. Some say he was moving too fast, going too big. He was raided in April 2019 by a posse of law enforcement led by Steve Carney—who, Big J said, had a vendetta against him. He paid the county's stupid fine—three-quarters of a million—in cash. One of his entities did a small trim deal with a new operator, a Type 7 cannabis-oil manufacturer, called Cruz Science.

Big J has described his approach to business as a "pod mentality." Here's how he explained it: "I swim in the ocean. We swim in the ocean. My team swims in the ocean. And if we're in the ocean, we swim with sharks. But *we're* not sharks. We're whales. Killer whales. We are fucking orcas. . . . I preach this. This is a philosophy: that the pod protects the pod. Our protection is in numbers. We are all equal in the pod, and we're all responsible to each other in the pod. And occasionally we swim with the sharks, and occasionally we eat a shark. We take their livers out. The most badass sharks in the ocean, the great whites, they're on our fucking dinner menu. We eat their livers. Look it up. . . . For the last six or seven years? They've been finding great whites washed up with a little sliver taken out of their back, almost like an incision. They're cut, and their livers are extracted, and they're left to die. Takes them days to die, sometimes." Then he sharpened his metaphor, saying that he organized the cannabis world into these binary pelagic categories out of necessity. "Are you *with* the pod, or are you a shark? That's how we identify things. We have to do that quickly, we have to be able to understand that quickly, because our *life* could be in jeopardy at times in the industry we're in. If you're a shark that is *dressed* as an orca, that's not going to work. . . . You're not part of the pod."

As for what Big J thought of Tushar Atre, Big J didn't really have an answer. He'd never once met, or even laid eyes on, Tushar Atre, he said—had never even heard the name Tushar Atre until the day of the man's tragic murder.

52. Hot Hemp

Sam LoForti was sometimes called Santa Cruz County's cannabis czar, though his official title was somewhat less grandiose: manager of the county cannabis-licensing office. He'd taken over the position in December 2018 after a stint working under his own shingle as a consultant for nascent cannabis start-ups. His niche had been licensing and permitting, helping those start-ups navigate California's regulatory labyrinth following the passage of Prop 64.

Tushar Atre was a client. LoForti had helped Interstitial obtain local use permits and building permits, as well as its state licenses. In that time, Tushar and LoForti had become friends. They'd grab lunch; they'd hang out in the evenings, drinking wine on the deck at the Pleasure Point house, gazing out at the surf breaks. LoForti, too, was an avid surfer, and he knew of Tushar before he'd ever met him. As an undergraduate at UCSC in the mid-2000s, LoForti had a college friend who had a low-level job at AtreNet. The friend described Tushar as intense, demanding, batshit crazy, so when LoForti met Tushar years later, he knew to keep him a little at arm's length.

One night at the Pleasure Point house, Tushar told LoForti he had something he wanted to show him. He went to his computer and brought up a website: Monterey Bay Agricultural Research Institute, MBARI. It had a logo, a woman carrying a sheaf of wheat. It had a mission: "the discovery of new hemp technologies." Tushar was going to register the Summit property as a hemp-research facility. LoForti, Tushar said, had given him the idea! LoForti vaguely recalled a previous conversation about how the 2018 federal farm bill had spurred California to establish a program for hemp research. Each county could, as it saw fit, register research groups that cultivated hemp for scientific purposes. The spirit of the program was to allow universities and other research entities to grow hemp without fear of being raided. Both types of cannabis, drug and nondrug, look exactly the same; hemp produces flowering colas almost indistinguishable from the THC-laden kind. And, of course, hemp contains all kinds of cannabinoids, such as CBD, that have still-not-very-well-understood effects.

Tushar beamed, smiling his infectious smile and flashing his piercing green eyes. It was like he was high, but he wasn't high. *Isn't this fucking awesome? MBARI!*

LoForti looked at the website. *Uh, Tushar? You do know that this acronym has already been taken, right? MBARI, em-bar-ee? Like, the marine biology institute that operates the world-famous aquarium? The Monterey Bay Aquarium Research Institute? You can't steal their acronym, dude!*

Oh, I can totally steal it! Tushar said. LoForti laughed but had the uncomfortable feeling this was not going to end well.

He told Tushar, *You're taking this too far, dude.*

Too Far. LoForti didn't know that that was one of Tushar's nicknames. Did not know that his other nickname, because of his sometimes pitiless cunning, was Two Sharks. Nor did he know what Tushar had going on at the Summit property, though he was well aware that wily black market operators were abusing California's hemp-research programs. Around this time, LoForti and Steve Carney were in the middle of an investigation into an unlicensed grow down in Watsonville, run by a former associate of Big J. Carney's team wound up seizing more than four hundred plants, though the grower was hollering and carrying on and claiming it was hemp. Tests soon revealed that it was not hemp. This was happening all over the state. And there were even more sophisticated versions of the scheme: growers growing actual hemp, and then spraying the plants, coating them, with high-THC distillate. Voilà. Psychoactive hemp, passed off as weed. Suitable, of course, only for the black market. There was even a term for it: hot hemp.

But at the time of this evening at Pleasure Point, LoForti did not suspect that Tushar was growing unlicensed weed under the guise of hemp research. Had he known, he would have been in a pickle. He would have been forced to investigate a friend.

THE CHOPPER SWUNG DOWN LOW over the Summit, rudders thudding. Believing it to be law enforcement, the guys planting the plants looked up, smiled, and waved. Damn near made eye contact with the motherfucker driving that bird. *You got no business here, cops! This shit's hemp!* That's how John Lapine described the encounter to Sam Borghese, anyway. This unlicensed pot farm was protected because it was a registered hemp-research facility!

Borghese had started working for Tushar a few months earlier, quickly becoming something like his new boss's right-hand man, though he often he felt more like a gofer, or a manservant. Borghese, then twenty-three years old, had just graduated from UCSC with a degree in computational mathematics that June. For his final undergraduate year, he'd found and rented a bedroom at this big, somewhat irregularly renovated house in Felton. Tushar Atre, this tech maven, he soon learned, was his landlord. Before long, Borghese was trying to butter up the guy, glean some entrepreneurial secrets from him, until Tushar, impressed with Sam's mathematical acuity, one day asked if he wanted to come work for him, for Interstitial, for the cannabis start-up. Borghese was like, *Are you kidding?* Borghese was curious, though: Why Interstitial? What did that mean? And Tushar explained that it had to do with . . . *sand* . . . and the air molecules that formed the *interstitial areas* between each grain of sand!

Tushar was a surfer and was always on the beach, Borghese nodding as Tushar explained.

Tushar put Borghese in charge of entry-level hiring—he needed low-cost, back-office labor to support the lab, to conduct sales calls, to work on marketing. *We've got to staff up*, Tushar said. But it turned out that nearly every friend Borghese brought in Tushar fired. Not just fired, but humiliated prior to firing.

This bothered Borghese, but he stuck it out. For one thing, it was temporary. He was heading off to UCLA to get a master's in economics in early September. For another, he was being mentored by this business dynamo, learning the entrepreneurial secrets of making money, learning what hard work really looked like. He was routinely putting in ten-, twelve-hour days, making twenty dollars an hour. He did whatever Tushar asked. Create a pitch deck for one of the crazy new weed business ideas Tushar was always coming up with? Sure thing! Help dig holes at the black market pot farm? No problem! Hire some grunt workers to help out? You got it!

In the office at Fern Street one day, Borghese picked up the phone and got to talking with a telemarketer trying to sell solar panels or something—a kid, sounded like—and Borghese starts fucking with him. *Oh man, I wish I could improve my home with solar energy, but I'm* homeless, *bro.* Soon Borghese showed mercy, ending the gag. *I'm bullshitting you, dude*, he said. *I work for a cannabis start-up*. And the kid was immediately interested. Borghese told him his boss needed workers. It would be shit work. Manual labor. Fifteen dollars an hour. But he'd probably end up logging sixty-five hours a week. That's what Borghese was putting in. And the kid said, *Sounds better than what I'm doing now*. And the very next day, the kid and the kid's brother drove up from Los Angeles for an interview, Tushar hosting them for an hour or so at his oceanfront pad, showing them around, showing off the view. They sat around the kitchen table and discussed their work histories, and Tushar's expectations. Soon they were sleeping in one of the bedrooms at the Felton house, which was becoming like a barracks for Tushar's employees.

•

TUSHAR'S NEW EXTRACTOR, the new guy in charge of the lab after Evan Scott and Brian Kenny, was another veteran of the Santa Cruz weed scene. Everyone called him Big Ben. He was covered in tattoos, had a chin-strap beard like a Mennonite, and was really tall, six six in socks. He had growing experience, brokering experience, extraction experience. He'd achieved all the degrees of a Wookiee hash education, though he did not consider himself a Wook. Now he was in charge of revving up this gleaming, state-of-the-art Ferrari of an extraction lab. This should have been a great job. It paid well—ninety grand a year. Except it came with a catch: one big, volatile Tushar Atre–shaped catch. What had he gotten himself into?

In Big Ben's first week on the job, Tushar asked him for help in sourcing clones on the down-low for a crop he wanted to plant at property he owned up at the Summit. Seriously? This guy had an unlicensed grow? Not a good idea. A black market grow op could jeopardize Tushar's rare and expensive Type 7 license. If his pot farm were raided, the state could and probably would revoke his license, destroying the Cruz Science start-up, which Ben knew had received millions in investment money from a VC group. Not to mention it would put Ben out of a job. And Big Ben needed this job. He had small children, and his wife wasn't working. So he told Tushar that he knew a guy, a black market grower in Santa Cruz who sold seedlings, and made the intro. They struck a deal for a hundred plants or so, and Tushar took delivery—and then he proceeded to *not pay* this black market grower! Said he didn't like the "quality" of the clones!

Not smart, Tushar, Big Ben tried to tell him. *Not fucking smart at all.*

•

SAM BORGHESE AND THE TWO KIDS FROM L.A. were driving a rented box truck from Santa Cruz to this remote town in bumfuck Humboldt County where the cell signal vanished, like, forty-five minutes before you even got there. Their destination was a nursery called Plant Humboldt. A legal, licensed nursery, Plant Humboldt was having a late-season sale on these huge marijuana clones, big as saplings, already in flower, forty dollars apiece. Tushar had already gotten the hundred clones through Big Ben, but he wanted more. Way more.

A day earlier, in Santa Cruz, Tushar had laid it all out for them. Prop 64 did not replace Prop 215. It merely sat atop it. Marijuana was still medicine, according to the law. And get this: If you had a medical condition, you could, technically—according to the letter if not spirit of the law—grow as much weed as you wanted for your own personal use, or as much weed as a doctor deemed necessary to treat your condition! The law didn't spell out any kind of limit! Truly! Tushar was not a spirit-of-the-law kind of guy. He had found a website, one of many such websites—they came and they went. Through this website, you could, for just $150, buy a doctor's recommendation for medical cannabis. Borghese and the two guys from L.A. went to the website and logged on to a video call with some sort of medical professional who asked them a series of boilerplate questions. Coached by Tushar, they complained of serious problems sleeping . . . unless they smoked weed, lots of weed. Like they needed an ounce a day—almost twenty-three pounds per year!—in order to sleep. Ever since a precedent-setting legal case many years earlier, it had been understood in the cannabis world that cops in California wouldn't bust people with doctor's recommendations if they grew fewer than one hundred plants. And so the number ninety-nine became this numerological amulet. If you grew max ninety-nine plants you were cool; the law wouldn't touch you. It turned out that this was a myth. But the myth was strong, and, via email, Borghese and the others each received a letter from the medical professional that stated they be allowed to legally grow their own medicine—specifically, ninety-nine marijuana plants each—so they could sleep.

Tushar had found Plant Humboldt, too, perhaps the only nursery in California that would sell to a regular person as many pot plants as a doctor was willing to recommend. He had given Borghese cash, roughly twelve thousand dollars in hundred-dollar bills. On the drive up to Humboldt, someone saw a billboard for a casino and joked that they should take Tushar's cash to the roulette table and put it all on black. At the nursery, a worker sent the bills through their automated money counter—*pfffft*—as other workers loaded 297 specimens of Asphalt, Sour Diesel, Blue Nile, Sour Orange, and Blueberry Muffin—a whole menu of high-THC strains—into the truck. Then they headed back to the highway for the return trip to the Summit. One of the L.A. kids asked what they should say if a cop pulled them over, and they came up with a bunch of crazy stupid answers, and maybe because they were exhausted and their nerves were fried they were cackling with laughter when they noticed the flashing red light behind them. A cop was pulling them over. One of the truck's taillights was out. The cop wanted to know what was in the truck. And one of the kids piped up: *Weed plants, officer*. And they handed over their doctor's notes and the Plant Humboldt receipts. The cop scrutinized them. *In all my time*, he said, *no one has ever handed me the paperwork*. And then the cop let them go.

They'd been on the road ten hours when finally they reached the Summit, unloaded the plants, got back into the truck, turned it around, and, after catching a few winks, immediately headed back to Plant Humboldt. On three successive days they made this trip—August 16, 17, 18—spending more than thirty thousand of Tushar's money, transporting 891 plants, ninety-nine times three times three. On each new day, you could buy another round of your doctor's recommended quantity of clones. That was how Plant Humboldt chose to interpret the law, anyway, since nowhere in the law did it say you couldn't.

After more than thirty hours in the box truck, the three of them got to know one another a little. The two guys, it turned out, were not brothers but brothers-in-law. The older one, Nick Lindsay, was married to the sister of the younger one, Kaleb Charters. They'd both recently joined the army reserves and had just gone through boot camp. Kaleb came from a devout religious family, evangelical Christians, and his parents had served almost twenty years as missionaries. The family had lived in St. Petersburg, Russia, then in a small town in the interior of El Salvador. Nick had grown up mostly in Las Vegas. He'd had a wild childhood, great and then awful: His mother and stepdad were mortgage brokers, were rolling in money—until the day, Nick was still a little boy, just ten years old, when men in jackets that said "FBI" on them broke down the front door and put his mom and stepdad in handcuffs and took them away. They were charged with fraud. The family lost everything, fell into poverty. Nick told of having to shoplift food, sprinting out of the supermarket carrying bunches of bananas, jugs of milk. Eventually his mom and stepdad went to prison, and Nick went to live with relatives.

Holy shit, man, Borghese thought. *Who the hell did we just hire?*

53. The Good Doctor

November 22, 2019

A man calling himself Dr. Bomi Joseph contacted the family of the victim on or about November 22, the Santa Cruz County Sheriff's Office would come to learn. Dr. Joseph wanted to express his condolences. But, begging their indulgence, he also wished to make them an offer.

Dr. Joseph, "close friend" of Tushar Atre, yet another successful and highly educated Silicon Valley entrepreneur in the victim's wide circle of such people, was aware that the Atre family wished to sell the Summit property. And Dr. Joseph was offering to take the land and its liability off their hands. He even offered terms. Half a million now, then another seven hundred thousand dollars paid out over the next eight or nine months. An easy way for Tushar Atre's estate—for which the victim's mother, now seventy-nine years old, was the executor—to unload the property and the debt owed on it. There was one catch, however. Discussions for a possible deal with Dr. Joseph needed to begin posthaste because Dr. Joseph would be "out of the country" for six months, maybe seven months, departing California on January 14, 2020. He was on the board of Doctors Without Borders, he said, and he was scheduled to be in Africa on a mission of humanitarian assistance.

Dr. Joseph was a busy, important man. That November and early December, he ingratiated himself with the Atre family. But then someone associated with the family apparently did some basic due diligence on Dr. Bomi Joseph—an online search. Bomi Joseph, it turned out, was not on the board of Doctors Without Borders; indeed, he appeared not to have any connection to the organization at all. Nor, apparently, was he a licensed physician, MD or DO, nor had he ever been.

He was, therefore, not leaving the country on January 14, 2020. What he, in fact, was doing on that date was surrendering to authorities of the US Bureau of Prisons so he could begin serving a twelve-month sentence. He'd pleaded guilty to a single count: making a false statement in application for a passport, a federal charge on which he'd originally been indicted—by a grand jury in the Northern District of California—on August 2, 2018, the day after he'd attended Tushar's forty-ninth birthday party, the one with the bluegrass band at the Pleasure Point oceanfront house. ("It was a great party!" Bomi Joseph had texted Tushar the next day, the day of his indictment. "Wonderful friends.")

Passport fraud? What? Why?

It seemed that this was a man who'd had many names, many identities: Bomi Joseph, Joseph Bomi, Revi Shastri, Moses Sunith Prasad Joseph, Moses Sunith Prassad Joseph. The reason this man needed a new passport was easy enough to ascertain once you started digging. He was trying to shed the skin of previous "serious crimes." "Joseph is a serial fraudster with little regard for the judicial system or his community," wrote a federal prosecutor in a court document filed as part of the passport case in 2019. In the early 2000s—at the peak of Silicon Valley's dot-com-bubble era—the man who was then known as Moses S. Joseph launched an elaborate scam. For five years he'd posed as a venture capitalist, defrauding "numerous banks, companies and individuals," according to an investigation report, including Wells Fargo and Eastman Kodak. "He routinely submitted false documents, forged signatures, fabricated audits, falsified tax returns, and produced fake marketing materials." According to the FBI, he bilked his victims out of twenty-two million dollars. He took the case to trial and lost. A jury convicted him on twenty-two counts, including grand theft, securities fraud, embezzlement, forgery, and preparing false evidence. Sentenced to more than fifteen years in prison, he wound up serving just four and a half, emerging on probation in 2014, at which point he "began falsely holding himself out as a physician," the prosecutor wrote in the 2019 filing. He also undertook the pursuit of a new and exciting entrepreneurial vision based on the discovery—or, rather, the rediscovery—of an ancient and miraculous strain of hops from the remote Arunachal Pradesh region of India. . . .

After Joseph's history came to light, the Atres promptly cut ties with him. But it didn't end there. Nothing in this story ever just ends there. This man calling himself Dr. Bomi Joseph was persistent, relentless. And litigious. He had sued many people. He had sued a former business partner, sued a former employee. He had filed bar grievances against a former lawyer. Now Joseph was making a claim against the Tushar Atre estate in probate court in a bold attempt to obtain ownership of the Summit property. He claimed to have a document, a promissory note, showing that he'd loaned Atre one million dollars in December 2017 so that Atre could close on the deal to acquire the Summit. Joseph claimed that Atre had not paid down this debt; the property therefore should belong to him.

In June 2020, the Atre family took all this information to the Santa Cruz County Sheriff's Office. A year and a half later, in January 2022, Bomi Joseph was pleading guilty to two counts of forgery with the intent to defraud. The "promissory note" was a fake. He'd also doctored text messages he'd received from Atre before his death as a way to support his fraudulent claims. "What kind of depraved person attempts to steal from the grieving family of a murder victim?" Tushar's sister said in court at Bomi Joseph's sentencing, reading from a statement. "This was taking advantage of someone's loss of life at the hands of others very violently . . . trying to take advantage of a family who could hardly figure out what was up or what was down."

For his crimes against the Atre estate, Joseph found himself behind bars yet again, entering custody in May 2022 to begin serving a three-year sentence in Santa Cruz County Jail. He almost certainly would have been somewhere on the list of persons of interest in the Atre case had Detective Miyoshi and his colleagues not already zeroed in on a far likelier set of suspects.

54. Powder Drugs

She'd almost canceled the trip. Rachael was planning to spend ten days or so in Santa Cruz during the first week of September, helping Tushar with the grow at the Summit and taking care of some other things, like getting a leak fixed on her BMW and updating its registration. She was about to close on a piece of land in Lenox, Massachusetts, in the heart of the Berkshires. She was using a modest inheritance from her mother to cover the down payment. The property would serve as the base of Benevolence Bound, her cannabis start-up that would bring together the things that mattered to her—weed, healing, and Cynthia's artwork. Lenox was an ideal location, equidistant between Vermont, where most of her family lived, and New York City, where Tushar's family was living. Because she was broke, Tushar was paying her an allowance—nothing extravagant, she thought, just covering her monthly credit card bill. But he'd bought her first-class tickets. She decided to go ahead and make the trip.

She felt a jolt of joy seeing him again in their old stomping ground. But in the days that followed, as Tushar took her to visit all the key sites of his burgeoning cannabis empire, it started to gall her a little, seeing him make real all the ideas she had given to him, while she was still reliant on him, and still without her name on the Summit title, without even a fraction of a percentage point of equity in Interstitial Systems, even though he continued to promise that those things were coming. Was he delaying just to keep her trapped, believing she would never dump him until she had a piece of the asset?

They went to the Salinas warehouses where big things were happening. Tushar was working on yet another deal with another licensed cannabis start-up founder, a big muscular guy named Alex Rowland, who was also a Silicon Valley entrepreneur. He and Tushar wanted to create a giant CBD-oil-extraction facility inside the middle warehouse. A construction crew was already busy framing out the interior. They went to Fern Street, of course, and Tushar showed her around the submarine, a series of chambers crammed with chemistry. A second Iron Fist closed-loop system had just been installed. This nice man Neil Ide, an engineer of some kind, was busy erecting, wrench in hand, a colossal steam-engine-looking thing, an extraction machine that used ethanol to extrude oil from plants—much less flammable than butane or propane. Some typical Tushar drama had unfolded, as well: The day before, a Fern Street employee had gone berserk and stolen a laptop, and Tushar had had to make a report to the police! Tushar also said he wanted to fire his current lab manager—yet more turnover at the lab. So Rachael and Tushar did a video call with a young woman from Colorado named Murphy, a live-resin-extraction guru with bottle blond hair and tattoos who was famous on Instagram; Tushar wanted to hire her as a consultant. Tushar had recently had some of the techs at Fern Street put remnants of Rachael's fresh-frozen biomass, which he'd found in the freezers at his house, through the systems at the lab, and wow. The resulting extracts were aromatic and amazing, he said, and would "create delicious benevolence-bound-worthy high terpene cartridges."

Then they drove up to the Summit. They toured the crop rows, and Rachael offered counsel. She felt weird, like a consultant herself. On the other side of the meadow, Tushar took her to a new element he'd had installed: a beautiful deck, like an open-air stage, made of wide, smooth planks, milled on-site from old redwood that had, across eons, lived and died on the property. She and Tushar had always wanted a deck like this, situated in this very spot, a platform for their custom-made yurt. From that spot, on an elevation above the meadow, there were magical, 180-degree views of the surrounding ridges and forests. As they stood there, Rachael felt that old fleeting feeling again, like this was where she belonged, in Santa Cruz with Tushar, when he tossed something in her direction. It was a black T-shirt emblazoned on the front with a logo designed by a friend: a Demeter figure clutching a sheaf of wheat with the words *Monterey Bay Agricultural Research Institute* in a circle around the goddess. Rachael held up the shirt and looked at it. She felt a surge of happiness. The goddess's face was her face.

She was smiling as she pulled the MBARI shirt over her head. *Come back to Santa Cruz and be my partner in everything*, Tushar said, and just at that moment his cell phone rang, and he took the call, and broke the spell. He began pacing around the planks listening to this caller. Whoever it was was yelling at him. She could hear the caller's raised voice from across the deck. Then Tushar was saying something furiously into the phone, trying hard not to explode, his lips pursed, the veins in his temples popping. It was typical Tushar, but more so.

Who was that? she said when he hung up.

He took a breath, composed himself. *Those guys*, he said.

What guys?

The guys he'd leased the Summit to, he told her, the guys who'd operated the trim scene and were packaging the biomass. He hadn't told her this part yet: how the trimming and packaging had ended earlier than planned, after just a few weeks, how he'd come up here one day to check on things and found *those guys* not just packaging weed but . . . *other* types of product! As in *powder drugs*. His meaning was clear. Coke, meth, fentanyl, something like that. Tushar went on: When he saw what these guys were up to, he did what he had to do. He kicked them off the property. *Get the fuck outa here*, he told them. And they did. But that wasn't all. Tushar decided to keep the rent that the group had already paid him! *Because, come on*, he said, *that's a legitimate deal-breaker*.

This was a lot to take in. It was clear to Rachael that Tushar was being threatened. Threatened by a group of coke dealers or meth dealers. Tushar didn't tell her who they were, didn't name names, and she didn't press him to tell her. But she wondered who it could be. Latif Horst and his crew? She never liked that guy, didn't trust him. Or was it some new gang of dangerous people Tushar had taken up with after she left? Panic rose through her body. As they drove back home, she started crying. She felt sick. She remembered the words of the psychic in Marin: *He'd made some group angry. . . . They were coming*. Then, as she was stepping out of the truck in the driveway of Pleasure Point, she saw this weird thing in the bed of the pickup, and it clicked. *Is that why you have* this *in the back of the truck?* she said, pointing at a thick black bat—a truncheon.

Yes, Tushar said, he had it for protection. They were inside the house now. He was visibly disturbed, pacing around again. He said he felt like *those people* might come around and try something, like a robbery. And he hated guns, so *this*, the club, was the next best thing. Rachael was kind of an expert on this sort of lifestyle, so he asked her: *If you were in this situation, if you thought you were going to be robbed, what would you do?*

I'd call the police! she said.

But Tushar shook his head. *The police won't help me*, he said as he walked out of the room.

55. Salinas

The market was crashing. In some ways, this was expected; Tushar had expected it. There would be, at some point, a "macro correction," he'd warned. Legalization would spark overproduction, then a glut, then a crash in prices—ordinary market forces at work. But this was different. This crash was specifically in the markets for hash-oil and distillate. It started in April 2019, when dozens of people fell ill in Illinois after smoking black market vape pens likely made in California. Over the course of ten months, sixty-eight people died and more than twenty-eight hundred were hospitalized. The federal government stepped in. The Centers for Disease Control and Prevention determined that the distillate used in the vapes contained toxic quantities of vitamin E acetate, used by some black market vape makers as a thickening agent, a way to cut the drug. When the deaths hit the news, demand for vape pens plunged, and then distillate and oil prices plunged.

Tushar's decision to underwrite Neil Ide's creation of an ethanol machine for the extraction of monstrous amounts of hash oil now seemed unwise. Brainstorming one day, Tushar and Ide came up with an idea for a pivot. They could use Ide's giant machine to extract CBD oil from hemp. Because regulations didn't allow for CBD production in the same lab as hash-oil production, they would need to relocate it from Fern Street. Tushar had the perfect spot: Salinas.

Tushar had recently met a guy: Alex Rowland, yet another Chad, yet another tech entrepreneur who'd moved into weed. Born in Norway but raised in the United States, Rowland was the size of a Viking, with a gym-built physique and silver swept-back hair. He was in the middle of launching his own licensed Type 7 extraction lab when Tushar proposed they merge their two companies. Why beat each other up competing when they could join forces instead, the ultimate Chads? Silicon Valley was in their veins. Both wanted to *achieve scale.* Both understood that to satisfy the dream of every Silicon Valley founder—the big money exit—they had to attract the right kind of buyer, and both understood that the right kind of buyer wasn't interested in anything less than a company generating a hundred million dollars in revenue a year. *Scale.*

Amid the rumblings of the vape crisis, Tushar intrigued Rowland with a joint venture to produce CBD oil instead of hash oil. They could use this ramshackle tin-roofed warehouse outside Salinas that Tushar owned. They could use this huge ethanol-extraction machine that Tushar had commissioned. It was at Fern Street now, but they could bring it down to Salinas. They shook hands on a deal. Tushar would provide the space, Rowland the cash to build out the empty middle warehouse and transform it into a facility that could wring CBD oil from ten thousand pounds of hemp per day. Rowland personally delivered a cardboard box filled with a hundred thousand dollars in cash to Tushar at his office at Fern Street. Throughout the summer of 2019 they made frequent trips to Salinas to check on the progress of the construction. Rowland noted that Tushar still had a couple of tenants in the warehouse complex, including an auto-body repair shop, called 101 Collision & Restoration, operated by a group of Polynesian Islanders. Tushar said, *Just let them do their thing and stay out of their way*. Rowland didn't give it another thought. In the warehouse, Tushar was very involved with his contractor and his contractor's team, interested in the smallest details, unafraid to offer ideas, dictate changes. Rowland could tell that Tushar was a micromanager, a control freak even, but, at the time, he considered that a good thing. In his experience, micromanagers tended to be successful. They understood how to get things done; they understood how not to get ripped off.

IN A SECRET LOCKED ROOM adjacent to 101 Collision & Restoration, a guy named Tommy Speziale was dropping off vape cartridges. Tommy's boss was not Elijah Esteban, the owner of 101 Collision. Tommy was working for Odie, the owner of Island Pharmz.

Tommy had a special machine, cost him twenty-five thousand dollars. He was a one-man assembly line. The machine injected distillate into these little cartridges. In a long day, Tommy could fill as many as two thousand of them. He himself had formulated the recipe, the unique mixture of terpenes and flavonoids that created the distillate's taste and aroma.

Tommy was another journeyman in the Santa Cruz/Monterey weed scene. Half Italian, half Mexican, and 100 percent Californian, he had grown weed, brokered weed, extracted hash oil from weed. He was once involved in a weed-smuggling operation with a ring of professional surfers. He was a devotee of this mystic plant. In a Santa Cruz rite of passage, he'd been busted by the Santa Cruz County Sheriff's Office for felony marijuana sales in 2011.

Small world: For more than a decade, Tommy had worked closely with Big J's organization, which didn't end well. After that Tommy went to work for Evan Scott's new company, which Scott had christened Consolidated Oil, as if it were a robber baron's nineteenth-century petroleum trust. This was some months after Evan Scott and his crew had rebelled against Tushar Atre, a story that Tommy heard more than once.

And then Tommy had moved on yet again, now working with Danny O'Brien, aka Odie, the Irish Samoan, making vape carts for Island Pharmz. From Evan Scott's point of view, Tommy had poached Odie from Consolidated Oil. Whereas Consolidated Oil had previously sold distillate to Odie, now Tommy was doing the same, but for cheaper. The

Consolidated Oil crew was not pleased. Because of Tommy, they had lost a big client, one with the potential for an even bigger future.

Odie was ambitious. He was trying to bring Island Pharmz into the legal market once and for all, to create a vibrant cannabis brand that would leverage Pacific Islander culture and urban California culture. But there had remained his one big obstacle, the same problem he'd been wrestling with since Prop 64. Odie, of course, had all these priors, which would make it difficult for him to obtain a California state cannabis license. Tommy knew all about Odie's past—the meth trafficking, his Samoan brothers and cousins who'd gone down for similar crimes, the decade-long prison sentences. Odie was not shy about telling these stories; it gave him cred. Along the way Odie met some guys with tech experience, Internet entrepreneurs, who agreed to serve as the business managers of Island Pharmz. Odie and this group had found a spot to manufacture Island Pharmz vape carts in the warehouse district of Los Angeles, just south of downtown. The scion of an L.A. real estate mogul had developed the building into a campus for weed companies, but with a twist. He held all the licenses. For a cut of your company's equity, the scion gave you licensed space in which to operate. Tommy would come to spend a lot of time in L.A., helping Odie and his group design the vape-making and packaging facility. Tommy was in line to join the Island Pharmz C-suite, he believed, with a six-figure salary and a slice of the company's equity, too.

For the time being, however, Tommy made do in Salinas. Odie always paid his bills on time, at least. He seemed flush with cash. But Odie was hard to pin down, always on the move, driving different cars, sometimes even a rental. Odie the broker, buying trim from growers, doing deals with extraction labs, selling some of the oil and distillate to others, and bringing some of the distillate back to Tommy, who would fill Island Pharmz vape carts with it. At one point, as payment in kind for Tommy's services, Odie gave him a late-model Mercedes CLS 550.

Tommy never saw Tushar at the Salinas warehouse. They'd only met once, very briefly, outside the Point Market. As for the Esteban auto shop,

Tommy noticed some repair work to the occasional banged-up vehicle, a few big dudes hanging out watching TV, other dudes coming and going. Tommy just kept his head down. Didn't want to know too much.

Therefore Tommy would not have known that a white BMW X3 SUV, registered to Rachael Lynch, was being repaired by Elijah Esteban at the shop. He would not have known that Tushar had decided, almost a year earlier, to lease the space to Esteban against the advice of Evan Scott, who was back on speaking terms with Tushar. Tommy would not have known that Tushar, in his own words, had "multiple irons in the fire with" Esteban, or that one of Odie and Elijah's brothers, who was busted in 2003 for meth trafficking in the case that also involved possession of the kinds of silencers that don't have serial numbers, had registered an LLC called J.E.T. Merchandise Distribution to the address of Tushar's warehouse.

56. The Felton House

November 2019

The Felton house was kind of a madhouse. The detectives were able to glean this much after interviewing several of its residents. At one point, a military veteran slept in a trailer in the yard. Then a woman moved in along with her horse. There was a retired professional big-wave surfer who was in recovery, and a Santa Cruz glassblower who specialized in bongs, pipes, and dab rigs. Sam Borghese lived in one of the upstairs rooms. The two kids from Southern California, the "army guys," slept downstairs. They'd come home from the Summit every night, after who knew how many hours of manual labor, looking like zombies. They were polite but reserved. They'd retreat to their lower-level quarters and stay there. Until one day in August when they were gone. Just . . . gone.

Nick Lindsay and Kaleb Charters said they needed a break from the relentless fourteen-hour days at the Summit. They were going to a friend's birthday party in L.A. for the weekend. Unfortunately, they fucked up and brought the key to Atre's Toyota Tacoma with them by mistake. When Atre found out, he was irate. He canceled their paychecks—fourteen hundred apiece—which they only discovered when they tried to cash the checks at the bank. *Fucking Tushar.* After the weekend, Nick and Kaleb drove back to the Summit to return the key to Atre. They were contrite. Atre sent them back to work, but they refused to do anything more until they were paid. *No*, Atre said. *You will go back to work for me now, and I will decide how much I'll deduct due to your fuckup with the lost key!*

Fuck this, they thought, and they left.

Atre, however, wouldn't let it go. He needed workers—and those guys were good workers. As detectives would later learn from the download of Atre's iCloud, he sent them a text: "Please come back," he wrote. "I'll pay you then, ok?" He also enlisted Sam Borghese to convince them to return. Borghese called them and said, *Look, if you show regret and that you learned a lesson, Tushar will take you back, and he'll pay you the money he owes you.* Nick and Kaleb returned to Santa Cruz to get their money and met Atre at Fern Street. They apologized, laid it on thick. Atre was receptive, said in fact he'd pay them *three* thousand dollars each, but there was a catch. There was always a catch. *You guys are ex-military, right?* Atre said. *Get down on the floor and give me two hundred push-ups.* What the fuck? Was this guy for real? But money is money, so they dropped and gave him two hundred push-ups. *Great*, Atre said. *Now go with Sam to the Summit. There's a lot of work to be done.* No way. Nick and Kaleb refused. They were headed to Las Vegas to meet up with Kaleb's brother. They were thinking of starting a cannabis-delivery service there. They were going to be entrepreneurs, inspired by Atre. Atre tried one last time to persuade them to stay, but it was no use. He paid them out, three hundred dollars less than what he'd agreed to, and they parted cordially. *Consider it a credit*, Atre said. *You can collect it when you come back here and work for me again.*

57. Strange Trip

The cops wouldn't help Tushar because he'd cried wolf too many times. That was his theory: He'd called them on a kid who'd stolen a laptop from the Fern Street lab not long ago, he'd called 911 and badgered the SCSO about Adam Jones earlier in the year, and then there was the sting operation he'd cooked up, dragging that posse of sheriff's cars up to the Summit.

At least, Rachael told him, he should make notes, create a Google Doc, leave a paper trail. *That's a good idea*, he said. She realized she was angry at him because he seemed to be in danger. Was this an emergency? It felt like an emergency. But maybe not? Whatever the case, she told him: *You need to make good with these people*, with "those guys," whoever *those guys* were. He needed to pay them back, to *over*pay them. The people Tushar kicked off at the Summit that day were probably going to tell their bosses, whoever *they* were! One set of lower people always led to a set of *higher-up* people, and those were the people you *really* didn't want to piss off. Maybe she didn't press Tushar to clarify, to tell her exactly who *those guys* were, because she was afraid. Maybe she didn't want to know who they were.

From the beginning, she'd worried about this. Tushar was too much of an *office* guy for the weed business. And too much of an asshole. At first she thought she could protect him. Then she thought she could get him to wake up. Tushar was trying to play it down. Don't worry, this was nothing new, he got threatened all the time. Nothing ever came of it.

Then he returned to his question. What would Rachael do if she knew people were trying to rob her? For one thing, she said, she'd *make this place like Fort Knox*. Cameras, alarms, a deluxe security system. He said he'd do it. She'd withdraw a bunch of cash from the bank and have the bills marked somehow. If intruders demanded money, *give them those bills*. He liked that idea. She'd given these scenarios a lot of thought, actually: What would she do if armed thieves came for her? What would she do if she were *kidnapped* by people who wanted to know where her weed was, where her money was? Shit like that happened in this crazy business.

But then the trip turned even weirder, scarier. This big tall guy—yet another tall guy, *so many tall guys* in this story—stood across the street from the house, on his phone, speaking a language Rachael didn't recognize. Greek? Russian? Arabic? She hadn't really noticed him until the second time she saw him. And then on the third or fourth day, she and Tushar were returning from a restaurant, holding hands, and there he was again, watching the house. And Tushar lost it. He broke away from her, strode up to the guy, got in his face, Rachael backpedaling and walking fast toward the door and going inside, not liking this at all. She did not hear what they'd said to each other. Then the man was gone. Tushar had run him off.

That was it for Rachael. The trip had become an incubator of fear, a prolonged panic attack. She hadn't been able to sleep; she didn't want to leave the house. It was as though Santa Cruz itself had become sinister. She needed to get away. Her fear expressed itself as anger. He was engaging in weed business that he hadn't told her about, black market weed business, keeping secrets. Why was he doing that? She yelled at him—again—for wasting time, for taking these stupid risks, for still not making good on his promises to give her her rightful share. She didn't see how she could ever marry him now. She wanted to break up with him, once and for all.

Now Tushar went into panic mode. *Don't leave me*, he begged. He wanted to be the father to her children, to raise a family with her, to keep her safe, to make good on all his promises to her and to everyone. . . . They were in the living room. He walked to the front door but did not open it, and, as if addressing the strange man who was no longer there, he fell to his knees as he screamed, *I'll sell it all! I'll fucking sell everything!*

She changed her flight to an earlier departure. On the day she was to leave, Tushar convinced her to go with him to Land of the Medicine Buddha. They walked up to the Ksitigarbha shrine, then to a nearby gong. He took photos and recorded a video. In the video, she is straining to smile. She looks tired. But she musters some enthusiasm, and she gongs the gong.

58. The Sock Monkeys

December 4, 2019

Detective Ethan Rumrill activated his body-worn camera. He was standing at the front door of Unit 6, had come here with three SCSO colleagues and two local cops, to this bland, desert-beige townhouse complex on the north side of North Las Vegas, right where the grid ended and the vast desert wastes began. The two kids from L.A. and a woman—Nick Lindsay; his wife, Kelsey; and her brother Kaleb Charters—were all apparently living here together. Rumrill knocked. His body cam captured Nick Lindsay opening the door. Flashing his badge, Rumrill did the talking. Santa Cruz County Sheriff's Office, homicide investigation, Tushar Atre, mind if they asked a few questions? And damn near the first thing Lindsay said was something to the effect of: *I'm not sure if this is the right time, but Tushar owed us some money? And I wanted to ask about how I can get the money he owed us.* Rumrill explained, politely, that Mr. Atre's financial affairs were being handled by his family and their attorney, *but sure, we can discuss the matter further at a later time, sure.*

At NLVPD, in a secure interrogation room, Miyoshi had Nick Lindsay run through his life story: a difficult childhood, Mom went to prison for mortgage fraud, he went to live with his biological father, an army soldier stationed at Fort Hunter Liggett in Monterey County. Graduated from King City High School, forty-five miles south of Salinas, where he was a pretty good wide receiver and safety, had football dreams, wanted to play in college, but he was not recruited. He enrolled at a series of community colleges, in Lancaster, California, then in Pasadena, but he did not win a scholarship and struggled to pay the tuition, so he dropped out, but not before meeting his future wife at the college in Lancaster—Kelsey Charters, Kaleb's older sister.

The Charterses were a Christian family, their father a preacher, their parents missionaries. Nick and Kaleb became friends, Nick said. Kaleb was like a brother to him. Both were trying to find a focus in life. They'd joined the army reserves together, went through boot camp at the same base, Fort Jackson in South Carolina. Afterward, still searching, they found temporary jobs as telemarketers, a dead end that lasted a day or two when Kaleb had this crazy phone call with some guy named Sam who worked at a weed company and who offered them jobs. It was like a winning lottery ticket, almost, and they decided to pack up and head to Santa Cruz.

Nick's story of working for Tushar Atre, and quitting working for him, comported closely with Sam Borghese's version of events. Nick told Miyoshi about starting out at the Fern Street cannabis lab, sweeping floors, cleaning toilets. They got to work under the cool lab director, Big Ben, got to work with the lab equipment, loading the weed biomass into these nylon sleeves, or socks, which went into these stainless steel columns, butane suffusing the columns, and the oil with the THC in it slowly dripping out into a big glass beaker. "Sock monkey" is what they called the job. Seemed pretty clear Nick had liked what he was doing at this point, was excited about working under Tushar, who spoke about mentoring him and Kaleb in business. As Miyoshi would later learn, Nick texted his wife in mid-August, saying the job was "really cool, I enjoy it, it can be fun and we take millionaire membership classes." But then, after only a few days, Tushar reassigned the pair to this land he owned in the middle of nowhere because he'd decided to . . . grow pot.

And Miyoshi cut in to reassure the kid that he and the other detectives didn't give a shit about any weed illegalities Nick might have been privy to—they were homicide investigators, not narcs.

Nick nodded and kept going, describing how he and Kaleb would go up to the Summit and work their asses off in the hundred-degree heat of the Santa Cruz Mountains in late summer. And he described the three round-trip drives they did between Santa Cruz and Humboldt in a truck, ferrying a thousand marijuana plants back to the property, then putting them in the ground, a crazy amount of work. Then the incident with the misplaced keys, and how Tushar withheld their pay and fucked with them. Tushar had shown his true self by then. He treated people, Nick told Miyoshi, like they were "retarded."

How did Nick find out that Tushar had been murdered? Miyoshi wanted to know. Nick said he'd been trying to find Tushar's phone number online one day. Nick said he'd lost the phone number. Had lost all his contacts, in fact. Lost them back in August when he found out that Tushar had canceled their paychecks and got so mad he smashed his cell phone against the steering wheel of his car, shattering the phone's glass. Anyhow, that's how he found out. Looking up Tushar's name online and seeing the news.

The last question Miyoshi asked was where Nick was on October 1. The kid had a quick answer: the gym. He and the Charters guys had been working out a lot in recent months.

It was "kind of spooky," Nick added, to be sitting here talking to a police officer investigating the killing of his former boss. And Miyoshi laid it on a little, telling Nick not to worry, he and his detective brethren were spooking a lot of people these days, interviewing them and trying to exclude them as fast as possible because there were so many suspects.

Nick agreed to give a DNA sample. So did Kaleb, who sat in another room at the station, telling his story to Detective Rumrill. At one point, near the end of the interview, Nick needed to use the bathroom. When he returned, he asked one of the local Vegas cops if they had any Pepto-Bismol.

59. Monster

On the road, early September, Tushar and Sam Borghese were driving Tushar's Tacoma pickup with a flatbed trailer hitched to the back. They were transporting several massive AC units from a place near Yosemite to the Fern Street lab, where they would go on the roof and work to cool the building with its extraction processes that demanded frigid temps. Somehow the conversation turned to girlfriends, relationships, marriage, children. Tushar said his girlfriend would be coming for a visit in the next couple of days. She lived somewhere on the East Coast. And Tushar ended up telling the story to Sam, parts of it anyway, of Rachael's 2018 pot farm at the Summit, the crop stolen by this scumbag who'd promised to extract oil from it, how Tushar reacted badly to this, chewing Rachael out, letting her have it. *Really* letting her have it. *How could you be so stupid?* Seemed like all his relationships ended this way, Tushar said, with him excoriating the woman. Sam replied, *If you're always breaking up with your girlfriends for the same reason . . . then it's probably something about you. Like, statistically speaking.*

Well, this time would be different, Tushar said. That's why he was growing all this weed at the Summit. To rebuild the farm after last year's catastrophe, to keep it in working order. Integrate it all together into Interstitial. And then Rachael could run the farm again. *I rebuilt it for her*,

Tushar said. He was putting her name on the title for the Summit property, something he should have done from the start.

And then they were going to get married.

AT FERN STREET, a young web developer was writing code for an input-output calculator that would measure the lab's workflow. He was a new Cruz Science hire, but he'd actually worked for Tushar before, for AtreNet, back in 2016, even lived with a few other employees at Tushar's penthouse apartment in San Francisco, but he ended up quitting the AtreNet job and had never received his final paycheck. Then, almost three years later, down on his luck, living out of his car, running deliveries for Postmates, he'd called Tushar Atre out of the blue and asked if he had any job openings. Tushar told him to come to Santa Cruz.

And now it was happening again, a payday coming and going without a paycheck. He had nowhere to live in Santa Cruz, so he moved out of his car and started living at Fern Street. He slept on an air mattress in an upstairs office and cooked his meals in the microwave in the break room. Still no pay from Tushar. When the web developer asked Tushar about it, Tushar kept delaying, delaying, delaying . . . until the day the developer snapped. He took the MacBook Tushar had provided to him for his work and used it to bludgeon an HP desktop. Another office worker wrestled him to the ground, and he and Tushar hustled the developer out of the lab, onto the street. But the developer still had the laptop clutched in his hands, and somehow he escaped.

That evening, September 4, 2019, Sam Borghese got a phone call. Borghese no longer worked for Tushar. He was heading to Los Angeles, to grad school, but Tushar needed him. *Have you ever done a smash and grab?* he asked Borghese. *Uh, no.* The young developer wanted a ransom, some thousands of dollars in back pay, in exchange for the laptop. At one of the east side beaches, they met the developer. Tushar showed him the money, and the developer handed over the laptop—*Look, I didn't even jizz on it!* the kid said—and then Tushar snatched the device from his hands and raced back to the car—*Go! Go! Go!* And Borghese peeled out, fishtailing into the street, the developer giving chase in *his* car, Borghese blowing through red lights, Tushar yelling to head for the PCH, the developer still following, so close now their bumpers were tapping—and then they heard the Klaxon, and a cop's voice blaring through a loudspeaker: *Pull! Over!* The young developer came across as unhinged. Tushar came across as a multimillionaire tech CEO. The cop arrested the web developer.

Soon he was sitting at a table in a room inside the Santa Cruz County Sheriff's Office, talking to a deputy. The developer was not in a great headspace. In his distress, he decided to unload onto this officer of the peace everything he thought he knew about his boss, Tushar Atre. Did the deputy take anything the developer said seriously? The developer told the deputy about how, three years earlier, in 2016, at Atre's San Francisco penthouse, he'd found a brick of cocaine. Tushar had accounted for the presence of the brick by saying something like, *Side hustle!* He told the deputy about the endless supply of weed available at the San Francisco penthouse—a supply that came from Tushar Atre's own pot farms somewhere. How during the November 2016 election Tushar had said he'd voted *against legalization.* According to the developer, Tushar explained his position by saying, *I don't like it. It's going to mess with my business.*

The developer told the deputy: *Tushar Atre is a drug dealer!*

His nickname was Blades. That's what he wanted everyone to call him. Great guy, Blades. Little ball of energy, an extraction technician. Blades had been working the distillation machines for Latif Horst's Herer Group, but then he and a coworker were traded like baseball players to this other team, this other company, Cruz Science, right around the corner. They literally wheeled the equipment down the street on dollies from Latif's place, which was being abandoned, to Fern Street, and suddenly Tushar Atre was their boss, not Latif Horst, though it was clear to Blades that Tushar and Latif were in business together, some kind of partners.

Tushar was cool at first. A hipster entrepreneur. But then things took a turn. He became demanding. And he said things that made you feel cold inside. Like one time he told Blades, *Some people are meant to be rich, and some people are meant to be poor, and poor people are meant to serve the rich.* The *fuck* was that shit? Then one day Tushar asked Blades and his coworker if they could work over the weekend. Tushar had something like twenty kilograms of old hash oil stored in his garage. Blades thought, *That's a shitload of hash oil to be keeping in your garage, bro!* Tushar asked if Blades could clean it up for him with the Herer Group distillation machine. Could Blades put it through the pipes and make it into something salable? Blades knew this had to be a black market op. No paperwork, no State of California manifest numbers, nothing tracking the origin of the oil. And Tushar, unsurprisingly, was vague on where he'd gotten the oil from. Some of it had come from his girlfriend, he said, the rest from . . . somewhere else.

Blades could not have known that the oil had been made by Evan Scott at the trap labs at Thirty-Eighth Avenue and Salinas, that the oil was Tushar's last remaining share of those runs. Off and on ever since, Tushar had been trying and failing to sell it.

Now Blades took over. All of Saturday, Sunday, and into Monday, he and his coworker tag teamed the job. They slept at the lab. They got it done. Maybe nineteen mason jars of material, according to what Blades remembers, easily more than thirty-thousand grams, clean and honey colored. Now that was something you could sell, likely to some black market vape-cart brand. At the going rate of twelve or thirteen dollars a gram, this was something like four hundred thousand dollars' worth of distillate. Tushar examined the material. He pulled out the fat wad of cash he kept in his fanny pack and peeled off a couple hundred bucks for a bonus.

•

THE TEXT MESSAGE DINGED in the middle of the night, two or three in the morning, late September. Evan Scott saw it was from Tushar. They'd spoken a few times since the breakup of their partnership more than a year before. At one point Tushar told Evan about renting space to Odie's brother. *Bad idea*, Evan thought. Then, earlier in the year, around May, Tushar asked if Evan wanted to join forces again. *This company is your baby, too*, Tushar had said, but Evan declined.

Now a text at this crazy hour. Tushar had written something like: *Hey, I can't sleep at night knowing what I did to you.* And: *I've done some things to people in business that I regret, but you're the only one that keeps me up at night.*

Evan replied in kind. Sort of. Said he respected Tushar's *business drive* and his *business acumen. . . . We just have different views on ethics.*

What Evan did not know was that Tushar had recently made a list of all the people—all the people he could think of, at least—he'd hurt or disrespected over the years and was systematically contacting each person and apologizing to them. "It was a substantial list," said one acquaintance (not Evan) who was also on the list. "He was in some process of, like, spiritual cleansing."

BIG BEN SURVEYED THE POT FARM at the Summit, Sunday afternoon, September 29. Standing among the crop rows, he took a cola in his hand and stroked its gluey textures. Tushar stood on one side of him, Ben's wife on the other. This crop was . . . *not healthy.* Big Ben's career was also, at this moment, not healthy. Two weeks earlier, Tushar had fired him, though it was more like a demotion that Big Ben had refused to accept. At any rate, he was no longer manager of the Fern Street lab. Tushar had replaced him with Murphy Murri, the young extraction phenom and social media celebrity from Colorado who'd helped pioneer live resin. Big Ben's time at Fern Street was turbulent. A problem with the lab's chillers had developed; the lab was overheating, hobbling their ability to run batches. Super high-strung during the whole of Ben's employment, pushing Ben and his crew to run the machines faster, faster, Tushar confessed to Ben why he was concerned: He needed to show cash flow to his investors, the Ohio guys.

Big Ben was in many ways relieved when Tushar fired him—"that job was hands down the most demeaning, soul-crushing thing I've ever done for employment"—but he'd lost his ninety-thousand-dollar salary. Ben and his family needed cash flow, too, and now here came Tushar again, offering him some. Ben had a good deal of experience as a cultivator. Tushar wanted to rehire him on a temporary basis to oversee the harvesting of this sickly weed.

There was more. Tushar told Ben he wanted to freeze the plants, create fresh frozen, and then make live resin out of the fresh frozen. Could Ben source some portable cold storage solutions? Create a spreadsheet, list all the costs associated with the harvesting and the freezing? Ben was considering saying yes to Tushar. But he did have a question of his own: What would Tushar *do* with the fresh frozen? Because running black market biomass through the licensed lab would be insane. Tushar told him not to worry about that; he'd figure it out.

ON FRIDAY AFTERNOON, September 27, Tushar swaggered into the coffeehouse at Abbott Square, his spirits high. He had come to meet Sam LoForti for their semiregular chat over coffee. Tushar was "jazzed," LoForti remembers. Cruz Science had just locked down its biggest client order to date, a massive series of shipments that would begin arriving today, more than two thousand pounds of trim in total, which his lab would convert into extracts for a princely sum. *Cash flow*. This was a turning point, maybe *the* turning point, Tushar was saying. There would be more biomass where this came from, too. Much more. This customer was a whale, one of the biggest cultivators in the state. Tushar said Latif Horst had helped him win the deal, but he didn't—or wouldn't—tell LoForti who the big customer was.

More great things were happening, too! *Rachael and I are getting back together*, Tushar told LoForti. She was coming back to Santa Cruz, coming back to him.

THAT WEEKEND, September 28 and 29, Neil Ide, along with his wife, daughter, and mother-in-law, were all staying at Tushar's glamorous house on Pleasure Point Drive. Neil and Diana, his wife and business partner, were in the final stages of assembling the ethanol-extraction machine at the Fern Street lab. In the evenings, Neil and Tushar had been having deep conversations about parenthood and the tricky undertaking of combining marriage with business.

Tushar and the Ides' five-year-old daughter, meanwhile, were having an aces time, opening and closing the trapdoors and exploring the secret passages that, like a fort, he'd built into his house. Tushar measured the girl's height on a doorjamb in the kitchen with a pencil and said he dreamed of the day he would have a little daughter or son (or both!) of his own.

ERNESTO, THE ORIGINAL CARETAKER of the Summit property, the guy Tushar had fired the previous summer after he got into a bar fight, was back in the area, doing some landscaping for one of the places that neighbored Tushar's land. On Saturday afternoon, September 28, Ernesto walked down the driveway to the main road, when who should he run into but none other than Tushar Atre himself. Tushar started right in, accusing Ernesto of stealing from him the year before. It didn't make sense. He was acting crazy. Stealing? Tushar said he knew Ernesto had kids, so he should consider himself lucky that Tushar hadn't had him arrested! Ernesto told Tushar to back off. He told Tushar, *One day you're going to mess with the wrong person.* And, *You know what, Tushar? All this stuff you're telling me is a reflection of* you.

Then Tushar stared into the space above Ernesto's shoulder, silent for a moment, and when he spoke again it was in a quiet voice, almost a whisper.

I am that monster, he said.

On Monday morning, September 30, Tushar Atre arrived at Fern Street bright and early. He had a big day ahead, a big week, the biggest yet in the short history of Interstitial Systems d/b/a Cruz Science. Once she got to town from Denver, Murphy Murri would spend all day and night scrubbing down the lab, filling up the columns in the Iron Fist closed-loop systems with the biomass from the gigantic shipment of trim that had just arrived. Tushar wanted to show off the lab to some important visitors the very next day.

Big J's people were coming. Murphy Murri was a little nonplussed that this huge transaction with Big J's group, Monterey Botanicals—like all of Cruz Science's deals, in fact—wasn't clearly documented. Yes, the shipments from Monterey Botanicals and the other clients were put through California's track-and-trace system; the shipments did appear to have manifest numbers. But there were no contracts, as far as she knew.

That afternoon, Diana Ide observed Tushar changing the passcode on the security system at Fern Street twice in the span of thirty minutes. Someone else saw him change the code behind people as they walked out the door. He was acting paranoid. He'd earlier complained to one lab worker that he was sick of Latif Horst and his people just walking into Fern Street unannounced, like they owned the place. He asked another for help in selling some lab equipment fast, as though he badly needed the cash.

And then, later that day, Latif showed up, and he and Tushar could be heard arguing. Tushar told Latif he was changing the terms of their agreement. Tushar would now take a bigger cut of the Herer Group's business—a 75 percent bigger cut. Furthermore, Tushar wanted it paid to him in cash. By jacking the price on Latif, Tushar must have known he was jacking the price on Latif's network, on Big J's pod, on the Santa Cruz cannabis community itself. The Herer Group's customers and trading partners had become Cruz Science's customers and trading partners, Latif's network merging with Tushar's network, Tushar's network based on Evan Scott's network, all of it interconnected, its people webbed together in business and in life, each person a story, each person layered with stories, each person's story touched now by that consummate Chad—or *was* he a Chad?—Tushar Atre.

Cannabis Transportation Manifest No. 52358: More than fourteen kilos of hash oil leaving 211 Fern Street, freshly processed for a Sacramento company called Friendly Farms, except the oil isn't going to Friendly Farms; it's headed to a warehouse in San Francisco, a licensed cannabis-distribution facility owned by a man who goes by the name of Harry Resin, as in the gooey fibrous texture of a cannabis flower, "a merry Canadian," according to a 2010 profile in *GQ*, but also a longtime resident of Amsterdam, a weed and psychedelics writer, proselytizer, trafficker, with experience dancing into and out of certain realms controlled by what you might call organized crime. "I'm an outlaw," Harry says, and he tells a story about a bad trip that turned into a good trip, involving an excursion to a nightclub in Mexico City that turned into a sex club in the wee hours, controlled by members of a drug cartel, the night ending with Harry "not getting killed but fucking getting high-fived and loved by all the cartel people."

But Harry at the time of the Friendly Farms trade with Tushar is no longer living in Amsterdam; he's living in the Bay Area, drawn to California grass, and has partnered with Friendly Farms because they don't have a license yet, so they're using Harry's in exchange for a percentage of Friendly Farms' sales. Harry never even meets Tushar Atre, doesn't even know about Friendly Farms' deal with Tushar Atre, and then after the horrible events of October 1, Harry Resin will be one of the handful of weed entrepreneurs invited to visit 211 Fern Street to see about buying it, but he won't buy it. Instead, he'll be expelled from the United States.

Cannabis Transportation Manifest No. 71674: A shipment of fifty kilos of freshly extracted Cruz Science hash oil going to another Type 7 lab in Monterey County, this one owned by an extraction pioneer, originally from the affluent Washington, DC, suburb of Potomac, Maryland, where he'd operated a large-scale pot-trafficking organization while still in his early twenties, whose trading partners included a professor of criminology at a large nearby university and a group of Hasidic Jews who, incidentally, were also the biggest ecstasy dealers in Baltimore. The extraction pioneer moved to Santa Cruz after the heat in Potomac got too intense, where he built a well-known extracts company and eventually became a board member of WAMM.

Cannabis Transportation Manifest No. 46812: Nearly two thousand pounds of mixed trim going from Fern Street to a distributor in Santa Rosa—or, rather, two thousand pounds that are *supposed* to go to the distributor in Santa Rosa until Tushar screws it all up. This is Alex Rowland's trim—biomass purchased by Rowland that his lab didn't have the capacity to process. At the last minute, Rowland has found another buyer for the trim at a decent price, decides to flip the two thousand pounds. This is normal, biomass traded between extractors and brokers, passed around. Tushar understands. He stands to earn a percentage of the profit. But then the driver for the Santa Rosa buyer shows up at Fern Street and waits. And waits. One hour, two hours, four hours, the driver sitting in his truck, Tushar not even inviting the guy into the Cruz Science building for a cup of coffee. Eventually the driver gets fed up and leaves. And then the Santa Rosa buyer says, *Fuck you, deal's off* . . . and Rowland is *furious*. And the company that was supposed to buy the weed, whose executives were so frustrated that they spiked the deal? It turns out that one of their vice presidents is the son of the legendary Santa Cruz smuggler who'd flown down to Colombia in the time before Pablo Escobar, and who was a close friend of Mike and Valerie Corral from the old days, and who went by the name Miles Morgan.

Cannabis Transportation Manifest No. 75042: The last in a series of shipments of biomass from Monterey Botanicals to Fern Street arrives in a Mercedes Sprinter van. The biomass was grown, most likely, at the sprawling greenhouse complex owned by Big J on Fuji Lane in the Salinas Valley, the greenhouse complex he bought with more than a million dollars cash. Twenty-two black garbage bags filled with the trim of many strains—True OG, for example, and OG Kush Breath, and Jack Herer—are carried into the storage vault at 211 Fern Street at 10:50 p.m. on Friday night, September 27, 2019.

The door to the vault is closed and locked. The lights are turned off. It is the last known shipment of weed that Tushar Atre will receive.

60. The Cartel

May 24, 2022

THE STORM HAD BLOWN THROUGH the day before, its winds scrambling the ranks of motor coaches and travel trailers arrayed across the vast Ohio macadam of Buckeye RV, America's RV dealer. For many months, ever since I began researching the magazine article that would give rise to this book project, I'd been trying and failing to talk to Jeff Walker Sr. He'd met all my messages to him with silence. But on this day, it turned out, I was in luck. A salesman manning the front desk disappeared into an interior office to fetch the boss. From a door in the wall on the other side of Buckeye RV's capacious showroom, Jeff Walker emerged, a small man with a mullet, striding urgently across the floor.

"I read your article" was the first thing he said, still some distance away, in his southwest Ohio drawl. "You *missed it*, man. Tushar was in debt to a Mexican drug cartel."

Seasoned reporters will strive in such situations to stay cool. Too much excitement risks curdling the relaxed atmosphere in which sensitive information flows. I, however, was not cool. "*Are you serious?*" is what I said.

For almost two years, OWC had been locked in hostile litigation with Atre's estate, trying to gain control of Cruz Science, its bank accounts, and the lab at 211 Fern Street, trying to recoup its $4.25 million investment. Terabytes of data and documents had been exchanged in discovery. But then, in February 2022, three months before my visit to Buckeye RV, the parties had settled out of court. OWC finally owned the Fern Street lab outright. Now Jeff Walker was dropping this explosive tip, adding that Tushar didn't have nearly as much money as people thought. The goddamn storm had ripped through his lot the day before, things were a shit show, he had to deal with all these insurance hassles, adjusters coming in—"Let's meet tomorrow," he said. And then the next day Walker canceled that meeting and rescheduled. And then over the following weeks and months, he pulled back further, he wasn't comfortable talking about it now but maybe later, and then finally the text message came: "I will be unable to discuss the matter with you at any point. Please do not contact me again."

Did Jeff Walker back away because of the confidentiality agreement he'd signed as part of the settlement with the Atre estate? Or out of fear?

"THE CARTEL IS a dirty word in the industry." "The cartel is everywhere." "They have their tentacles in everything." I'd heard these and similar statements from many of the weed operators in California I interviewed for this book. The idea of the cartel haunts the California weed business. It is almost always spoken of as *the* cartel, as if there were only one cartel, and never a specific cartel—Gulf? Juárez? Tijuana? Jalisco? Sinaloa? Michoacana? I've been told that cartels in the California weed business "operate just like normal people. . . . They're just dudes. They don't have business cards that say 'Sinaloa Cartel' on them." Claims of "cartel grows" operating in the wildernesses of California are ubiquitous. Enormous illegal cannabis farms in deserts, in redwood forests, in mountainous backwoods, in state parks, on federal lands, are raided by law enforcement every year, sometimes with dead bodies turning up. In the ensuing press statements, law enforcement will often describe the busted operations as "cartel grows." But then you delve into the cases, you review the court documents, and evidence linking those grows to an actual, specific Mexican drug-trafficking organization is almost always circumstantial or absent. The cartel allegations often seem based on circular reasoning. The police know this farm is a cartel farm because it bears the "characteristics" of a cartel farm. What are those characteristics? The police cite use of banned pesticides, pirated water, undocumented labor. But that kind of rule breaking is common among all unlicensed pot growers. Then they cite the Latin American immigrants who work on unlicensed farms and refuse to talk when apprehended. Law enforcement officials say the workers refuse to talk because they fear they will be killed, that their families in Mexico will be killed. But this lack of testimony means that rarely has an investigation of an illegal pot grow on US soil followed the money back to a specific cartel in Mexico. Claims of "the cartel's" omnipresence on US soil have become political, a reason to take a hard line on immigration, or a reason to denounce the corruption and racism of the drug wars and drug warriors. There is even a book, *Drug Cartels Do Not Exist* by Mexican academic Oswaldo Zavala, who advances a somewhat semantic argument for the claim made by its title. There is a hallucinatory quality, a conspiracy theory quality, to the cartel's existence or lack of existence in the California weed business, this secret monstrous force that can be glimpsed only occasionally, after the proper initiation.

And yet at some point my reporting began running into what might be termed specifics. It's true and obvious that Mexican cartels make most of their profits in the worldwide distribution of hard drugs, not weed. But their origins lie in weed: The Guadalajara Cartel, which begot the Sinaloa Cartel, made its first big money by growing and smuggling industrial quantities of brick weed into the United States in the 1970s to service the exploding demand among young Americans. And although American demand for such brick weed has since declined, neither the Sinaloa Cartel nor its rivals have stopped shipping it north. I've been asked rhetorically: *Do you think just because prohibition has ended in California that the cartel would just walk away from the weed business, a business they had a hand in inventing?* Of course not.

Eduardo Escobedo-Silva, aka El Mago, the Magician, born in East L.A., a US citizen by birth, who served almost five years in federal prison on charges related to the trafficking of more than eleven tons of weed, said to be El Chapo's son's good friend and the chief weed mover in the United States for the Sinaloa Cartel, was gunned down in the Los Angeles warehouse district in 2023 by unknown assassins.

A black market cannabis operator from Los Angeles who has certain friends-and-family connections—I'll call him Lex—tells me that a handful of licensed cannabis companies in California were secretly bankrolled by cartels. The cartels are on their cap tables in the names of the adult children, American citizens born in the United States, of Mexican narcos, the children having gone to elite universities and come back with MBAs, who are tasked not with laundering the cartel's profits but investing its *already laundered* profits in an industry they thought they knew. Lex also tells of another kind of arrangement, debt not equity. He knows of legal weed operators struggling financially who have borrowed money from cartels. (Lex is not the only person who will describe this kind of deal to me.) The borrowers may not even have realized that they'd taken money from a criminal group, the group shielded behind innocuous names and suave proxies. And when the borrowers failed to pay their debts, the cartels didn't kill them. They simply took over their companies. When I ask for the names of any of these licensed California cannabis entities, Lex looks at me, shakes his head. He's afraid to say. "And don't try to name the companies!" he warns. "You don't want to die. Or get kidnapped." Is this real? Is it paranoia? Is Lex's fear even real? Or is he using the idea of fear to conceal his own lack of knowledge?

A cannabis chemist who has worked as a consultant for hash-oil extractors tells me about the time in 2017 when he was approached by a friend of a friend who had a job for him. A group of people in Mexico had access to *supercheap trim*. Like, four dollars a pound. And they wanted to build a massive extraction lab in Mexico to make hash oil out of this supercheap Mexican-grown weed. Would the chemist/consultant be interested in helping them do it? All he needed to do was come with the Mexicans down to Hermosillo or San Carlos a couple hundred miles south of the border with Arizona. The Mexicans would pay him well. "And I said: The people in Mexico who have access to four-dollar trim—when we were paying upward of four hundred dollars per pound—are cartel folks, and I'm not interested," this chemist told me. "Rather than write me a check, they could just bury me in a shallow grave."

A different longtime West Coast extraction expert tells the story of a quiet man sitting in the corner of a trap lab in San Diego, taking notes. It is 2017 or 2018. The extraction expert has been hired to help design this unlicensed lab. The lab's supposed American owner pulls the expert aside. *This is all cartel*, the "owner" says. The quiet man taking notes in the corner is the cartel's man, here to babysit this cartel asset. The quiet man then approaches the expert and asks him to join him on a trip to Mexico—right now; he has a plane standing by—to advise the cartel on the construction of an advanced extraction facility for the manufacture of hash oil. This expert, too, declines the invitation. "Like, that's a *bad idea*. That's, like, Jesse Pinkman." The quiet man tries to reassure the expert. His organization doesn't work in this way. Though the expert refuses to get on the airplane, he nevertheless agrees to act as a consultant *remotely*. He is paid in a series of bank wire transfers from an entity that is only a number. The expert cannot say which cartel. He doesn't know. No way was he going to ask these men that question.

A former black market extractor from California describes a Zoom meeting with two men who live in Mexico. They want to bring the extractor to a town across the border. They will pay him a very good fee if he shows them how to make high-quality distillate. This is in 2018, before the vape crisis, when the price of distillate is still very high. The men's faces are blurred, their voices distorted. The California extractor has turned his camera away so they can't see him. He doesn't give his name. He listens to them talk for ten minutes or so, then he says, *Let me think about it*. And then never contacts them again. The California extractor, who is also at this time a large-scale broker of black market extracts, will also come to learn that the Sinaloa Cartel is smuggling tremendous amounts of unrefined hash oil—made in Mexico—into the United States, where it is distilled in trap labs and then distributed across the nation for use in black market vape pens. There are specific details about this operation that the California extractor tells me—names, places, methods. But he warns me not to divulge those details. "I'm talking about things that, if you were to publish them in a certain way, it could put a legitimate target on both of our backs and anyone else you write about. You can use your imagination. The first people they'd talk to are the people that the crude oil was being delivered to. Then they would figure out everyone those people had ever done business with or talked to on Instagram or email or phone calls or text messages over the last however many years. They're thorough, man. They don't fuck around. They protect their shit."

You can use your imagination. His fear is real, and it is contagious. It also threatens to stymie reporting. "Do your due diligence," another source warns me. Meaning: Anyone you approach for an interview could be secretly affiliated with a cartel. If the cartels' power is real, and a reporter pushes too hard, or asks the wrong person the wrong question, could the reporter *really* put sources' lives at risk? Put his life—*my life*—at risk? You think about the films you've seen. The TV series. The gory news dispatches from the border towns, headless corpses dangling from overpasses.

A law enforcement official with deep experience in Santa Cruz County tells me that specific cartels control or "own" specific territories in the United States. Santa Cruz County, he says, is "owned" by La Familia Michoacana, a cartel originally from that Mexican state but now with a presence throughout the hemisphere. Its roots were in the rugged Sierra Madre del Sur, one of the earliest weed-growing regions in Mexico. Its founder was a teetotaling Christian zealot who published his own book of parables that he forced his soldiers to study and master. La Familia, the law enforcement official says, has long had operatives living in Santa Cruz.

A man from the Bay Area—I can't be more specific—travels to a place in the continental United States that is not on the West Coast. The year is 2018. The details given to me about this trip are very specific; I cannot share them, either, but that the trip happened has been corroborated by another source. From the airport of a major US city, the California man is picked up and driven away. The drive takes more than one hour but less than six. He arrives at an estate on a large piece of land in a rural area where animals are being raised at great expense. There are barns and outbuildings. Four or five men from Mexico await the Californian in one of the barns. The men represent an organization that the Californian will later refer to, in English, as the Family. The Mexicans are interested in creating distillate out of the titanic amount of cannabis trim they have from their pot farms in Mexico. They want the help of the Californian, who has brought samples of distillate with him, and he shows the honey-colored liquid to the Mexicans. The Mexicans like what they see.

Three out of four of the above encounters between cannabis people in California and an alleged Mexican drug cartel involve people who, in one way or another, knew Tushar Atre. Either they did business with him, or worked with him, or knew someone who did. None of these people say they know anything about Atre having contact with a cartel, let alone becoming indebted to one, and I believe them. But the fact does seem to remain that one degree separated Tushar Atre from a Mexican drug cartel. A cloud of cartel activity indeed seems to have surrounded Tushar Atre and the California cannabis business in general. It is, after all, a small world. Up until the beginning of the vape crisis in mid-2019, Mexican drug cartels seem to have observed the elevated prices for distillate, hash oil, and trim, recognized an opportunity, and sought out the expertise of California's extractors in an effort to exploit it.

I had another encounter with someone I'd been trying to contact for a long time. A person who once briefly worked with Interstitial. I finally tracked down this person's phone number.

I won't disclose the person's name. I won't even disclose the person's gender. I will disclose that I subsequently learned that this person has had a troubled work history, has been accused of embellishing the truth, and worse.

When I reached this person, they seemed scared. They didn't want to talk. "There were some really bad people involved with what happened," they said, and then they said they had to go.

"But can I run one thing by you real quick?" I manage to ask.

"OK."

"Someone told me Tushar was in debt to a Mexican drug cartel."

Pause.

"Yes."

"He was?"

"Yes. And that's why I have to be very careful about what I say." The person refused to provide any details. Only two others knew the full story, they said. If the person were to expose Tushar's entanglement with the cartel, they would be risking all of their lives.

I asked if the cartel had anything to do with Tushar's murder.

"The cartels are not associated" with Atre's killers, the person said and then hung up. They have refused my entreaties ever since.

61. In the Way of Ourselves

Tushar was waking up in a panic every night at three in the morning, he told Rachael, having *weird thoughts*, overcome by the fear that people were coming for him, that people were coming to the Summit to cut down his weed crop. So agitated was he that he'd drive up to the farm and just sit cross-legged in the moonlight until the sun rose, breathing deeply, calming down, guarding the plants. Rachael phoned him every morning when she got up, to check in, feeling the same way she felt in the weeks before her mother died, consumed with anxiety that she kept trying to rationalize, her thoughts spinning. . . .

For three days in late September, from the twentieth to the twenty-third, just for a weekend, he flew across the country to see Rachael. It was three days of relative bliss. No arguing. The sense of foreboding dissipated in the Berkshires' crisp, early-autumn air. They looked at the Lenox property, now in contract: a tumbledown house Rachael would repair, on two and a half acres. There was even a nineteenth-century schoolhouse on the land, just like there had been on the other side of a stream from her mother's house in South Pomfret. She would grow weed here the following season, once her license from the Massachusetts state regulatory authorities came through. They spoke cheerfully, bullishly, about combining the companies, Santa Cruz and Lenox, creating a small, multistate cannabis operation. He spoke again about how badly he wanted children. He told her he'd undertaken a project; he was making amends with the people he had treated poorly over the years. She was, of course, number one on the list and the inspiration behind the project. The leaves in the Berkshires had begun to turn. They hiked a mountain trail toward a vista, Hashtag galloping along beside them. A family.

The last photograph of Rachael and Tushar together was a selfie, Tushar reaching out with his phone to snap them on this Berkshire hilltop, the sun shining, sweat freckling Tushar's brow, health in their faces, bright smiles, handsome couple. . . .

But once Tushar returned to Santa Cruz, the anxiety returned. And Rachael was angry with him again.

Just after eight on the morning of September 30, he called her. He was riding his bike, AirPods in his ears. The connection was poor. He couldn't hear her. She got irritated. An exchange of text messages quickly escalated, another text battle, a microcosm of their relationship for the last eight months. Tushar complained that she always turned on him so quickly, went nuclear, threatening for the thousandth time to dump him. He brought up an old grievance of his: *If only you cut me as much slack as you do old white guys.*

And then she did something she would come to regret, that would haunt her in more ways than one in the months and years to come. In a text, she brought up how Tushar had treated her during the tumult of the 2018 harvest. She accused him of stealing her Trinity money. *I cut you plenty of slack*, she said. After all, she added: *I almost shot you in the face.*

Shot me in the face? Tushar said. *Are you insane? Are you ever going to move past it?*

And then, like every other fight they'd ever had, every other explosive moment in their intense, volatile love affair, they made up.

It's all going to be fine, he said.

They spoke later that day on a video call and apologized to each other. Then Tushar quickly moved past it to expound again on the gorgeous THCA-isolate powder, of the *highest quality*, with the *best terpenes ever*, that Murphy Murri had extracted at Fern Street from the few pounds of Rachael's leftover fresh frozen, the remnants of the 2018 harvest. He showed her the stuff over the phone. A white sugary powder. Almost 100 percent pure. It was, Tushar said, *proof of concept*. Her concept. It was medicine. "We were really proud of us," Rachael would later recall.

That same evening, just before Rachael turned out the light to go to sleep, she and Tushar spoke again, and the fear and anxiety dissipated once more. She almost forgot about it. *Everything is going to be OK*, he said. She let herself believe, for now, for this night, that he was safe. That *they* were safe. He needed her to come to Santa Cruz to sign the legal documents that would make her whole. He was setting up an LLC shell company that would hold all the cannabis assets. She would own half of the LLC. He said he was even putting her in his will; he was *making good on his promise to Cynthia*. She let herself believe he had chosen love, that he had vanquished the monster inside him. He hinted at some surprise he had in store for her, something big. She suspected he was going to propose again—on October 13, her thirty-fourth birthday. She was going to say yes to him this time. They spoke about his next trip to the Berkshires. Maybe he'd stay longer than just a weekend. He wanted to stay longer, wanted to get away from Santa Cruz, from Fern Street. He was learning to delegate. Learning how not to micromanage. *I'm letting go of a lot*, he said. She reiterated what she'd already written him in a text earlier in the day, after they'd made peace: "We are often the ones in the way of Ourselves."

It was the last text she would ever send him.

•

HER CELL PHONE RANG, waking her. She reached for the nightstand. It was the first day of October, a month charged with meaning. She and Tushar had just spoken about that, too. The traditional month of the harvest. The month of Cynthia's death. The month of Rachael's birth, a day now forever subordinated to the day of her mother's death.

The area code of the incoming call was 831, Santa Cruz. It was 7:00 a.m. She instantly knew it could only be bad. Words were being spoken. *Sheriff's office. . . . Is this Rachael? . . . Tushar Atre. . . . His girlfriend? . . . A home invasion . . . possible kidnapping . . . pot farm. . . . Can you give us the address of the pot farm?*

Now she was standing. Probably she was standing. The memories she has of this morning are fragments of movement and sound and feeling. Feelings of terror. Moments of clarity. The pot farm. She said, *It's not a pot farm*. The deputy said: *Ma'am, we don't care about the pot.* Rachael told him that the actual numbers of the address of the property were useless; if you plugged them into a GPS, the algorithm sent you somewhere else. So go to the Summit Store, go south on the Soquel San Jose Road. *You guys know where it is! You were there just a few months ago!* Sideways is the way the phone call was going. There were multiple calls from sheriff's deputies that morning. She hung up on one of them, enraged because she thought the officer was being flippant. She called one of Tushar's friends, one who lived close to the Pleasure Point house, woke him up, and asked him please to go over to the house and tell the deputies what to do. Tell them to go to the Summit, the other places. *Bring them* to the Summit! The friend, frightened now, alert, said he was on it. Another deputy called her. More questions. *When was the last time you saw Mr. Atre, or spoke to him? What did you talk about?* She didn't answer the questions. Or maybe she did. She remembers saying: *You need to go to the Summit now! Go to the warehouses in Salinas now!* Those were the places *those guys* would probably take him!

What guys? the deputy said.

The kidnappers! she said.

In the electric kaleidoscope of thought spirals that had by then usurped her mind, one thought she had was that she'd known he was in danger yet she'd left him alone in Santa Cruz. She hadn't been there to protect him.

What have I done to you? She sank to the floor, got down onto her hands and knees, and she felt something, some energy, surrounding her head like a tight crown, like a squeezing, and she believed then, and still believes now, that the energy embracing her was him.

Four or five hours later, after 11:00 a.m. Eastern, Tushar was still missing, and she was speeding down a highway in upstate New York, on her way to JFK to catch the earliest possible flight to the Bay Area, when her cell phone rang, another 831 area code. It was the number of a friend of theirs, the woman who'd designed the MBARI logo, and Rachael put her on speaker. The woman said she had an acquaintance who worked at the sheriff's office, she didn't want Rachael to learn about it on the Internet or TV, she wanted Rachael to hear it from a friend. . . .

There was nowhere to pull over on this highway, just an enormous sheer-faced wall of rock, gray rock, granite probably, rising up into the sky from the western side of the southbound lane like the ramparts of an abyss. The woman was telling Rachael what Rachael already knew in her soul, that they'd found Tushar. Found his body. At the Summit. And he was gone. Above the din of the car engine, Rachael said, *OK*, and politely thanked the woman—*Thank you*, Rachael said, *thank you*—and the woman said if she needed anything, anything at all. . . .

How could any of this be real? Just when he'd changed, they'd killed him. Still she had nowhere to pull over. She gripped the wheel, cars and trucks flying past her, everyone in the middle of their routine days, and she drove on. The desolation rose up inside her, its raw dark power, and she screamed as she gripped the wheel, and then she went back to searching for a place where she could pull over and put the car in park and go on screaming until her voice ran ragged, and pound the wheel with the palms of her hands until they bruised—but for now she had no choice. There was nowhere to pull over. Trapped by the wall, she had to keep going.

62. The Confession

May 19, 2020

They wanted to make the arrests all on the same day, at the same time, just after nine in the morning Pacific, a coordinated operation. They'd staked out all the last-known addresses. They'd surreptitiously stuck GPS trackers to the undercarriages of the targets' cars. They wore tactical vests emblazoned on the back with the letters SCSO in bright yellow. In Burbank there was confusion. They had the wrong address; they had to scramble to find the right address. They sent Detective Christine Jones, former UCLA track star, blond, in plainclothes, no vest, no badge, to knock on the door of the apartment in the high-rise in downtown Burbank where they thought they saw a person matching Lindsay's description on the balcony. A young man opened the door.

"Nick?"

"Yes?"

Detective Jones stepped aside as a phalanx of cops swarmed into the apartment, putting Nick Lindsay in cuffs, his young wife, Kaleb's sister, sitting on the couch and possibly in shock. In St. Clair Shores, Michigan, a suburb of Detroit, where Kaleb Charters was now living in a shared apartment, from which he was commuting to his job at Home Depot on his skateboard, they discovered the teenager hanging out in his bedroom, barefoot. They put him in handcuffs without incident and brought him his socks and shoes. In Lancaster, California, a dusty L.A. exurb at the edge of the Mojave, inside a modest ranch house on Spahn Lane, they detained Joshua Camps, twenty-three, a friend of Kaleb's brother, Kurtis Charters, and also, as of the last two months or so, his roommate. In a search of Joshua Camps's bedroom, the cops found a knife; a .22-caliber Marlin rifle; a .45-caliber Springfield handgun with one bullet in the chamber; a Mossberg twelve-gauge pump-action shotgun, five rounds in the magazine, and another five in the sidesaddle shell holder attached to the butt; a Beretta PX4 nine-millimeter handgun, loaded; a Glock 19 nine-millimeter handgun, loaded; spent and unspent .223-caliber rifle ammunition, same caliber as the casings found near the body of Tushar Atre at the Summit on the morning of October 1; and multiple pairs of Safariland flex-cuffs, same type and brand as those that had bound Atre's wrists. Elsewhere in Lancaster, as all of this was happening, the SCSO deputies' local L.A. County brethren, dome lights whirling, pulled over a car they'd been following and hollered for the driver to emerge with his hands in the air, which Kurtis Charters did do, and they restrained his wrists behind his back as the normal citizens of Lancaster in their passing cars rubbernecked and wondered what this kid had done.

They took Kurtis Charters to a Los Angeles County Sheriff's Department substation in the neighboring city of Palmdale and put him in an interrogation room. Kurtis Charters, twenty-two, would soon come to learn that his friend and roommate Joshua Camps was sitting in another room in the same substation, that his brother was being held by St. Clair Shores PD, and that his brother-in-law, Nick Lindsay, was confined to a similar room in Burbank. The SCSO detectives conducting the interrogations—Miyoshi, Rumrill, Fulton, and others—were in constant communication, Palmdale, Michigan, Burbank. In Burbank, Lindsay immediately invoked his right to an attorney, saying nothing to his chief inquisitor, Miyoshi, saying nothing to any law enforcement officer, ever.

But in the other three rooms, the interrogations went differently. They did not invoke their rights to attorneys. They answered the cops' initial softball questions. Then they lied, dissembled—told bits and pieces of the truth—and then cracked. In each room, the detectives said some version of: *This is between you and God at this point, whether you decide to tell the truth or not.* Sitting at a table across from Ryan Fulton and his partner in a small bland room in the Palmdale station, Kurtis Charters hugged his stomach with his arms, doubled over. "What I hate about this is it makes people seem so evil," he said through tears. And then, in despair, almost singing: "He wasn't supposed to be there!"

By the time it was over, Kurtis Charters had spent five hours telling his story. Only portions of what he and his brother and Camps said to detectives during their "custodial interviews" on May 19, 2020, have been made public. But from those excerpts and other evidence presented in court hearings, a story takes shape:

The plot was hatched in Las Vegas—or, more accurately, in North Las Vegas—in September 2019, when Nick Lindsay and his wife, Kelsey, and her two brothers were all living together in their communal home. "We were a team," Kurtis told detectives. But they were also adrift. The Charters boys were estranged from their parents, estranged from their church, the church of their father, the preacher and missionary who had himself shifted careers, if slightly, who had become a hospice chaplain "specializing in end-of-life spiritual care." In North Las Vegas, there were money struggles. They were living off their army reservist's pay and wages from Kurtis's job at a Pizza Hut.

Then one day the idea sprang into one of their minds. The evidence suggests it was Nick Lindsay's mind—Lindsay who had become something like the patriarch of this little family unit, whom the others looked up to and maybe even slightly feared. In the interrogation room, Kurtis told detectives that Lindsay had "some sort of vendetta." Kurtis believed that the purpose of their plan was merely to rob the rich man. To punish Tushar Atre by taking just a little of his tech-and-weed millions. He could afford it. They knew he carried rolls of hundred-dollar bills in his fanny pack. They "knew he dealt in cash a lot." They knew he had money spread out all over the oceanfront house; Kaleb and Nick had seen it firsthand,

Tushar opening a kitchen drawer on the very first day they'd met him and giving them each a hundred-dollar bill. He was in the pot business, so he had to have lots of cash lying around. And probably lots of product, too.

Kurtis told the detectives that he believed Atre would not be at home on the day they had chosen for the burglary, the wee hours of October 1, because Nick Lindsay told him that Tushar would be on the East Coast, visiting his girlfriend.

The Las Vegas three—Kurtis, Kaleb, and Nick—had decided they needed a fourth man. They needed some "brawns," as Kaleb called it, some muscle, and Kurtis knew that his old church friend Josh Camps had the heavy tools. The plan was to travel from their home in North Las Vegas and stop in Lancaster to meet up with Camps. Lancaster was the Charterses' hometown, more or less, and Lancaster Baptist Church, a megachurch on the north end of town, where the Mojave begins in earnest, the church with its walled and gated campus like a ribat in the desert among the uncanny Joshua trees, was more or less the Charterses' ecclesiastical home base. Kurtis's father had preached at this church, which had sponsored the Charterses on their mission to El Salvador. And it was as members of this congregation that Kurtis and Camps had first met. They kept their plan a secret from Kelsey, to protect her.

On September 26, Nick, Kaleb, and Kurtis drove west across the desert on a trip to recruit Josh Camps. Nick and Kaleb had this former boss up in Santa Cruz who was a "P.O.S." of the worst kind, they told Camps, and "had a million in cash in his safe." Camps said no way. He had dreams—ironic, the way it turned out—of a career in law enforcement; these aspirations had inspired him to assemble an arsenal at his house. But then Camps, for some reason, said fuck it. His mom had just died; he didn't feel in his right mind. To Camps, the Charters brothers made it sound like the former boss "was some gangster dude and he would have muscle at his house." And so Camps decided to bring the heaviest of his heavy tools: the AR-15 long rifle. They also brought a pair of his black Safariland flexcuffs. If they happened to be wrong, if Atre was, in fact, not traveling, if he was at home, Camps and his rifle would be their "contingency plan." They would bind Atre's wrists and brandish the rifle and threaten him with it, force him to tell them where the money was. "Plan B is if he's there, this is something to scare him," Kaleb Charters told detectives in his interrogation room in Michigan. Each of the four also armed themselves with a knife.

They were, Kurtis said, "supposed to be in and out and gone."

On the evening of September 30, at approximately 8:00 p.m., they piled into Camps's blue Toyota Camry and drove north through the night.

It is, without traffic, a five-hour drive.

THEY HOPE TO ENTER THE OCEANFRONT HOUSE by using the passcode. Kaleb says he thinks he knows the code, that he remembers overhearing Tushar talking to someone about it. The passcode is 1985, which the occupants of the Camry cannot know is the year that Rachael was born. But what if Tushar changed it? To confirm the code, Kaleb calls Sam Borghese, but Borghese doesn't pick up.

Two minutes later, the Charters brothers receive a group text. Kelsey, their sister, is apparently worried. "You guys have been gone a really long time???" she writes. One of them responds by sending her a meme, a reaction-image meme of a Claymation pirate. "Well yes but actually no," reads the caption, like a koan.

They arrive in Pleasure Point at 2:25 a.m. Three of them exit the Camry—Nick, Kurtis, Josh. This is all part of the plan. Kaleb takes the wheel and drives alone to the Summit property, a place he knows well. He will wait there in the night for the others. The others are supposed to borrow one of Tushar's cars, the Tacoma pickup most likely, taking the keys from the house, filling the truck with their stolen booty, and driving it to the Summit for the rendezvous with Kaleb. Then quickly they will transfer the treasure to the Camry, leave the pickup at the Summit, and escape into the night, no one the wiser.

This is the plan.

Their plan is full of holes. Three of them have brought their cell phones. Only Nick has left his behind. Do they not know that cell phones, even when powered down, can be tracked? Something has taken over their minds, obliterating reason. They are like zombies, automatons. It is as though they've been called into being by the gruesome worldview that Atre subscribed to for most of his life: *Some people are meant to be poor.*

Nick walks in the lead, the three of them striding single file down the sidewalk on Pleasure Point Drive, Kurtis in the middle with a duffel bag, Josh in the rear with his rifle strapped around his chest, a SWAT wannabe. Nick pulls on a pair of gloves as they reach the house. At the front door, he punches in 1-9-8-5. The lock beeps; invisible gears whir. Tushar hasn't changed the code! Kurtis has the feeling, he later tells the detectives, that maybe this is not a good thing.

They enter the darkened household. All is quiet. Nick of course has been here once before, just two months ago, back in August, the day that he and Kaleb first interviewed with Tushar. Just forty-nine days earlier had been his and Kaleb's first day on the job. But Kurtis has been at this house before, too. He had joined Kaleb and Nick for their trip to Santa Cruz to interview with their potential new boss . . . and Kurtis, too, remembers the house, the basics of its layout, the wall of windows, the thundering ocean, the master suite back there. They need to check the master suite, Kurtis not liking any of this, because they're just supposed to grab some cash and be in and out and gone, Kurtis in a spell of terror, he wants to leave . . . but he doesn't leave, he can't leave. He follows Nick, creeping now into the master bedroom, their eyes having already adjusted to the darkness, and there in the king bed lies a form under a blanket. Tushar is home, but *he's not supposed to be at home.*

And this is when time trips, when free will falls through the warp of the now and comes out the other side as destiny.

Lights come on, a sudden blazing, clear and harsh. There is shouting; Nick is shouting. There is confusion. Tushar is confused, dazed with sleep. Then he's out of the bed and down on his knees. Does he recognize Nick? Kurtis? He's asking Nick what he wants, asking Nick how he can make things right. Somehow the red athletic shorts Tushar was sleeping in have fallen to his ankles. Kurtis pulls the shorts back up, and one of them binds Tushar's wrists behind his back with the zip ties, Josh by now probably pointing the AR-15 at Tushar while someone shouts: *Where's the safe? Open the safe!* It's Kurtis's job to search the house for cash, so frantically he proceeds to walk around the bedroom, the living room, the kitchen, opening and closing drawers and cabinets. He spots Tushar's cell phone, his wallet. He sees an array of expensive-looking acoustic guitars hanging on a wall. He sees an expensive camera. A fugue state. Mindless, automatic movements. He or one of the others walks out onto the deck into the chill of the night, the surf roaring, and hurls the phone and the wallet into the roar. Back inside the bright bedroom, more confusion. They need a car. Where are the keys to the white BMW in the driveway? Camps at some point jams a sock in Tushar's mouth. There is a safe in the walk-in closet in the master suite. Gun safe, tall as a fridge. They pull out the sock and demand the code. Tushar tells them the code, and the sock goes back in. The code works, the safe opens. There are stacks of cash inside the safe. Also dozens of bottles and an uncountable number of little vials stored in cardboard cartons. Nick must know that the bottles contain hash oil, that the little vials are vape carts. Kurtis and Nick start pulling out cash, stuffing the cash into the duffel bag. Later they will count what they took: twenty thousand dollars. Josh takes Tushar by the elbow and walks him back to the bed and tells him to lie down.

The job is done. They want to get out of there. Everyone moves to leave—except Nick, who grabs Tushar, pulls him out of bed. Does Nick want to take Tushar with them to the meeting point at the Summit? Does Nick want to take him hostage? *What the fuck?* Josh says. *Not the plan!*

It is now, Nick says.

Twelve minutes have passed since they entered the house.

Then Tushar's gone.

He has escaped.

From the front door, Kurtis sees Tushar fleeing into the dark of Pleasure Point Drive. Nick, the former high school football player, chases and then headlong tackles him to the pavement in the middle of the street. Josh runs toward the fallen pair as Nick gets up and retraces his steps toward the house.

Slit his throat, Nick says to Josh.

The white SUV in the driveway yelps unlocked. Kurtis and Nick both get in, Nick taking the wheel. They drive the fifteen yards to where Tushar is lying on the street, but Tushar is no longer lying on the street; he's struggling to his feet and staggering and trying to run. But then he collapses, and Kurtis is out of the SUV and grabbing Tushar by the sweatshirt and lifting him up. And, with the others, he shoves Tushar into the SUV's passenger seat.

Nick speeds away, following the route familiar to him and his captive—northbound on the twisting, climbing Soquel San Jose Road, into the night-black mountains, past the turnoff to Land of the Medicine Buddha, past Laurel Glen Road and the Latif Horst homestead, past the properties where Big J had his showcase grow, past Subud Santa Cruz, past Bonefire Bob's flamethrower-art studio, past Dharma Ridge and into the Summit with its conifer-serrated ridges and ancient indigenous springs and San Andreas Fault zone and the cloistered hippie garths where the kush has long been grown. . . . Tushar sits in the passenger seat. Kurtis and Josh are in the rear. But the rear seats have been folded down, the cargo area expanded, because the SUV is loaded with furniture—a chest of drawers, a small table, a small chair—so Kurtis and Josh are kneeling, Kurtis on the passenger side, when he notices a dark sticky wetness covering everything—his hands, the seat, the doors, the floorboards, his clothing, the head and shoulders and body of this man that they've taken. A horror of blood—what Josh Camps will later call "artery blood"—welling up from Atre's neck in shocking cardiac intervals. Kurtis presses his hands to the sodden wound, a futile intervention. Still he presses hard, as if trying to gather up the life and push it back into the body of the bleeding man. Estranged though he is from his father's church, Kurtis will later tell detectives that he retains a certain faith, and he begins talking to Tushar, administering a haphazard last rite.

Tushar is conscious. And at some point during the trip to the Summit, according to the later testimony of Josh Camps and Kurtis Charters, Tushar begins to cry. He seems to know now—everyone knows now—that he will die.

Describing these scenes to detectives, Kurtis will say it is "like a nightmare" in which he is "permanently" trapped. He will break down in sobs. "I should have stepped in and been a leader and prevented this from happening." He will call out, "I don't want to go to hell!"

They arrive at the gate. The gate is open. The BMW moves up the switchbacking driveway, climbs the hill to the plateau and the large tepee, and there is Kaleb standing like a ghoul in the dark beside the Camry. The night is pitch; there is no moon. In the end Josh is the one who guides Tushar Atre by his cuffed hands in a dream walk down a gentle incline and into a stand of towering pines, and the others will hear the crack of gunfire, and someone will shout *Go! Go! Go!* and all four will pile into the Camry and drive the five hours back to Lancaster in an apocalyptic silence, none of them saying a word.

But before that happens, just as the BMW is coming to a stop on the plateau near the tepee, Kurtis remains for a moment in the car with the dying Tushar, talking to him. Because of the trauma, the blood loss, the physical pain, Tushar by now is "out of it," is losing consciousness or entering an altered state of consciousness. It is the arrival we all must make—sublime, appalling—at the brink of the void. What has brought him here? What contingencies? Has this been a crime of circumstance? Random? Without meaning? Or has there been a secret chain of cause and effect? Has some dark force put these four fools, or even just one of them, up to it? There is, in the end, no evidence for that. No evidence that any of the four ever knew a cartel operative, no evidence that they'd ever been in contact with a Samoan gangster, no evidence that in their brief time as laborers at the lowest, sock-monkey level of the Santa Cruz weed world they ever met or knew Miles Morgan's son or Odie or Latif Horst or Big J or Bomi Joseph or Evan Scott or Rachael Lynch, or anyone associated with any of them. Only these four are present for the end of this trip, this life, Kurtis Charters bearing witness to the dying Tushar, murmuring to him, fearing for his soul, for all their souls, and asking him: *Will you go to heaven, or will you go to hell?*

EPILOGUE

Within the Santa Cruz weed community, the arrests of Lindsay, Camps, and the Charters brothers were met with something close to disbelief. Who even were these guys? They were from somewhere else, not Santa Cruz. They weren't even *of* the business. Four randoms, two of whom had briefly worked for Tushar's hash oil company? It couldn't have been them. And if it was them, some other powerful person or entity must have put them up to it. The reluctance to accept the outcome of the investigation as conclusive says something about the paranoia that saturates the cannabis trade. As William S. Burroughs, the writer and outlaw, once said, "A paranoid might be defined as someone who has some idea as to what is actually going on."

To those who were one-time persons of interest, the arrests came as a huge relief. Evan Scott felt so persecuted locally by gossip and innuendo that he escaped to Fiji for almost a year. Now, finally, he could return home. Rachael felt the heat of suspicion directed toward her from Tushar's family and his loyal friend group. Suspicion soon turned to wrath when, in January 2020, even before the arrests, she filed a probate claim against Tushar's estate and then, in October of the same year, a lawsuit. She was seeking to recover the life savings she'd poured into the Summit property and Tushar's cannabis business. After more than two years of motions, pleadings, and depositions, the parties reached a settlement. Its terms were private, but Rachael was likely paid an undisclosed sum by the Atre estate. From court filings, it seems Shaku Atre could not shake the notion—which lacked any factual foundation—that Rachael somehow knew the accused killers, had somehow been involved in her son's murder.

Rancorous litigation would come to define the posthumous story of Tushar Atre. There was the matter of Bomi Joseph, who made false claims against the estate that weren't fully put to rest until his prosecution in 2022. Then there was OWC, Tushar's Ohio venture-capital investors, who also filed a probate claim and then sued, attempting to gain control of 211 Fern Street, the lab into which they'd poured all those millions of dollars. After another vitriolic legal battle that lasted nearly two years, the parties also settled. OWC took over the lab and attempted to restart operations but has struggled to make that happen. For years it looked as though the Fern Street building had been abandoned. But then, in June 2025, the facility finally came back online, churning out hash oil for the first time since September 2019.

The long delay was likely not the Ohioans' fault. After 2019, the entire American cannabis economy entered a depression. It started in California and, like a financial contagion, spread from there. In essence, what Tushar and many others had foretold came true. Legalization aroused so much opportunistic desire among both Chads and traditional market operators that they cultivated far too much flower and manufactured far too much extract. Such an enormous glut of product was created that prices collapsed not just in California but nationally. The pandemic helped, at least at first, sparking demand from home-bound consumers. But that didn't last. High-end indoor flower that sold for $2000 a pound in 2019 was selling for $500 in 2021. Cannabis taxes, licensing, and permitting fees on the state and local levels vaporized profit margins. As of 2025, the market has still not recovered. The black market couldn't dodge the crash, either. Supply is supply. As Tushar and many others recognized, black market weed prices were artificially high and profit margins artificially wide. And so the backstop that had helped many cannabis companies in California stay afloat—namely, selling weed out of state on the black market—also eventually tanked.

Like an asteroid, the crash sparked an extinction event. Since 2020, an estimated 77 percent of licensed cannabis companies in California have gone out of business. Dan Herer's conspiracy theories had a grounding in fact. Those with the most capital in reserves have been best positioned to survive, which included many (but not all) of the biggest corporate players. Asset values collapsed along with weed prices. Even Big J has struggled mightily. He has largely abandoned California, switching his focus to New Mexico, where business hasn't been much better. As he told me in 2023, "This has been the most challenging part of my career—way more challenging than being chased around Mendocino by helicopters."

Very few of the cannabis businesspeople in this book remain in the cannabis business. The Herer Group is no more. With Fern Street a crime scene, the company was forced to cease operations. Dan and Latif parted ways. Latif has gone back to tech sales, refashioning himself as an AI guru. Dan has tried to forge on with the Jack Herer brand but has been mired in litigation with other people and groups who have laid claim to his father's name. Danny O'Brien is out of the weed business. Brian Kenny is out of the weed business. Alex Rowland has given up on hash oil extraction. Evan Scott struggled to keep Consolidated Oil going before falling out with his partners. Rachael left the business behind after Tushar's death and has worked instead to relaunch her mother's art brand. The vast greenhouse complexes of the Salinas Valley again stand mostly empty.

Four years and eight months after the arrests of Tushar Atre's accused killers, the first of them, Nick Lindsay, went on trial in Santa Cruz County Superior Court. The four had been held without bail in the county lockup since their arraignment. The wheels of justice grind slowly even under the best of circumstances, but this case took so long to proceed first because of the pandemic and then because there were four defendants, each with their own court-appointed counsel who mounted vigorous defenses. The prosecution, meanwhile, was not offering deals of any kind—life without parole, take it or leave it—a stance that all but guaranteed no guilty pleas. At first, Lindsay, Camps, and the Charters brothers were to be tried together. But in late 2024, the judge in the case, Stephen S. Siegel, Ben Rice's old law school classmate, ruled in favor of a motion by the defendants to sever the cases into four separate trials.

Lindsay would go first.

Would it matter, the assistant district attorney, Michael McKinney, asked during jury selection in December 2024, if it came out during the trial that the victim was, as one potential juror put it, "an asshole"?

The trial took place over the course of six weeks between January and March 2025. A parade of personalities from the investigation raised their right hands and testified for the prosecution: Dr. Lauren Zephro, Lieutenant Nicholas Baldrige, Lieutenant Daniel Robbins, and Sgt. Erik Miyoshi, who was in many ways the prosecution's star witness. For three and a half days Sam Borghese sat in the witness box answering questions on direct and on cross and on redirect and then on recross. Kelsey Charters, now divorced from Nick Lindsay, testified against her ex-husband. Other key witnesses included the houseguests: Murphy Murri, Chris Berry, Neil and Diana Ide. Latif Horst was subpoenaed to testify for the defense, but in the end he did not. What questions the defense would have asked him is anyone's guess. (Neither Lindsay nor his defense attorneys responded to my requests for interviews.) Horst himself was confused about the subpoena. Indeed, Lindsay's defense immediately rested, calling no witnesses after all.

Sitting in the gallery for closing arguments, Tushar's sister, in apparent agony, put her head in her hands. At other times, she got up and left the courtroom altogether. Shaku Atre was not there. She had died in November, at eighty-four. "The death of our son has turned our golden years into a time of misery," Shaku had written, devastatingly, in a 2023 court filing, "which will only cease when we die."

"Tushar Atre was at home in bed on October first . . . he had no idea that four men had left Lancaster earlier that night on a mission," Michael McKinney, the prosecutor, said at the start of his two-and-a-half-hour closing argument. "He ran and fought for his life—twice—trying to avoid the ultimate action that has brought us all here today."

At ten in the morning on March 5, the jury began deliberations. By three in the afternoon, they had reached a verdict: guilty of murder in the first degree. Lindsay stood silently, without emotion, his hair trimmed military short, wearing a pair of horn-rimmed glasses. Audible sighs rose up from the friend group. One stomped his foot in celebration. They hugged. On the defense side, Lindsay's mother, Eve, stared at the back of her son's head.

At a hearing the following month, Judge Siegel would sentence Lindsay to the statutory maximum, life without the possibility of parole.

If that seemed like an ending, it wasn't. Then the order was reshuffled. Kurtis Charters would now go on trial next, then Kaleb, and then Camps. On September 18, after three weeks of testimony, Judge Siegel read the verdict to the courtroom. Kurtis Charters, too, was guilty on all counts and later sentenced to life without parole. As of this writing, his brother's trial had just begun, and unless there are guilty pleas, Camps's trial will possibly extend into 2026—almost a decade after Tushar Atre first made the fateful decision to enter the weed business.

Endings, in this story, are hard to come by.

Santa Cruz
October 2025

Legalization in California: A Timeline

1915

The California legislature amends its Poison Act to ban the sale of "flowering tops and leaves, extracts, tinctures and other narcotic preparations of hemp."

1937

Cannabis prohibition on the federal level effectively begins with the passage of the Marihuana Tax Act, championed by Harry Anslinger, the founder of the federal agency that would become the US Drug Enforcement Administration.

1969

The US Supreme Court overturns the Marihuana Tax Act in a case brought by the psychedelic activist Timothy Leary, who was contesting his arrest at the Mexico border in 1965 for possession of less than half an ounce of marijuana.

1970

President Richard Nixon signs into law the Controlled Substances Act, which strengthens weed prohibition by classifying cannabis as a Schedule I narcotic.

1972

Proposition 19, or the California Marijuana Initiative, makes it onto the state's ballot. California becomes the first state in the nation to attempt to legalize weed by plebiscite. A two-thirds majority rejects the initiative.

1983

The California Department of Justice forms the Campaign Against Marijuana Planting (CAMP) as a multiagency effort to destroy cannabis production in the state.

1992

The Santa Cruz County Sheriff's Office raids Valerie and Mike Corral's pot garden, politicizing the couple and triggering the medical-necessity defense that would pave the way for:

1996

Voters in California narrowly approve Proposition 215, resulting in the Compassionate Use Act, which legalizes cannabis for medical purposes in the state. In Santa Cruz County, the initiative passes by a 74 percent margin.

2003

The California legislature passes Senate Bill 420, which clarifies regulations around medical marijuana in the state, and establishes the "rights of patients" to form cannabis collectives.

2006

The City of Santa Cruz effectively decriminalizes cannabis, making violations of marijuana laws the lowest law enforcement priority for city police.

2009

A memo by Attorney General Eric Holder indicates that federal law enforcement agencies will not pursue cases against producers and distributors of cannabis that operate within local laws.

2010

Another version of Prop 19 goes on the ballot in California but is again rejected by the electorate, 53 percent to 46 percent.

2012

Voters in Colorado and Washington choose to legalize recreational cannabis, the first two states in the nation to do so.

2016

Voters in California finally legalize weed for recreational use, saying yes to Prop 64, which results in the enactment of the Adult Use of Marijuana Act.

2018

The first legal recreational weed sales in California begin on January 1.

AUTHOR'S NOTE

This book is the result of four years of reporting and research, and is based on interviews with more than two hundred people, as well as the examination of thousands of pages of court records and other documentation. Every major scene in the book is drawn from the account of a person (or people) who witnessed the event firsthand. Material that appears between quotation marks was either heard by me, or came from court documents or published sources. Where dialogue was based on the memory of a participant, it is rendered in italics. Every part of the book has been extensively fact-checked, and whenever possible, passages were read back to the people who participated in the events. In very few instances, I agreed to change the names of sources (these changes are indicated in the text). Writing about secret worlds occasionally requires such accommodations.

NOTES

1. Persons of Interest

1 *wasn't discovered until 1988*: The breakthrough came in the laboratory of the neuropharmacologist Allyn Howlett, at St. Louis University. For a good roundup of the origins and development of the science around the endocannabinoid system, see Roger G. Pertwee, "Cannabinoid pharmacology: the first 66 years," *British Journal of Pharmacology* 147, supplement 1 (January 2006): S163–71, pubmed.ncbi.nlm.nih.gov/16402100.

1 *whenever something new, important, or meaningful is encountered*: In a TEDx Talk on the neuroscience of addiction, behavioral neuroscientist Judy Grisel explained that the endocannabinoid system acts as a "neurological highlighter," releasing neurotransmitters in regions associated with learning, memory, and reward, in moments we find meaningful—such as a good meal or a great line of poetry. She posits that endocannabinoid receptors are so widespread throughout the brain because we never know which experiences we'll find important. Judy Grisel, "Never Enough: The Neuroscience and Experience of Addiction | Judy Grisel | TEDxPSU," TEDx Talk, posted February 24, 2020, by TEDx Talks, YouTube, 12 min., 14 sec., www.youtube.com/watch?v=rnt1eb9vQxA.

1 *enigmatic host of cannabinoids*: Some weed enthusiasts and scientists have asserted that the panoply of active compounds in weed work together synergistically to influence the quality and character of a person's high. That different cannabinoids (and terpenes) may combine in this way has been called the entourage effect, though scientists have yet to find conclusive evidence that it exists.

1 *As of this writing, 301 have been discovered*: This number comes from Lumír Ondřej Hanuš, retired professor of chemistry at Hebrew University in Jerusalem, who has studied cannabinoids for half a century. Indeed, his research is responsible for confirming the existence of the endocannabinoid system itself. See https://lumirlab.com/prof-lumir/.

2 *possible hallucination and psychosis*: Claims about the dangers posed to mental health by cannabis consumption have long been controversial. For a discussion on how dopamine itself produces such effects at superhigh doses, see, Paul Bernard Foley, "Dopamine in

psychiatry: a historical perspective," *Journal of Neural Transmission* 126, no. 4 (February 13, 2019): 473–79, www.researchgate.net/publication/331076984_Dopamine_in_psychiatry_a_historical_perspective. As for cannabis's relationship with psychosis, see Kat Petrilli et al., "Association of cannabis potency with mental ill health and addiction: a systematic review," *The Lancet Psychiatry* 9, no. 9 (September 2022): 736–50, pubmed.ncbi.nlm.nih.gov/35901795.

2 *a posse of sheriff's deputies began their approach*: The description of the search of Atre's property at the Summit on the morning of October 1, 2019, is largely based on testimony by sheriff's deputies and forensic staff in court during the 2025 trial of one of the accused killers, as well as during a preliminary hearing, which took place over the course of four weeks in October and November 2021.

4 *Hungarian psychologist Mihaly Csikszentmihalyi*: Mihaly Csikszentmihalyi, *Flow: The Psychology of Optimal Experience* (Harper & Row, 1990). Csikszentmihalyi's ideas have long found purchase in Silicon Valley. *Wired* magazine was seeking out his wisdom on, of all things, website design as early as 1996—see John Geirland, "Go With The Flow," *Wired*, September 1, 1996, www.wired.com/1996/09/czik—the same year Tushar Atre moved to California to begin his career in web design.

5 *one of the hundreds of cannabis start-ups launched in the state between 2017 and 2018*: The Department of Cannabis Control issued temporary licenses for retail, distribution, cultivation, and manufacturing to around twenty-five hundred distinct entities.

7 *Drug Enforcement Administration to be included on its short list of approved suppliers*: As of this writing, there are only seven such suppliers. Three of the seven suppliers are based in California.

9 *sometimes by a factor of ten or more*: According to one California weed operator, a kilogram of hash oil in Massachusetts circa 2019 was going for thirty thousand dollars, compared to just two thousand dollars in California.

12 *preserve the integrity of the crime scene for the forensic people and the detectives*: The first detective to examine Atre's body at the crime scene was Nick Baldrige, a veteran Santa Cruz investigator who'd clocked many hours with the county narcotics squad bringing down dope rings.

2. Dropping In

22 *he'd told the* Santa Cruz Sentinel: Michael Iacuessa, "Web design company CEO finds best of both worlds here," *Santa Cruz Sentinel*, March 14, 2001.

24 *used to create a substitute for mother's milk*: Hemp is a nutrient-dense seed, and some maintain that hemp-based formulas can be helpful alternatives for formula-fed babies with allergies to cow's milk. But no such formulas are available commercially in the United States, and homemade hemp-formula recipes presented online have come under scrutiny. Sutton A. Davis et al., "Homemade infant formula recipes may contain harmful ingredients: a quantitative content analysis of blogs," Public Health Nutrition (June 2020): 1334–39, https://pmc.ncbi.nlm.nih.gov/articles/PMC10200673/.

3. The Houseguests

26 *They were still wearing their pajamas and sleeping clothes*: The descriptions of the houseguests' movements in the immediate aftermath of the home invasion, including their interviews with detectives at Santa Cruz County Sheriff's Office headquarters, are based on testimony of detectives at the 2021 preliminary hearing of the accused killers; testimony of Christopher Berry, Murphy Murri, and Neil Ide at the 2025 trial; various court documents summarizing the houseguests' statements to police; and author interviews.

26 *massive machine that used ethanol as the solvent*: Neil and Diana had named the system the Nyborg Machine, a tongue-in-cheek portmanteau of their first names plus *cyborg*.

29 *elevated to detective in 2018*: After his promotion to detective, Miyoshi was assigned to the Person Crimes Unit. Santa Cruz County didn't have enough murders to warrant its own murder squad, so in addition to homicides, Person Crimes sleuths also worked assaults, burglaries, domestic violence—anything involving bodily harm.

4. Call Ben Rice

34 *or you could join a patients' collective*: Such collectives were enshrined into law by a second piece of medical marijuana law, known as SB420, enacted in California in 2003.

34 *known as clubs or dispensaries*: The somewhat cloying term *dispensary* is a self-consciously olden-times word, chosen by medical-weed providers precisely because it hearkens back to the nineteenth century when apothecaries sold, across their countertops, any number of now illicit substances, including cannabis.

34 *came to have hundreds and then thousands*: One of the biggest 215 era collectives, CannaCanHelp in Goshen, California, had more than fifteen thousand members.

5. A New Partner

37 *They called this break Sewers*: Also known as Sewer Peak, it is a notoriously locals- and experts-only wave. "Don't join the line up if you're a kook," wrote one Santa Cruz surfer in a blog post.

38 *read the statute*: California Health and Safety Code 11379.6, which covers the production of all sorts of drugs, from hash oil to meth.

41 *One of the Pleasure Point otters, a female, would become world-famous*: Born in captivity at the marine biology institute at UCSC, raised at the Monterey Bay Aquarium, and dubbed Otter 841 there, the creature was eventually released into the wild at Moss Landing in 2020 and ended up stealing surfboards and having a baby.

42 *they were called Chads*: The etymology of this pejorative term is not totally clear. It may have leached into the cannabis world from online culture, where it refers to alpha bros generally and tech bros specifically. According to Evan Scott, in the weed context, outsiders from the corporate world trying to start legal weed companies were originally referred to as "Chads and Brads," as if they'd just emerged from the country club with

pink sweaters draped over their shoulders. To be fair to the Chads, the traditional market was full of Trevors and Travises and Dustins and Bryces.

43 *on Tushar's Onewheels*: Future Motion Inc., the company behind the Onewheel, was launched in Santa Cruz in 2014 with a Kickstarter fundraising campaign.

43 *that said "Zissou" on the uppers*: These were replicas of the footwear worn by Steve Zissou, the character played by Bill Murray in the 2004 Wes Anderson film *The Life Aquatic with Steve Zissou*. Adidas released a limited edition of the sneaker in June 2017. Jake Woolf, "Adidas Made Steve Zissou Sneakers and Actually Sold Them to the Masses," *GQ*, June 28, 2017, www.gq.com/story/adidas-senakers-steve-zissou-life-aquatic.

6. The Safe

46 *A handful of Baldrige's colleagues were already on the premises*: The descriptions of the search of the Pleasure Point house and its contents at the time of the murder are based on testimony of detectives at the 2025 trial of one of the accused killers, crime scene photos displayed during the trial, as well as testimony during the 2021 preliminary hearing, and interviews with sources with direct knowledge of the events.

7. Being Values

50 *Cynthia had added two values of her own invention*: In addition to "Order," she'd added "Resolution," which she defined as "Dichotomy transcendence, acceptance, transform contradictions into collaboration."

53 *past the Subud Santa Cruz spiritual center*: Subud is an obscure quasi-Buddhist movement founded by an Indonesian guru whose global adherents often lived together as blended communal family units.

53 *Bob Hoffman, aka Bonefire Bob*: Bonefire is a veteran participant of the Burning Man festival. In 2003, he was given the highest Burning Man honor: With his flamethrower, he ignited the Man. There are deep connections between Burning Man and the Santa Cruz weed trade. Local black market weed tycoons had long bankrolled many of the festival's wilder installations and sound systems, the successors of Owsley Stanley, the famed LSD chemist and concert audio engineer, who developed the Grateful Dead's Wall of Sound. Joel Hersch, "GLOW," *Good Times*, October 16, 2013, www.goodtimes.sc/glow-mah-festival-of-fire-and-light; Russ Megowan, "Downtown Santa Cruz Closer to Burning Man," *City on a Hill Press*, January 31, 2008, cityonahillpress.com/2008/01/31/downtown-santa-cruz-closer-to-burning-man.

8. Blindfold

55 *This, to Evan, seemed insane*: Although law enforcement had less energy to investigate weed crimes given recreational legalization, they still went hard after unlicensed labs because of the danger of explosions.

58 *all came from other industries, legitimate industries*: The companies that made the stuff often had no idea these West Coast stoners were repurposing their gear for use in a clandestine manufacturing process deemed by many jurisdictions to be illicit. The simplest example: beakers and other standard lab glassware. A more complex example: a kind of refrigerant pump made by a company, Dorin, in Compiobbi, Italy. To extract the highest quality oil using hydrocarbons, the system needed to be very cold.

58 *It was arguably risky*: Based on consultation with his lawyers, Kremerman maintained that it was not illegal to sell extraction-lab equipment or to buy it. What was illegal was building an unlicensed commercial extraction lab with it.

58 *If, for instance, law enforcement were ever to visit Summit Research*: Since time immemorial, cops have similarly targeted hydroponics stores. It wasn't illegal to sell fertilizer. But, as every hydro shopkeeper knew, cops were known to hang around in unmarked cars outside and attempt to follow the stores' customers to their clandestine cultivations.

59 *Operation Shattered Dreams*: As part of the yearlong undercover investigation centered on San Diego County, DEA agents not only surveilled suspected unlicensed labs, but tracked supply chains, as well, monitoring the movement of chemicals and equipment associated with hash-oil labs.

59 *of his own design*: In time, Kremerman would file applications for sixty-nine patents on the devices he'd developed, mostly in the realm of short-path distillation, in which he is considered a pioneering figure. He never once referenced cannabis or cannabinoids in the language of the claims. But times have changed. Cannabis-related patents were once considered unenforceable due to marijuana's Schedule I status, but the US Patent and Trademark Office has indeed issued hundreds of such patents as legalization has spread across the states.

61 *a* trap house: The apartment above the Point Market had been a trap house for a while. The previous tenant had also been a large-scale Santa Cruz black market pot dealer. Yet another eccentric, he would walk around town with a parrot on his shoulder. When Tushar filed to incorporate Interstitial Systems as a nonprofit collective with the California secretary of state, he made the company's official business address the trap house's address.

63 *which led to a year in prison*: One of Kogon's prison buddies was the Wolf of Wall Street, Jordan Belfort, from whom, Kogon says, he learned a few options-trading tips.

65 *Kogon called this particular model the "Bizzy Beest"*: Each of the Beest's columns could hold ten pounds of weed, yielding hash oil in amounts that weighed anywhere from 5 percent to 10 percent of that, typically.

9. The Casings

66 *Zephro had taken control of the crime scene*: This chapter is based on the testimony of Zephro at the 2025 trial and Fulton at the 2021 preliminary hearing.

66 *a civilian employee of the sheriff's department*: Lauren Zephro's specialties included fingerprints and skeletal remains. "Determining the Timing and Mechanism of Bone Fracture in Bovine Bone" was the title of Zephro's dissertation for a PhD in forensic anthropology from the University of California, Santa Cruz, where she studied under Alison Galloway, who'd helped cracked the Laci Peterson case in the early 2000s, one of those sensational murders of bygone years that would attract blanket cable-TV news coverage.

10. Alternative Therapies

68 *widely believed (without evidence) to be a cure for cancer*: The first promising studies on anticancer properties of cannabinoids in animal models emerged in the seventies, but excitement over cannabis as a cancer-fighting agent has outpaced the evidence. Despite decades of case studies, there is still insufficient data showing cannabis as an effective cancer treatment in humans. Jordan Guggisberg et al., "Cannabis as an Anticancer Agent: A Review of Clinical Data and Assessment of Case Reports," *Cannabis and Cannabinoid Research* 7, no. 1 (February 10, 2022): 24–33, www.ncbi.nlm.nih.gov/pmc/articles/PMC8864433.

70 *trademarked under the name Kriya*: In a trademark form filed in September 2022, Bomi is identified as "Bomi Joseph M.D." Bomi, LLC, "Kriya," registration number 6206207, filed August 7, 2018, and registered November 24, 2020.

11. Illuminati

73 *underground handbook*, Cannabis Alchemy: The real name of D. Gold, the author of this classic 1973 text, is David Hoye, who went on to found, many years later, a company called Berkeley Bio-Organic Research Laboratories, which, according to *Bloomberg*, "develops and produces non-psychoactive cannabinoid medicines . . . for cancer treatments." As noted in the body of the handbook's text, there are indications that the book was originally titled *Marijuana Alchemy*, not *Cannabis Alchemy*.

73 *Timothy Leary's* Terra II . . . A Way Out: Written while Leary was serving time in Folsom Prison on charges of possession of half an ounce of weed, and excerpted in *High Times* in June 1974: Timothy Leary, "Terra II," *High Times*, Summer 1974, 23–25.

74 *son of jazz clarinetist George Koenig*: For a bit more information on George Koenig, see "George Koenig," Discogs, www.discogs.com/artist/258699-George-Koenig.

74 *"free of all the old middle-class Freudian hang-ups"*: From the title essay "Slouching Towards Bethlehem," in Joan Didion, *Slouching Towards Bethlehem* (Farrar, Straus and Giroux, 1968).

75 *Neil Plante, his old lady, Joyce*: Within a year, according to Chris Daly, the couple had disappeared from the Deer Creek area. Later, Daly heard that Joyce had been arrested in Colombia for attempting to smuggle cocaine out of the country.

75 *Ken Kesey's writing cabin*: By the mid-sixties, Kesey had famously stopped writing novels and turned instead to LSD explorations and the acid tests and a kind of performance art that involved the famous Day-Glo bus on which the Pranksters crisscrossed the country, freaking out the squares.

75 *"homegrown grass"*: Mountain Girl's *The Primo Plant* was published in 1977 by Wingbow Press, of Berkeley, California.

76 *smuggled into the country in increasingly elaborate, expensive, and dangerous operations*: Often enough, the smugglers were Californians, including Jerry Kamstra, a local who lived down in Capitola, the beach town next to Santa Cruz, or the surfers of the gonzo Brotherhood of Eternal Love out of Laguna Beach in Orange County. See Kamstra's classic memoir of the smuggler's life, *Weed: Adventures of a Dope Smuggler* (Harper & Row, 1974).

77 *Alba Mark*: Alba was not his real name. He was called Alba because he lived on Alba Road.

77 *into the lungs and minds of famous bands*: In addition to the Band, Bill Graham, the rock impresario and owner of the Fillmore, was a big Alba Mark customer. Nearly every grower of weed in the Santa Cruz Mountains of a certain generation will also tell you a Neil Young story or two. Young was, apparently, a prodigious buyer of locally grown pot. For years, Young lived on ranch in the range, across the county line in San Mateo.

78 *On the autumnal equinox of 1983*: Although CAMP didn't officially launch until 1983, state and federal narcotics agents were already teaming up to conduct aerial raids as early as 1982. "California's Marijuana Fields Raided but Effect Is Doubted," *The New York Times*, October 26, 1982, www.nytimes.com/1982/10/26/us/california-s-marijuana-fields-raided-but-effect-is-doubted.html; *1993 Domestic Cannabis Eradication/Suppression Program*, Office of Investigative Support, Drug Enforcement Administration, US Department of Justice, www.ojp.gov/pdffiles1/Digitization/152429NCJRS.pdf.

78 *worth almost as much as gold*: In 1987 and 1988, the average price of gold was $442 an ounce, according to data from the World Gold Council, very close to the per-ounce wholesale price Daly says he was fetching in those years. "Historical Gold Prices—1833 to Present," National Mining Association, September 2016, nma.org/wp-content/uploads/2016/09/historic_gold_prices_1833_pres.pdf.

79 *a major police raid on a bulk-psilocybin-production facility*: Koenig was never charged with a crime, as his longtime Santa Cruz lawyer—Ben Rice, of course—would later attest.

80 *a handful of Santa Cruz weed entrepreneurs*: They included the owner of the biggest chain of hydroponics stores in Santa Cruz County; the owner of Herbal Cruz, one of the first dispensaries in town; and a cultivator, hash maker, and retailer all-in-one who'd come to Santa Cruz from Utah years earlier.

81 *former concrete plant*: An industrial complex now given over wholly to cannabis companies, it started life as an R&D facility for experimental cement mixtures. In the early 2000s, it became the site of a (failed) nuclear energy start-up. Finally it became a weed-industry business center, housing dozens of cannabis cultivators and extractors, conceived of by Mike Bitar, the founder of a Salinas dispensary called East of Eden, along with Nader Agha, the owner of the Moss Landing building complex. Agha, a Syrian immigrant now in his eighties, is a wealthy Monterey real estate developer and antiques dealer. He and Bitar have since fallen out savagely, going to combat in Monterey County Superior Court in a series of lawsuits so byzantine and interminable they may have forgotten the original reason for their falling out.

81 *old port town of Moss Landing*: The village has a storied smuggling history. Rum-running during Prohibition. Weed from Mexico and Asia during the sixties. Cocaine from Latin America in the seventies and eighties and beyond. According to local scuttlebutt, just after the events described in this book, tunnels were discovered underneath the marina area of Moss Landing, with dead bodies inside the tunnels. There are no news accounts of this discovery, nor any criminal case that I could find.

12. The Girlfriend

83–84 *Miyoshi recalled*: The details in this chapter are based on Erik Miyoshi's testimony in 2021 in the preliminary hearings for the accused killers, and the first trial, which took place in 2025.

13. Fresh Frozen

85 *Evan Scott was out of town*: He was in Costa Rica, actually, attending the Envision Festival, an annual eco-dance-music gathering. As a matter of course, Evan made it a habit *not* to be involved in the transportation of weed and to not be present for drop-offs and pickups—a strategy to insulate himself from legal risk.

86 *were preparing to grow more cannabis here*: Another pioneer of industrial-scale cannabis cultivation in the Salinas Valley was Steve DeAngelo, the founder of the enormous Oakland weed dispensary Harborside, who, with his long braids and porkpie hats, has been a very public Bay Area weed operator since the medical marijuana era. Thomas Fuller, "Marijuana Goes Industrial in California," *The New York Times*, April 15, 2017, www.nytimes.com/2017/04/15/us/california-marijuana-industry-agriculture.html.

87 *They identified as Samoan*: That is, members of a population group with origins on islands in the South Pacific. These include the islands of Samoa, an independent nation, and American Samoa, a US protectorate. The Estebans hailed from the latter, according to Elijah Esteban.

89 *A thousand pounds of fresh frozen*: This was the approximate total wet weight of the weed shipped to Tushar and Evan, not to be confused with the dry weight, which is generally used to describe quantities of cannabis in flower or trim form.

14. Mothers

90 *who had recently taken to writing her memoirs*: Excerpts and a summary were posted on Shaku's personal website. Shaku died in November 2024. She was eighty-four.

91 *"I'm going to make a lot of money," Shaku explained*: Many of the details of Shaku's early life and career were drawn from an interview she gave in 2017 on a podcast formerly called *Legends and Losers*, hosted by Christopher Lochhead, a close friend of Tushar's.

92 *"The doctor was worried and splashed water on him"*: This quote is drawn from an account of Tushar's life, and the impacts of his sudden death on the Atre family, that Shaku later wrote for a document filed in court, in her wrongful death lawsuit against the accused killers. "Maybe he somehow knew that his life would be cut short," Shaku wrote, after recounting Tushar's many and varied interests, from German architecture to low-carbon living to cheese and chocolate. "He packed so much in his 50 years of life."

15. The Compliance Manager

95 *The lab was a "free for all," with "people coming in and out all the time."*: Quoted material in this chapter comes from the 2021 preliminary hearing and the testimony of Nick Baldrige.

16. Sons of Samoa

97 *For their highly anticipated meeting with Odie*: Odie says he does not recall this meeting.

98 *Weed brands had existed for many decades in California*: There are myriad examples, stretching back into the 1970s. They include, to name a few, Mad Jag, Beaver Brand, Sense of Humor, Bud Brothers, Bigg Ass Buds, and Popo de Oro.

99 *He'd seen a lot in life*: Biographical details about O'Brien are derived from public court documents.

99 *of at least five states*: Hawaii, California, Utah, Mississippi, and Virginia.

100 *two of his adoptive Salinas brothers*: Everett Napoleon also pleaded guilty; he was allegedly the leader of this particular Mississippi meth-trafficking op and was sentenced to more than sixteen years.

100 *spent nearly ten years in federal prison*: Odie did a chunk at the penitentiary in Victorville, California, where he made interesting friends, including Freeway Rick Ross, the Los Angeles kingpin ensnared in the CIA-contra-crack-cocaine conspiracy of the 1990s, and John Walker Lindh, the American Taliban member, whose parents were Marin County hippies. Almost every day Odie and Ross would stroll the courtyard track, two OGs trading stories and wisdom.

18. The Footage

105 *did not lack for security cameras*: Details on the events and timing of the kidnapping are drawn from detectives' testimony in court and surveillance footage captured by Tushar's neighbors. The Santa Cruz County Sheriff's Office released clips of the footage on Facebook in November 2019 and asked for the public's help in identifying the suspects caught on tape.

19. A Warning

107 *born during a blizzard on a ranch in Montana*: Not only does Evan Scott's story start like a Western, it was, he says, the setting of an actual one: The ranch where he was born would later serve as the backdrop for the TV show *Yellowstone*.

108 *a hermit*: A female hermit was almost unheard of among the many eccentric wild-eyed men who'd sought permanent solitude in the wildernesses of the West since the days of Lewis and Clark. Men, for example, like Ted Kaczynski.

111 *Would-be weed entrepreneurs flocked to the county*: One guy had been a New York City yellow-cab driver—he had actually owned an expensive and difficult-to-obtain taxi medallion—which he used as a front for his citywide black market pot-delivery service. In the 215 era, he became a Santa Cruz pot grower with a farm in the Boulder Creek area.

112 *Yakuza's presence*: Stories about yakuza mobsters buying Santa Cruz weed in bulk come from a black market broker who spoke on condition of anonymity. "It was like Christmas when the Japanese came to town," he said.

112 *the vacation home of the Santa Cruz County administrative officer*: This was Susan Mauriello, who served in that position for thirty-seven years. Jondi Gumz, "Susan Mauriello, creative Santa Cruz County leader, leaves a legacy," *Santa Cruz Sentinel*, last updated September 11, 2018, www.santacruzsentinel.com/2017/06/24/susan-mauriello-creative-santa-cruz-county-leader-leaves-a-legacy.

113 Whoever has the most plants wins: One of the twins has said that this comment was misunderstood. What the twin meant when he said it was that whatever cultivator has the most *kinds* of cannabis *strains*—and thus the most genetic diversity—wins, because then they will have healthier plants.

113 *Mt. Crushmore*: The twins' weed plantation above Deer Creek Road came to an end in 2016, when half the crop burned in a wildfire that started in an adjacent canyon.

113 *were given over entirely to indoor grow rooms*: One of the twins contests that the main house had any grow rooms.

113 *Parties were thrown at the ranch*: One of the twins contests that the parties were as big or wild as described here.

114 *first independent forays into extraction*: During one of those early runs is when Evan suffered the only extraction accident of his career, when gas expanded, a bolt broke, and oil erupted from the malfunctioning machine, coating his face in hashish goo and leaving him with a nasty eye infection.

115 *more than twenty million dollars a year*: Evan Scott is quick to point out that he had to spend a lot on overhead, so his profit margins were quite slim. He had to pay rent to landlords and wages to employees. He had to purchase equipment. Biomass raw material was his most significant expenditure.

21. The BMW

118 *stood at the Summit property*: This chapter is based on the testimony of Detective Ryan Fulton and criminalist May Cheung during the 2021 preliminary hearing as well as the 2025 trial.

22. Two Sharks

122 *airlifted to Bay Area burn units*: In 2015, after responding to an explosion and fire at a Santa Cruz apartment complex, police found a clandestine BHO lab in the building's garage. A forty-eight-year-old man with serious burns requiring immediate medical attention was found hiding in his upstairs apartment with his wife and young child. His family, though home at the time of the explosion, was unharmed. Santa Cruz Police Department, "Butane Hash Oil Explosion," media release, December 16, 2015, www.cityofsantacruz.com/home/showpublisheddocument/49019/635859708281130000.

122 *had notes pinned*: This anecdote comes directly from Ben Rice, who has had enough clients involved in accidents that, while driving past a plume of smoke in Monterey one time, he thought to himself, *God, I hope that's not one of my clients.* The smoke turned out to be a fire raging in the greenhouse of a black market cannabis grow. The owner of the grow wasn't yet but would soon become a Rice client.

122 *yielding hundreds of kilos of oil*: Yields could fluctuate considerably based on any number of variables, not least of which was the relative quality and potency of the biomass itself.

23. Trap Queen

125 *From the playlist, her mother had some favorites*: According to Rachael, Cynthia was put off by hip-hop prior to the visit, mostly because she disliked the genre's seeming misogyny. After the visit, she changed her mind, and even thought some of the lyrics reached the level of poetry. Rachael's dog, Hashtag, also enjoyed the Fetty Wap track. To this day, whenever the song is played, Hashtag will howl along to the music in a tone that can only be described as sorrowful, as if mourning Cynthia.

24. The Lab

128 *Terry Parker and Steven Robbins*: "Classic narc," Ben Rice said of Terry Parker. "Hated weed." Steven Robbins's son Daniel was one of the deputies working closely with Miyoshi on the Atre homicide investigation.

128 *bust that involved a smuggling ring*: The twelve tons of Thai pot was worth more than eighty million dollars. After receiving an anonymous tip from a hiker, the Santa Cruz County Sheriff's Department found the smugglers shuttling the precious cargo from an offshore ship to a beach five miles north of Santa Cruz. John Robinson, "Four local men indicted in big pot smuggling case," *Santa Cruz Sentinel*, November 17, 1989, www.newspapers.com/article/santa-cruz-sentinel-see-the-last-paragra/36354874; John Robinson, "Smuggler tells his tale," *Santa Cruz Sentinel*, April 10, 1990, www.newspapers.com/article/santa-cruz-sentinel/36355297.

129 *Carney ranked up there*: Another of his notable busts was a meth dealer he convinced to roll over on a major weed broker whose headquarters was an oceanfront manse in Santa Cruz. The broker, who had a six-figure wine cellar and shipped weed to New York City through the US Postal Service in the early 2000s, protested that he was just a provider of medicinal cannabis, helping people in need. "Marijuana trafficker Edwin Hoey being prosecuted for tax fraud," *Santa Cruz Sentinel*, last updated September 11, 2018, www.santacruzsentinel.com/general-news/20080812/marijuana-trafficker-edwin-hoey-being-prosecuted-for-tax-fraud.

129 *a certain mutual respect*: Their relationship reminded Rice of "the old cartoon with the chicken hawk and the dog."

129 *physically fit*: Early-bird county employees coming to work at dawn would catch glimpses of Carney sprinting up and down the five flights of stairs in the county administrative building—a brutalist icon erected in 1967.

130 *had actually busted him once before*: Big J's lawyer in this 2002 case was not Ben Rice but Ben Rice's rival/mentor in Santa Cruz criminal defense, the legal eminence Paul Meltzer.

131 *the massive use of money orders*: Big J and others have long argued that legal weed businesses are forced to use money orders to pay their bills because banks either refuse to take them as clients or charge outrageous, usurious fees.

131 *were somewhat counterintuitive*: The case Carney built against Big J did not accuse his organization of engaging in black market sales, per se, or in interstate commerce, a federal crime.

131 *If you snuck a bunch of unlicensed pot onto the books of your licensed company*: You could also inflate your cash flow and make your company that much more attractive—with a consequently higher valuation—to a potential corporate buyer.

131 *quickly settled the case*: Big J also agreed to the banishment of his weed businesses from the unincorporated areas of Santa Cruz County. Because this was a Santa Cruz County case, his Monterey businesses could continue to operate, and that apparently was where this mound of weed in the Fern Street storage room had come from.

25. Revolt

133 *a consultant*: They'd hired a policy wonk named Sam LoForti, a UCSC grad who liked weed and used to work in compliance for mining companies, to guide them through the regulatory labyrinth. The same Sam LoForti who would go on to become Santa Cruz County's cannabis czar.

26. The Cloud

136 *flung the device into the churning sea*: The details in this chapter are based on the testimony of detectives at the 2021 preliminary hearing and various court documents containing segments of police reports written by the detectives as the murder investigation was unfolding.

27. Summit

139 *a scientific journal that detailed recent research findings*: A number of such studies were published in the early to mid-1970s, investigating THC's effects on several kinds of rodent brain. See, e.g., M. E. Corcoran et al., "Acute antiepileptic effects of 9-tetrahydrocannabinol in rats with kindled seizure," *Experimental Neurology*, August 1973; M Ten Ham et al., "Acute and chronic effects of beta9-tetrahydrocannabinol on seizures in the gerbil," *European Journal of Pharmacology*, March 1975; and GB Chesher et al., "Interaction of delta9-tetrahydrocannabinol and cannabidiol with phenobarbitone in protecting mice from electrically induced convulsions," *Journal of Pharmacy and Pharmacology*, August 1975.

139 *a regular cannabis-consumption regimen*: Valerie also read Paavo Airola's *How to Get Well*, a bestseller at the time, one of the first popular works to harp on diet as a contributor to inflammations. She followed its guidelines, changed what she ate, went outside and touched her bare feet to the grass, or the soil, just standing there for a half hour every morning. "Cannabis didn't work singularly," she says today. "It was diet, everything."

142 *Original Haze*: Many years later, according to Robert Clarke, the creators of Haze were dubbed the "Haze Brothers" by a person who was seeking to "squat" on the Haze genetics, which were unclaimed, and essentially part of the public domain. Cannabis lore is famously convoluted and difficult to sort.

142 *migrated north . . . Santa Cruz Mountains*: Once in Santa Cruz, Watson and his wife took organic-gardening classes with famed UCSC horticulturalist Alan Chadwick. Watson told me he never discussed cannabis cultivation with Chadwick or any of the other students. But, Watson added, "I'm sure Chadwick taught many people who used the knowledge to grow better cannabis."

142 *Brotherhood of Eternal Love*: For more on this psychedelic cult of surfer drug traffickers (originally from Laguna Beach, but with Santa Cruz connections) see *Orange Sunshine: The Brotherhood of Eternal Love and Its Quest to Spread Peace, Love, and Acid*

to the World by Nicholas Schou (Thomas Dunne Books, 2010). After fleeing California and setting up shop in Hawaii, the BEL created—or are credited with creating—a cannabis strain that became popular in the 1970s: the iconic Maui Wowie. "Since its beginnings in the island's volcanic soil, Maui Wowie has spread across the world to bless us with its sweet pineapple flavors and high-energy euphoria," writes Leafly, the excellent cannabis review website. Members of the BEL were also strain hunters on the Hippie Trail in central Asia, and were early, pioneering extractors of hash oil. They operated industrial-scale labs in pre-war-torn Afghanistan, then smuggled the stuff into the United States, using the profits to finance their wacky LSD evangelism. Their extraction efforts in Afghanistan are shrouded in mystery, but it's likely they would have used methods similar to those described by D. Gold in *Cannabis Alchemy*.

143 *A marijuana researcher*: The judge in the case described Watson as the Luther Burbank of weed. Burbank was the nineteenth-century botanist who created hundreds of flower and vegetable strains, including the potato used to make McDonald's fries. Burbank did most of his hybridizing in Santa Rosa, California.

143 *until his death in 2025*: Watson, whom I interviewed at length in 2023 after months of trying to convince him to tell his story, died unexpectedly in January 2025 while on his annual visit to Santa Cruz from his home in Amsterdam. He was seventy-five years old.

143 *Clarke would go on to dedicate his life to cannabis research*: Clarke has written a string of seminal cannabis texts, including *Marijuana Botany* (1981), *Hashish!* (1998), and his magnum opus, with the longtime University of Hawaii botanist Mark D. Merlin, *Cannabis: Evolution and Ethnobotany* (2013).

144 *high-altitude farms in the Sierra Madre del Sur*: The original weed cultivators of the rugged Sierra Madre took to carrying "AR15 rifles . . . to protect their fields from the occasional army patrol," wrote Jerry Kamstra in his memoir *Weed*. Kamstra, a would-be Beat Generation writer who for decades made his home in Santa Cruz County, smuggled literally tons of Acapulco Gold into California in the 1960s and '70s. On his smuggling trips to Mexico, he befriended many paisanos. "The truth about marijuana is money," one of those paisanos told Kamstra. "It is the best crop we can grow in the mountains now, because of you gringos."

144 *Cannabis cultivation in Africa began*: This is from Chris Duvall's cultural and scientific survey, *Cannabis* (Reaktion Books, 2014), 46. A professor of geography at the University of New Mexico, Duvall is an expert on the history of African cannabis use and production. See also his *The African Roots of Marijuana* (2019).

144 *often appears in classical Islamic literature*: Duvall, *Cannabis*, 45: "In Old Arabic works from the Islamic Golden Age (800s–1200 CE), banj referred generically to any psychoactive plant and was associated in stories with crime, dark magic and poisoning." For this, Duvall himself cites the Yale professor of Arabic literature Franz Rosenthal, *The Herb: Hashish Versus Medieval Muslim Society* (1971).

144 *Marco Polo*: The Italian adventurer describes the myth of the Old Man of the Mountain and the cult of the assassins in his thirteenth-century narrative *Book of the Marvels of the World*.

145 *full of shit*: There is no evidence in the historical record that the assassins ever actually used hashish. The hash element of their story was apparently disinformation created contemporaneously by the sect's enemies within Islam, and was later embraced by the Crusaders and disseminated throughout Europe, most importantly by Marco Polo. The sect's colloquial name is how it became known in Europe, and is apparently a bowdlerization of the Arabic *hashshashin*, or hashish user, a pejorative term in the Islamic world. Many have argued that this erroneous claim, that the assassins consumed hash, has slandered cannabis itself down through Western history, propagating the falsehood that cannabis induces violence, which in turn was cynically used by Harry Anslinger, the founder of the DEA's predecessor agency, to bring about marijuana prohibition in 1937 so as to advance his own career.

145 assassin: For more on the assassins, see volumes two and three of Steven Runciman's magisterial three-volume *A History of the Crusades* (1951); *The Assassins: A Radical Sect in Islam*, by Bernard Lewis (1967); and *The Assassins: Holy Killers of Islam*, by Edward Burman (1988). The etymological origins of the word *assassin* were established in 1809 by the French linguist Antoine-Isaac Silvestre de Sacy, though he also propagated the myth that the sect's murderous initiates were fueled by prodigious hash consumption.

145 *The Arab world, in turn, likely discovered cannabis*: This summary of the ancient migrations of drug cannabis is based chiefly on interviews with Robert C. Clarke, as well as on Clarke and Mark D. Merlin's *Cannabis: Evolution and Ethnobotany*; Duvall's *Cannabis*; and Martin Booth, *Cannabis: A History* (Picador, 2005).

145 *Possible references to it . . . Vedic texts*: That the Vedic texts actually refer to cannabis is controversial. The sacred beverage soma may have included other, different intoxicants, not cannabis.

145 *some have posited*: See, e.g., Julian Jaynes, *The Origin of Consciousness in the Breakdown of the Bicameral Mind* (Mariner Books, 1976).

146 *"Indian killer"*: According to Ibn Buttata in his writings, the locals referred to the mountain range as the Hindu Kush because slaves taken there from India often died "on account of the intenseness of the cold." See *The Travels of Ibn Buttata*, translated by Samuel Lee, 1829. https://archive.org/stream/b28406084/b28406084_djvu.txt.

146 *In late September 1978*: One of the growers arrested at the Summit, whose case was dismissed because it was determined that law enforcement had conducted a warrantless search, was represented by a young Santa Cruz attorney named Art Dudley, who would go on to represent, more than forty years later, one of Tushar Atre's alleged killers.

147 *Norman Dillon*: An appellate court in Norman Dillon's case found the life sentence excessive given Dillon's age and that the shooting was the result of panic, not premeditation. *People v. Dillon*, 668 P.2d 697 (1983), state-law-research.org/case/people-v-dillon.

147 *Their story after that is well-known*: See, for example, Michael Pollan, "Living with Medical Marijuana," *The New York Times Magazine*, July 20, 1997, and Peter Hecht, *Weed Land: Inside America's Marijuana Epicenter* (University of California Press, 2014).

148 *One of their lawyers had the idea . . . medical necessity defense*: Paul Meltzer, éminence grise in the Santa Cruz cannabis law realm, Harvard Law, 1977, was the attorney who came up with the idea. Meltzer was one of Ben Rice's mentors and, later, rivals in the Santa Cruz cannabis legal-defense industry.

148 *at a community center in downtown Santa Cruz*: Immediately after each WAMM distribution event at this same community center, Narcotics Anonymous would hold its meetings, and WAMM was eventually forced to find new quarters.

148 *elite unit*: Members included Alan Hopper, then of the American Civil Liberties Union, and Gerald Uelmen, a law professor at Santa Clara University, who was part of O. J. Simpson's defense team.

148 *including, of course, Ben Rice*: Rice says he was only a minor player in the WAMM drama, and that other attorneys did the heavy lifting. He does recall, however, that he and the others were "licking our chops" to depose John Ashcroft, then the US attorney general under George W. Bush, as part of WAMM's litigation against the federal government, but the case was won before that could happen.

149 *WAMM struggled to reinvent itself*: Those struggles may now be over. In 2023, WAMM partnered with a licensed Santa Cruz cannabis retailer called Treehouse so they could continue to dispense free or low-cost weed to people with health problems.

28. Driving Off a Cliff

151 *seemed to influence their decisions*: Tushar also filed incorporation documents for a "nonprofit mutual benefit corporation" called Interstitial Systems Inc. with the California secretary of state in May 2017—the registration filing that listed Evan Scott's trap house above the Point Market as its corporate address. Rachael was unaware of this, however, and I could find no evidence that the Interstitial "collective" had any patient members, let alone a structure to distribute cannabis to them. Such filings were extremely common in the Prop 215 and early Prop 64 eras as weed operators hoped to use these nonprofit documents as a means to shield themselves from prosecution for unlicensed or black market pot sales.

154 *dispensary-finder websites*: Such as Leafly or Weedmaps.

155 *Light dep accelerated*: The hippies of Deer Creek Road—and all over California—had been doing light dep at least since the eighties, though not Chris Daly, who considered any cannabis not grown under the sun's true analog arc to be inferior.

155 *using organic farming methods*: Earlier in the spring, before the cannabis growing season began, Rachael had infused the soil with nitrogen by planting legumes.

157 *obscure work of anthropology*: It could also be considered a how-to guide for tepee construction. Reginald Laubin and Gladys Laubin, *The Indian Tipi: Its History, Construction, and Use* (University of Oklahoma Press, 1957).

29. Trinity

160 *She was eighteen years old, class of 2004*: Around this same time, across the continent in Santa Cruz, Tushar Atre, thirty-five, had purchased his first oceanfront home, for two million dollars.

163 *Rachael planted her garden*: The term *garden* is a euphemism preferred since at least the 1960s by cannabis growers of even great commercial scale.

165 *One of the hands she'd hired was Hank*: Hank had been the head grower for a different weed entrepreneur who'd migrated from Vermont to California during the Prop 215 Green Rush. Rachael recruited him away from her rival.

165 *reputed ally of certain cartels*: For more on the Mexican Mafia's links to La Famila, see this federal case from 2013: United States Attorney's Office, Central District of California, "13 Linked to Mexican Mafia and La Familia Indicted," August 6, 2013, https://www.justice.gov/usao-cdca/pr/13-linked-mexican-mafia-and-la-familia-indicted-after-investigation-reveals-plot-join. A January 2025 indictment against six members of the Mexican Mafia alleges that the prison gang agreed to provide protection for incarcerated Sinaloa Cartel members—including Joaquín "El Chapo" Guzmán—in exchange for drugs supplied from Mexico. Nearly all major prison gangs in the United States have connections to cartels, according to law enforcement, and not just the Sinaloa Cartel. United States Attorney's Office, Eastern District of California, "California La eMe Members and Associates Indicted for Racketeering and Controlled Substance Trafficking through a Partnership with the Sinaloa Cartel," January 17, 2025, www.justice.gov/usao-edca/pr/california-la-eme-members-and-associates-indicted-racketeering-and-controlled.

30. The Autopsy

168 *October 7, 2019*: This is the date, less than a week after Tushar's death, that his autopsy results made the local news. Nicholas Ibarra, "Kidnapped entrepreneur Atre was fatally shot; death ruled homicide," *Santa Cruz Sentinel*, last updated October 10, 2019, www.santacruzsentinel.com/2019/10/07/kidnapped-entrepreneur-atre-was-fatally-shot-death-ruled-homicide.

168 *Dr. Stephany Fiore*: A California native whose specialty training in forensic pathology began in New York City as a fellow, examining the remains of the victims of the 9/11 World Trade Center attacks. Stephen Baxter, "New forensic pathologist starts in Santa Cruz County," *Santa Cruz Sentinel*, last updated September 11, 2018, www.santacruzsentinel.com/2014/07/21/new-forensic-pathologist-starts-in-santa-cruz-county.

168 *In the grainy, ghostly footage*: The details of Tushar's injuries and the manner in which they were sustained are based on court documents, publicly available footage of the attack, and the testimony of Detective Erik Miyoshi in the 2021 preliminary hearings for the four accused killers.

31. Dabs

172 *these guys in Oregon*: This outfit, called Skunk Pharm Research, was founded by a prominent figure in the underground development of hash-oil-manufacturing systems, an engineer who goes by the alias Graywolf.

173 *leaving his family behind*: "He had some really interesting partnerships with people who could have killed him at any moment for the slightest infraction" is the way Brian Kenny would later describe his father's perpetual situation in life. Family legend indicates that David Kenny fled California following the felled-oak-tree incident, made his way to Singapore, and spent seven years there. Family legend also indicates that during those years, David Kenny and his good pal, a guy from Hawaii, embarked on a caper to smuggle a shipment of cocaine and heroin and weed from Mexico and California via Hawaii to Japan, where David's friend had yakuza connections. Family legend further indicates that the shipment—secreted inside a shipping container on a cargo vessel—was discovered and seized in international waters, and that Interpol and other law enforcement bodies foreign and domestic launched investigations into the origins of this attempted smuggling operation, which David Kenny was never implicated in.

174 *and now it was after midnight at Brian's house*: Brian Kenny doesn't clearly recall any of this, his memories muddled by the amount of dab smoking he was doing in those years, including on this intoxicated night with Tushar in late July 2018, but there is a digital record of the event in the form of text messages.

32. Forty-Ninth

175 Whether you experience heaven or hell: A close paraphrase from a line in the introduction of *The Psychedelic Experience: A Manual Based on the Tibetan Book of the Dead* by Timothy Leary, Ralph Metzner, and Richard Alpert.

178 *large, reliable labor pool*: Rachael says she did not pay foreign workers any less than American workers. At other farms, trimmigrants have been known to set up their own informal labor unions, negotiating their wages as a group.

181 *Kyle was also a weed broker*: Kyle denies he was a weed broker, though this contradicts multiple other sources. Kyle claims he was merely a hash-oil extraction "consultant."

181 *Santa Cruz was an important brokering hub*: One such black market broker—everyone knew him as Wale (pronounced WALL-ay)—rode around in a Lamborghini Urus SUV with an entourage of dudes and brought in quantities said to exceed a thousand pounds per deal, according to people who knew him. Wale was a whale. Based in Los Angeles, he owned property in Mendocino County. He owned a twin-engine Cessna 650 jet, which he used to ship weight east, selling it in states where full-scale prohibition still existed, which of course produced the highest profits. Then in 2022, Wale's flashy style caught up with him. He was indicted in federal court on drug-trafficking

and money-laundering charges, causing no small disruption in the national and even global cannabis black markets.

182 *OG cultivator*: OG, of course, stands for Original Gangster, another piece of Black American urban slang co-opted by the weed world and used to refer to older-generation pot farmers and operators, as in the ones who pioneered the domestic pot trade in the 1960s, '70s, '80s.

33. The Reward

185 *Unnamed private parties*: The excerpt printed here is taken from the article "$25,000 reward offered in Pleasure Point kidnapping-turned-murder case," by the *Santa Cruz Sentinel*'s ace crime and courts reporter Jessica A. York, who covered the Atre homicide investigation and subsequent court case for her paper with vigor and aplomb starting on the day of the discovery of Atre's body and ending only in January 2025, when she died at forty-three of a rare form of cancer.

185 *the reward was increased*: The sum being offered to potential tipsters was increased to $150,000 on November 18, 2019, and then to $200,000 on January 29, 2020. On that same day, the Santa Cruz County Sheriff's Office publicly released footage taken from one of the Pleasure Point Drive security cameras. The video shows an unidentified man on a bicycle stopping outside Atre's house at just after midnight on October 1, 2019. The rider, a thin person, probably male, wearing a hoodie, appears to gaze at the entrance to the house for about ten seconds, as if casing the place, and then moves on. Detectives never identified this mysterious rider.

34. Fire

188 *engulfed by flames*: Videos of the accident have been available online for years, including here: Rebecca Atkins, "Former marijuana dispensary employee sues owners after lab explosion," *KRQE News*, May 12, 2017, www.krqe.com/news/former-marijuana-dispensary-employee-sues-owners-after-lab-explosion.

190 *owners and operators of secret marijuana plantations*: See, for example, Thomas Fuller, "California's 'Green Rush' Takes Hmong Back to Their Opium Growing Roots," *The New York Times*, June 3, 2017, www.nytimes.com/2017/06/03/us/hmong-marijuana-california.html; Paige St. John, "Hmong pot growers in Siskiyou County seeking identity, profit—or both," *Los Angeles Times*, September 10, 2017, www.latimes.com/local/california/la-me-hmong-marijuana-siskiyou-20170910-htmlstory.html.

190 *Then came the day that Brian arrived home*: Kenny's wife does not recall this specific incident and says that Kenny was aware of her business practices.

35. Harvest

193 *would form encampments*: For an excellent depiction of life as a trimmigrant on a California pot farm in the medical marijuana era, see Matthew Gavin Frank, *Pot Farm* (University of Nebraska Press, 2012).

193 *developed into the Emerald Cup*: Tim Blake, a longtime pot farmer in Mendocino County, started hosting harvest parties at the site of his farm collective outside the town of Laytonville. Part of the festivities included a friendly competition among area weed growers to see who'd produced the best bud that year. Bobby Black, "Growing Culture: The Emerald Cup," *Leaf Nation*, May 24, 2021, leafmagazines.com/profiles /growing-culture-the-emerald-cup.

193 *In Big Sur*: Details about Big Sur's famously secretive cannabis-farming community and its annual harvest celebration come largely from Oliver Bates, a grower and surfer from Santa Cruz who has lived in Big Sur for years and knows many of the region's "elders," as he calls the old-timers. Legends abound. For example, it is said that a member of the Hearst family grew weed on a large scale in Big Sur as early as the 1950s. Big Sur may also have been the place where high-potency, seedless weed—also called sinsemilla, borrowing from the Spanish—was first grown in the United States. In 1970 or 1971, it is said, a Big Sur pot grower named Patrick Cassidy destroyed his male plants so they couldn't pollinate the females, and the females could instead focus their energies on producing flowers, not seeds. Potency spiked, and the always undesirable seed content nearly vanished. Cassidy supposedly had heard about this technique from strain hunters who'd traveled through Afghanistan and seen the slaughtering of the males practiced there. Cassidy, it was said, called his new strain Holy Weed because it was so mind-blowing you could perceive the Eternal. Or maybe not. There is a competing legend, which tells of a Catholic monk named Perry—no one knows his last name, a member of New Camaldoli Hermitage, a Benedictine retreat that hangs to a crag high above the Pacific in the middle of Big Sur. Perry had lived previously in a monastery in Mexico, where he'd kept an apothecary's garden and learned from the locals how to grow all sorts of medicinal plants—including sinsemilla cannabis, or so the story goes. And so it was Perry the holy man who may have created the strain that came to be known as Holy Weed, which is at least as famous as Haze and Skunk.

197 *Each turkey bag held a pound of weed*: Technically speaking, each bag could hold more than two pounds of product, but according to Rachael, industry practice was to fill up each bag only halfway—equivalent to about a pound of weed—so it could be twisted shut.

36. The Trimmer

202 *sent the Santa Cruz County aircraft*: Santa Cruz residents have complained about the constitutionality of airborne surveillance since the CAMP days of the 1980s and '90s.

202 *but they couldn't find anything*: Carney's team did end up locating—on a parcel about a dozen miles from Tushar Atre's property—a sprawling hoop-house operation containing almost ten thousand illegal plants. It had sophisticated irrigation systems. It used fertilizers and pesticides. It was being operated by a handful of undocumented people from Mexico. It bore the hallmarks, therefore, of a "cartel grow." The land was raw land, owned by the CEO of a *licensed* cannabis-cultivation company up in Humboldt County—not connected to Atre in any way.

37. Venture Capital

204 *hard-partying, bong-hitting, business-majoring variety*: Miami University is unquestionably a party school. "If you blow off studying to rage your face off it's not a big deal," wrote one Miami student in an anonymous online testimonial. "I have more friends whose parents own companies than don't. This obviously leads to perpetually irresponsible binges."

204 *OWC Ventures, which stood for OpenRoads Wealth Capital*: Or possibly it stood for Ohio Wellness Cultivators, another limited liability company formed by Jeff Walker Sr. in 2017.

207 *took pains to describe the Fern Labs team, including Nick Montoya*: This and other details about the pitch made by Brian Kelly and Tushar to OWC, as well as their subsequent interactions as they negotiated, derive in large part from court documents generated by the long and complex litigation battle waged between OWC investors and Atre's estate, as well as interviews with some of the participants.

38. A Proposal

209 *the rear tire thumped over his thigh*: Jones denies running over Tushar. The way Jones remembers it, Tushar didn't fall down. Instead, Tushar ran back to the truck he was driving, put it in gear, and accelerated headlong toward Jones in the Tacoma. There was a chase, and Tushar lost control, crashing into a ditch, and that's how Jones got away.

39. The Investor

216 *Jack Heekin arrived in Santa Cruz*: Heekin's interview with detectives was described during Miyoshi's testimony at the preliminary hearing in the Atre case on October 12, 2021.

40. A Deal

219 *this was atypical*: "I would have tanked the deal," said one person with expertise in the world of venture capital.

41. Weed and Thieves

223 *but a meth lab*: Kyle's father was charged with manufacturing methamphetamines in Oregon in 2001, but pled guilty to a lesser charge: unlawful manufacture of a destructive device. He was sentenced to thirty-six months probation.

223 *It was obvious to her*: Kyle denies this. He says that Rachael's biomass went to another extraction lab entirely—Emerald something—and he doesn't know what happened to it after that. Rachael says Kyle is lying.

42. The Caretaker

226 *Eager to help*: The details describing this portion of the investigation are taken from court testimony by SCSO detectives Erik Miyoshi and Ryan Fulton made during the preliminary hearings for the accused killers in 2021.

226 *received a text message*: Tushar's phone was never found, and detectives were never able to solve the mystery of the phantom text message and unopenable attachment.

43. Betrayal

229 *It ruined the centrifuge enterprise*: Nick Montoya has denied Brian Kenny's allegations and declined to comment further.

229 *company called Iron Fist*: Founded by an eccentric but highly accomplished welder in the town of East Wenatchee, Washington. Like the barkeeps at certain New York City dive bars, Schenk was not known for his customer service. Inevitably, Iron Fist was one of Boris Kogon's biggest rivals.

229 *sweat equity in Interstitial*: Documentation included in OWC's lawsuit against the Atre estate shows that both Brians were each to receive 138,100 shares of Interstitial/Cruz Science. That quantity of stock equated to 10 percent of the company each for him and Kelly.

44. Cannabis Karma

231 *convoluted scheme involving a shell company*: According to Rachael, Tushar's plan, which he eventually does appear to have halfway executed, was to create a shell company, which he called Monterey Storage Solutions LLC, which would hold Tushar's equity stake in Interstitial/Cruz Science. Then, Tushar would make Rachael a partner in Monterey Storage. Voilà, she would have equity in the extraction company.

45. The Memorial

234 *She wore a dress*: Rachael wore the same dress to her mother's funeral in Vermont in 2017.

235 *a ceremonial paddle out*: Tushar's memorial in Monterey Bay appears to have been based on the traditional Hawaiian sea burial, which often involve surfers paddling out to sea to spread the departed's ashes.

46. A New Lease

236 *Salem, Massachusetts*: In 2016, more than a century after it became the first state to criminalize marijuana, Massachusetts voters approved a ballot measure to legalize recreational use—the same year that Proposition 64 passed in California.

238 *Latif was trying to convince him*: This is not how Latif Horst remembers it; he says he was looking for employee housing.

238 *Latif . . . was involved in other kinds of business*: The Santa Cruz weed community is a cauldron of gossip and rumor, and the Horst clan has featured in certain vibrant strains of it. From several different people with no connection to one another, I heard, in essence, that the Horsts were allegedly members of a drug-smuggling hippie cult and were forced to flee to England because they were being investigated by law enforcement.

Latif Horst cackled with laughter when confronted with these rumors. He said, "That is the most ridiculous, bizarre thing I've ever heard. How would anyone even come up with that? No. There's absolutely zero chance of that whatsoever. My dad was not into anything like that, for sure."

The Horsts were, in fact, members of Subud, one of the many Eastern spiritual communities that have been drawn to the Santa Cruz Mountains. Said to be a portmanteau of the Sanskrit words *susila*, *buddhi*, and *dharma*; Subud was founded in Indonesia by a man who had a religious vision in 1925 and then traveled the world proselytizing, building Subud into an international movement that came to have particular sway in bohemian circles in 1950s London and then in 1960s California. His acolytes called him Bapak, Javanese for "father." Actors and musicians joined his group, including Roger McGuinn, founder of the seminal psychedelic rock band the Byrds, and Lewis Arquette, father of the actors Rosanna, Patricia, and David Arquette. In the seventies, the local Santa Cruz branch of Subud built its headquarters on a small campus off Soquel San Jose Road, the Subud Santa Cruz spiritual center. A half dozen Subud families lived in the hills around the center. Names were sometimes changed to indicate spiritual conversion. Latif's father, for example, was Joshua Horst, but also at other times Sequoia Horst and Hamid Horst.

But when it came to cannabis, or any drug for that matter, Subud was unequivocal. Bapak, Subud's founder, prohibited all drug use on penalty of expulsion from the movement.

As for the rumors of criminal activity, the most absurd (and also alluring) involved the Horst family fleeing Santa Cruz for England in the 1980s following the crash of an airplane that was carrying bulk quantities of weed. Or possibly cocaine. Or both. Crashes of airplanes carrying great cargoes of illicit drugs were in fact an entire genre of aviation incident in the seventies and eighties. Domestic traffickers had evidently discovered they could acquire decommissioned World War II aircraft for cheap and then repurpose them as efficient drug-ferrying vehicles, so long as they knew what they were doing. But often, alas, they didn't. Tennessee, Georgia, Florida, Virginia, West Virginia—the crashes seemed to occur mostly in the American South, but in California also—old B-25s and Lockheed Lodestars and small civilian single-engine jobs, and big decrepit DC-3s, too, were falling out of the sky and scattering tons of bud and kilos of coke across the land. The film *Cocaine Bear* is based on the true story of one of these crashes, in Tennessee.

There is no evidence that Joshua Horst moved his family to the United Kingdom in order to avoid a US federal investigation into the crash of an airplane carrying weed or anything else. In fact, far more mundanely, Latif's father, an architect and engineer, had been hired to manage a large-scale hotel construction project near Windsor.

47. The Gofer

239 *Detectives already knew Sam Borghese*: As a witness for the prosecution, Borghese testified at great length on the stand at the 2025 trial of one of Atre's accused killers. Much of the information in this chapter is taken from that testimony, as well as my own interviews with Borghese.

48. Jack Herer

241 *The book was called* G.R.A.S.S.: It was published in 1973 by something called Primo Publications, of Melrose Avenue, Hollywood, California. "We feel that grass is for fun," Herer wrote along with his coauthor, Al Emmanuel, at the start of the book, "but remember, no matter how high you go, you are going to come down, and, conversely, no matter how far down you go, you always come back up."

242 *The story of Jack Herer's conversion is well-known*: Herer's life story is chronicled in the 1999 documentary *Emperor of Hemp*.

242 *Proposition 19*: The California voter guide for 1972 contained a litany of arguments against it: "The hallmark of marijuana use is flight from reality and its assassination of ambition," wrote one opponent. "Even one marijuana trip is dangerous because marijuana is the vehicle for crossing the psychological barrier to drug abuse." Two-thirds of voters agreed and voted against the measure.

244 *refused to plead guilty*: A summary of the case against Herer and others at the protest that day can be found in the US Court of Appeals decision from 1983. See https://law.justia.com/cases/federal/appellate-courts/F2/700/1253/117179/.

244 The Emperor Wears No Clothes: It has apparently gone through fourteen editions, at least according to what it says on the cover of my copy, which was published by Herer Media & Publishing, Inc., an entity created by Dan Herer.

245 *a secretive cannabis breeder in Amsterdam*: Not David Watson. This strain was created by a *different* secretive cannabis breeder from California who'd fled to Amsterdam.

There were, perhaps not surprisingly, many such Californians in Amsterdam at one time.

245 *Ben Dronkers, an idealistic hippie and strain hunter*: Dutchman Dronkers traveled across the Middle East and central Asia, including Pakistan and Afghanistan, in the 1970s, collecting landrace cannabis seeds. He would later largely be responsible for pushing the law in the Netherlands that allowed for the sale of cannabis seeds in the country. For more details, see "Will you be the next Jack Herer or Ben Dronkers?" Sensi Seeds, last updated December 22, 2020, sensiseeds.com/en/blog/will-next-jack-herer-ben-dronkers.

245 *Dronkers's son Che refused*: The Dronkers did not respond to requests for comment.

246 *called Dr. Delights*: Though the company is now defunct, the brand's Instagram page—which features a lot of stylish photos of young, fit women hanging out with one another on what are clearly Santa Cruz beaches, laughing and happily holding Dr. Delight vapes between their fingers—is still up. The last post was on November 30, 2019, two months after Tushar's murder.

247 *terpenes are believed*: That terpenes might affect a cannabis user's high is contentious. It is difficult, if not impossible, even to study such a topic. If terpenes do impact a user's psychotropic experience, it's likely through the entourage effect. According to researchers from the Hadassah Medical Center in Israel, increasing amounts of the terpene myrcene in cannabis are linked to an increased couch-lock effect. Dr. M. Sruthi, "What Do Terpenes Do for Your High?" MedicineNet, accessed July 14, 2025, www.medicinenet.com/what_do_terpenes_do_for_your_high/article.htm; Lumír Ondřej Hanuš and Yotam Hod, "Terpenes/Terpenoids in Cannabis: Are They Important?" *Medical Cannabis and Cannabinoids* 3, no. 1 (August 10, 2020): 25–60, pmc.ncbi.nlm.nih.gov/articles/PMC8489319.

247 *experiment with a whole palette of terpenes*: There are companies that do nothing but produce cannabis terpenes for just this purpose.

49. The Brit

250 *some kind of "incident"*: Details on Horst's interview with detectives come from Horst himself as well as Miyoshi's testimony at the 2021 preliminary hearing. Horst was interviewed at least twice by detectives during the homicide investigation. He was also subpoenaed by defense attorneys to testify at the 2025 trial of one accused killer. But the defense ended up not calling him as a witness. Horst told me he has no idea what they would have wanted to ask him. The defense team, meanwhile, did not respond to my requests for an interview.

50. Fiftieth

251–252 *The application that Tushar would later submit*: "Our research is focused on improving the wellness of our planet and all of its inhabitants," MBARI's research-permit application grandly stated.

51. The Pod

255 *In November 2018, a service drop from a utility pole*: Information about this incident comes from Carney's search warrant affidavit, obtained from Santa Cruz Superior Court.

256 *Calvary Chapel*: "Founded in Costa Mesa, California, in 1965, Calvary Chapel combined popular fundamentalism with a hippie community outreach which was called the 'Jesus Movement,'" writes Paul Tutwiler in his monograph, *Santa Cruz Spirituality* (fourth edition, 2012). Tutwiler lists several Calvary Chapels in Santa Cruz, but not the San Lorenzo church that was once pastored by Peter Rich, Big J's father.

257 *notorious for its general outlawry*: See *Marijuanaland: Dispatches from an American War*, by Jonah Raskin (High Times Books, 2011). "If you want to find true criminals, that's where they are," a local source told Raskin. "They get out of the state pen and settle in Covelo."

257 *Having registered as a patient collective, he obtained*: This is according to a capsule Josh Rich bio on the website of the cannabis brand RICH&ROSE, which is run by Big J's daughter. "About," RICH&ROSE, accessed July 14, 2025, www.richandroseofficial.com/about.

257 *the first jurisdiction in the nation ever to issue such legal authorizations*: Two years later, Mendocino halted the permitting program, under threat of legal action from the US Department of Justice, and then fought the federal government's efforts to subpoena the county's list of medical marijuana growers in 2012. Federal agents targeted the permit holders from the beginning—the DEA raided the farm of the first person to register, in 2010. Mendocino County, California—Code of Ordinance, Ord. No. § 2 (2017), library.municode.com/ca/mendocino_county/codes/code_of_ordinances?nodeId=MECOCO_TIT9HESA_CH9.31MEMACURE; Joe Mozingo, "Mendocino County spars with feds over conflicting marijuana laws," *Los Angeles Times*, January 20, 2013, web.archive.org/web/20200902132658/https://www.latimes.com/local/la-me-mendo-pot-20130122-story.html.

259 *with a box containing*: According to the seller, Nader Agha, Big J was short by a single hundred-dollar bill. See *Nader Agha v. Mike Bitar*, in Monterey County Superior Court, specifically Bitar's May 12, 2022, motion for a new trial. In these documents, Bitar alleges that the purpose of the transaction was "laundering Josh Rich's cash," "for which he [Agha] was paid handsomely." Big J's group, which bought the King City property from Agha in a deal brokered by Bitar, went on to convert the King City buildings into a licensed cannabis-distribution facility.

259 *a rival Santa Cruz weed baron*: This particular Santa Cruz weed baron also happened to be an officer in the fire department of a nearby city.

259 *Accused of being part of a ring that was allegedly smuggling . . . the subordinate gave up nothing*: Charges against him were eventually dropped.

260 *man cave*: The building formerly belonged to a tech lord who used the space to store his exotic cars.

261 *We eat their livers. Look it up*: Big J's orca science, it turns out, is largely accurate. Killer whales do in fact remove the livers of great white sharks, though the fish are believed to perish soon after the attacks, not linger on for days. See, for example, Stephanie Pappas, "Why are killer whales ripping livers out of their shark prey?" Scientific American, April 11, 2023, https://www.scientificamerican.com/article/why-do-killer-whales-rip-out-shark-livers/.

52. Hot Hemp

263 *Both types of cannabis, drug and nondrug*: As both Tushar and LoForti were aware, hemp *is* cannabis, just without any THC, or with trace amounts of THC. (The DEA defines hemp as cannabis with less than 0.3 percent THC based "on a dry weight basis.")

264 *Believing it to be law enforcement*: In fact, the Santa Cruz County Sheriff's Office doesn't have a chopper. According to Sam LoForti of the county cannabis-licensing office, it was most likely a Pacific Gas & Electric (PG&E) helicopter that the people on the ground mistook for cops.

267 *Tushar had laid it all out for them*: The details describing the medical-marijuana-card program come from the California Department of Public Health and NuggMD websites, while those on the purchase of the clones and the legality of the transactions are drawn from interviews with Sam Borghese and the owner of Plant Humboldt.

268 *how Plant Humboldt chose to interpret the law*: What if you got in an accident and all the plants in your truck were destroyed, and so you had to buy another round? Or maybe thieves had come to your farm in the night with their own box truck and stolen them all, and so you needed to buy more.

53. The Good Doctor

271 *surrendering to authorities*: The case against Bomi Joseph for passport application improprieties, filed on August 8, 2018, in federal court in the Northern District of California, is *United States v. Bomi Boban Joseph aka Moses Sunith Prasad Joseph*.

271 *wrote a federal prosecutor in a court document*: This quote and the previous "serious crimes" quote are from the government's sentencing motion in the passport case against Bomi Joseph.

271 *launched an elaborate scam*: A good summary of Bomi Joseph's yearslong fraud scheme in Silicon Valley from the early 2000s can be found in the government's sentencing motion in the passport case. See, in particular, Exhibit 1 in that filing.

272 *"began falsely holding himself out as a physician"*: A Moses S. Joseph did actually receive a PhD in food science and nutrition from Ohio State University in 1986, according to the appendix to the proceedings of the 1986 board-of-trustees meeting, listing all the degrees conferred.

272 *sued a former business partner*: This lawsuit, filed in federal court in San Jose, California, in July 2018, is *Peak Health Center v. Jared Berry and CBD Naturals*.

272 *sued a former employee*: Bomi Joseph filed this lawsuit in Santa Clara County Superior Court, on August 17, 2021. For more details on this litigation, see https://unicourt.com/case/ca-scl-casebi0a2525e0395c-1310323?init_S=c_relc.

272 *filed bar grievances*: See *Allen Baden v. Bomi Boban Joseph*, filed in Santa Clara County Superior Court on November 12, 2021, for a description of the bar grievances made by Bomi Joseph.

272 *in January 2022, Bomi Joseph was pleading guilty to forgery with the intent to defraud*: See *People of the State of California v. Bomi Boban Joseph*, filed in Santa Cruz County Superior Court on August 26, 2020.

55. Salinas

278 *fell ill in Illinois*: For more on the vape crisis, see this September 2019 report by the Centers for Disease Control and Prevention: https://www.cdc.gov/mmwr/volumes/68/wr/mm6839e2.htm, as well as Chris Kirkham and Jeffery Dastin, "One possible culprit in vaping lung illnesses—'Dank Vapes,'" Reuters, September 13, 2019.

279 *yet another Chad, yet another tech entrepreneur*: Rowland's businesses in the square world involved digital-media trading—the rather abstruse practice of buying and selling online ad space, as if digital ads were a commodity on a financial market, which they pretty much had become. This was lucrative but also, in Rowland's words, "pretty soul-destroying." He was also partly motivated by politics. The war on drugs, he said, was a "massive waste of human resources" and the "primary vehicle that people have used to incarcerate entrepreneurs in low-income neighborhoods. . . . The whole notion that, frankly, any drug should be illegal is farcical."

280 *Tommy was working for Odie, the owner of Island Pharmz*: Elijah says the Island Pharmz space was not on the premises of his auto-repair shop, but in a different, nearby unit inside Tushar's warehouse.

280 *a devotee of this mystic plant*: Tommy was a member of the local branch of a spiritual movement called Santo Daime, founded in Brazil by a seven-foot Black man, a rubber tapper for rubber conglomerates in the Amazon rainforest, who, circa 1922, befriended an indigenous tribe who in turn introduced him to a sacred substance. Santo Daime was an ayahuasca religion. Recognized as a religion by the United States after a court battle, it had a temple in Aptos, in the Santa Cruz Mountains (where else?), where Tommy met the future mother of his children, where he participated in days-long ayahuasca retreats that sometimes involved pregnant women, where he entertained important Santo Daime *padrinos* traveling to Santa Cruz from Brazil, "psychedelic warriors," Tommy called them. The *padrinos* would, in turn, have their minds blown by this giant young Californian and the hash-oil dabs of his creation that he offered to them with the deference of a disciple.

56. The Felton House

283 *was kind of a madhouse*: This chapter is based on my interviews with residents of the Felton house who spoke to detectives during the murder investigation.

283 *professional big-wave surfer who was in recovery*: Originally from Laguna Beach, this particular surfer had once traveled the world for the sport. He won events at Puerto Escondido, saved a man from drowning at Biarritz, and slashed his groin on his board's blade-sharp fin in a gnarly wipeout in Brazil. Then he fell on hard times. He suffered a head injury in a hit-and-run accident and became addicted to hard drugs. He was falsely accused of arson, did time in jail, and lived on the streets, a member of Santa Cruz's substantial homeless population. But he'd worked his way back from addiction with the help of both Flea, the Santa Cruz big-wave surfer and recovering addict who'd founded the well-known rehab center FleaHab, and, to a small but important degree, Tushar Atre. Tushar had given him a place to live in the Felton house.

283 *who specialized in bongs, pipes, and dab rigs*: The glassblower used to have a studio and storefront in downtown Santa Cruz where he displayed his water-bong, dab-rig, and hash-pipe creations, until it was invaded by an armed assailant who pistol-whipped the glassblower and cleaned the place out.

57. Strange Trip

286 *Cameras, alarms, a deluxe security system*: Tushar had started looking into installing all of this but never got around to it.

58. The Sock Monkeys

288 *activated his body-worn camera*: The descriptions of the investigators' trip to Vegas and their learnings are based on court documents citing police reports and testimony in court by Detective Erik Miyoshi, Deputy Ethan Rumrill, and Kelsey Charters.

289 *wanted to play in college*: "I've struggled with many things in my life and have shown true perseverance and I wish I could display that at the next level," Lindsay wrote in a personal statement on one of the many websites for high school players hoping to be recruited by college programs.

289 *"we take millionaire membership classes"*: This quote is taken from the court testimony of Deputy Ethan Rumrill during the 2021 preliminary hearings of the accused.

290 *Pepto-Bismol*: This detail comes from an investigative report written by Detective Erik Miyoshi, after the arrest and questioning of Nick Lindsay. The report was included by a defense attorney in a court pleading in the Atre murder case.

59. Monster

293 *Tushar had said he'd voted*: against legalization: According to one longtime traditional-market operator, "Most people working in cannabis voted against legalizing it. I voted to legalize 'cause I'm hella woke."

298 *He asked another about selling some lab equipment*: This comes from Chris Berry's testimony on the stand at the 2025 trial.

299 *according to a 2010 profile in* GQ: This hilarious article was written by Wells Tower. Wells Tower, "My Kushy New Job," *GQ*, August 15, 2010, www.gq.com/story/wells-tower-on-marijuana.

300 *expelled from*: "Have you ever gone through a deportation?" Harry asked me when I spoke to him. "It ain't fun!"

300 *whose executives were so frustrated*: Miles Morgan's son, himself a Santa Cruz hash oil pioneer, told me that he doesn't recall this particular trim deal gone sour.

60. The Cartel

302 *I began researching the magazine article*: Scott Eden, "He Chased Silicon Valley Dreams Amid the Cannabis Boom. But Did His Ambition Lead to His Murder?" *Inc.*, March/April 2022, www.inc.com/magazine/202203/scott-eden/he-chased-silicon-valley-dreams-amid-the-cannabis-boom-but-did-his-ambition-lead-to-his-murder.html.

303 *many of the weed operators in California I interviewed for this book*: More than a hundred people at all levels of the business, from trimmers to CEOs, from brokers to growers to extractors.

304 *"characteristics" of a cartel farm*: According to Steve Carney, among the clearest indicators of cartel grows are the cultivation style and the remote locations. The cartel grows he's raided were all about scale, with multiple plants growing out of each hole in the ground, on remote terrain that's all but inaccessible.

304 Drug Cartels Do Not Exist: Zavala's book, translated into English by William Savinar and published in 2022 by Vanderbilt University Press, questions whether the cartels are just a distraction from the true beneficiaries of the drug war—the governments and politicians that gain power and profit from its continuation.

304 *The Guadalajara Cartel, which begot the Sinaloa Cartel*: See, for example, Patrick Radden Keefe, "The Hunt for El Chapo," *The New Yorker*, April 28, 2014. See also Larry Rohter, "In Mexico, Drug Roots Run Deep," *The New York Times*, April 16, 1989.

305 *El Mago, the Magician*: El Mago didn't just move weed. He allegedly laundered money for the Sinaloa Cartel by purchasing luxury cars and shipping them back to the capital city of Culiacán, the *Los Angeles Times* reported. See Matthew Ormseth, "'El Mago,' drug trafficker linked to son of Sinaola cartel kingpin, gunned down in L.A.," *Los Angeles Times*, November 24, 2023.

306 *come with the Mexicans down to Hermosillo or San Carlos*: Logistically, it would also be much easier for the cartel to move oil across the border than massive quantities of trim.

306 *That's, like, Jesse Pinkman*: This is a reference to one of the main characters in the TV series *Breaking Bad*.

306 *from an entity that is only a number*: "They were superpolite people," the extraction expert says of his encounter with a cartel. "Everything was just like business, like normal. They had bank accounts and normal fronts here. You'd never know."

307 *La Familia Michoacana, a cartel originally from that Mexican state*: LFM has experienced many reversals of fortune since the group shocked the world in 2006 by tossing five severed heads onto the dance floor of a nightclub. Though it was first organized as a civilian vigilante group aimed at eliminating narcos because the local police were too corrupt, the group's members quickly transformed into narcos themselves. Later, the cartel's charismatic leader, Nazario Moreno González, aka El Chayo (a "chayo" is a kind of edible gourd), was rumored to have been killed in 2010, only to be confirmed dead in a shoot-out in 2014. Since 2019, LFM has found new life under new leadership.

307 *Its founder was a teetotaling Christian zealot*: He wrote three books, actually: *Código de los Caballeros Templarios de Michoacán* (Code of the Knights Templar of Michoacán), *Pensamientos* (Thoughts), and *Me dicen el mas loco* (They call me the crazy one). El Chayo wanted his soldiers to be warriors for justice. According to *Vice News*, he also paid religious writers and speakers to give lectures to his gang members.

62. The Confession

315 *They wanted to make the arrests*: Details on the arrests and interrogations of the accused are drawn from court documents, interrogation recordings, and testimony in court of the arresting officers during the 2021 preliminary hearings and the 2025 trial.

317 *Sitting at a table*: The interrogations of Kurtis Charters, Kaleb Charters, and Joshua Camps on May 19, 2020, were video recorded. Portions of the videos were played in open court during the 2021 preliminary hearings. A handwritten confession by Camps was later made public in a court filing by Nick Lindsay.

320 *cell phones, even when powered down, can be tracked*: Detective Erik Miyoshi obtained search warrants for Camps's, the Charterses' and Lindsay's cell phone records, including hits on cell towers around Pleasure Point during the days leading up to and following Tushar's murder. According to court documents filed by Kaleb Charters's defense team, Miyoshi cited the lack of activity on Lindsay's phone during that time period as one of the reasons he became a person of interest in the case.

320 *Nick walks in the lead*: Surveillance footage played in open court during the preliminary hearing, as well as the trial in early 2025, shows a man leading two others down the Pleasure Point Drive sidewalk. The prosecution argued that this man could only be Nick Lindsay. Lindsay's court-appointed defense lawyers tried to counterargue

that it was impossible to determine from the video the identity of any of the figures walking on the sidewalk toward Atre's house.

321 *one of them binds*: It is contested which one of the three assailants bound Tushar's wrists. Some court documents indicate it was Kurtis; in others, it is Lindsay.

322 Slit his throat: This line of dialogue and a handful of other details in this chapter come from a handwritten confession by Josh Camps, which was made public in a court filing by Nick Lindsay in May 2025.

324 Will you go to heaven, or will you go to hell?: That Kurtis "witnessed to" Tushar as he was about to die is described in several motions filed by defense attorneys at various times as the case has dragged on, especially Kaleb Charters's motion to sever, filed on September 6, 2024, as well as in a police report written by one of the detectives who interrogated Kurtis, published in one of the pleadings. The motions contain summaries of the portion of Kurtis's and Kaleb's confessions where each brother tells detectives about Kurtis's last talk with Tushar before Camps takes him away.

ACKNOWLEDGMENTS

This book would not have been possible without the generosity of the many people who shared their stories with me, despite the obvious perils in doing so. Many friendly spirits in the Santa Cruz cannabis underworld gave me the education I desperately required, even while others fled into the hills when they heard I was coming.

The clerical staff at the Santa Cruz County Superior Court helped immensely with the wrangling of documents. Indeed, the court and its people might be the easiest for a journalist to work with in the Western world.

Jeff and Rainbow, the surfer-bartenders at Santa Cruz's Hotel Paradox, provided important insight into the local breaks and their subcultures.

Jessica York, the crime and courts reporter at the *Santa Cruz Sentinel*, added immensely to my understanding of the local criminal justice community. Rest in peace, Jessica. You were a Santa Cruz treasure.

Ty Wenger, the greatest of magazine editors, is responsible for the origin story; he not only assigned the piece that led to this project but offered sage counsel all along the way. I am deeply grateful to David Granger, my agent, who perceived the power of this story from the beginning and supplied a crucial narrative breakthrough. Brett Forrest helped solve thorny reporting conundrums. Sam Nicholson championed the project in a formative stage. No publisher could have offered better support than the one founded by Cindy Spiegel and Julie Grau, the legend, my editor, who took an ungainly sprawler and made it flow. Her strength and clarity of mind propelled the project to the end. Devon Halliday gave much help and good cheer. Mona Houck applied her calming diligence. Kate Wheeling, my reporting assistant and fact-checker, is in many ways a coauthor. She conducted interviews, ran down documents, and saved me from diverse grave embarrassments. (Any errors are mine alone.)

My thanks to Patsy and Jack Tucker, of Costa Rica, and a host of moral supporters, including Tim Hickey, Paul Winner, John Brandon, Rafi Kohan, Ben Ryder Howe, Keith Newton, Matt Dellinger, Isaac Morris, Kevin DiCamillo, Joe Mulligan, Aimee Eden, Ryan Morris, Michael Geertson, and Brian Krowicki. Deep gratitude goes to Justin and Patty Becker, who took me into their home on I don't know how many reporting trips to the Bay Area, allowing me to contemplate the verities in peaceful surroundings.

My mother's love has always kept me going. My father's way of being inspired me to write; he died before he could read this book in its entirety. It is dedicated to his memory. And, as always, to Leyla: Every word is for you.

ABOUT THE AUTHOR

Scott Eden is an award-winning journalist whose work has focused on crime, corruption, injustice, business, science, technology, and the dark side of sports. He's written for *ESPN The Magazine*, *GQ*, *Wired*, *The Atavist Magazine*, *The Believer*, and many other publications, and his stories have been anthologized in *The Best American Sports Writing* and in *The Believer*'s best-of collection *Read Hard*. He is also the author of *Touchdown Jesus*. He lives in New Jersey.